Plate A

Plate B

Plates A and B are computer-generated images of two woodcut prints selected out of a series of landscapes, Thirty-Six Views of Mt. Fuji, made by Katsushika Hokusai (1760-1849). He is one of Japan's most famous *ukiyo-e* artist of the Tokugawa Shogun era (1615-1868), and is best known for this series.

Ukiyo-e literally means "pictures of the floating world", and depicts everyday life of ordinary people in woodcut prints. The word "floating" also meant "modern" and *ukiyo-e* artists created very fashionable style of pictures including those shown here.

Creation of *ukiyo-e* images in computer graphics required a lot of skills such as simulating woodcut printing- and paint brush- effects.

These images were generated under the direction of Prof. Dr. Tosiyasu L. Kunii by the following members of the Kunii Laboratory of Computer Science at the University of Tokyo, Mr. Naohiro Oshima, Mr. Tsukasa Noma, Mr. Kazunori Yamaguchi, Mr. Naota Inamoto and Miss Yukari Shirota. The equipment used was provided by the Software Research Center of Ricoh Co., Ltd., and consists of Seillac-3 graphic systems, VAX 11/780 and 11/750 computers running UNIX (UCB 4.2 bsd version) and a Summagraphics digitizing tablet. All programs are written in C language.

Plate A is *Kanagawa-Oki Nami-Ura*, or "Stormy Sea off Kanagawa", and features boats being tossed on raging waves with Mr. Fuji in the background. Plate B is *Aka Fuji*, literally "The Red Mt. Fuji", often known as "Mt. Fuji on a Fine Day with Breeze."

Frontiers in Computer Graphics

Proceedings of
Computer Graphics Tokyo '84

Edited by Tosiyasu L. Kunii

With 266 Figures
82 of them in Color

Springer-Verlag
Tokyo Berlin Heidelberg New York
1985

Dr. Tosiyasu L. Kunii
Professor & Director
Kunii Laboratory of Computer Science
Department of Information Science
Faculty of Science
The University of Tokyo

ISBN-13:978-4-431-68027-7   e-ISBN-13:978-4-431-68025-3
DOI: 10.1007/978-4-431-68025-3

Library of Congress Card No.: 84-23637

All rights reserved, No part of this publication may be reproduced or transmitted in any form or by any means, electronic or mechanical, including photocopy, recording, or any information storage and retrieval system, without permission in writing from the publisher.

© by Springer-Verlag Tokyo 1985
Softcover reprint of the hardcover 1st edition 1985

Preface

Computer graphics as a whole is an area making very fast progress and it is not easy for anyone, including experts, to keep abreast of the frontiers of its various basic and application fields. By issuing over 100 thousand calls for papers through various journals and magazines as well as by inviting reputed specialists, and by selecting high quality papers which present the state of the art in computer graphics out of many papers thus received, this book "Frontiers in Computer Graphics" has been compiled to present the substance of progress in this field. This volume serves also as the final version of the Proceedings of Computer Graphics Tokyo '84, Tokyo, Japan, April 24-27, 1984 which, as a whole, attracted 16 thousand participants from all over the world; about two thousand to the conference and the remaining 14 thousand to the exhibition.

This book covers the following eight major frontiers of computer graphics in 29 papers: 1. geometry modelling, 2. graphic languages, 3. visualization techniques, 4. human factors, 5. interactive graphics design, 6. CAD/CAM, 7. graphic displays and peripherals, and 8. graphics standardization.

Geometry modelling is most essential in displaying any objects in computer graphics. It determines the basic capabilities of computer graphics systems such as whether the surface and the inside of the object can be displayed and also how efficiently graphical processing can be done in terms of processing time and memory space. Various advanced geometry models such as surface models, solid models and surface/solid interface models are presented by six papers to cover the essential technological breakthrough in this area.

Graphic languages are devices for users to actually handle graphical objects based on geometry modelling. Two advanced high level languages are presented. The first one is a high level data flow language. This provides designers with a natural and concise way of parallel manipulation of graphic objects. An application example shown is the simulation of a robot manipulator movement which involves parallel control of several joints. The other language presented is Mira-Shading. This is a structured high level language for synthesizing and animating realistic images. Mira-Shading has been used to produce computer animated movies. As you see, advanced languages drive 3D geometry models interactively to generate images of moving bodies on graphic displays.

Visualization techniques show you varieties of approaches which have been developed to present information graphically. Four papers cover cases of visualizing dynamic phenomena (such as material flow) and geographic relief, and also methods to realize artistic visual effects.

Human factors are well known as a typical area which is still under development in spite of their importance. Starting from human factor design and evaluation illustrated by the first paper, we look into human factor aspects of input peripherals which is roughly sketched in the second paper, and finish up with user interface design supported by geometric models as described in the last paper.

Interactive graphics design is another human-oriented technical area. Two papers give overviews of graphics design, one on an educational aspect and the other on an office automation application.

Advances in CAD/CAM, one of the fastest growing industrial application areas of computer graphics, are extensively covered by five papers. The first two papers illustrate the status of 3D CAD/CAM in practice at factories. The third paper is a case study of the artistic use of CAD in bottle design. A very advanced VLSI CAD system is presented by the fourth paper. The last paper concludes the story by looking into the future of CAD in the context of fifth generation systems. As you see, 3D CAD/CAM is growing into an actual practice area with some of the flavor of artists' dreams.

Reflecting the rapid progress of VLSI technology, graphic displays and peripherals are becoming more and more versatile in their functions and more economically accessible by the increasing number of users, including personal computer users. A new intelligent 3D graphic display architecture with image processing capability is presented by the first paper. The second paper describes the architecture of a pipelined very high speed image analyser for real-time image processing. The third paper is on a graphic output peripheral. It reports an experimental development of a low cost color hard copier using an ink jet printer. The fourth and last paper proposes a new graphic input device based on a mechanical feedback touch sensor.

The last area covered is graphics standardization. Reflecting recent progress of graphics standardization activities within ISO (the International Standardization Organization), the first two papers talk about the commercial implications and applications of ISO's graphics standard GKS (the Graphics Kernel System). The last paper looks into the problems of and requirements for standardizing animation commands. This is a good example of the recent rapid increase in social needs for standardization.

Computer graphics is a young area, and still making very fast progress. I believe this volume helps the readers to catch up with its major progress.

Tosiyasu L. Kunii, Editor

Cover Design: Botanical tree images are drawn by the 3D Botanical Tree Image Generator, developed by M. Aono and T.L. Kunii at the University of Tokyo, sponsored by Software Research Center of Ricoh Co., Ltd.

Table of Contents

Chapter 1
Geometry Modelling 1

A Hierarchical Data Structure for Representing the Spatial Decomposition of
3D Objects
(I. Carlbom, I. Chakravarty, D. Vanderschel) 2

Boundary File Generation from Octree Encoding
(K. Yamaguchi, T. Satoh, T.L. Kunii) 13

A Representation of Solid Design Process Using Basic Operations
(H. Chiyokura, F. Kimura) 26

Bridge Edge and Triangulation Approach in Solid Modeling
(F. Yamaguchi, T. Tokieda) 44

A Procedure for Generating Contour Lines from a B-Spline Surface
(S.G. Satterfield, D.F. Rogers) 66

An Automated Finite Polygon Division Method of 3D Objects
(Y. Ota, H. Arai, S. Tokumasu, T. Ochi) 74

Chapter 2
Graphic Languages 89

A Data Flow Language for Intelligent Graphic Displays
(N. Inamoto, K. Yamaguchi, T.L. Kunii) 90

MIRA-Shading: A Structured Language for the Synthesis and the Animation of
Realistic Images
(N. Magnenat-Thalmann, M. Fortin, L. Langlois, D. Thalmann) 101

Chapter 3
Visualization Techniques 115

"Steam Plume" Simulation
(H. Kishino, K. Tanaka) 116

Computer Graphics Techniques for Three-Dimensional Flow Visualization
(K.A. Kroos) 129

Geomatic: A 3-D Graphic Relief Simulation System
(S. Motet, D. Laurent) 146

Realistic Effects with Rodin
(H. Huitric, M. Nahas) 159

Chapter 4
Human Factors 169

Human Factors Redesign and Test of a Graphics System
(P. Reisner, G.G. Langdon, Jr.) 170

Toward the Standardization of Input Peripherals in the Urbanistic Design Process
and Person-Machine Interaction
(M. Salvemini) 188

User Interface Management System with Geometric Modeling Capability:
A CAD System's Framework
(T. Takala) 198

Chapter 5
Interactive Graphics Design 211

Critical Issues in Computer Graphics Education for Graphics Design
(R.G. King) 212

New Office Automation Environment: In-House Graphics and Publishing
Capabilities
(A. Bernhard) 224

Chapter 6
CAD/CAM 239

A Practical Application of a Computer to Industrial Design
(K. Hatakenaka, M. Yano, A. Kotani, K. Yamada, M. Ishibashi, Y. Shibui,
Y. Kugai, K.M. Jones, K. Kobori, K. Sakashita) 240

Development of a Total 3D CAD/CAM System for Electric Appliances
(K. Kobori, Y. Nagata, Y. Sato, K.M. Jones, I. Nishioka) 254

Bottle Design Arts System
(Y. Sato, M. Akeo) 266

Interactive VLSI Chip Floor Design Using Color Graphics
(K. Ueda, Kitazawa, I. Harada) 281

On Fifth Generation Systems and Their Implications for Computer Aided Design
(D.B. Arnold) 294

Chapter 7
Graphic Displays and Peripherals 309

New Trends in Graphic Display System Architecture
(E.M. Kaya) 310

Morphological Binary Image Processing with a Local Neighborhood Pipeline Processor
(W.K. Pratt, I. Kabir) 321

Continuous Color Presentation Using a Low-Cost Ink Jet Printer
(S. Kubo) 344

Mechanically Feedbacked Touch Sensor for Electronic Painting by Skilled People
(S. Kimura) 354

Chapter 8
Graphics Standardization 361

GKS, a Standard for Software OEMs
(C.N. Waggoner) 362

A Standards Solution to Your Graphics Problems
(M.G. Rawlins) 375

Standardization of Animation Commands for Computer Animation System
(H. Sato) 417

Author Index 431

Subject Index 439

List of Contributors

The page numbers given below refer to the page on which contribution begins.

Makoto Akeo   266
Hiroshi Arai   74
David B. Arnold   294
Alice Bernhard   224
Ingrid Carlbom   2
Indranil Chakravarty   2
Hiroaki Chiyokura   26
Mario Fortin   101
Ikuo Harada   281
Kenji Hatakenaka   240
Hervé Huitric   159
Naota Inamoto   90
Manabu Ishibashi   240
Kenneth M. Jones   240, 254
Ihtisham Kabir   321
Ender M. Kaya   310
Fumihiko Kimura   26
Shigeru Kimura   354
Robin G. King   212
Hirohiko Kishino   116
Hitoshi Kitazawa   281
Kenichi Kobori   240, 254
Akio Kotani   240
Kenneth A. Kroos   129
Sachio Kubo   344
Yutaka Kugai   240
Tosiyasu L. Kunii   13, 90
Glen G. Langdon, Jr.   170
Louis Langlois   101
Daniel Laurent   146
Nadia Magnenat-Thalmann   101
Serge Motet   146

Monique Nahas   159
Ikuo Nishioka   254
Toshio Ochi   74
Yoshimi Ota   74
William K. Pratt   321
Mark G. Rawlins   375
Phyllis Reisner   170
David F. Rogers   66
Kiyoshi Sakashita   240
Mauro Salvemini   188
Hidemaru Sato   417
Yoshinobu Sato   254
Yoshio Sato   266
Toshiaki Satoh   13
Steven G. Satterfield   66
Yuichi Shibui   240
Tapio Takala   198
Katsumi Tanaka   116
Daniel Thalmann   101
Toshiya Tokieda   44
Shinji Tokumasu   74
Kazuhiro Ueda   281
David Vanderschel   2
Clinton N. Waggoner   362
Kazuo Yamada   240
Fujio Yamaguchi   44
Kazunori Yamaguchi   13, 90
Motokuni Yano   240

Chapter 1
Geometry Modelling

A Hierarchical Data Structure for Representing the Spatial Decomposition of 3D Objects

Ingrid Carlbom and **Indranil Chakravarty**
Schlumberger-Doll Research
Old Quarry Road
Ridgefield, CT 06877, USA

David Vanderschel
Schlumberger-AEC
12175 Technology Blvd
Austin, TX 78727, USA

Abstract

A generalization of the octree data structure for representing polyhedral objects is described. This data structure, called the polytree, is a cellular spatial decomposition of the object space into primitive cells containing edge and vertex intersection information. The increased complexity of primitive cells results in several advantages over octrees, while, at the same time, retaining most of the desirable features of the octree structure. A recursive subdivision algorithm for the creation of a polytree from a boundary representation is presented.

1. Introduction

Two types of hierarchical representations of graphical objects are prevalent in computer graphics: one is based on the decomposition of objects into their constituent parts, and the other is based on the decomposition of object space into regularly shaped subspaces. The first representation, hierarchical decomposition of objects, dates back to Sutherland's Sketchpad System [11]. Since then, many vector and raster graphics systems have provided both software and hardware support for hierarchical (or structured) graphical data. Hierarchical representations are convenient for positioning objects and their components in space and for moving objects relative to one another. In addition they offer considerable memory savings when objects and object components occur several times in a scene. Each such object and object component needs to be defined only once, and can subsequently be instantiated by the application of linear transformations in the hierarchy.

Image synthesis algorithms, such as clipping and visibility calculations, can also benefit from using the spatial coherence in a hierarchical object representation [1]. Each object and object component in the hierarchy is enclosed in a bounding volume. In the case of clipping, a bounding volume is compared to the clipping volume. If the bounding volume is either entirely inside or outside the clipping volume, the object components in the bounding volume can be trivially accepted or rejected respectively, and no further clip processing is required. Similarly, in the case of visible-surface calculations, the sorting process can be speeded up by sorting the bounding volumes and only performing visibility tests on those components of the object which are likely to be visible. As in the case of clipping, the content of a bounding volume can be removed completely from consideration if the bounding volume is completely blocked from view by other objects. In addition, Clark [1] has suggested other methods for improving image synthesis algorithms by using bounding volumes for representing "levels of detail" and for managing "graphical working sets."

In the hierarchical representations discussed above the leaf nodes typically contain edges, polygons, and possibly surface patches. Rubin and Whitted [8] propose a scheme whereby the object space is represented only by bounding boxes. The leaf nodes are rectangular paralellepipeds and form an approximation of an object component. The creation of the bounding boxes is a rather tedious process that requires a human operator. Once the objects are decomposed, however, the resulting representation can be rendered efficiently using ray-tracing techniques.

The second kind of hierarchy, the decomposition of object space, has been the focus of much recent research. In this case the entire object space is divided repeatedly into cubes [5,9], or rectangular parallelepipeds [10] resulting in a tree structure. As in the Rubin and Whitted scheme, the leaf nodes do not contain primitives such as edges and polygons, but approximate the object components by repeated subdivision into cubes or parallelepipeds to some degree of precision. Hierarchical space decomposition does not provide the memory savings offered by object decomposition, nor does it provide any structure for managing or interacting with components of a complex object. However, the spatial decomposition provides a representation applicable to a wide class of objects and allows geometrical properties to be computed rapidly.

Clip testing is performed by testing each of the nodes in the tree in a top down fashion against the clipping volume. If a node is completely inside or is completely outside the clipping volume, all subnodes can be trivially accepted or rejected, respectively. When a leaf node crosses the clipping boundary, the actual clipping operation is trivial. Similarly, visible surface algorithms require no sorting; the surfaces are sorted at the creation of the tree, and by traversing the nodes in the correct order the visible surfaces are rendered correctly.

The most common spatial decomposition of this type, the octree, is discussed further in the next section.

2. The Octree Data Structure

The octree[1] is a regular cellular decomposition of the object space (universe). The universe is subdivided into eight equally-sized cells. If any one of the resulting cells is homogeneous, that is the cell lies entirely inside or outside the object, the subdivision stops. If, on the other hand, the cell is heterogeneous, that is intersected by one or more of the object's bounding surfaces, the cell is subdivided further into eight subcells. The subdivision process halts when all the leaf cells are homogeneous to some degree of accuracy.

The octree representation has several advantages. First, any arbitrarily shaped objects, convex and concave with interior holes, can be represented to the precision of the smallest cell. Second, geometrical properties, such as surface area, volume, center of mass, and interference are easily calculated at different levels of precision. Third, because of the spatial sorting and the uniformity of representation, (only three distinct node types are required) operations on octrees are efficient.

Nevertheless, the octree structure suffers from several limitations. In particular, the leaf cells in an octree representing a volume are all homogeneous. The bounding surface of an object is represented by the set of square facets between the empty and full cells, and is therefore an approximation of the original surface by square polygons which are parallel to the sides of the original universe space. For objects with complex detail, the octree requires a large number of cells to represent the object accurately. Yet, regardless of the number of subdivisions, an octree is still an approximation of an object, and only approximate properties of the object can be calculated. Precise detail, such as surface curvature, is often lost in the rendering process.

A major limitation of the octree data structure is the difficulty in incorporating it in existing graphics software systems. For example, CAD/CAM systems are built typically either around a boundary representation scheme or around primitive solids that can be combined into complex objects by

---
1. The 2D corresponding structure, the quadtree, has many similar properties. The quadtree is, however, not described here.

constructive solid geometry operations [6]. An object created on such a system and transformed into an octree to take advantage of set operations, can no longer be reconstructed exactly for conversion into a boundary representation scheme. The irreversibility of the transformation is a serious drawback for using octrees in conjuction with existing CAD/CAM systems and databases.

The hierarchical decomposition described in the next section, the <u>polytree</u>, retains most of the advantages of the octree data structure, while having few of its disadvantages.

3. The Polytree Data Structure

The polytree data structure (introduced by Vanderschel [13] and by Hunter [4]) is a regular cellular decomposition of the universe. As in the case of the octree, the root cell corresponds to the entire universe. The universe is subdivided until the leaf cells are <u>sufficiently simple</u>. In the octree data structure, sufficiently simple means homogeneity, that is, a cell is either full or empty. In a polytree, the leaf cells are more complicated and can be one of five types:

1. Full Cell - Homogeneous cell which lies entirely inside the object.

2. Empty Cell - Homogeneous cell which lies entirely outside the object.

3. Vertex Cell - Contains one vertex and a set of edges which are all connected to the vertex (see Figure 1.)

4. Edge Cell - Contains either one edge with one polygon or one edge with two polygons sharing a common edge (see Figure 2.)

5. Surface Cell - Contains a planar surface intersecting the interior of the cell (see Figure 3.)

Cells that do not satisfy the above criteria are called partial cells and correspond to nodes in the tree. Further definitions for the remaining discussion are:

1. Real Vertex - A vertex that is part of the original object definition.

2. Pseudo Vertex - A vertex that is not part of the original object definition, but is introduced during the subdivision process.

3. Real Edge - An edge that is part of the original object definition.

Figure 1. Vertex Cell

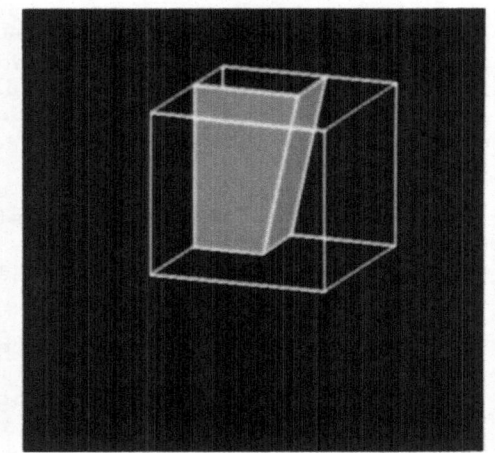

Figure 2. Edge Cell

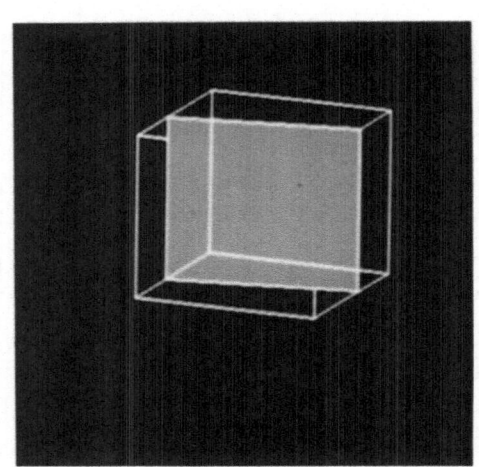

Figure 3. Surface Cell

4. Pseudo Edge - An edge that is not part of the original object definition, but is introduced during the subdivision process.

The primary difference between the octree and the polytree is the difference in the leaf complexity. This gives the polytree a number of advantages over octrees. First, the increased cell complexity can result in substantial memory savings. Second, the polytree provides an exact representation of polyhedral objects and surfaces because planar facets are represented exactly, instead of approximated by homogeneous cubes. Thus any geometric operations performed on polytrees will also result in an exact polyhedral object. Third, since polytrees retain the coordinate data of a polyhedral object, a boundary representation can be reconstructed from the polytree. This means that the polytree can be used in conjunction with other existing representation schemes, and algorithms for simulation or for dynamic display can be applied without modification. Finally, polytrees maintains the hierarchy and the spatial sorting inherent in the octree structure. Although clipping and visible surface calculations are slightly more complicated than in the octree case for the leaf cells, clipping need only be performed for the edges and surfaces in the leaf cells that intersect the clipping volume, and visibility tests need only be applied to edge cells and vertex cells.

4. <u>Conversion from Boundary Representation to Polytree Representation</u>

A scene is assumed to contain a set of objects, which are in turn described by a set of polygons. The object can either represent a surface or a bounded volume. The algorithm comprises of two parts: first the boundary representation is divided into a polytree representation, and second, if the boundary representation represents a volume, the cells interior to the object are identified as full and the cells exterior to the object are identified as empty.

The first part of the algorithm is based on the Sutherland-Hodgman clipping algorithm [12] which uses a divide and conquer strategy. The polygons are successively clipped against the clipping volume boundaries and at each successive step a polygon representing the portion of the polygon inside the volume is reconstructed and the portions outside the clipping volume are discarded.

In our algorithm[2], there are three clipping boundaries for

---
2. Fujimura and Kunii have, in parallel, worked on algorithms for the polytree data structure [3]. They propose an alternate first step to the algorithm. In their algorithm, the polytree boundary representation is created in three

each cell at each level of subdivision. The clipping planes are parallel to the sides of the universe, all intersecting the center point of the cell, dividing the cell into eight equally sized subcells. As in the Sutherland-Hodgman algorithm, each of the three boundaries is clipped successively. A polygon which intersects a clipping boundary is divided into two polygons, each with a pseudo edge that lies in the clipping plane. The subdivision continues until the leaf cells are sufficiently simple according to the criteria in the previous section. In summary the algorithm proceeds in four steps:

1. Divide the cell into two parts along a plane parallel to the yz-plane through the center point of the cell.

2. Divide each of the two parallelepipeds resulting from (1) into two parts along a plane parallel to the xz-plane through the center point of the cell.

3. Divide each of the four parallelepipeds resulting from (2) into two parts along a plane parallel to the xy-plane through the center point of the cell.

4. Test each of the resulting eight cells for the leaf node conditions described in the previous section. If the sub-cell is a partial cell return to (1).

In the resulting polytree some cells are homogeneous, either completely full or completely empty. Each surface cell contains one polygon, all of whose edges are pseudo edges. Each edge cell contains one real edge which is a portion of an edge in the original object representation. The edge cell contains one polygon if the real edge lies on the boundary of a surface; otherwise it contains two polygons. Each vertex cell contains two or more polygons connected to a real vertex. The result of the subdivision of a wedge represented by six triangular polygons is shown in Figure 4(a-c). In Figure 4(a) the red lines represent the original edges, in Figure 4(b) the green lines delineate the pseudo edges introduced during the subdivision process and in Figure 4(c) the white lines delineate the cell boundaries.

The second part of the algorithm uses ray-casting to separate the full and empty cells for objects that represent volumes. Such a scheme is described by Roth [7] and is not discussed here.

The algorithm has been implemented for objects representing surfaces. The primary implementation difficulty lies in keeping track of edges that are common to more that one polygon

---

steps: the vertices are divided into a polytree, next the edges are added, and lastly the surfaces of the polygons are added.

Figure 4(a). Real Edges
and Vertices of the Wedge

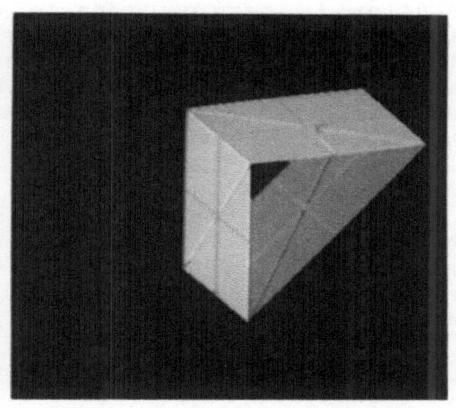

Figure 4(b). Pseudo Edges of
the Wedge (after subdivision)

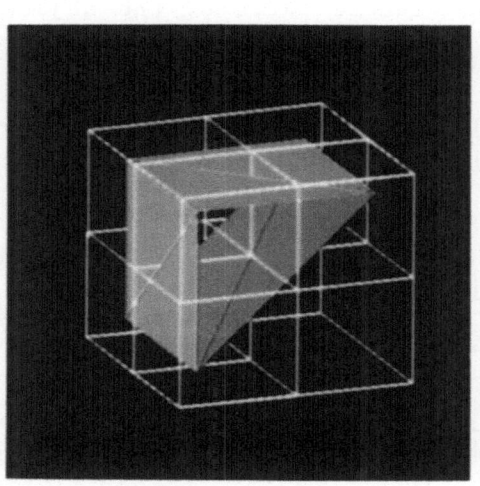

Figure 4(c). Cell Boundaries
of the Polytree for the Wedge

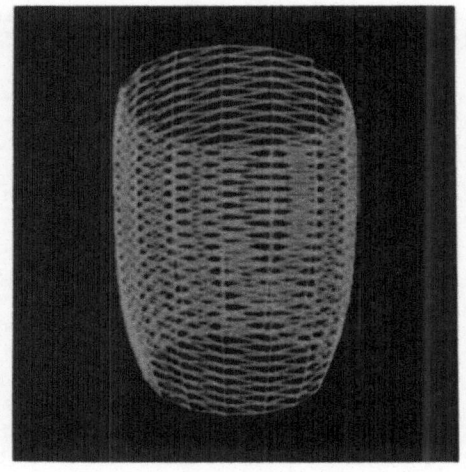

Figure 5. Triangulated
Surface Test Case

in the original object and in the resulting pseudo edges. The solution is to keep adquate bookeeping information associated with the cells during the division process. In addition, vertices and edges that are "close" in the the original representation may require many levels of subdivision; such situations require special testing so that the subdivision does not exceed the resolution required for the application under consideration.

The algorithm has been implemented on a VAX-11/780 in C. The surface of revolution in Figure 5 is triangulated by 375 vertices and 720 polygons. The resulting polytree contains 375 vertex cells, 11757 edge cells, 4449 surface cells and 5040 partial cells.

5. Display of Objects in a Polytree Data Structure

Octree display algorithms can be classified into two types; (i) back-to-front traversal and (ii) front-to-back traversal [2,5]. The former, although inefficient, is easier to implement and simply traverses the tree structure in a back-to-front order and paints the leaf nodes on the screen. The display algorithm that we propose is very similar to the octree rendering algorithms. The algorithm exploits the spatial sorting of data structure and traverses the tree back-to-front, that is, in a manner such that the visible parts of the object are written last on the screen. The ordering of the cells is dependent upon the position of the viewer.

In rendering each leaf cell of the polytree, we need to consider the visibility of the individual polygons for each of the three leaf types. To determine the visibility we compute the distance of the polygon with respect to the viewer so that the polygons may be painted on the screen in the correct order.

1. Surface Cell - Contains a single surface which divides the cell into two parts. There is no visibility determination - the boundaries of the cell (pseudo-edges) describe the polygon to be projected and shaded onto the screen space.

2. Edge Cell - Contains a single real edge common to two polygons or one real edge which is part of one polygon. If there is only one polygon, there is no visibility determination. In the case of two polygons, visibility consists of traversing each polygon and determining from the coordinate position of each vertex the polygon closest to the viewer.

3. Vertex Cell - This is the most complex cell and contains a single vertex and multiple polygons. Polygons may only intersect along the real edges. Sorting the polygons consist of sorting the real edges by their coordinate

position and then ordering the polygons by the order of real edges.

6. Summary and Future Work

This paper describes work in progress on a generalization of the octree data structure. By increasing the complexity of the leaf cells, an exact representation of polyhedral objects and surfaces is possible within a hierarchical object space decomposition. The advantages over the octree structure include reduced memory for the resulting representation as well as the capability to calculate exact geometrical properties of objects. The polytree data structure is also more compatible with other graphical data representations. Initial results indicate that this approach to object representation can result in considerable space savings and increased versatility for representation of polyhedral objects.

There are many ways to extend the ideas presented here. First, the data structure itself could be extended. The notion of <u>sufficiently simple</u> was chosen here to mean surface, edge, and vertex cells. Other possible definitions could be added easily: for example, the leaf cells could contain surface patches with some limited curvature thereby allowing exact representations of curved surfaces.

Algorithms other than display algorithms should be investigated. The polytree data structure allows geometric set operations in a fashion similar to octrees, which consist of traversing the tree and comparing cells to decide properties of union, intersection, etc. For polytrees the comparison operation between cells is somewhat more complex than in the octree case, that is, we need to test for intersection among the polygons in the cell structure. However, the greater complexity of these operations may be offset by the fewer number of cells required and by the fact that the resulting object can now be described by the exact intersection boundaries.

7. Acknowledgment

The authors would like to thank Dr. Peter Will, Director System Science, for his encouragement during the course of this work.

8. References

1. Clark, J.H., "Hierarchical Geometric Models for Visible Surface Algorithms," *Communications of the ACM* 19, 10 (Oct. 1976) pp. 547-554.

2. Doctor, L.J., and J.G. Torborg, "Display Techniques for Octree-Encoded Objects," *IEEE Computer Graphics and Applications* 1, 3 (July 1981) pp. 29-38.

3. Fujimura, K. and T.L. Kunii, *Personal Communication*, Department of Information Science, The University of Tokyo, Japan (1984).

4. Hunter, G.M., *Geometrees for Interactive Visualization of Geology: An Evaluation*, Research Note, Schlumberger-Doll Research, Ridgefield, CT (April 1984).

5. Meagher, D., "Geometric Modeling Using Octree Encoding," *Computer Graphics and Image Processing*, 19, (1982) pp. 129-147.

6. Requicha, A.A.G., "Representations for Rigid Solids: Theory, Methods, and Systems," *Computing Surveys*, 12,, 4 (Dec. 1980) pp. 437-464.

7. Roth, S.D., "Ray Casting for Modeling Solids," *Computer Graphics and Image Processing* 18, 2 (Feb. 1982) pp. 109-144.

8. Rubin, S.M. and T. Whitted, "A 3-Dimensional Representation for Fast Rendering of Complex Scenes," *Computer Graphics* 14, 3 (July 1980) pp. 110-116.

9. Srihari, S.N., "Representation of Three-Dimensional Digital Images," *Computing Surveys* 13, 4 (1981) 399-424.

10. Srihari, S.N., "Hierarchical Data Structures and Progressive Refinement of 3D Images," *Proc. IEEE Conference on Pattern Recognition and Image Processing*, Las Vegas, NV (June 1982) 485-490.

11. Sutherland, I.E., *SKETCHPAD: A Man-Machine Graphical Communication System*, SJCC 1963, Spartan Books, Baltimore, Md, p. 329.

12. Sutherland, I.E. and G.W. Hodgman, "Reentrant Polygon Clipping," *Communications of the ACM*, 17, 1 (Jan. 1974) pp. 32-42.

13. Vanderschel, D.J., *Divided Leaf Octal Trees*, Research Note, Schlumberger-Doll Research, Ridgefield, CT (March 1984).

Boundary File Generation from Octree Encoding

Kazunori Yamaguchi, Toshiaki Satoh and Tosiyasu L. Kunii
Faculty of Science
Department of Information Science
The University of Tokyo
3-1, Hongo 7-chome, Bunkyo-ku
Tokyo 113, Japan

ABSTRACT

This paper describes an algorithm for generating a boundary representation from an octree representation. This algorithm includes some useful algorithms, such as how to find cubes adjacent to a given cube in an octree.

I. INTRODUCTION

Octree encoding [1] of a three dimensional solid object has been studied over the past few years. Octree encoding is a method used to represent a solid object by a set of cubes in hierarchically organized sizes. Each cube is represented by a node of a tree: the operation on a solid object represented by the tree is mapped to an operation on the tree. Many useful operations on the solid object such as boolean operations, can be converted to tree traversal operations, which can be executed faster than the original operations.

Octree representation is also used as a primary data representation in some applications. Examples include three dimensional data extraction from images created by Nuclear Magnetic Resonance (NMR) scanning [2] and three dimensional rough data input [3]. For such applications, it is sometimes necessary to generate other representations from the octree encoded data. One such representation is the boundary representation [4], which is a well-studied and developed data representation. In order to eliminate hidden line that images from the octree data, we have to generate lines that surround the objects. Sometimes, conversions are part of algorithms such as algorithm to convert the octree to a boundary representation.

One algorithm to convert the octree representation to a boundary representation is quite simple. In this algorithm, a boundary representation is generated that corresponds to each cube in the octree. A union operation is then performed on the cubes in the boundary representation. This algorithm is very inefficient. Octree encoding is good at performing boolean operations, but the target of the conversion is not the octree but a boundary representation. We have found a better approach which combines the structures of the octree and boundary representations so that the intermediate calculations can be done on the octree. The time required to perform conversion using this algorithm is proportional to the number of nodes and leaves in the octree. Thus, the algorithm is optimal except for a constant factor.

Section II defines the octree and boundary representations used in this paper. Section III describes the algorithm to generate a boundary representation from the octree representation. Section IV concludes this paper with a remark on the boundary representation.

II. DEFINITION OF OCTREE AND BOUNDARY REPRESENTATIONS

In this section, we define the octree and boundary representations.

Octree Representation

The octree o is defined as a tree with out-degree eight, excluding leaves. A set of octrees SO is defined formally as follows:

1. $0 \in SO$,
2. $1 \in SO$,
3. $(o_{0,0,0}, o_{0,0,1}, o_{0,1,0}, o_{0,1,1}, o_{1,0,0}, o_{1,0,1}, o_{1,1,0}, o_{1,1,1})$
   $\in SO$ if $o_{x,y,z} \in SO$ for $x,y,z \in \{0,1\}$.
4. SO does not include any element which is not constructed by repeatedly applying rules 1 through 3.
   (In the following, we do not explicitly repeat this rule.)

We call 0 and 1 __leaves__ and other octrees __nodes__. Leaf 0 is called empty and the leaf 1 is called full. If $ot = o_{x,y,z}$ then (x,y,z) is called a __child node position__ of ot in o. Sometimes we call the empty and full leaves, empty and full nodes, respectively. In that case, the node is called a __heterogeneous__ node to make the distinction.

A three dimensional object $E(o)$ associated with the octree $o = (o_{0,0,0}, o_{0,0,1}, o_{0,1,0}, o_{0,1,1}, o_{1,0,0}, o_{1,0,1}, o_{1,1,0}, o_{1,1,1})$ is called an __octree object__ and recursively defined as follows:

1. $E(0) = \emptyset$,
2. $E(1) = [0,1[^3$,
3. $E((o_{0,0,0}, o_{0,0,1}, o_{0,1,0}, o_{0,1,1},$
   $o_{1,0,0}, o_{1,0,1}, o_{1,1,0}, o_{1,1,1})) =$
   $\bigcup_{x,y,z \in \{0,1\}} H((x,y,z), E(o_{x,y,z}))$.

Here, $[x,y[$ is a range $\{a | x \leq a < y\}$ and the scaling function $H((x,y,z), A) = \{((x'-x)/2+x, (y'-y)/2+y, (z'-z)/2+z) | (x',y',z') \in A\}$.
   $E(o_{x,y,z})$ is called an __octant__.

Example:

The octree $o = (1,(0,0,1,0,0,0,0,0),0,0,1,0,0,0)$ and the associated object is shown in Figure 1.

Boundary Representation

The boundary representation consists of seven sets. Body, Plane, Edge and Vertex are a set of body, plane, edge and vertex identifiers (ids for short). The relationships between these sets are described in the sets: BodyPlane $\subseteq$ Body$\times$Plane$\times\{-1,+1\}$, PlaneEdge $\subseteq$ Plane$\times$Edge$\times\{-1,+1\}$, and EdgeVertex $\subseteq$ Edge$\times$Vertex$\times\{-1,+1\}$. A body, plane, edge and vertex are oriented to each other. An element in {-1,+1} of the BodyPlane, PlaneEdge and EdgeVertex sets shows whether or not the orientations of the body, plane and edge agree with that of the plane, edge and vertex. This field is called _dir_. When the orientations of an edge and vertex agree, the edge has the vertex as a starting point.

III. BOUNDARY REPRESENTATION GENERATION

In this section, we explain an algorithm that generates a boundary representation from an octree representation. We extend an octree representation so that body, plane, edge and vertex identifiers (ids) can be stored at each node. In the extended octree, each leaf has the following information i($\underline{o}$).

i($\underline{o}$) ∈ BodyxPlane^{3}xEdge^{3}xVertex.

The meaning of the data i($\underline{o}$) = ($\underline{b}$,$\underline{p1}$,$\underline{p2}$,$\underline{p3}$,$\underline{e1}$,$\underline{e2}$,$\underline{e3}$,$\underline{v}$) is as follows: $\underline{b}$ is an object to which this cube belongs. A cube has six planes, each of which is shared by exactly one other cube. Thus, one cube has to keep information on the three planes of the cube. $\underline{p1}$, $\underline{p2}$ and $\underline{p3}$ are the planes which belong to this cube. A cube has twelve edges, each of which is shared by three other cubes. $\underline{e1}$, $\underline{e2}$ and $\underline{e3}$ are the edges which belong to this cube. A cube has eight vertices, each of which is shared by seven other cubes. $\underline{v}$ is a vertex which belongs to this cube. Specific value NOTEXIST indicates that an entity does not exist. UNDEFINED indicates that an entity is not specified yet. The body, plane, edge and vertex information attached to a cube is shown in Figure 2. Because each cube holds only a part of its body, plane, edge and vertex ids, we need to create an empty cube for representing an object. For example, a single cube is represented as shown in Figure 3. The advantages of using this representation are:

1. Sometimes we need to create an empty cube. However, in most cases when we are treating a connected object, there is a non-empty adjacent cube and it is not necessary to create an empty cube.

2. There is no redundancy in the representation, which makes it simple to update data.

3. It is necessary to refer to the adjacent cube to update plane, edge and vertex data related to the cube. However, it is easy to determine the adjacent cube's data if we follow a tree properly as shown later. Even if each cube has its own body, plane, edge and vertex data, it is necessary to locate adjacent cubes to update the shared plane, edge and vertex data.

Boundary representation generation is performed in several steps.

Step 0: Converting octree data to extended octree data

Octree data is converted to extended octree data by simply replacing the full leaf of an octree with (UNDEFINED, UNDEFINED, UNDEFINED, UNDEFINED, UNDEFINED, UNDEFINED, UNDEFINED, UNDEFINED).

Step 1: Connected Component Identification

The body id of each leaf is determined in this step checking adjacent cubes so that connected cubes are assigned the same body id. This is a hierarchical three dimensional version of region labelling.

The following notation is used in the algorithm. p_i is the projection function for the i-th element. For a leaf o, o.body, o.plane[X], o.plane[Y], o.plane[Z], o.edge[X], o.edge[Y], o.edge[Z] and o.vertex are used to refer to $p_0(i(o))$, $p_1(i(o))$, $p_2(i(o))$, $p_3(i(o))$, $p_4(i(o))$, $p_5(i(o))$, $p_6(i(o))$, and $p_7(i(o))$, respectively. $o[x,y,z]$ stands for $p_{zyx}(o)$. The algorithm is described in a PASCAL-like control structure with informal statements for readability.

Algorithm A: Recursive Region Labelling Algorithm

```
labeling(o)
begin
  equivalence <- ϕ;
  connect(o);
  Decide the representative element of each equivalence class and then
  change all body ids in a tree to the representative element.
  All body ids are stored in the Body set.
end;

connect(o)
begin
  if o = full then
    begin
      if o.body = UNDEFINED then o.body <- new_object;
      for each adjacent cube ot in X,Y and Z direction do       ...(1)
        begin
          if ot.body = UNDEFINE then ot.body <- o.body;
          else equivalence <- equivalence ∪ {(o.body,ot.body)};
        end;
    end;
  if o = node then
    begin
       for each x,y and z in {0,1} do connect(o[x,y,z]);        ...(2)
    end;
end;
```

New_body is a function to generate a new body id. We use the following algorithm to locate the adjacent node at part (1) in this algorithm.

<u>Adjacent Node Locating Algorithm</u>:

The method used to find the adjacent nodes in the octree representation is not straightforward. There are three cases, which depend on the size of the adjacent cube. Figure 4 shows the three cases.

It is possible to use the node address of a cube to find the adjacent nodes. Here, the node address is a sequence of child node positions approaching to the target node. The node address of node $o[x_1, y_1, z_1]...[x_n, y_n, z_n]$ is $(x_1, y_1, z_1)...(x_n, y_n, z_n)$. In this representation, the adjacent node in the x direction has a node address $(x_1', y_1, z_1)...(x_n', y_n, z_n)$ where $x_1'...x_n' = x_1...x_n+1$. This addition is performed in binary representation. This covers cases (a) and (b) in Figure 4. In the case (c), the adjacent cubes have node addresses $(x_1, y_1, z_1)...(x_n', y_n, z_n)(0, y_{n+1}, z_{n+1})...(0, y_m, z_m)$ for $y_{n+1}, z_{n+1}, ... y_m, z_m$ {0,1}. By updating the adjacent cube information for each node n when a target node n changes, we can find the adjacent nodes without calculation. Of course, updating the adjacent cube information increases the overhead and slows down execution. However, it is still necessary to update the node address information when the target cube changes in the node address method. And in order to reach the adjacent node, it is necessary to follow a pointer, which slows down execution at a factor of log(n), where n is the number of nodes and leaves in the tree.

The following is the algorithm used when the target node's (x,y,z) child node is made a new target node. Here, ao holds information about the node which is adjacent to the node. ao has to be correctly specified when execution starts.

```
Update(ao,x,y,z)
begin
        if x = 1 and y = 0 and z = 0 then
            if ao <> empty then begin
                    if ao <> full then
                            ao <- ao[0,0,0]
                    end
            end;
        ... {other cases} ...
        (Figure 5 illustrates this operation)
end;
```

This program is inserted in position (2) in algorithm A. If the adjacent node is neither full nor empty at position (1) in algorithm A, then follow adjacent node ao to the near side to reach adjacent nodes. For the x direction, perform the following operation.

```
find_cubes(ao)
begin
  if ao = full then do something.
  if ao = heterogeneous then
    begin
      find_cubes(ao[0,0,0]);
      find_cubes(ao[0,0,1]);
      find_cubes(ao[0,1,0]);
      find_cubes(ao[0,1,1]);
    end;
end;
```

Step 2.0: Plane Generation, Split and Removal

In order to perform the plane connectivity check, all nodes that have plane ids have to exist. In this step, a node corresponding to a plane is generated if it does not exist.

If a cube is smaller than the adjacent cube which has plane information on the cube, then we divide the adjacent cube until the adjacent cube becomes the same size as the cube.

The object field of the generated cube is set NOTEXIST. If a plane sits between two existing cubes, the plane does not actually exist in the final boundary representation. In this case, the plane is removed by setting the plane id to the specific value NOTEXIST.

This algorithm also scans through an octree with adjacent node information.

Algorithm B: Remove Unexisting Planes

```
remove(o)
begin
  if o = full then
    begin
      for adjacent node ao in x direction do
        begin
          if ao = full then o.plane[x] <- NOTEXIST;
          if ao = heterogeneous then
            if all adjacent nodes exist then o.plane[x] <- NOTEXIST.
        end;
    end;
end;
```

Step 2.1: Connected Plane Identification

The plane[X], plane[Y] and plane[Z] fields of each leaf are determined in this step. By checking the planes of adjacent cubes the connected planes of cubes are assigned the same plane id. This algorithm is similar to step 1.0. The created plane ids are stored in the Plane set.

Step 3.0: Edge Generation, Split and Removal

In order to perform the line connectivity check, we have to have all the nodes holding the data corresponding to lines of an object. This is performed in a manner similar to step 2.0.

Step 3.1: Connected Edge Identification

The edge[X], edge[Y] and edge[Z] fields of each leaf are determined in this step. By checking the edges of the adjacent cube, shared edges of connected cubes are assigned the same edge id. This algorithm is similar to step 1.0. The created plane ids are stored in the Edge set.

Step 4.0: Vertex Generation and Removal

The vertex field of each leaf is determined in this step. This step is similar to step 2.0. The generation and removal of a point have to be performed in a manner similar to step 3.0.

Step 4.1: Vertex Identification

Each vertex is given a unique vertex id. All vertex ids are stored in the Vertex set.

After this step, all data will be ready. Data is stored in boundary files in the following steps.

Step 5:   Vertex Data Generation

The coordinate of each vertex is stored in a table in this step.

Step 6:   EdgeVertex Data Generation

By traversing the octree, the relationship between edge and vertex ids is determined in this step. The direction of o fan edge e is decided so that for the start vs and end point ve for the edge e, $vs < ve$ holds. Here, the order between vertex ids is determined from the chronological order in which vertex ids were created. If all tree traversal is done in a negative to positive direction, each edge points in the positive direction of one of the axes.

Step 7:   PlaneEdge Data Generation

The relationship between plane and edge ids is identified by traversing the octree. The direction of the plane is checked against that of the edge and stored in the _dir_ field. Figure 6 shows some examples of this.

Step 8:   ObjectPlane Data Generation

By traversing the octree, the relationship between object and plane ids are identified and stored in the ObjectPlane set. The direction of the plane for a full object is clockwise and that of an empty object is counterclockwise. The direction of a full cube is + and the direction of an empty cube is −. The direction of the object is checked against the plane and stored in the _dir_ field. Figure 7 shows some examples of how the _dir_ field is determined.

IV. CONCLUSION

In this paper, we described the conversion of data from octree data to a boundary representation. Samples are shown in Figure 8.

In the algorithm described in this paper, we generate a table so that an edge can be shared by two non-adjacent cubes. Figure 9 shows this situation. This is because we want to retain the semantics of the original data as much as possible. Some of the boundary representation based on the winged-edge data structure break with the semantics of the data by imposing the restriction that each edge be shared by exactly two planes. In our implementation, the target is a table that does not impose such restrictions on the data.

ACKNOWLEDGEMENT

We are grateful to Dr. Hideko S. Kunii of RICOH Co. Ltd for her technical support and to RICOH Co. Ltd for financial support.

REFERENCES:

1. K. Yamaguchi, T. L. Kunii, K. Fujimura, and H. Toriya,
   "Octree Related Algorithms and Data Structures,"
   IEEE Computer Graphics and Applications, Jan., 1984, pp.53-59.

2. M. M. Yau and S. N. Srihari,
   "A Hierarchical Data Structure for Multidimensional Digital Images,"
   Comm. ACM., Vol. 26, No. 7, July, 1983, pp. 504-515.

3. K. Yamaguchi, N. Inamoto, H. Kunii and T. L. Kunii,
   "Three-Dimensional Data Input by Selection of Hierarchically Defined Blocks,"
   submitted to Eurographics 84.

4. A. Baer, C. Eastman and M. Henrion,
   "Geometric modelling: a survey,"
   CAD Vol. 11, No. 5, Sept. 1979, pp. 253-272.

Fig. 1. Sample octree

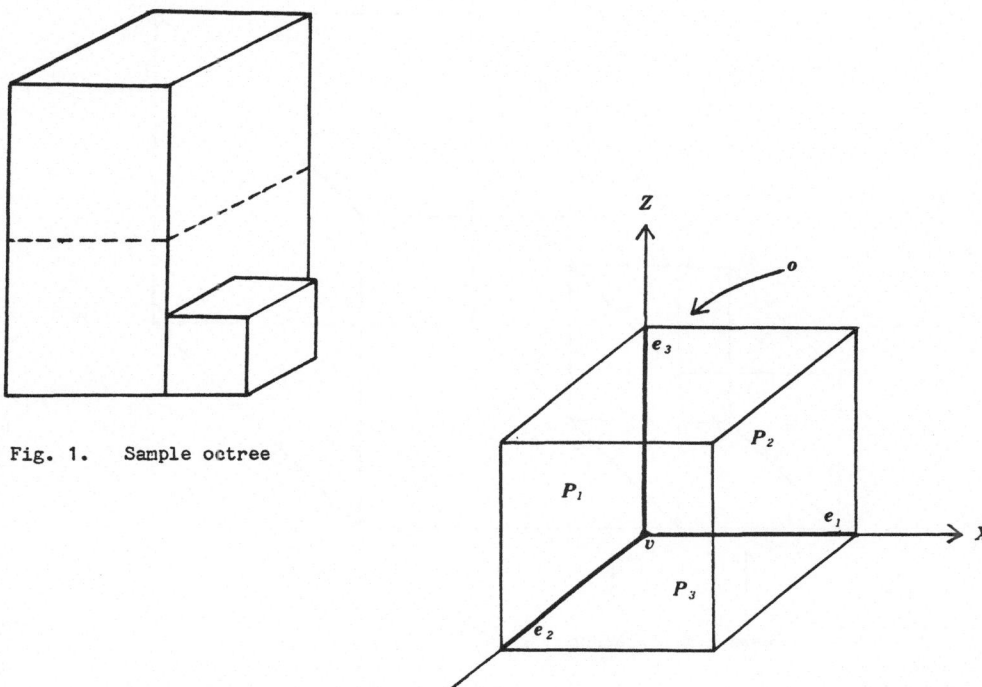

Fig. 2. Extended octree with its object, planes, edges and vertex

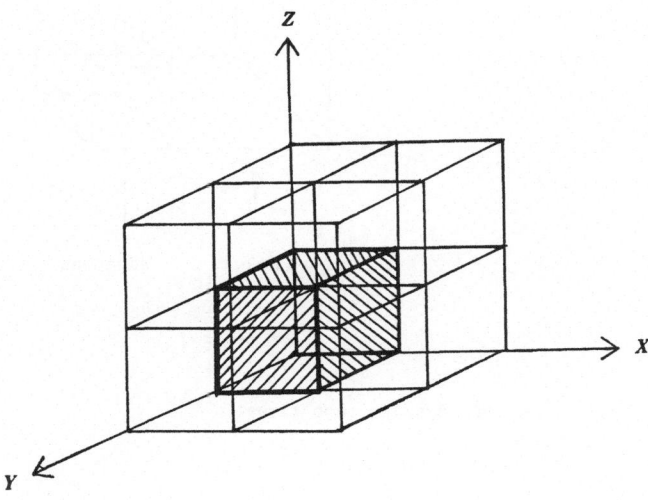

Fig. 3. Cube and empty cubes

22

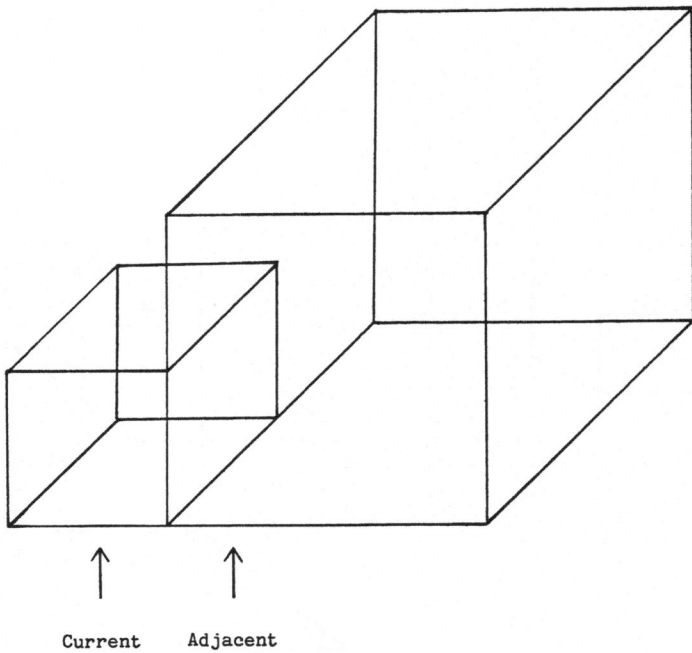

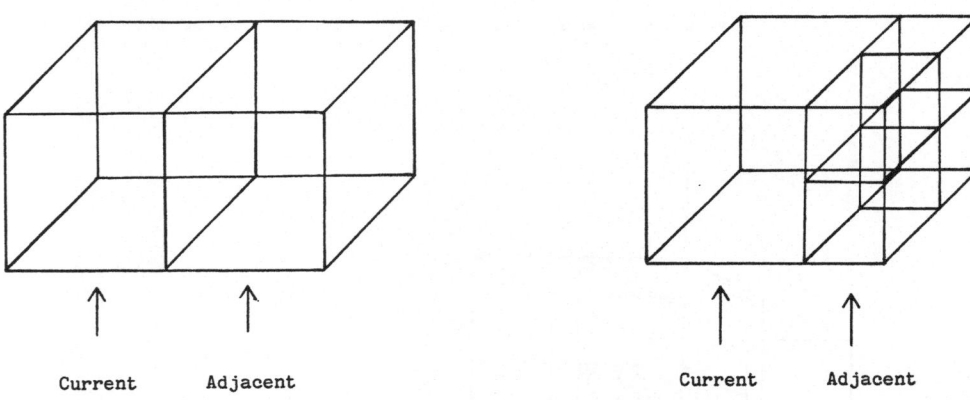

Fig. 4. Three cases of adjacent cube sizes

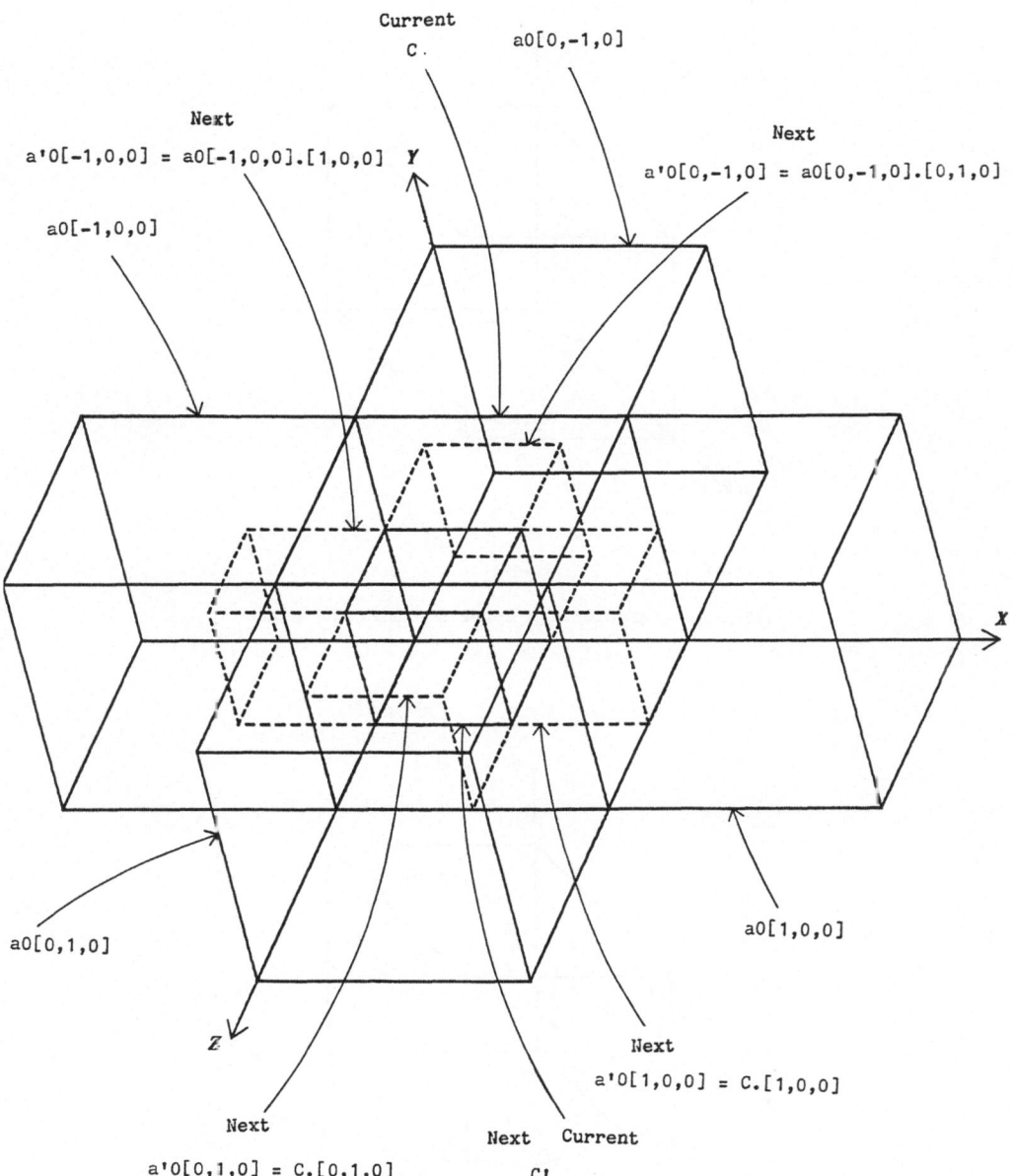

Fig. 5. Adjacent cube calculation

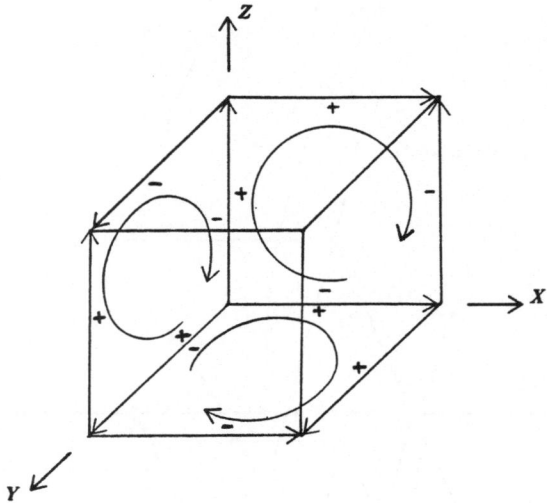

Fig. 6. Relationship between planes and edges

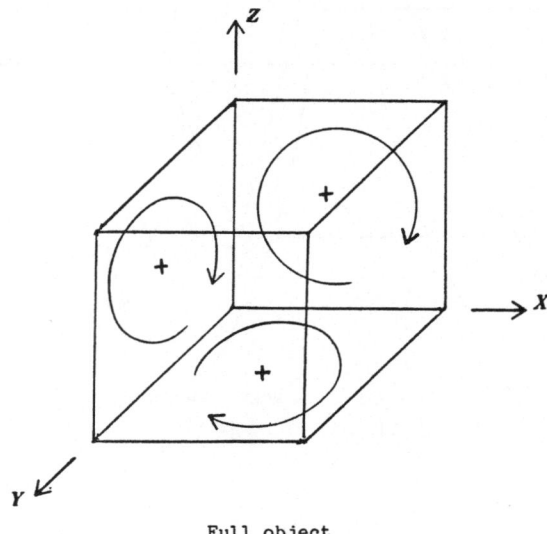

Full object

Fig. 7. Relationship between object and planes

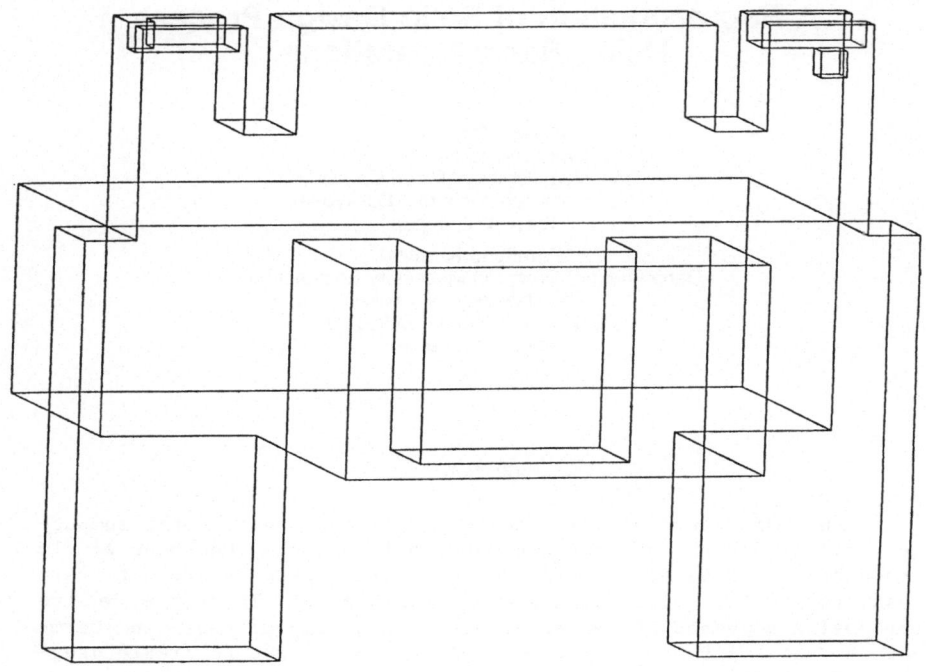

Fig. 8. Example of conversion

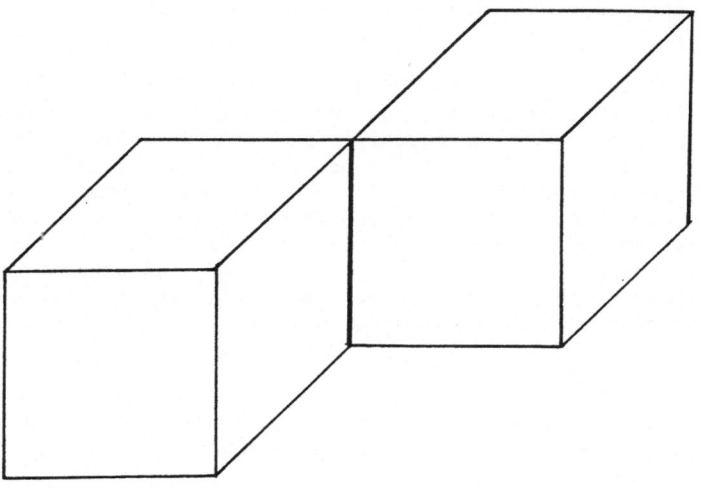

Fig. 9. Edge shared by two non-adjacent touching cubes

A Representation of Solid Design Process Using Basic Operations

Hiroaki Chiyokura
Software Research Laboratory
Technology Division, Ricoh Co., Ltd.
1-17, Koishikawa 1-chome, Bunkyo-ku
Tokyo 112, Japan

Fumihiko Kimura
Department of Precision Machinery Engineering
The University of Tokyo
3-1, Hongo 7-chome, Bukyo-ku
Tokyo 113, Japan

ABSTRACT

The importance of using solid modeling systems in the computer aided design of three-dimensional objects has been widely recognized. However, current solid modeling systems are not very easy-to-use for interactive geometric design. Therefore, we are proposing a method of representing solid design process in terms of a set of basic operations, which can be used to create user-friendly modeling systems.

The basic operations which are fundamental to our method are primitives for changing solid shapes. Each operation has an inverse operation. In our system MODIF, all operations (for example, set operations and local operations) change the solid shapes through basic operations. The basic operations which have been invoked are then stored as the leaves of a binary tree structure. This structure is used to represent the solid generation process itself.

If this representation and a boundary representation are used together as the internal representations in a solid modeling system, the system can quickly regenerate previous solids in the design process. The design process usually includes many trials and errors. Sometimes a solid is accidentally broken by the user. Therefore, in interactive geometric design, it is important that the system can regenerate previous solids. Also, since in our system the programs for all operations are independent of the data structure of the solids, it is easy for an implementer to develop the operations. This adds to the reliability of the solid modeling system.

KEYWORDS AND PHRASES : Computer aided design, Solid modeling, Boundary representation, Euler operation

1. INTRODUCTION

The importance of using a solid modeling system (SMS) in the computer aided design (CAD) of three dimensional objects has been widely recognized. A solid model which completely represents the shape of the solid is much more useful than a conventional wire-frame model or a surface model in many engineering applications. However, there are a number of problems in using current SMSs in interactive geometric design. Especially, as important problems, these include the response time for interactive operations, the geometric coverage of the generated solids, the usability for designers, and the reliability of the system. The response time will improve as advances are made in hardware design. As for geometric coverage, we have previously proposed one method for solving this problem[3]. The problems of usability and reliability are related to the basic design of the solid modeling system. In this paper, we propose solutions to these last two problems.

Regarding the problem of usability, we are proposing a method of representing the solid design process as a list of basic operations. Since our system MODIF uses this representation, it can quickly regenerate a solid from earlier in the design process. This is important for the user of a SMS, because the design process usually includes many trials and errors. Also, the user wants to recover easily from operational errors. The problem of reliability is also alleviated through the use of basic operations for all shape changes. This is because the coding of these operations can be kept independent of the solid data structure. This makes it easier for an implementer to develop or modify operations, and increases the reliability of the system.

2. BACKGROUND

In previous solid modeling systems, solids have been internally represented by using either constructive solid geometry representations (CSG-reps) or boundary representations (B-reps) [5]. CSG-reps have the advantage of requiring less memory for representing solids. Also, modifications such as that shown in Fig.1 are easy for the user to make, because CSG-reps store the definition process for the solids. However, it is not easy to use non-set operations (i.e., local operations) in CSG based systems. For a designer, it is desirable that all types of operations for changing shapes are available in a system.

In this regard, systems using B-reps as an internal representation can make use of a wide variety of operations. This is a major advantage of B-rep systems. However, since B-reps are only representations of solid shapes, it is not easy for a user to make modification such as that shown in Fig.1. In order to do this in B-rep systems, a user must first erase the hole by adding a proper solid, and then make a smaller hole by subtracting a cylinder. This troublesome procedure must be followed, because B-rep systems do not contain information about the generation process of the solid. Also, many difficulties can arise when a user make a mistake in a B-rep system. For example, if a mistake occurs in the positioning of solids for a set operation, important parts of the original solids might have to be erased. Fig.2 shows this type of mistake in a set operation. While Fig.2(c) shows the solid generated by the correct operation, Fig.2(d) shows a solid generated with an error. In this case, after erasing the rectangle, the user must reconstruct part of the original solid. Also, if a user makes mistakes during local operations, self-intersecting objects will sometimes be generated, as shown in Fig.3. In most such cases, the user can regenerate the original solid by local operations. But occasionally it is very difficult to regenerate the original solids. Because of these difficulties in B-rep systems the designer must be very careful in specifying operations, keeping in mind that the solid might be broken by the an error.

In order to deal with this problem, the following methods have been previously employed. The first method is to store the solids data in external storage at each stage of the design process. However, if the solid is complicated, the amount of data can be quite large. If the solids are saved many times during the design process, a very large data area is used. So this method is undesirable. The second method is to store all commands which a user enters while generating a solid. But if a solid from earlier in the design process must be regenerated, all the operations must be computed again from the beginning. This takes a lot of time, and is therefore not feasible for interactive design.

We propose to solve this problem by representing solids internally as lists of basic operations, as well as B-reps. Basic operations are primitives for generating and modifying solids. Each basic operation has an inverse operation, for reversing any changes. In our system, set operations and local operations always use these basic operations to change the solid shapes. The basic operations which have been invoked are then stored as the leaves of a binary tree structure. This structure represents the solid generation process.

By using this representation of the solid generation process, the system can quickly regenerate the previous solid in the design process. In a system with this facility, the user does not have to worry that an error might destroy the solid. So he or she can easily use an SMS as part of interactive CAD.

3. BASIC OPERATIONS

Basic operations are either topological, geometrical or global. Each operations always has its inverse.

3.1 Local elements of a solid

For most basic operations, the local elements of a solid are specified. In our system local elements of B-reps are described. B-reps represent the boundary faces of a solid. Faces can be defined by loops. We distinguish P-loops, representing face boundaries from C-loops, representing holes in a face, as shown in Fig.4. A face has always one P-loop. These loops are a series of edges. The nodes of the edges are called vertices. Therefore, the local elements specified in basic operations are loops, edges and vertices.

3.2 Topological operations

Topological operations generate and modify the topology of a solid. Although our descriptions of these operations are almost the same as Euler's[1,2,4], there is one difference. In Euler operations, a hole in a face is called a ring, and a face boundary is distinct from a ring. However, in our operations, both a face boundary and a ring are called loops, and they are treated without distinction in many processes. The details of the topological operations are described below. In the operation parameters, ^ and v mean output and input respectively.

```
           ^  ^  v v v
1) MEL(E1,L1,L2,V1,V2)
```
Edge E1 is drawn between V1 and V2 in loop L2. (See Fig. 5.) At the same time, loop L1 is created. Although loop L2 may be either a P-loop or a C-loop, loop L1 is always a P-loop.

```
           v  v  ^ ^ ^
2) KEL(E1,L1,L2,V1,V2)
```
Edge E1 is deleted. (See Fig. 5.) At the same time, loop L1 is deleted. This is the inverse of the MEL operation.

```
        ^  ^  v v v v
3) MVE(V1,E1,E2,x,y,z)
```
Vertex V1 is created at a point (x,y,z) on edge E2. (See Fig. 6.) At the same time, edge E1 is created.

```
        v  v  ^ ^ ^ ^
4) KVE(V1,E1,E2,x,y,z)
```
Vertex V1 is deleted. (See Fig. 6.) At the same time, edge E1 is deleted.

```
            v  v
5) KLcMLp(L1,L2)
```
This procedure changes C-loop L2 to P-loop L2. (See Fig. 7.) P-loop L1 was the face to which C-loop L2 belonged.

```
            v  v
6) KLpMLc(L1,L2)
```
This changes P-loop L2 to C-loop L2. (See Fig. 7.) P-loop L1 is the face to which C-loop L2 belongs.

```
        ^  ^  v v v v v
7) MEV(E1,V1,V2,L1,x,y,z)
```
Edge E1 is drawn between vertex V2 in loop L1 and a point (x,y,z). (See Fig. 8.) At the same time, vertex V1 is created at point (x,y,z). Loop L1 may be either a P-loop or a C-loop.

```
        v  v  ^ ^ ^ ^ ^
8) KEV(E1,V1,V2,L1,x,y,z)
```
Edge E1 and vertex V1 are deleted. (See Fig. 8.)

```
           ^  v  v v v
9) MEKL(E1,L1,L2,V1,V2)
```
As shown in Fig.9(a)(b), edge E1 is drawn between vertex V1 in loop L1 and vertex V2 in loop L2. Loops L1 and L2 must be of the same type. When the loops are C-loops, they must belong to the same face. If loops L1 and L2 are of different types, KLcMLp are used, as shown in Fig.9(c).

```
           v  ^  ^ ^ ^
10) KEML(E1,L1,L2,V1,V2)
```
As shown in Fig.9, edge E1 is deleted, and loop L1 is created. The

type of loop L1 is made the same as that of loop L2.

11) MEVVL(E1,V1,V2,L1,x1,y1,z1,x2,y2,z2)
Edge E1 is drawn between a point (x1,y1,z1) and a point (x2,y2,z2). (See Fig. 10.) At the same time, vertices V1, V2 and loop L1 are created.

12) KEVVL(E1,V1,V2,L1,x1,y1,z1,x2,y2,z2)
Edge E1 is deleted. (See Fig. 10.) Vertices V1, V2 and loop L1 are deleted at the same time.

3.3 Geometrical operations

1) TV(V1,x,y,z)
Vertex V1 is translated. The translation vector is (x,y,z). (See Fig. 11.)

2) CLZ(E1,x1,y1,z1,x2,y2,z2)
This procedure changes a straight line edge E1 into a cubic Bezier curve. Here, the control points of the Bezier curve are (x1,y1,z1) and (x2,y2,z2). (See Fig. 12.)

3) CZL(E1,x1,y1,z1,x2,y2,z2)
This changes Bezier curve edge E1 into a straight line. (See Fig. 12.)

4) TZ(E1,i,x,y,z)
This translates i-th (1 or 2) control point of Bezier curve edge E1. The translation vector is (x,y,z). (See Fig. 13.)

The edge shapes used in MODIF are straight lines and cubic Bezier curves. If new types of edge shapes are added to the system, basic operations for changing the shapes of the new edges must also be added.

3.4 Global operations

1) TS(A,x,y,z)
Solid A is translated. The translation vector is (x,y,z).

2) RS(A,i,θ)
Solid A is rotated about i-axis (x, y or z). Here, the rotation angle is θ.

3) NS(A)
All faces of solid A are turned over so that the normal vectors of the faces are changed to the opposite direction. This operation is used in set operations, and in the generation of a mirror image described later.

4) CS(A,B,C)
Solid A and solid B are combined, and solid C is generated. The geometry and topology of solids A and B are not changed. The only ef-

fect of this combination is that the two solids are considered as one solid in the data structure. This basic operation is used in combinational operations on two solids, such as set operations and glue operations.
$$v\ v\ v$$
5) SS(A,B,C)
By separating the data structure of solid C, two solids A and B are generated. This operation is the inverse of 'CS'.

4. Internal representation of the solid generation process

MODIF has two kinds of representations of each solid. One is a representation of the solid's shape, called a B-rep. The other is a representation of the solid generation process, in the form of a binary tree structure. This representation is called a basic operation tree. Fig.14 shows how this tree changes as the generation of the solid proceeds.
(1) Solid A is generated. At this time, one node of the tree is created. This node contains the name of the solid.
(2) Two faces of solid A are lifted. The basic operations and variable values used in the lifting are stored as the right leaf of the tree.
(3) Solid B is generated, and all faces are turned over by basic operation 'NS'. At this point, one node of solid B is created, and then basic operation 'NS' is stored as the right leaf.
(4) Solid A and solid B are combined by a glue operation, and new solid C is generated. A node representing the combination of two solids is created. Next, a node for solid C is created and connected to the combination node. Basic operations used in the glue operation are stored as the right leaf of the node of Solid C. At this point, the B-reps of solid A and B will disappear.

The nodes of a tree representing a solid generation process are of two types. One contains the name of a solid. The right leaf of this node contains basic operations and their variable values, which were used to change the B-rep of the solid. The other type of node represents the combination of two solids. This combination means that two solids are now regarded as one solid. No topological or geometrical changes are made.

If the solid generation process is represented in this way, the system can quickly regenerate the B-rep of the previous solid by using the inverse operations. Also, it is easy to regenerate the current solid from the B-rep of the previous solid. However, the user does not need to know that the solid generation process is represented by using trees and basic operations. He or she only has to know that the system contains representations of both the solid shapes and the solid generation process. To generate a previous solid, first the system shows the names of the previous solids and a number N, that represents numbers of operations (for example, set operations and local operations) used for changing the respective solids. After a user examines this information, he or she enters the solid name and a number M ($1 \leq M \leq N$), that represents the number of the operations to be used for represents the solid. Then, the system automatically regenerates the shape representation of the earlier solid. Because of this capability, the user does not have to worry about a mistake destroying the solid. Therefore, a designer can easily use this system as the basis of an interactive CAD system.

In the current version of our system, in order to change the B-rep of a previous solid, we must delete the representation of generation process, from the previous stage to the current one. It is desirable for a designer to have access to the representation of the entire solid generation process even after changing a previous solid. We are working on adding this capability to the system.

5. THE STRUCTURE OF MODIF

Fig.15 outlines the program structure of the MODIF system. In this figure, ◯ indicates the data representing solids, and ▭ indicates the program modules. The user gives commands to the geometric modeling (GM) program, in order to generate or modify a solid. Local operations and set operations are part of the GM. Then, the GM changes the B-rep of a solid, using the basic operations. At the same time, the tree processor (TP) records the basic operations in the tree structure, and the display program (DP) draws the resultant solid for the user. The DP does not directly read the information for drawing the solid from the B-rep, but receives its information from the reference program (RP). The RP formats the solids data, to make the implementation of the GM and DP as easy as possible. For example, when describing a loop, the RP gives which edges and vertices are attached to the loop. Or when describing a vertex, the RP gives which loops and edges are attached to the vertex. Similarly, the application program (AP) also receives its information from the RP. A program for generating cutter path data for NC machining is being used as an example in the current version of the AP.

The B-rep in our system uses a winged-edge structure [1]. However, the implementers of the GM, DP and AP do not have to know this, because the GM, DP and AP are independent of the characteristics of the B-rep structure. Therefore, the implementation of the GM, DP and AP in our system is easier than in a conventional system. In addition, it will be possible to use the GM, DP and AP with another B-rep system, if the basic operations and the RP are reimplemented.

Mantyla and Sulonen [4] have proposed a method for using Euler operations in the construction of a solid modeling system. Our system differs in that the B-rep can only be changed by using the basic operations, and cannot be changed directly. This allows for the reversal of any changes, by the use of the inverses of those basic operations.

6. IMPLEMENTATION OF HIGH-LEVEL OPERATIONS FOR CHANGING SOLIDS

This section shows how various high-level operations for changing solids are implemented in MODIF, using combinations of the basic operations.

6.1 Lifting

A lifting is an operation for sweeping local elements of solids, such as faces, edges and vertices. Fig. 16 shows how the lifting of a face is implemented, using basic operations.

6.2 Generation of a mirror image

Many engineering objects are symmetric. So it is important that a modeling system can generate the mirror image of a solid, as shown in Fig.17. This operation is again accomplished by using the basic operations. First, an identical solid is generated, by a copy operation. Next, all vertices and all control points of curved edges are translated, using the basic operations 'TV' and 'TZ'. Finally, the faces of the solid are turned over, using basic operation 'NS', and a mirror image of the original solid has now been generated.

6.3 Glue operation

In a glue operation, two solids which are attached to each other are combined to make a single solid. However, the two solids must not be interfered - in other words, they must not overlap the same three-dimensional area. The same operation can be accomplished by using set operations, however, set operations require much computational time, and also there are some problems in the reliability of the implementation. But, in a glue operation, many of the processes used in set operations are not necessary, because the glue operation has the restriction that the two solids will not be interfered. This simplifies the algorithm, so the response time is shorter than for set operations. Futhermore, the reliability of the program is better. Therefore, a glue operation is important in a system which uses B-reps as the internal model of solids.

Fig.18 shows a glue operation, implemented using basic operations. Fig.18(a) shows two solids which are to be glued. Although the solids in the figure do not seem to be attached to each other, they were only drawn this way for purposes of illustration. In fact, their adjacent faces are common. First, as shown in Fig.18(b), four edges of zero length are generated, and the two solids are combined treated as a single solid. Next, unnecessary edges are deleted, as shown in Fig.18(c). Finally, unnecessary vertices are deleted, and the glued solid shown in Fig.18(d) is generated.

If a user makes mistakes in the positioning of two solids, and interfered solids are combined in a glue operation, a self-intersecting solid is sometimes generated. It is difficult to regenerate the original solids from the self-intersecting solid, using conventional operations. However, since our system records the history of the solid generation process, the original solids can be quickly regenerated.

6.4 Rounding operation

The authors [3] have elsewhere proposed the rounding operation as a method for generating free-form shapes in a solid modeling system.

This operation is again implemented by using basic operations, as shown in Fig.19. Fig. 19(a) shows three edges E1, E2 and E3 that are to be rounded. First, the faces which are attached to these edges are divided by new edges, as shown in Fig.19(b). Next, unnecessary edges on the vertices of the original solid are deleted, and curved edges are generated as shown in Fig.19(c). Then unnecessary vertices on the new dividing lines are deleted, and these edges are curved. This completes a curve model for representing the desired free-form shape, as shown in Fig.19(d).

6.5 Set operation

This section shows how set operations are implemented, through the combinations of basic operations. Fig.20 shows a union in set operations. In Fig.20(a), two solids are interfered. The union is accomplished in the following manner:
(1) Intersection lines of the two solids are computed, and they are added as edges on the faces of the solids (Fig.20(b)). These edges and their vertices are called double-edges (D-edges) and double-vertices (D-vertices) respectively.
(2) The interfering parts of the solids, bordered by the D-edges, are deleted (Fig.20(c)).
(3) As in the glue operation, edges of zero length are generated between corresponding D-vertices, and the two solids are combined (Fig.20(d)). Then, unnecessary edges and vertices are deleted, and the union of two solids is completed (Fig.20(e)).

The three set operations are union, difference (DIF) and intersection (INT). DIF and INT are implemented by combining a union and a NS which turns over all the faces, as follows:
 DIF(A,B) = NS(UNION(NS(A),B))
 INT(A,B) = NS(UNION(NS(A),NS(B)))
where, A and B are solids.

The implementation of set operations in conventional systems is dependent on the characteristics of the B-rep structure. If a set operation fails due to a fault in the program, the data structure of the solids will sometimes be broken. It is difficult to recover the original solids in these systems. However, in our system, the original solids can quickly be regenerated, using the history of basic operations stored in the tree structure. Since the algorithms for set operations are complicated, it is not easy to implement perfect programs. Therefore, the ability to recovery previous solids is an important function in a solid modeling system.

7. CONCLUSION

In this paper, we have proposed a method for representing the solid generation process itself, as a tree of basic operations. By using this representation, the system can quickly regenerate solids from earlier in the design process. In a system with this capability, the user need not worry about accidentally causing a solid to be broken. He or she can easily use the system as a tool in interactive geometric design.

In addition, we proposed a method of implementing a solid modeling system through the use of basic operations. In our system, the implementer of the geometric operations does not have to know the detail of the solid data structure, since all operations are specified by basic operations. This simplifies the implementation of the system, and improves its reliability.

In order to make the solid modeling system more user-friendly, new efficient operations should be added in the future. Therefore, it is important that the system is able to incorporate new operations, and that their implementation is easy. This is true for our system, because the basic operations can be used as simple tools for implementing new high-level operations.

In this paper, we described the usefulness of inverse operations in solid modeling. They are particularly important in the design of free-form shapes, which is subject to a great many trials and errors, and where often the designer can not remember the previous free-form shapes. Therefore, we are developing efficient operations for changing free-form curves and surfaces, and the inverse of these operations.

ACKNOWLEDGEMENTS

We would like to thank Prof. T.Sata in the university of Tokyo for his valuable suggestions. In addition, we thank T.Takamura for his support in making a final version of this paper.

REFERENCES

[1] Baumgart,B.G. : A Polyhedron Representation for Computer Vision, AFIPS Conf. Proc., Vol.44, pp.589-596, May 1975.
[2] Braid,I.C., Hillyard,R.C. and Stroud,I.A. : Stepwise Construction of Polyhedra in Geometric Modelling, Mathematical Methods in Computer Graphics and Design (Ed. by K.W.Brodlie) Academic Press, pp.123-141, 1980.
[3] Chiyokura,H. and Kimura,F. : Design of Solids with Free-Form Surfaces, Computer Graphics (Proc. SIGGRAPH'83), Vol.17, No.3, pp.289-298, July 1983.
[4] Mantyla,M. and Sulonen,R. : GWB : A Solid Modeler with Euler Operators, IEEE Computer Graphics and Applications, vol.2, no.7, pp.17-31, September 1982.
[5] Requicha,A.G. : Representation for Rigid Solids : Theory, Method and Systems, Computing Surveys, vol.12, no.4, pp.437-464, December 1980.

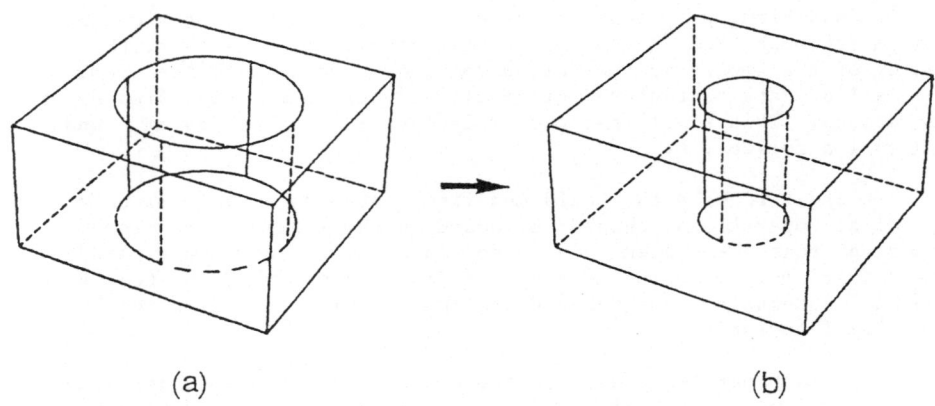

Fig.1. Modification of the shape definition

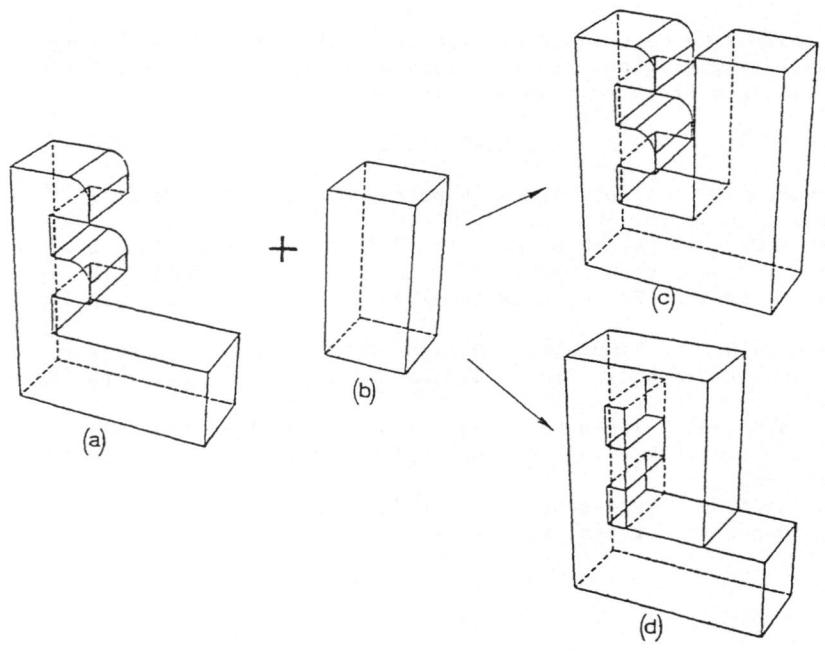

Fig.2. Mistake in a set operation

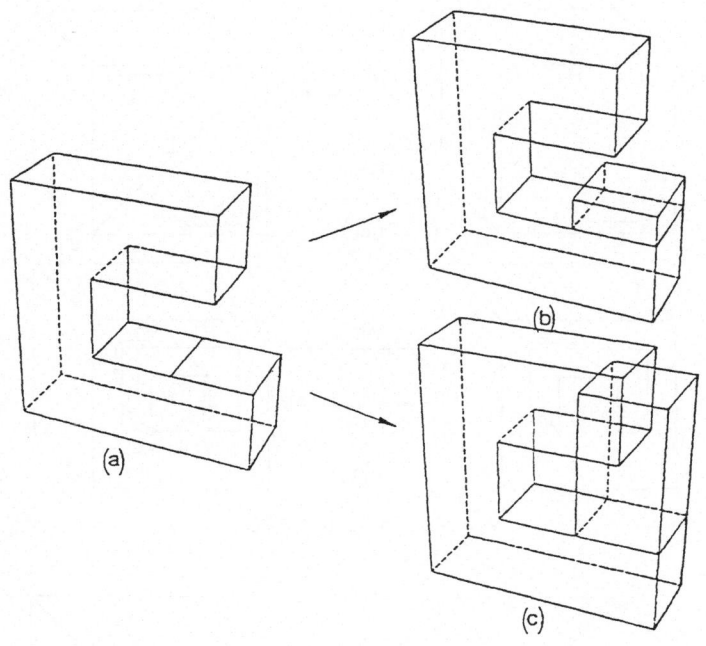

Fig.3. Mistake in a local operation

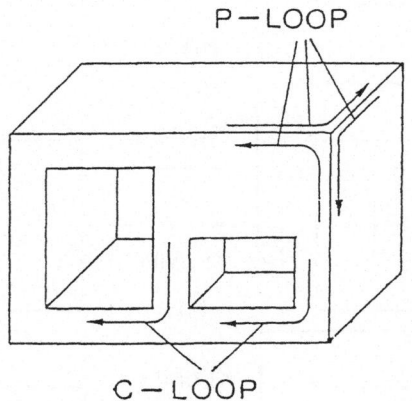

Fig.4. Types of loops

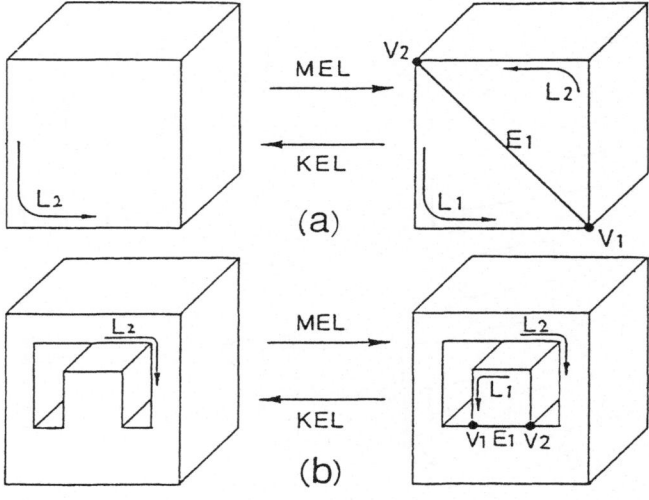

Fig.5. MEL and KEL

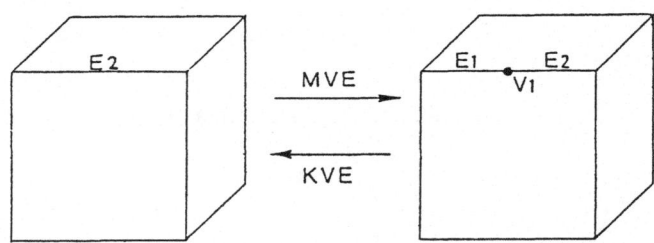

Fig.6. MVE and KVE

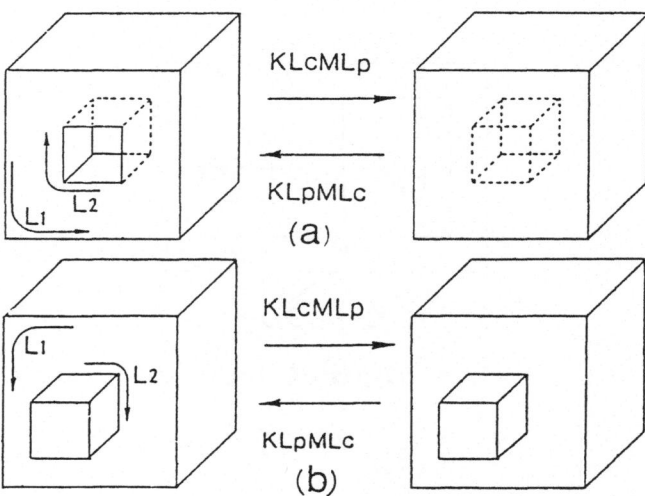

Fig.7. KLcMLp and KLpMLc

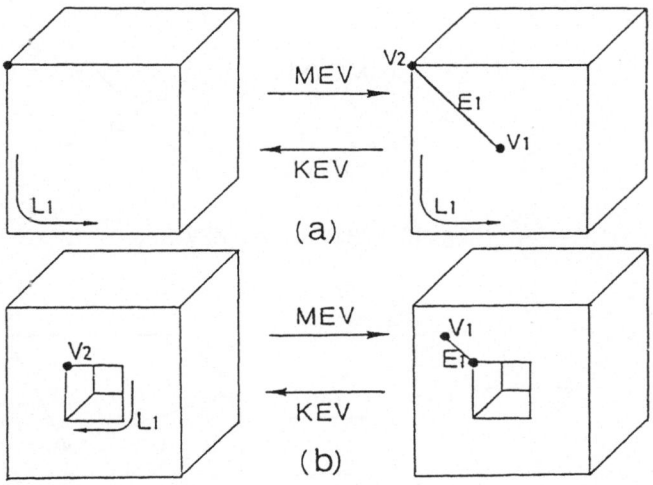

Fig.8. MEV and KEV

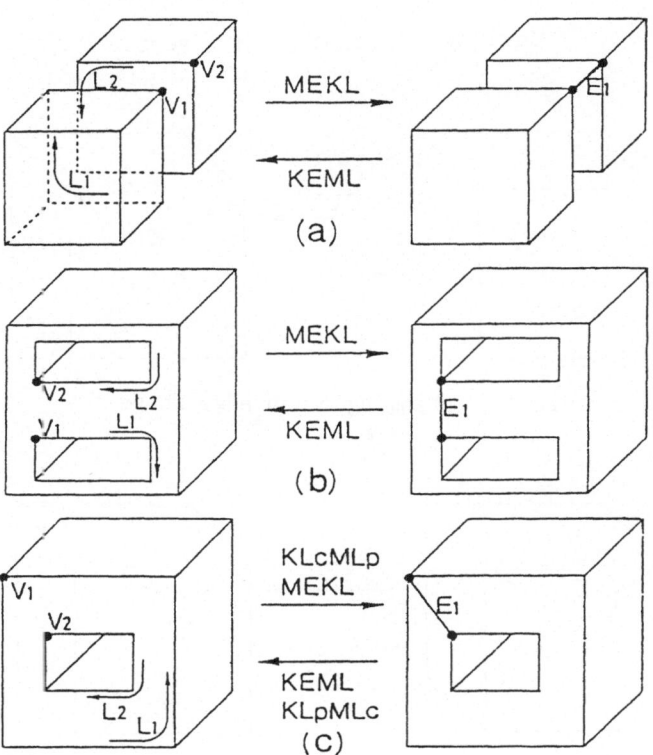

Fig.9. MEKL and KEML

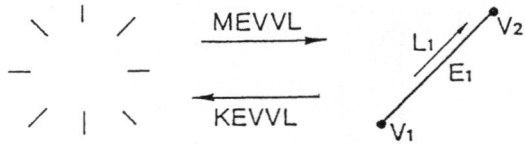

Fig.10. MEVVL and KEVVL

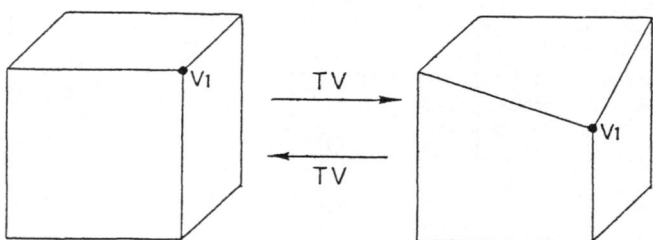

Fig.11. Translation of a vertex

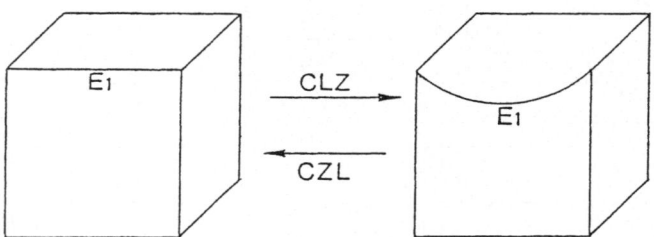

Fig.12. Changing of an edge shape

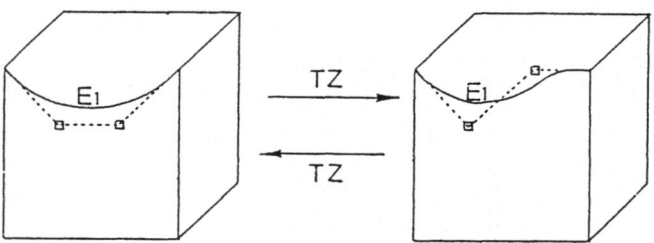

Fig.13. Translation of a control point of a Bezier curve

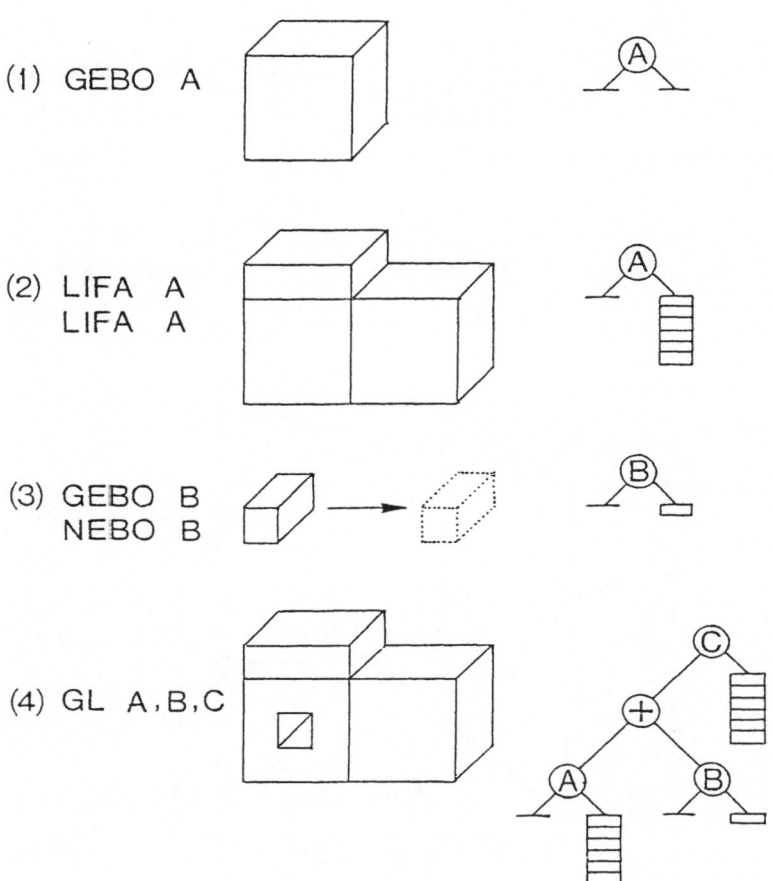

Fig.14. Process of solid generation

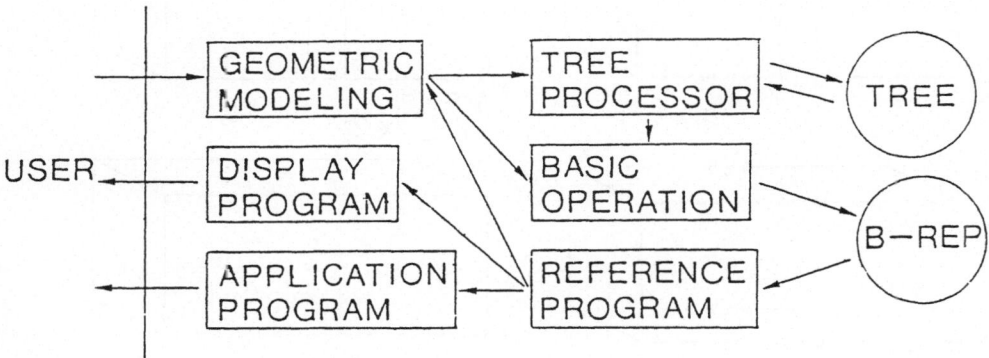

Fig.15. System structure of MODIF

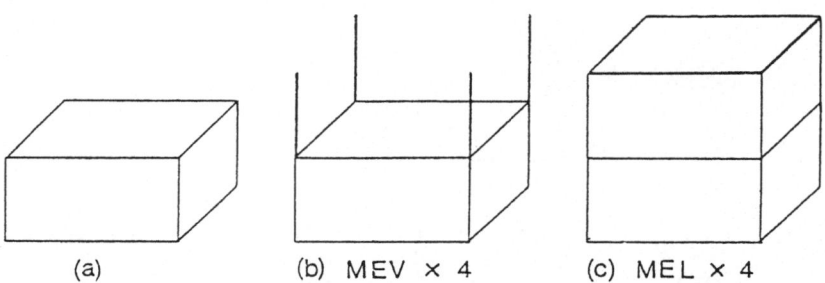

(a) (b) MEV × 4 (c) MEL × 4

Fig.16. Lift operation

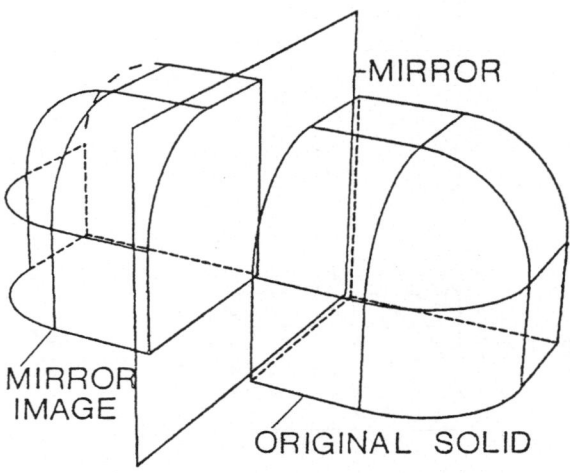

Fig.17. Mirror image

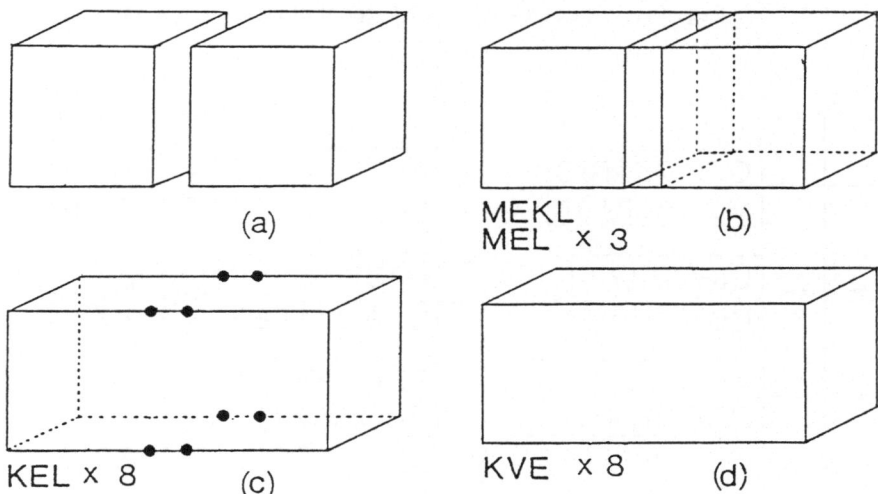

(a)

MEKL
MEL × 3   (b)

KEL × 8 (c)

KVE × 8 (d)

Fig.18. Glue operation

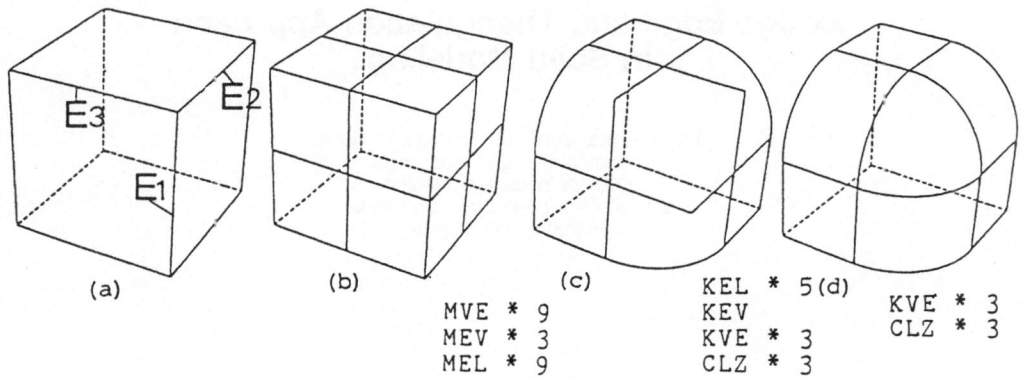

Fig.19. Rounding operation

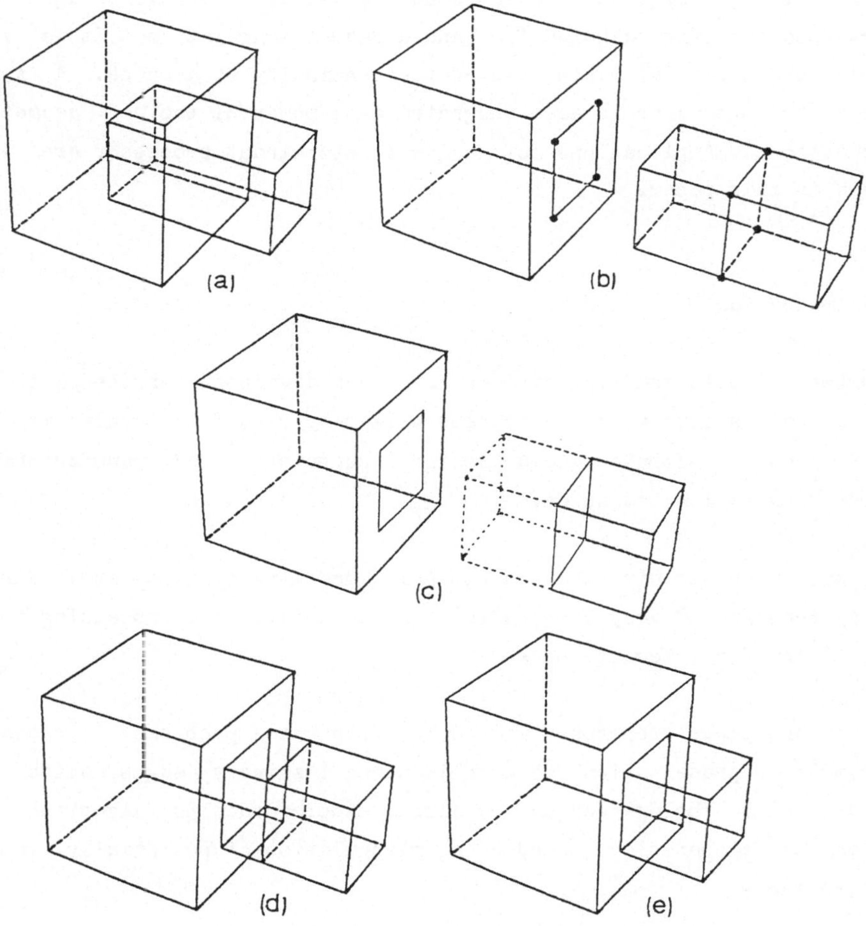

Fig.20. Set operation (UNION)

Bridge Edge and Triangulation Approach in Solid Modeling

Fujio Yamaguchi and **Toshiya Tokieda**
Industrial Design Department
Kyushu Institute of Design
9-1, Shiobaru 4-chome, Minami-ku
Fukuoka 815, Japan

Abstract

Boolean shape operations of a solid modeling system FREEDOM-II are described. The algorithm is based on the two techniques: bridge edge representation for a holed face and a face triangulation. It is very simple and efficient making use of the continuity of a shape. A 4 x 4 determinant processor is also suggested as a powerful tool of geometric computations. Applications of a 4 x 4 determinant processor are discussed in this paper.

1. Introduction

A number of solid modeling systems have been developed for the past few years. The solid modeling systems will play significant roles in the areas such as computer aided design, computer aided manufacturing, computer animation and so on.

Two main problems with the present solid modeling systems are, first, the systems are of very large size; and secondly, the processing speed is too slow for interactive use.

The present paper proposes a method to solve these problems. It presents a simple representation of a solid using imaginary edges which the authors call "bridge edge" and also a simple modeling algorithm for Boolean shape operations based on a triangulation of potentially intersecting faces.

First, the paper will explain the bridge edge representation of a solid along with data structure manipulating routines. The solid representation proposed is preferably used together with face triangulation. Secondly, a face triangulation method will be explained, and how the bridge edge representation and triangulation are utilized for the Boolean shape operations will be discussed. Thirdly, the paper will explain almost all of main geometric computations of the algorithm can be done by computing 4 x 4 determinants. The paper suggests that the solid modeling system will become simplified and very efficient by using a hardware 4 x 4 determinant processor or a more sophisticated "triangle processor."

2. Various Representation Methods of a Solid

Baumgart proposed a very nice representation method of a solid called Winged Edge Data Structure [1]. According to Baumgart a solid is represented by describing adjacent geometric elements with respect to each edge. The unique feature of the data structure is that an edge block has four pointers, PCW, PCCW, NCW, NCCW to the "winged edges" on both side faces in addition to the two pointers, PVT, NVT to its end vertices and to the two pointers, PFACE, NFACE to its side faces (see Fig.1). This data structure provides a basis for efficient geometric processing, making it possible to capitalize on the continuity of geometric element connection of a solid.

A difficulty arises, however, when we must represent multiply-connected faces, that is, holed faces. Baumgart split the face into a few pieces of simply connected faces. In order to cover a solid with multiply-connected faces Braid introduced a new geometric element "loop" into the representation of a solid [2], employing the basic concept of the Winged Edge Data Structure. According to Braid each face is bounded by one or more loops of edges. Each edge has two loop pointers, NLOOP, PLOOP instead of having two face pointers. Each face on both sides of an edge is associated with it through a loop (see Fig.2).

The present authors propose a representation method of a solid using imaginary edges. The Euler-Poincaré characteristic holds in a body with the faces triangulated. These generated edges in triangulation can be deleted without affecting the Euler-Poincaré characteristic until the number of the generated edges becomes equal to the number of holes in a face (see Fig.3). Which edges are left undeleted depends on the order of edge deletion. There can be many sets of edges left undeleted (see Fig.4). We will call these edges "bridge edge." The bridge edge is particular in that PFACE is the same as NFACE.

3. Bridge Edge Representation Method of a Solid

We consider a mechanism for a multiply-connected face to have a single circuit with respect to edges or vertices. For example each edge of the face in Fig.5 seems to be visited counterclockwise as the sequence of E_1, E_2, E_3, E_4, E_5, E_6, E_7, E_8, E_4, E_9, E_{10}, E_{11}, E_2, E_{12}, E_{13} and E_{14}. Because the bridge edges E_2, E_4 are visited twice, it is impossible to determine the next edge from E_2 or E_4 if E_2 or E_4 is specified alone. The same is true of the circuit with respect to vertices. It is impossible to visit vertices, for example, counterclockwise as the sequence of V_1, V_2, V_3, V_4, V_5, V_6, V_7, V_8, V_5, V_4, V_9, V_{10}, V_3, V_2, V_{11} and V_{12} because the end vertices of bridge edges, V_2, V_3, V_4, V_5 are visited twice.

If we visit each vertex and edge alternately counterclockwise, then the sequence is V_1, E_1, V_2, E_2, V_3, E_3, V_4, E_4, V_5, E_5, V_6, E_6, V_7, E_7, V_8, E_8, V_5, E_4, V_4, E_9, V_9, E_{10}, V_{10}, E_{11}, V_3, E_2, V_2, E_{12}, V_{11}, E_{13}, V_{12} and E_{14}. We notice in this sequence the pair of vertex and edge appears only once. This means that in bridge edge representation the topological position of a vertex or an edge round a face can be specified uniquely by a vertex-edge pair, not by a vertex or an edge alone. Having this precaution in mind we can make use of the data structure manipulating functions and procedures proposed by Baumgart, by adding adjacent vertex or edge information to the arguments. Some of the important ones are discussed in the following.

ECW, ECCW

ECW(E,F) or ECCW(E,F) is a function which outputs the next edge located clockwise or counterclockwise from the specified edge E respectively. In the bridge edge representation the argument E is not sufficient to specify the topological position of the edge in the edge circuit round F. We must further specify an adjacent vertex located either clockwise or counterclockwise. For example if we specify a vertex VT located counterclockwise from E in Fig.6, then the edge NE is output by turning the edge E clockwise at VT. A Pascal program for visiting all the edges round F might be written in Fig.6.

MKEV

MKEV is a procedure which attaches a new edge NE to the specified vertex V and creates a new vertex NV at its tip on the specified face F. In the bridge edge representation the vertex V is not sufficient to specify its topological position in a vertex circuit round F. An adjacent edge to the vertex, for example, an edge E located counterclockwise from V, must also be specified as an argument (see Fig.7). This edge information can be derived by making use of face triangulation during the processing of Boolean shape operations as will be described briefly in Chapter 4. Note that the faces (triangles) on both sides of an bridge edge are different while the face is triangulated.

MKFE

MKFE is a procedure which inserts a new edge NE between the specified vertices V_1, V_2 on the face F and creates a new face NF. In the bridge edge representation the arguments V_1, V_2 are not sufficient to specify their topological positions in a vertex circuit round F. For example edges, E_1, E_2 located counterclockwise from V_1 and V_2 must also be added to the respective vertex (see Fig.8). These edge information can be derived by making use of face triangulation during the processing of the Boolean shape operations as will be described in Chapter 4.

WING

WING is a procedure which sets wing pointers between an existing edge E_0 and a newly specified edge E_1. In the bridge edge representation the argument E_0 is not sufficient to specify the topological position in the edge circuit round the common face of E_0 and E_1. We must further specify an adjacent vertex V_0 located either clockwise or counterclockwise from E_0. Fig.9 illustrates eight cases of WING procedure.

4. An Outline of the Boolean Shape Operations Based on Face Triangulation

The following algorithm for the Boolean shape operations is based on a face triangulation. Followings are the advantages gained by the triangulation.

(1) As a standardization method of a polyhedron, face triangulation is much simpler than other methods, such as decomposition into an assembly of convex polyhedra.

(2) The algorithm for the Boolean shape operations can be largely simplified.

(3) The main processing unit of the algorithm is nicely amenable to hardware implementation as will be discussed in Chapter 5 and 6.

(4) Extra information required for the data structure manipulating procedures in the bridge edge representation method is derived by making

use of the face triangulation. While a face is triangulated, the side faces (triangles) of a bridge edge are different.

Face Triangulation

The face triangulation is simple and can be applied in the same way whether the face is simply connected or multiply-connected.

By using the function ECW or ECCW, find a concave vertex and try to triangulate with the two successive edges from the vertex and continue the process until the triangulation is impossible or the vertex becomes convex. Apply the above procedure to all the concave vertices. Then emanate edges from any one vertex to all the other vertices, and the triangulation is complete.

Let us call the edges temporarily generated in the triangulation "T-edge" and the other edges except B-edges and T-edges "R-edge."

An Algorithm for the Boolean Shape Operations

In connection with the discussion in chapter 5 and 6, an outline for the Boolean shape operations is described in the following. (For detailed description, refer to [3].) We suppose two intersecting polyhedral bodies in 3-space.

(1) Potentially intersected faces of the bodies are triangulated and intersecting triangle pairs are linked in a list called ITLIST.

(2) A triangle pair is taken out of ITLIST which has an intersecting R-edge. The intersecting point Q_1 is the initial point on an intersecting line loop. We denote the intersecting edge by EDR, the triangle having the edge by TRR and the other triangle by TRS.

(3) Find the next intersecting triangle pair (new EDR, new TRR and new TRS) by testing for intersection between TRR and adjacent triangles to TRS. If there is no intersection found, test for intersection between TRS and adjacent triangles to TRR. The pair of old TRR and old TRS is removed from the ITLIST.

If new EDR is T-edge, return to the beginning of (3). Otherwise the intersection point Q_i is computed, which is a point on the intersection line loop. The processed face is detriangulated and split by the intersection lines and split faces are marked inner or outer against the other body.

If Q_i is Q_1, the determination of the intersection line loop is completed. Otherwise return to the beginning of (3).

(4) There might be other intersection line loops to be processed. Check if there are some intersecting triangle pairs stored in ITLIST. If there are some, repeat the above process by returning to (2).

(5) Faces surrounded by an intersection line loop are either inner or outer faces. According to the Boolean operation specified, either inner or outer faces must be removed from the data structure. Then the data structures of the two bodies are reorganized into a single data structure.

5. Importance of 4 x 4 Determinant Computation in Geometric Processing

In the foregoing algorithm for the Boolean shape operations we notice the algorithm is fairly simple. The solid modeling part of the system Freedom-II utilizing the algorithm is of only 25KW program size. This compactness of the system is brought about by the simple representation method of a solid, i.e., bridge edge method and the simple processing based on the face triangulation. We further notice that several types of computations pertaining to triangles are repeated many times, which are listed in the following.

(1) In the face triangulation process each vertex is tested for concavity. As in Fig.10 this test can be replaced by a side test of the next vertex with respect to a plane constructed by the previous vertex, the present vertex and the point at infinity in the direction of the normal vector pointing outwards. As will be explained, this test can be done by computing a 4 x 4 determinant and testing its sign.

(2) In the face triangulation process vertices are tested for containment in a triangle. We notice this test is replaced by three side tests of a vertex with respect to three planes. This test can be done by computing three 4 x 4 determinants and testing the signs.

(3) In inserting a bridge edge when a hole is created, the edge is tested for intersection with all the edges making up the hole. This intersection test of two line segments on a plane can be replaced by four side tests.

Therefore, this test can also be done by computing 4 x 4 determinants.

(4) In many places of the algorithm two triangles are frequently tested for intersection. For one thing, prior to main processing, intersecting triangle pairs are checked and stored in ITLIST. For another thing, during the determination process of intersection line loops, adjacent triangles are tested for intersection with either TRR or TRS.

The test for intersection of two triangles can be carried out by repeating 4 x 4 determinant computations as will be described in Chapter 6.

6. 4 x 4 Determinant Processor and Triangle Processor

Suppose vertices of a triangle are numbered V_0, V_1 and V_2 counterclockwise, seen from the outside of the triangle. The equation of the plane of the triangle is expressed in determinant form as

$$\begin{vmatrix} x & y & z & 1 \\ x_0 & y_0 & z_0 & 1 \\ x_1 & y_1 & z_1 & 1 \\ x_2 & y_2 & z_2 & 1 \end{vmatrix} = 0 \qquad (1)$$

where $V_0 = [x_0 \; y_0 \; z_0 \; 1]$, $V_1 = [x_1 \; y_1 \; z_1 \; 1]$ and $V_2 = [x_2 \; y_2 \; z_2 \; 1]$ in homogeneous coordinates.

The normal vector N of the triangle pointing outwards is given by

$$N = [n_x \; n_y \; n_z] \qquad (2)$$

$$n_x = \begin{vmatrix} y_0 & z_0 & 1 \\ y_1 & z_1 & 1 \\ y_2 & z_2 & 1 \end{vmatrix}, \quad n_y = \begin{vmatrix} z_0 & x_0 & 1 \\ z_1 & x_1 & 1 \\ z_2 & x_2 & 1 \end{vmatrix}, \quad n_z = \begin{vmatrix} x_0 & y_0 & 1 \\ x_1 & y_1 & 1 \\ x_2 & y_2 & 1 \end{vmatrix}$$

We denote by S_{A012} the determinant in the left side of equation (1) whose first row is substituted with $V_A = [x_A \; y_A \; z_A \; 1]$, that is,

$$S_{A012} \equiv \begin{vmatrix} x_A & y_A & z_A & 1 \\ x_0 & y_0 & z_0 & 1 \\ x_1 & y_1 & z_1 & 1 \\ x_2 & y_2 & z_2 & 1 \end{vmatrix} \qquad (3)$$

and denote by V_N a homogeneous vector of a point at infinity in the direction of the normal vector. That is,

$$V_N = [n_x \; n_y \; n_z \; 0] \qquad (4)$$

(A) <u>A side test of a point with respect to a triangle made up of three points</u>

Since the equation (1) has an outward pointing vector as the coefficients, for a point (x_A, y_A, z_A) in the outside half space of the triangle plane

$$S_{A012} > 0 \qquad (5)$$

and for a point (x_A, y_A, z_A) in the inside half space of the triangle plane

$$S_{A012} < 0 \qquad (6)$$

By making use of this side test, the vertex concavity test in the face triangulation can be done as follows (see Fig.10). The convexity or concavity of V_1 is judged by carrying out a side test of V_2 with respect to a triangle made up of V_0, V_1 and a point at infinity in the direction of the outward pointing normal vector of the triangle.

For a convex vertex (x_1, y_1, z_1)

$$S_{201N} = -S_{N012} < 0 \quad \therefore S_{N012} > 0 \qquad (7)$$

For a concave vertex (x_1, y_1, z_1)

$$S_{201N} = -S_{N012} > 0 \quad \therefore S_{N012} < 0 \qquad (8)$$

where,

$$S_{N012} = \begin{vmatrix} n_x & n_y & n_z & 0 \\ x_0 & y_0 & z_0 & 1 \\ x_1 & y_1 & z_1 & 1 \\ x_2 & y_2 & z_2 & 1 \end{vmatrix} \qquad (9)$$

In this paper we will write the subscript order of "S" such that "N" comes first.

(B) <u>A containment test of a point in a triangle made up of three points</u>

We consider a condition for a triangle made up of three points V_0, V_1, V_2 to include a point V_A in its plane (Fig.11). Let us construct three triangles $V_0V_1V_n$, $V_1V_2V_n$ and $V_2V_0V_n$. A containment test can be carried out by doing three side tests of the point V_A with respect to the three planes of these triangles.

The condition for the triangle $V_0V_1V_2$ to contain the point V_A is,

$$(S_{A01N} \leq 0) \wedge (S_{A12N} \leq 0) \wedge (S_{A20N} \leq 0)$$

or in another form

$$(S_{N01A} \geq 0) \wedge (S_{N12A} \geq 0) \wedge (S_{N20A} \geq 0) \qquad (10)$$

(C) <u>An intersection test of two line segments on a plane</u>

We consider a condition of two line segments V_0V_1 and V_AV_B in a plane to intersect with each other.

Let us construct two triangles $V_0V_1V_n$ and $V_AV_BV_n$ (Fig.12). An intersection test can be carried out by doing four side tests. Two side tests are for V_A and V_B with respect to the plane of the triangle $V_0V_1V_n$. The other two are for V_0 and V_1 with respect to the plane of the triangle $V_AV_BV_n$.

The condition for the two line segments $\overline{V_0V_1}$ and $\overline{V_AV_B}$ to intersect is,

$$[\{(S_{A01N} \leq 0) \wedge (S_{B01N} \geq 0)\} \vee \{(S_{A01N} \geq 0) \wedge (S_{B01N} \leq 0)\}]$$
$$\wedge [\{(S_{OABN} \leq 0) \wedge (S_{1ABN} \geq 0)\} \vee \{(S_{OABN} \geq 0) \wedge (S_{1ABN} \leq 0)\}]$$

or in another form,

$$[\{(S_{NO1A} \geq 0) \wedge (S_{NO1B} \leq 0)\} \vee \{(S_{NO1A} \leq 0) \wedge (S_{NO1B} \geq 0)\}] \\ \wedge [\{(S_{NABO} \geq 0) \wedge (S_{NAB1} \leq 0)\} \vee \{(S_{NABO} \leq 0) \wedge (S_{NAB1} \geq 0)\}] \quad (11)$$

If the condition (11) is satisfied, the intersection point P is computed as,

$$P = V_A + \frac{S_{NO1A}}{S_{NO1A} - S_{NO1B}} \times (V_B - V_A)$$
$$= V_0 + \frac{S_{NABO}}{S_{NABO} - S_{NAB1}} \times (V_1 - V_0) \quad (12)$$

(D) <u>An intersection test of a triangle with a line segment</u>

We consider a condition for a line segment $\overline{V_A V_B}$ to intersect with a triangle $V_0 V_1 V_2$.

(D-1) First, we consider the case where the line is on the plane of the triangle (Fig.13).

There are three main cases of the relationship between the line segment and the triangle.

(D-1-1) <u>Complete containment of a line segment in a triangle</u>

This test can be carried out by doing the containment test of each endpoint in the triangle which was described in (B).

The condition of the complete containment is,

$$(S_{N01A} \geq 0) \wedge (S_{N12A} \geq 0) \wedge (S_{N20A} \geq 0)$$
$$\wedge (S_{N01B} \geq 0) \wedge (S_{N12B} \geq 0) \wedge (S_{N20B} \geq 0) \qquad (13)$$

(D-1-2) <u>Intersection with one or two edges</u>

This test can be carried out by repeating the intersection tests of two line segments on a plane which has been discussed in (C).

If the following condition is true, that is

$$[\{(S_{NijA} \geq 0) \wedge (S_{NijB} \leq 0)\} \vee \{(S_{NijA} \leq 0) \wedge (S_{NijB} \geq 0)\}]$$
$$\wedge [\{(S_{NABi} \geq 0) \wedge (S_{NABj} \leq 0)\} \vee \{(S_{NABi} \leq 0) \wedge (S_{NABj} \geq 0)\}] \qquad (14)$$

then, the line segment $\overline{V_A V_B}$ intersects with edge E_k (i.e., $\overline{V_i V_j}$), where $j = (i+1) \mod 3$, $k = (i+2) \mod 3$ with $i = 0, 1, 2$.

If the above condition is satisfied, the intersection point P_k with edge E_k is computed as

$$P_k = V_A + \frac{S_{NijA}}{S_{NijA} - S_{NijB}} \times (V_B - V_A)$$

$$= V_i + \frac{S_{NABi}}{S_{NABi} - S_{NABj}} \times (V_j - V_i) \qquad (15)$$

(D-1-3) <u>No intersection with the triangle</u>

If neither condition (13) nor (14) is satisfied, the line segment does not intersect with the triangle.

(D-2) Next, we consider the case where the line is not on the plane of the triangle. The conditions for the line segment $\overline{V_A V_B}$ to intersect with the triangle $V_0 V_1 V_2$ are,

(i) V_A and V_B are in the different sides with respect to the plane of the triangle.

(ii) An endpoint of the line segment $\overline{V_A V_B}$ is in the triangular pyramid which is constructed by the other endpoint of the line segment and the triangle $V_0 V_1 V_2$ (Fig.13).

Combining the above two conditions, we get,

$$[(S_{A012} \geqq 0) \wedge (S_{B012} \leqq 0) \wedge (S_{B01A} \leqq 0) \wedge (S_{B12A} \leqq 0) \wedge (S_{B20A} \leqq 0)]$$
$$\vee [(S_{B012} \geqq 0) \wedge (S_{A012} \leqq 0) \wedge (S_{A01B} \leqq 0) \wedge (S_{A12B} \leqq 0) \wedge (S_{A20B} \leqq 0)] \quad (16)$$

(E) <u>An intersection test of two triangles</u>

If any edge of a triangle intersects with the other triangle, then the two triangles intersect with each other. If no edge of the two triangles intersects with the other triangle, the two triangles do not intersect. All we have to do is just to repeat the intersection test which was discussed in (D).

We have found that almost all of the time-consuming computations repeated many times in the proposed algorithm can be processed uniformly by the computations of 4 x 4 determinants. Therefore, if the solid modeling system can make the most of a hardware processor computing 4 x 4 determinants, the processing speed of the system could be much improved. Furthermore, if the system can use a "triangle processor" computing simultaneously all or some of the "S"s discussed in Chapter 6, we can realize an ideal solid modeling system which is very efficient as well as very compact.

We are now in the process of building a triangle processor, of which the hierarchical structure is shown in Fig.15. This processor can be called in many ways, from the intersection test of two triangles (K=0) to the simple side test (K=8). This processor will be useful in many types of geometric interference problems such as solid modeling, hidden line and surface elimination, clipping,.... and various types of mass property computations.

7. Conclusion

In search of techniques to realize a compact and efficient solid modeling system we arrived at the three techniques: a simple representation method of a solid using bridge edges ,a Boolean shape operation algorithm based on a face triangulation method and a triangle processor. The Boolean shape operations can be applicable not only to planar or conic surfaces, but also to free form surfaces.

We proposed in this paper a 4 x 4 determinant hardware processor and a "triangle processor" based on the determinant processor which would be very powerful especially in a solid modeling system employing the methods presented in this paper.

8. References

[1] B.G.Baumgart, Geometric modeling for computer vision, Computer Science, Stanford Univ. (1974)
[2] I.C.Braid, R.C.Hillyard and I.A.Stroud, Stepwise construction of polyhedra in geometric modeling, Mathematical methods in computer graphics and design, Academic press (1980).
[3] F.Yamaguchi and T.Tokieda, A unified algorithm for Boolean shape operations, to appear in IEEE Computer Graphics and Application, May (1984).

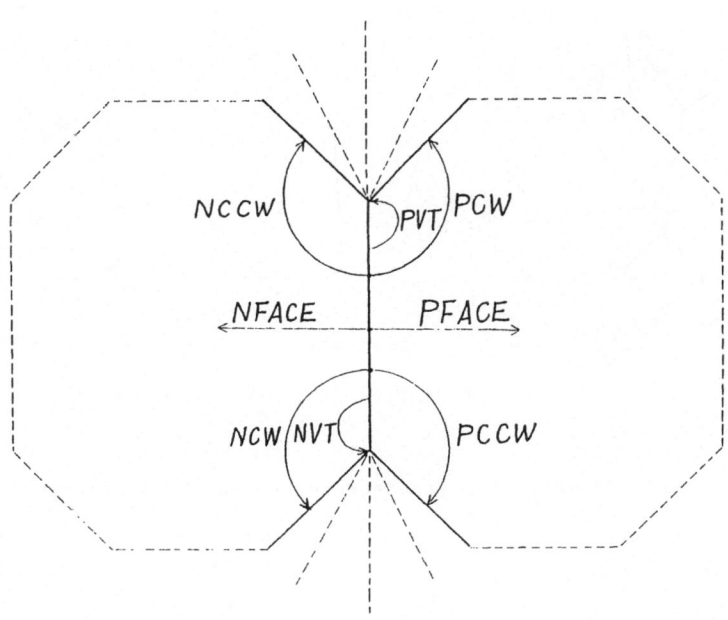

Fig.1 Winged Edge Data Structure

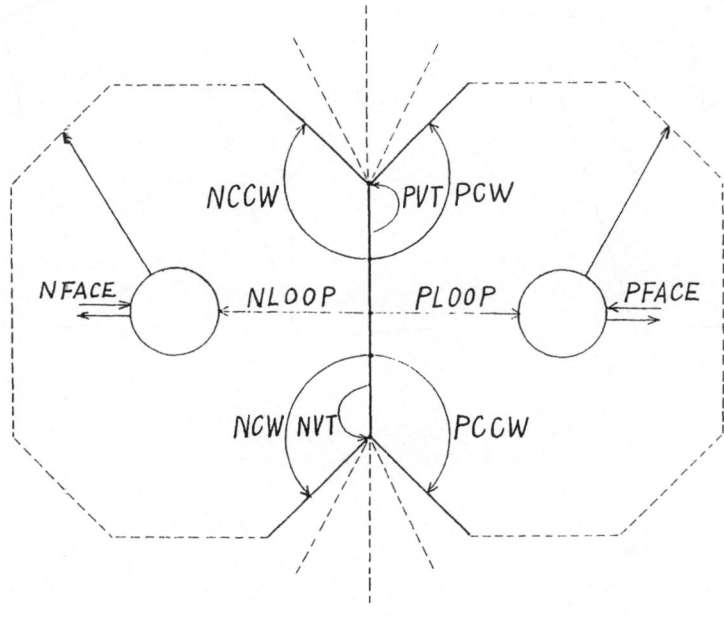

Fig.2 Introduction of loops in the representation of a solid

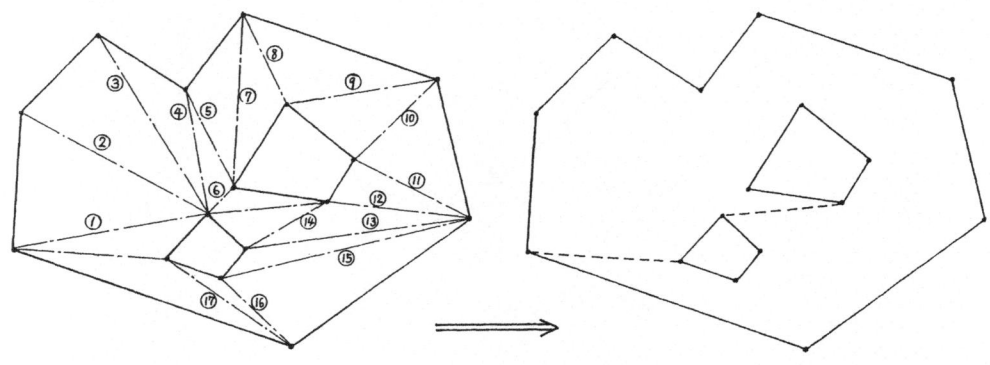

* Numbers indicate the order of edge deletion.

Fig.3 Deletion of generated edges in triangulation

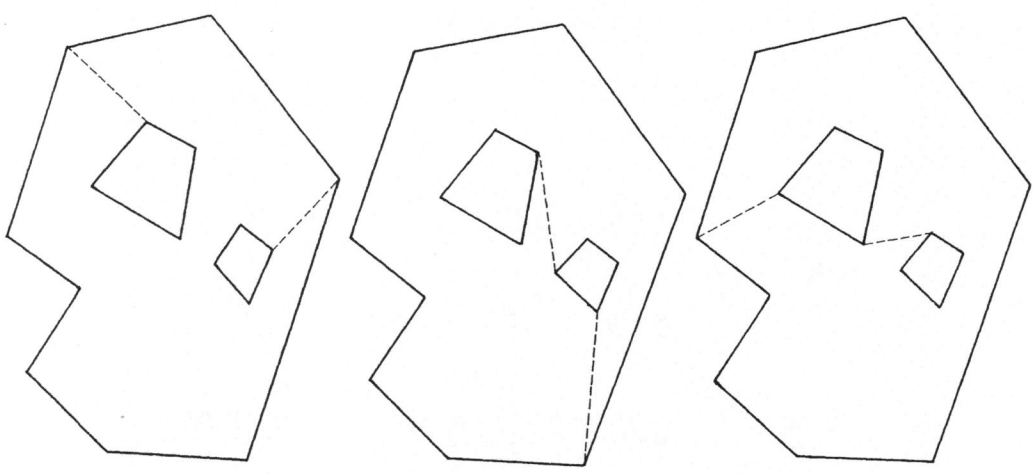

Fig.4 Bridge edges in a face

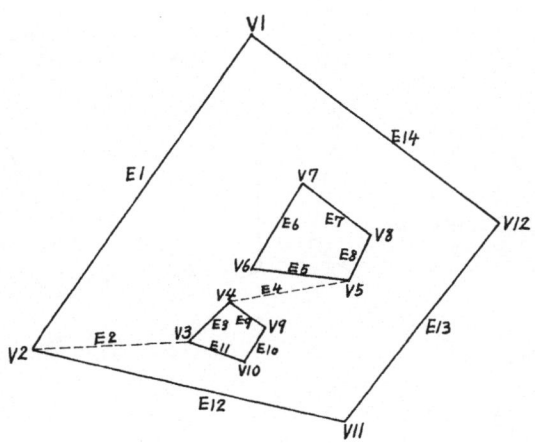

Fig.5 Circuits of edges or vertices round a face

```
E:=F↑.FPED; VT:=VCCW(E,F);
REPEAT
   NE:=ECCW(E,VT,F);  VT:=OTHER(VT,NE); E:=NE
UNTIL E = F↑.FPED;
```

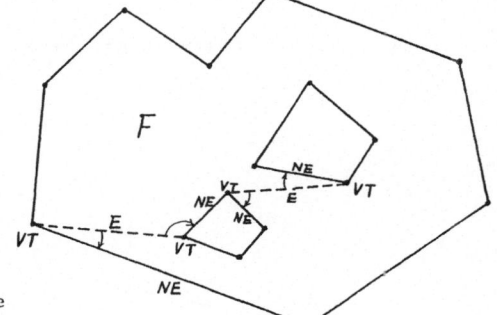

    VT: a pointer variable to a vertex
 E,NE: pointer variables to edges
     F: a pointer variable to a face
  FPED: a field name of a face block
        storing a pointer to one of the
        edges of the face
  VCCW: a function which outputs
        a vertex VT located counterclockwise
        from a given edge E about a given face F.
 OTHER: a function which outputs the other vertex
        except a given vertex VT about a given edge

Fig.6 ECCW

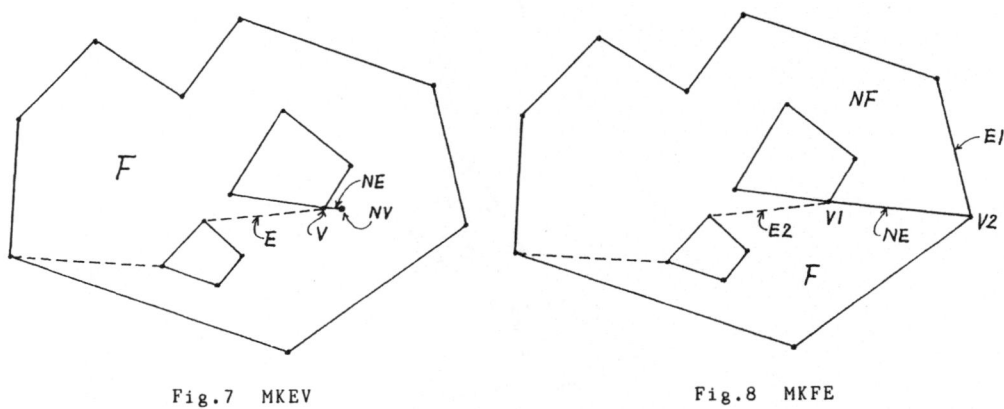

Fig.7 MKEV   Fig.8 MKFE

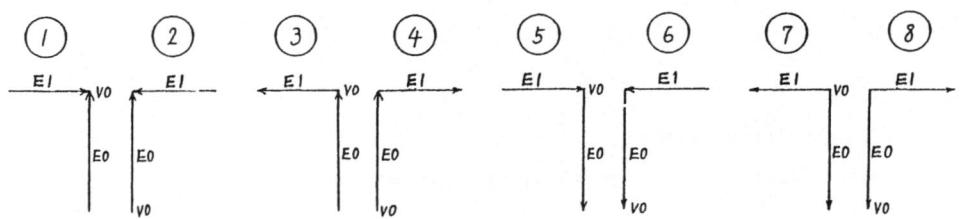

Fig.9 Eight cases of "WING" procedure

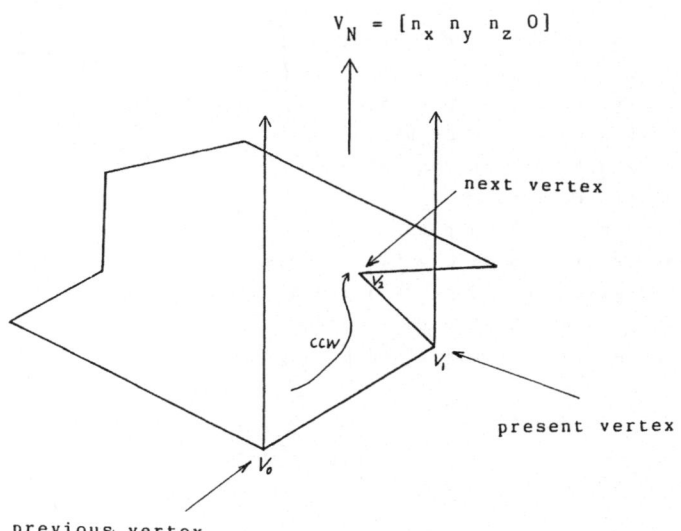

Fig.10 A convexity test of a vertex V_1

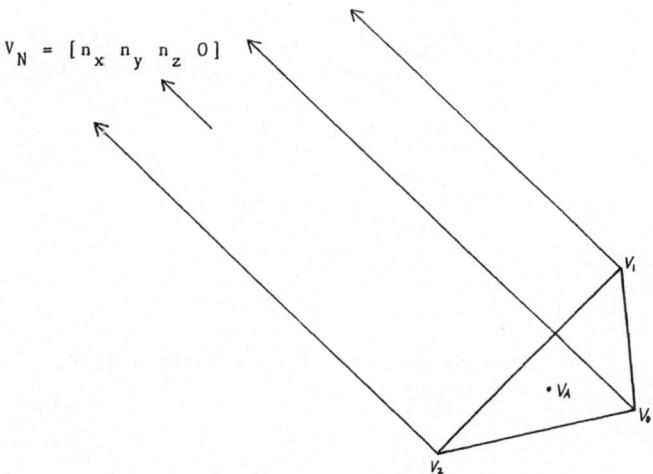

Fig.11 A containment test of a point in a triangle

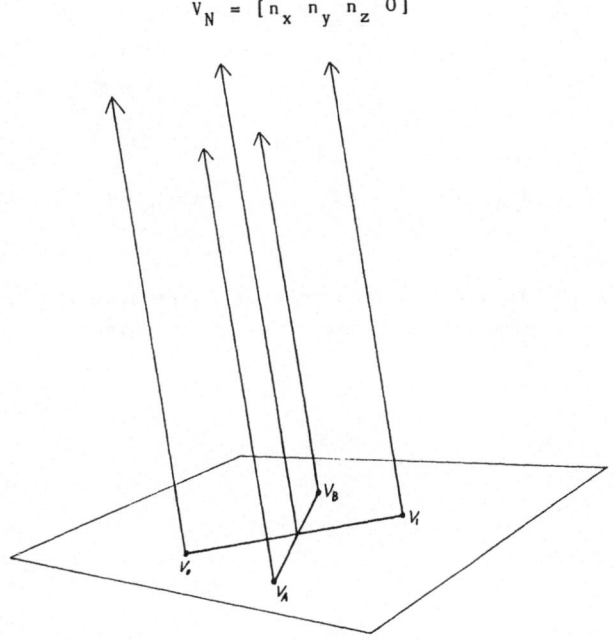

Fig.12 An intersection test of two line segments

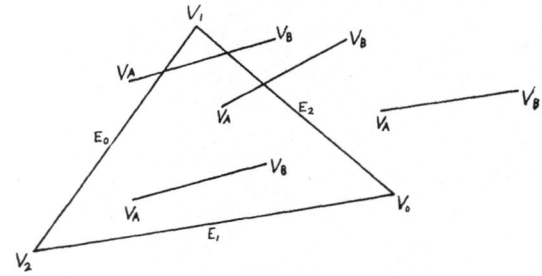

Fig.13　An intersection test of a triangle with a line segment on its plane

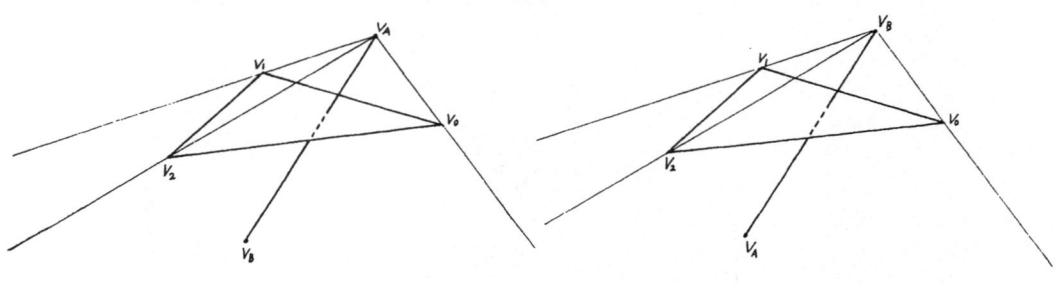

$(S_{A012} \geqq 0) \wedge (S_{B012} \leqq 0)$　　　　　　$(S_{A012} \leqq 0) \wedge (S_{B012} \geqq 0)$

Fig.14　An intersection test of a triangle with a line segment not lying on its plane

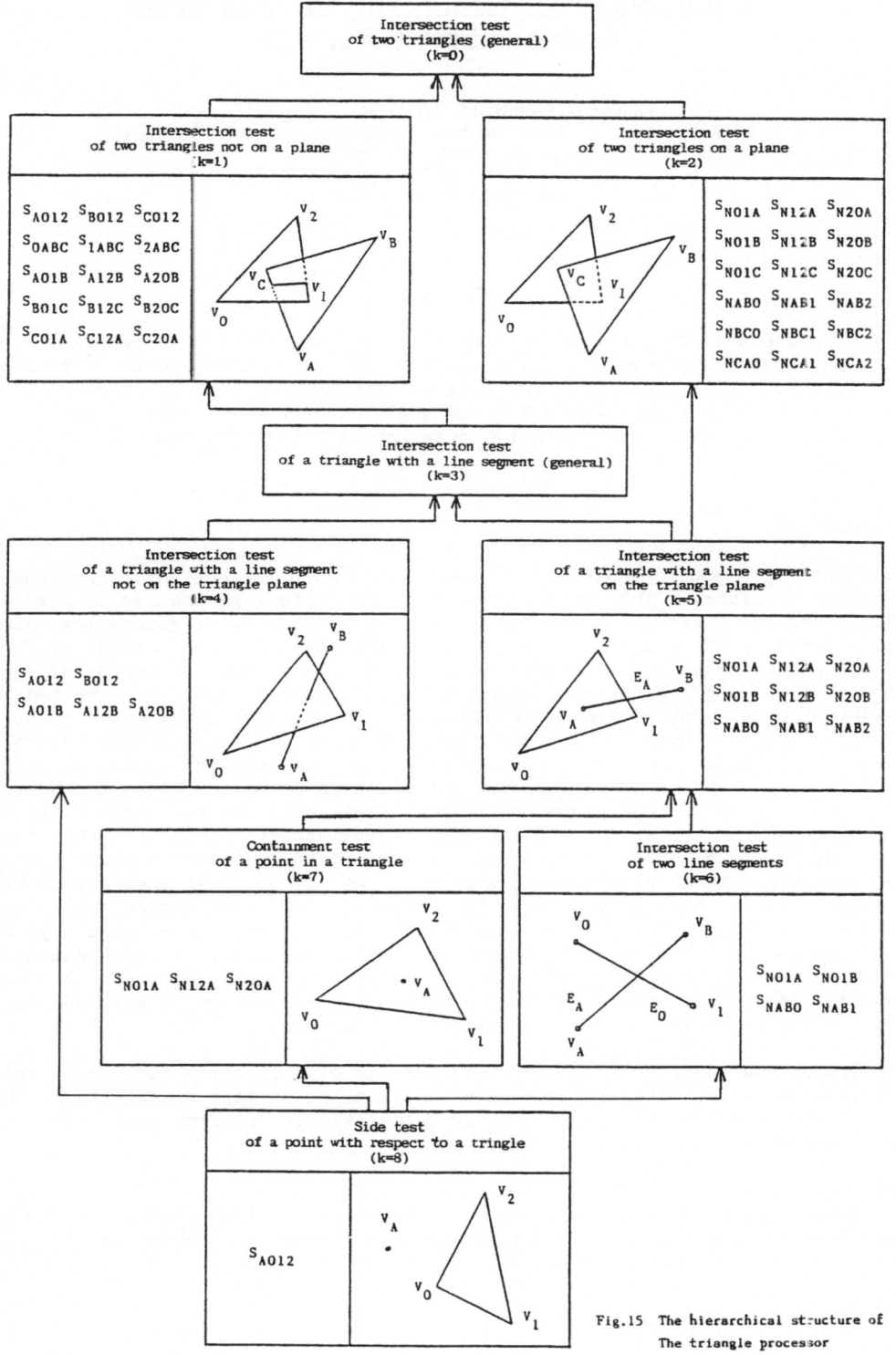

Fig.15 The hierarchical structure of
The triangle processor

A Procedure for Generating Contour Lines from a B-Spline Surface

Steven G. Satterfield[+] and David F. Rogers[++]
Computer Aided Design and
Interactive Graphics Group
U.S. Naval Academy
Annapolis, Maryland, USA

ABSTRACT

A procedure for generating accurate contour lines for a B-Spline surface is presented. The method is a two step process. The first step is a modification to a traditional routine for contouring over a triangular mesh. The second step uses B-Spline surface generation over a limited area to accurately produce the contour.

INTRODUCTION

This paper presents a procedure for generating parallel contour lines from a B-Spline surface. The details of B-Spline surface generation as used in this paper are given in References 2 and 5. The problem of generating contour lines would seem to be the same as intersecting the B-Spline surface with a plane. However, generating true contour lines requires more information than finding a group of planar points. The points must be connected in a logical order that "follows" the desired contour. For an arbitrary surface several disconnected contour lines may exist. Figure 1 shows an arbitrary B-Spline surface containing several hills and valleys. A set of contour lines for this arbitrary B-Spline surface is shown in Figure 2. Notice that some of the contour planes contain multiple disconnected contour lines. Contour lines are required in a variety of application areas. In the context of surface design it is often necessary to see cross section lines. For computer aided manufacture, parallel contour lines are frequently required for machining purposes. For computer aided manufacture, the accuracy of the contour lines is of considerable importance. The accuracy of the contour lines is associated with the number of points (or straight line segments) used to represent the contour line. To be useful in CAD/CAM applications, the procedure must be capable of generating very accurate lines without excessive memory or execution requirements.

The new contouring procedure described here is essentially a two step process. The first step preprocesses the B-Spline surface description. The second step performs the final contour calculation. The remainder of this paper describes these steps in detail.

[+]Computer Systems Analyst.
[++]Professor of Aerospace Engineering and Director of CADIG Group.
This work was partially supported by the U. S. Coast Guard under work order number MIPZ 70099-9-95726-7B

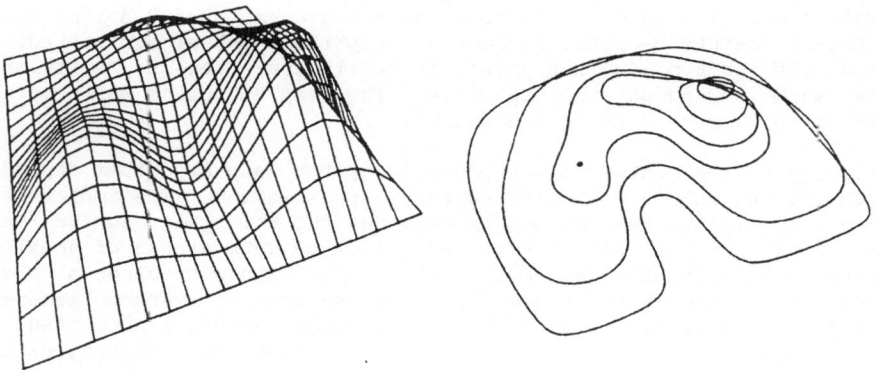

Figure 1 B-Spline Surface   Figure 2 Contour Lines

CONTOUR PREPROCESSING

In a paper by Heap (Ref. 1) an algorithm is presented for the production of contour maps. This algorithm produces contour lines from a triangular surface mesh polygonal approximation of the surface. The mesh consists of a set of triangular elements whose vertices are points lying on the surface. For each specified contour plane the algorithm follows the contour element by element. As each triangular element is found, the edges of the triangle are intersected by the contour plane. Figure 3 illustrates a single triangular element. P1, P2 and P3 are points lying on the surface. The solid curved lines indicate the true surface. The dashed lines indicate the approximating triangle. The contour line segment produced by the Heap algorithm at this element is the bold line segment joining two edges of the approximating triangle. Thus, the resultant contour lines are composed of straight line segments determined from each intersecting triangular element.

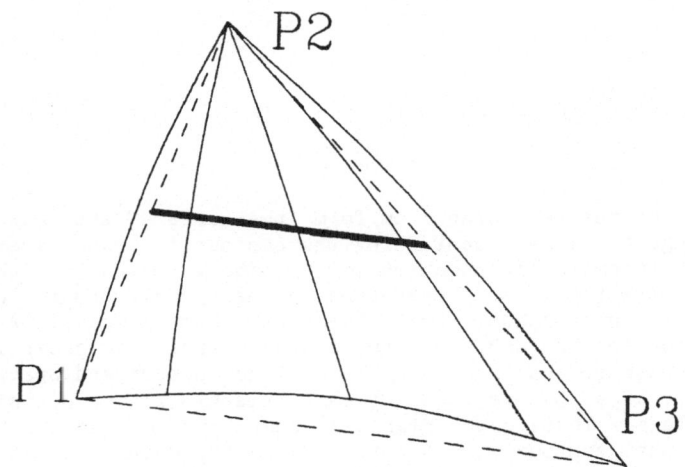

Figure 3 Single Triangular Element with Heap Intersection

This method can be used directly to produce contours for a B-Spline surface. From the parametric B-Spline surface description a set of surface points is produced. This set of surface points is easily converted to a triangular surface mesh as shown in Figure 4. The Heap algorithm may be directly applied to this mesh to produce contours.

The accuracy of the contour lines produced by the Heap algorithm depends on the density of the triangular surface approximation. The implementation given in the original Heap algorithm requires the triangular surface mesh to be stored in arrays along with several other data arrays of equal size. Therefore, increasing the accuracy of the contour lines requires a significant increase in memory requirements. In attempting to overcome memory restrictions on a small minicomputer, the Heap algorithm was implemented using direct access disk files. For test cases of moderate accuracy, execution time of this implementation is excessive. Hence, the implementation is impractical. Consequently, improving the accuracy of the contour lines without significantly increasing the number of triangles used to approximate the surface is of interest.

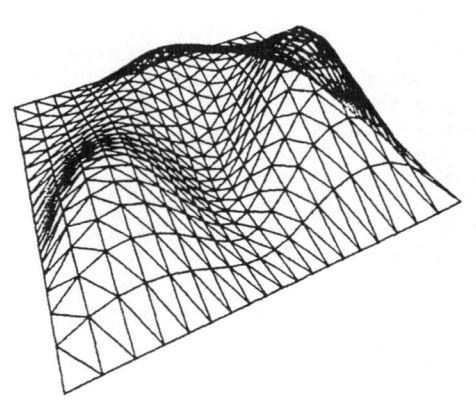
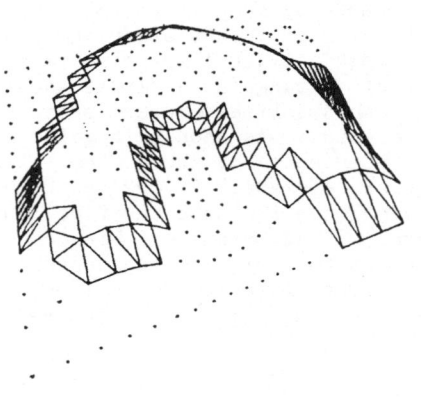

Figure 4 Triangular Mesh   Figure 5 One Triangular Contour

A modification to the Heap algorithm forms the basis of the new algorithm. As each triangular element containing the contour is found, instead of calculating the triangular intersection points, the vertices of the triangle are saved. These vertices, represented by their positions in the topologically rectangular grid space, form a triangular contour band. A single triangular contour for the arbitrary surface of Figure 1 is shown in Figure 5. The triangular contour band follows the desired contour and spans the actual contour plane, i.e. two vertices of each triangle lie on opposite sides of the contour plane. Thus, each triangular contour specifies a band within which the actual contour line exists. Since the data supplied to the Heap algorithm is a polygonal approximation formed from a small number of surface points, both memory requirements and execution time are significantly reduced.

In summary, the modified Heap algorithm preprocesses the surface to identify a limited surface area within which the desired contour line or lines occur. As a result of the algorithm "following" the contours, the correct order for the points on a contour is produced and the existence of multiple disconnected contours within a single contour plane is identified.

FINAL CONTOUR CALCULATION

The triangular contours produced by the modified Heap algorithm may now be used as the basis for a piecewise B-Spline calculation of the surface. Since the B-Spline calculation is controlled by parametric values, any subregion of the full surface can be calculated if the corresponding parametric values are known (Ref. 2). Since the triangle vertices are represented by grid positions, the corresponding parameter values may be computed using linear interpolation in the range of zero to the maximum parameter value. Thus, each triangular element is used to accurately identify a small region of the B-Spline surface that intersects the desired contour plane. Points on this sub-surface that intersect the contour plane are used to obtain an accurate contour line.

Figure 6 shows a single triangular element. The solid lines indicate parameter lines along the actual surface. The dashed lines indicate the approximating triangle. The orientation of the vertices produced by the Heap algorithm are such that the contour enters at the edge between P1 and P2. First the parameter line between P1 and P3 is computed. Using points along this parameter line, a series of parameter lines connecting to P2 are computed as shown. Since the entry edge is known, the proper contour order is maintained. Thus, the contour segment at this triangular element is produced from the corresponding set of parameter lines. This contour segment is shown by the bold solid line in Figure 6 connecting across the curved surface lines. Notice that the calculated contour points lie on the surface since they are calculated from the B-Spline parameter lines. Figure 7 illustrates the difference between the new algorithm and the original Heap algorithm.

Shown below is an outline of the algorithm for generating the contour line segment. For each of the surface parameter lines shown in Figure 6, a binary search is performed to find the actual surface point on the contour. A surface point is calculated at the mid-parameter value. If the height component of the computed surface point is within the desired accuracy of the contour height, then the contour point is found. Otherwise, the parameter value is adjusted and the process repeated. The value 'di' is an increment value determined by the number of parameter lines used. Since the parameter lines and corresponding points are generated from the contour entry edge to the contour exit edge, the sequence of points within each triangular element follows the contour.

```
# P1, P2, P3 are parameter values at the vertices
# pi, pj, pk are temporary parameter values
# sp is a calculated surface point
# sp(z) is the height component of sp
# level is the contour height
# z2 is the height of the surface point at P2

For pi= P1 To P3 Step di
    pj = pi
    pk = p2
    sp = surface point computed at pi
    While (abs(z2-sp(z)) > Desired Accuracy)
        pm = (pj+pk)/2
        sp = surface point computed at pm
        if (sp(z) > level)
                pj = pm
        else
                pk = pm
        Endif
        Output sp
    Endwhile
Next pi
```

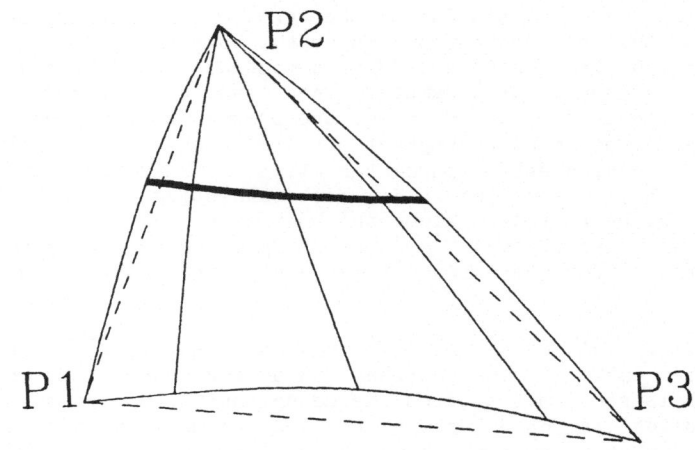

Figure 6 Single Triangular Element with New Intersection

PROCEDURE OVERVIEW

A brief overview of the entire contouring process is given below. The process has two inputs. The first input is a list of x,y,z triplets for the B-Spline control net. Using this control net and a B-Spline surface algorithm (Refs. 2 and 5), the desired surface is fully specified and can be easily recreated. The second input is a list containing the height for each desired contour. Before invoking the contouring algorithm, the surface is rotated and translated such that the contour planes are parallel to one of

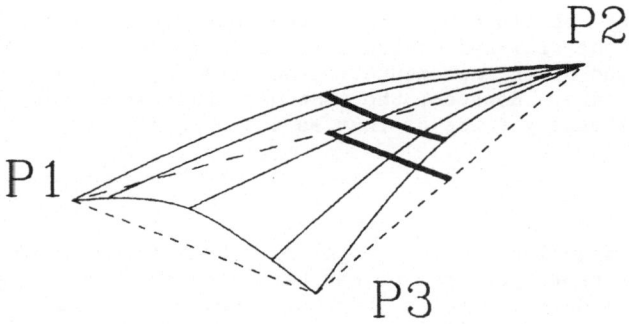

Figure 7 Comparison of the New and the Heap New Intersections

the coordinate planes. Hence, only a height value for each contour plane is required. The output is the desired set of contour lines represented by x,y,z triplets correctly ordered and separated into groups. The procedure follows.

> The B-Spline algorithm creates a set of surface points from the B-Spline control net. The surface points lie on a topologically rectangular grid. The number of points generated is small producing a coarse surface representation.
>
> The surface points are converted into a triangular surface mesh.
>
> The modified Heap algorithm produces a set of triangular contour bands at the specified contour heights.
>
> The B-Spline algorithm produces a series of contour line segments from each triangular element in each triangular contour band. The segments are produced from parameter lines generated for the small surface area defined by each triangular element.

COMPARISON WITH HEAP ALGORITHM

As previously stated, the original Heap algorithm can be used to produce contours by approximating the B-Spline surface with a triangular grid. In order to compare the new algorithm with the original Heap algorithm, a B-Spline surface description of a ship hull was generated. The basis for comparison is to produce twenty five contours (water lines) using both methods. The total execution time and memory requirements are then compared for contour lines of similar accuracy. Similar accuracy is determined by computing the total cross sectional area for each set of contour lines. For purposes of this discussion, cross sectional area is defined to be the area enclosed by each contour line.

For contours of the same desired accuracy, the Heap algorithm required approximating the surface with 10388 triangles. The new algorithm required only 1088 triangles to obtain the same accuracy. The additional surface definition required by the Heap algorithm used 1.5 megabytes of memory to store the various internal data structures. Execution times for the two algorithms were obtained by running the complete process from the B-Spline control net to the finished contours for each method in batch mode. Since file handling and other implementation details differ, the timing comparison is only approximate. However, the test case indicates that the new algorithm is approximately twice as fast as the original Heap algorithm.

APPLICATION

The techniques described in this paper have been implemented in a prototype system. This prototype system has been used for the production of towing tank ship hull models. Here, a ship hull form was created using an interactive B-Spline surface design program (Refs. 5 and 6). The contouring technique was used to produce a set of contour lines. See Figure 8. Ship hull models were then produced by numerically controlled milling of the contour lines (Refs. 3 and 4). A typical model as produced by the milling process is shown in Figure 9.

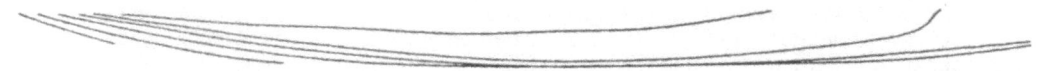

Figure 8   Contour Lines for a Ship Hull

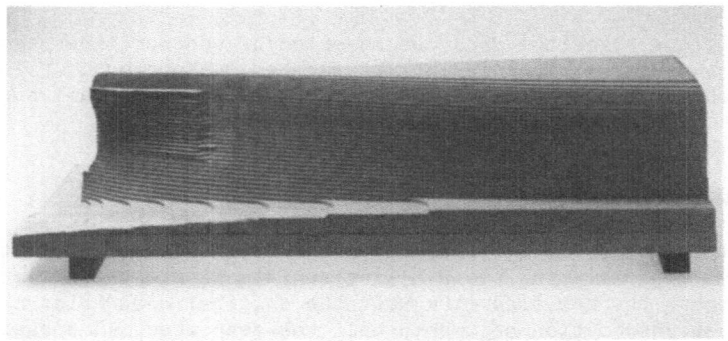

Figure 9   Typical Ship Model

EXTENSION

A logical extension to the described method is to apply the technique recursively to obtain increased local accuracy. Here, each triangular element of a given triangular contour is locally subdivided to obtain a new polygonal surface. The contour algorithm is then applied locally to the smaller surface approximation again producing a small local triangular contour band. Since the original B-Spline description is used, each triangle vertex point again lies on the surface. Thus a very accurate contour can be obtained without resorting to finer polygonal approximations for the entire surface.

CONCLUSIONS

A method for accurately producing contour lines from a B-Spline surface description has been described. A traditional contouring algorithm was modified to produce contours consisting of triangular elements whose vertices lie on the B-Spline surface and span the desired contour. The vertices of these triangular elements are transformed into parametric values. The parametric values allow a B-Spline surface to be accurately calculated over a limited surface area. By properly generating the surface parameter lines, a set of intersection points is formed which yields a properly ordered contour line. The new algorithm executes approximately twice as fast as traditional polygonal algorithms with one tenth the memory requirement for equal accuracy contour lines.

REFERENCES

(1) Heap, B.R., 'Algorithms for the Production of Contour Maps Over an Irregular Triangular Mesh', National Physical Laboratory, Report NAC 10, February 1972.

(2) Rogers, D.F. and Adams, J. A., Mathematical Elements for Computer Graphics, McGraw-Hill, New York, 1976.

(3) Rogers, D.F., Rodriguez, F. and Satterfield, S.G., 'Computer Aided Design and Numerically Controlled Production of Towing Tank Models', Proceedings of the 16th Design Automation Conference, June 1979.

(4) Rogers, D.F., Rodriguez, F. and Satterfield, S.G., 'A Simple System for the Design and Construction of Towing Tank Models', Proceedings of the 17th Numerical Control Society Conference, 1980.

(5) Rogers, D.F., and Satterfield, S.G., 'B-Spline Surfaces for Ship Hull Design', Proceedings of SIGGRAPH '80, Computer Graphics 14, 3 (1980).

(6) Rogers, D.F., and Satterfield, S.G., 'Dynamic B-Spline Surfaces', Proceedings of the Fourth Conference on Computer Applications in the Automation of Shipyard Operation and Ship Design IV (Rogers, D.F., Nehrling, B. C. and Kuo, C. ed.), North-Holland Publishing, 1982, pp 189-196 (ICCAS '82), June 1982, Annapolis, Md.

An Automated Finite Polygon Division Method of 3D Objects

Yoshimi Ota, Hiroshi Arai, Shinji Tokumasu and **Toshio Ochi**
Hitachi Research Laboratory
Hitach Ltd.
4026 Kuji-cho, Hitachi,
Ibaraki 319-12, Japan

Abstract

This paper presents an automated method of the finite polygon division of a 3 D object, defined by a geometric modeller according to the boundary representation scheme.
By applying this method to computer graphics, color shading data for a 3 D object defined by C A D can be generated automatically. The polygon data generated by the method can be utilized for calculating the mass properties of the object. According to this method, the precision of the calculation can be controlled arbitrarily by choosing the proper division parameter. Minimum errors of 0.001% for polyhedrons and 0.2% for a 3 D object with a curved surface have been attained.

1. Introduction

Computer graphics (C G) is widely used today for making movies and T V films. Finite polygon data are commonly input data to approximate real 3 D objects. Unfortunately, this method has required a considerable investment in man—hours because polygon data generation has not been automated.

On the other hand, C A D / C A M, closely related to C G, it is necessary to input precise data for 3 D objects related to a given product. The system used for this purpose is called a geometric modelling system or geometric modeller, where the wire frame model, the surface model and the solid model are well known methods for treating the geometric expression of a 3 D object in a computer.
The authors have already presented a geometric modeller H I C A D / 3 D, which can treat these three methods uniquely, such that the modelling data of any type are generated when and only when they are needed and they can be converted to one another between the different kinds of data according to the commands.

By the way, the most interesting model from the stand point of C G is the solid model in the three models mentioned above and especially the constructive solid geometry type (i.e. the C S G type of the solid model) is commonly utilized.

On the other hand, the boundary representation type (i.e. the B-rep. type of the solid model) is also used widely in CAD/CAM and adopted as a main algorithm in HICAD/3D: as to the solid modelling, it is now under development.

This is because the B-rep. model maintains detail topology data with respect to the face-edge-vertex relation as an internal description of an object; thus the model can adapt itself easily to any stage of the design and manufacturing and also because it can treat a 3D object of any shape, in contrast to the CSG type.

However, in this case, the method needed to generate CG data or mass property data of a given object is thought much more difficult than in the CSG model. Actually, no distictive methods have been presented thus far, nevertheless of their importance.

In this paper, first of all, an automated finite polygon division method for the B-rep. model is constructed in order to reduce time and cost for generating CG data. Secondly, as its direct utilization to CAD/CAM, it is applied to construct a method to caluculate mass properties of an object. These methods are to be presented according to HICAD/3D B-rep. scheme with numerical experiments and discussions..

2. B-rep. Scheme in HICAD/3D

In this section, the B-rep. scheme of a 3D object in HICAD/3D is described. The items listed below define the notation and the data structure of the internal expression of a 3D object constructed by the system and they are not corresponding to the construction procedure of a 3D object in the system.

(1) A 3D object is a 3D region in 3D Euclidean space.(See Fig. 1 (a).)

(2) The boundary surface of the object is composed of one or more faces. (See Fig. 1 (b).)

(3) A face is defined as a bounded plane or bounded curved surface on a given definition plane or a given definition curved surface sided by 0 ~ 4 definition lines. Then, edges of the faces are restricted to the definition plane/surface and each edge is given the direction so as to look at the inner part of the face to the left.(See Fig. 1 (c).)

(4) A definition curved surface is divided in meshes, and dealt as a set of one or more four sided patches (three sided patches are also included as a non-standard case.).
Each side line is called a patch boundary, and a partical face/edge split by the patch boundaries is called an face/edge segment.(See Fig.1 (c).)

(5) A definition line, a patch boundary, an edge, and an edge segment are defined as a chain of straight lines, arcs and cubic Bezier curves, where a cubic Bezier curve is equated parametrically as follows.[4]

$$C(t) = (1 - t + tE)^3 P_0, \quad 0 \leq t \leq 1 \tag{1}$$

where E is a shift operator such that $EP_i = P_{i+1}$. (See Fig. 1 (d).)

(6) A patch is expressed parametrically as a bi-cubic Bezier surface as follows.[4]

$$S(u,v) = (1-u+uE)^3 (1-v+uF)^3 P_{00}, \quad 0 \leq u, v \leq 1 \tag{2}$$

where E and F are shift operators such that $EP_{i,j} = P_{i+1,j}$ and $FP_{i,j} = P_{i,j+1}$. (See Fig. 1 (e).)

3. Finite Polygon Division

In order to get a finite polygon division of the surface of a given 3D object, you must have a method to divide a face, because of B-rep. scheme described in the previous section. Moreover, if the face is a bounded curved surface, then the method to divide it need only be a patch.

In the followings, two cases of the finite polygon division method are discussed. The first one is that for a face of bounded plane and the second is for a face (segment) on a patch. In both cases, it is assumed to have an integer n, which denotes the division ratio.

3.1 Case for Bounded Plane

In this case, the plane is considered as a plane segment on a virtual patch. Taking a (u,v) coordinate on the definition plane, then, the method goes as follows.

Step(1). Define a minimal square patch including the planar face, where corners of the square are to be parallel to u or v axis.

Step(2). Divide the patch by a mesh into n×n finite polygons of the same scale, shown in Fig. 2 (a).

Step(3). Divide (approximate) each edge of the face into a chain of straight line segments of almost the same length equal to the average length of the mesh corner lines.

Step(4). Construct a chain-refinement of the straight line segments by dividing each original segment to two or more parts if it intersects with the mesh lines. (Then, the objective face is covered by finite polygons with corners consisting of straight line segments and mesh lines. See Fig.2(b).)

Step(5). Extract all the polygon data, searching them along the mesh rows or columns.

3.2 Case for Patches

Let a given patch be a four-sided, standard patch. If treating the patch in correspondence with the square defined in the former case, then the finite polygon division in this case is conducted similarly on a (u,v) parametric coordinate for the patch.

However, it is difficult to follow Step(4) in this case, because it is time-consuming to try finding intersecting points between straight line segments and mesh lines on the curved patch and sometimes the process aborts because of the approximation error of edges and mesh lines. Then in order to reduce the drawback, Step(3A) and Step(5A) are placed next to Step(3) and Step(5) respectively.
The new steps are as follows.

Step(3A). Project the (u,v) patch and the resulting mesh and face to the (u',v') plane with the same normal vector as at the point $(u,v)=(1/2, 1/2)$ on the patch.(See Fig.3.)

Step(5A). Transform (u',v') data of selected polygons to (u,v) data.

4. Application of Finite Polygon Division

The finite polygon division method is applied to implement a color shading function and a mass property function in HICAD/3D.
This section will discuss two functions at some length:

4.1 Color Shading

The modeller (HICAD/3D) is principally based on the conversational operation. It utilizes GRADAS, an intelligent graphics terminal developed by Hitachi Ltd. to improve the efficiency of the conversational process for all commands. The color shading function utilizes the color printing function of GRADAS and is executed in the following steps.

First, a finite polygon division is needed. Second, sorting polygonal patches in the Z direction, it paints the patches from the far end to here on the display, where the normal vectors of the patches are determined by the corner points and the color is induced from the direction of the light and view. Figure 4 shows the construction procedure of a die-cast part step by step, where every step is shown as a wire-framed image. Figure 5 is a shading example of the die-cast part generated by the finite polygon division.

Also, other two shading examples are shown for a penguin doll in Fig.6. and Fig.7. These are made by the finite polygon divisions with the division ratio n=1 (coarse division) and n=4 (fine division) respectively in order to see the effects of the ratio.

In either case, detailed data around intersecting lines, which is a special property of B-rep. scheme, are exploited to generate clear display images.

Moreover, in the use for CAD/CAM, the precision control ability by the division ratio is advantageous, sometimes for saving CPU time and sometimes for creating a high quality image.

4.2 Calculation of Mass Property

Finite polygon data generated by the division process are utilized for determining mass property, such as surface area, volume, center of gravity, second moment and etc.

The method is as follows.

Let a 3D object be M, then the surface area of M can be equated as the following integral.

$$S_M = \int_{\partial M} ds \qquad (3)$$

where S_M surface area of M
      ∂M surface of M
      ds area of infinitesimal plane

Suppose, as the result of the finite polygon division, ∂M is approximated/covered by K-finite polygons ΔS_i ($i=1, K$), that is $\partial M \approx \bigcup_{i=1}^{K} \Delta S$
Then the following equation holds:

$$S_M \approx \sum_{i=1}^{K} |\Delta S_i| \qquad (4)$$

where $|\Delta S_i|$ is the area of ΔS_i. Moreover, assuming each ΔS_i to be a L-edged polygon, we have,

$$S_M \approx \sum_{i=1}^{K} \vec{n_i} \cdot \sum_{j=1}^{L} (\vec{r_{ij}} \times \vec{r}_{i,j+1}) \qquad (5)$$

where $\vec{n_i}$ unit normal vector of ΔS_i
      $\vec{r_{ij}}$ j th point vector of ΔS_i
      $\vec{r}_{i,L+1} = \vec{r}_{i,1}$

and where $\vec{r}_{i,j+1} - \vec{r}_{i,j}$ is a j th edge vector of ΔS_i, looking at the inner part of the polygon to the left.

Thus, given a finite polygon division, the surface area can be calculated easily according to the equation (5).

Also, for other properties (such as volume, center of gravity, and second moment), similar equations are introduced, in Table 1. Figure 8 shows the relation between the division size (n×n) and the error in the calculation of area and volume for a cylinder and a sphere. In either case, the error goes down according to increase in the division size, leveling off at around 0.2% error. By the way, if the 3D object is a polyhedron, the error must theoretically be zero regardless of the division size and actually it has been reduced to 0.001%. Figure 9 shows a displayed output of mass property data calculated for the die-cast part shown in Fig. 5.

Since this finite polygon division method can be applied to a 3D object of any shape, a very flexible color shading function and a mass property function can be introduced.

5. Conclusion

We have presented an automated finite polygon division method for a 3D object according to the B-rep. scheme of the geometric modeller HICAD/3D.
We have proved that the method can be applied effectively to color shading in CG and calculation of mass property of an object. Strong advantages to this method are the following:

(1) Applicability to a 3D object of any shape and

(2) Control ability in quality in image or precision in calculation versus response time.

Especially in the case of the color shading, high-quality color shading is possible around intersecting lines on a 3D object. And in the calculation of mass property, minimum errors of 0.001% for a polyhedron and 0.02% for curved objects are possible now.
Finally, this method allows you to control the division by division ratio (n) or division size (n×n) per patch (homogenious division using polygons of the same area could attain much better division). Good though this method is, it is still being imoproved.

Reference
1) Tokumasu, S. et al, "Implementation of a Geometric Modelling System: HICAD," Proc. I.G. '83, 1983.
2) Tokumasu, S. et al, "Solid Model in a Geometric Modelling System: HICAD," Proc. 20th Designing Automation Conference, IEEE Computer Society, 1984, pp. 360−366.
3) Okino, N. et al, "TIPS−1 Technical Information Processing System for Computer Aided−Design, Drawing and Manufacturing," Proc. of PRORAMAT '73, 1973.
4) Hosaka, M. et al, "Theory and Methods for Three Dimensional Free−Form Shape Construction," J. Info. Proc., Vol. 3, No.3. IPSJ, 1980, pp. 140−151.

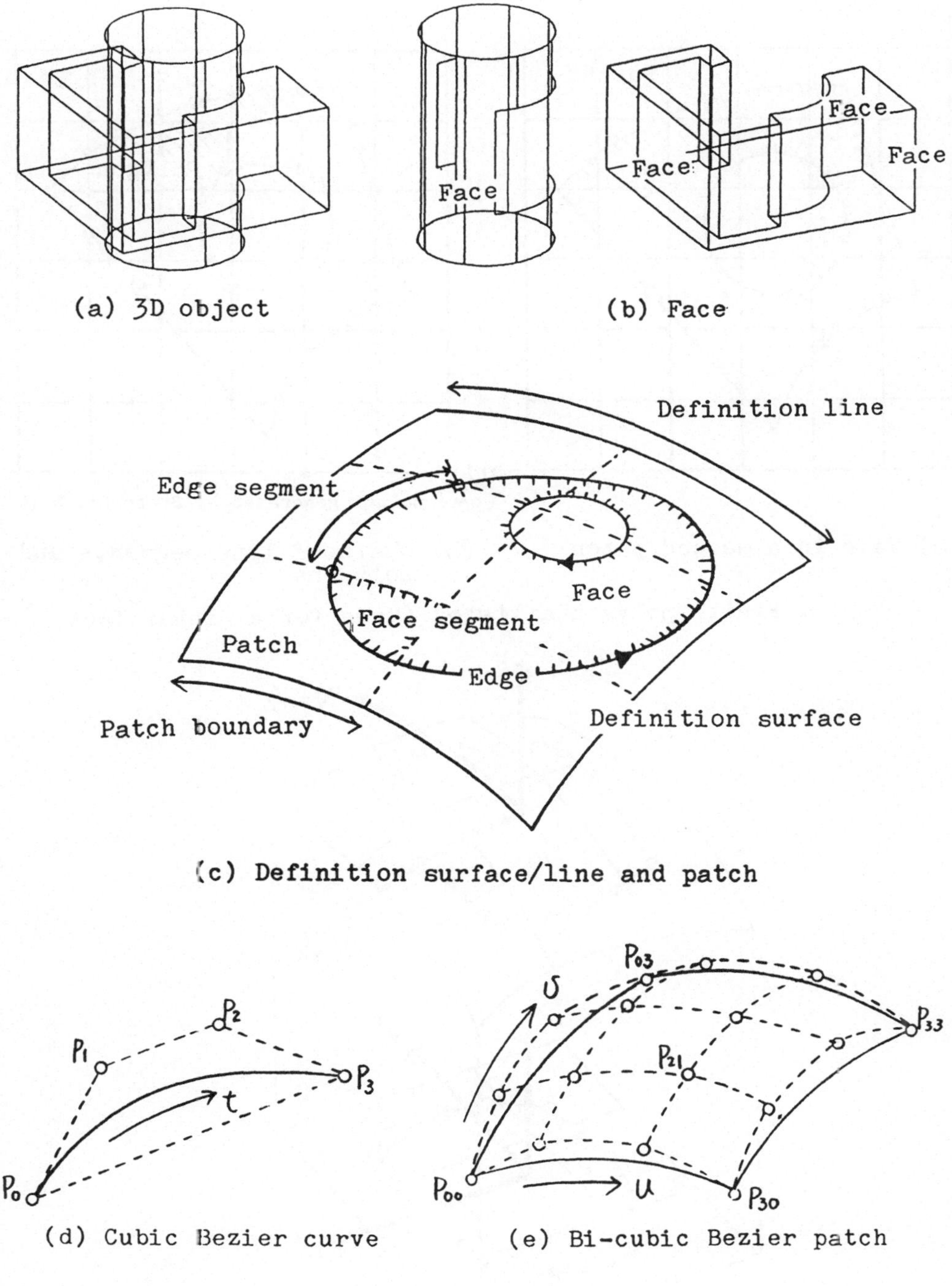

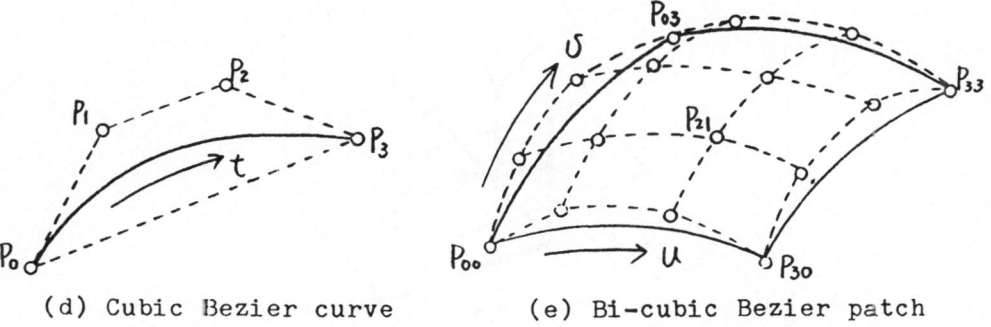

Fig.1. B-rep. scheme in HICAD/3D

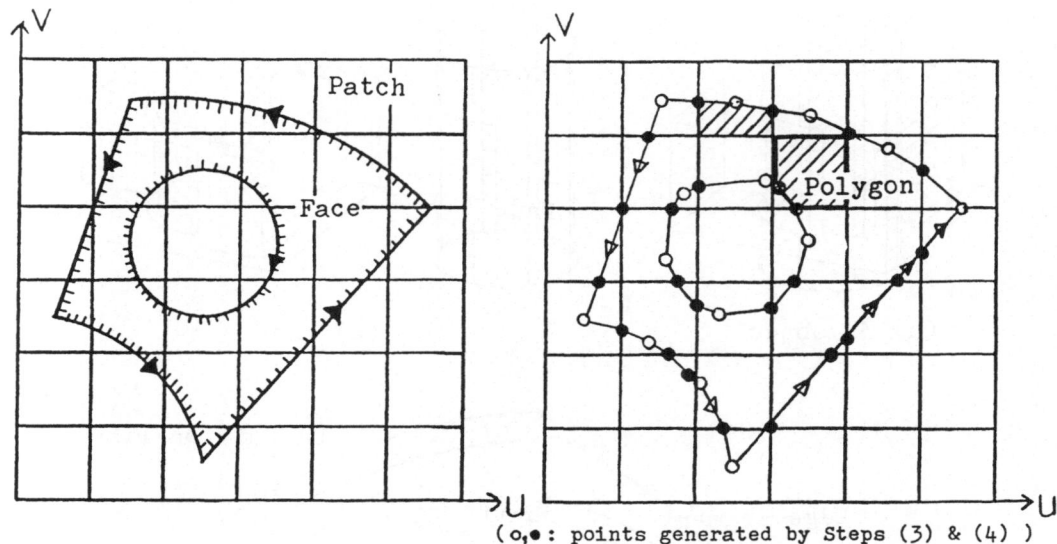

(a) Face in a meshed patch (b) Chain of line segments and polygons

(o,• : points generated by Steps (3) & (4))

Fig.2. Finite polygon division (Case for a planar face)

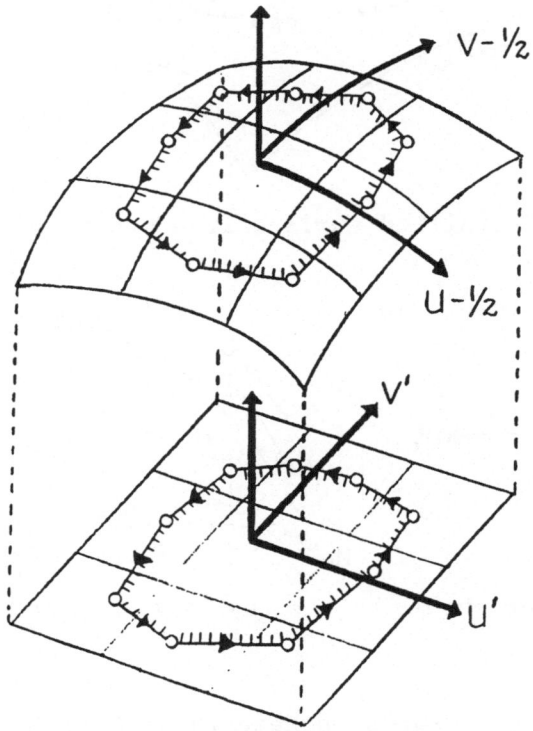

Fig.3. Projection of a curved patch on a plane

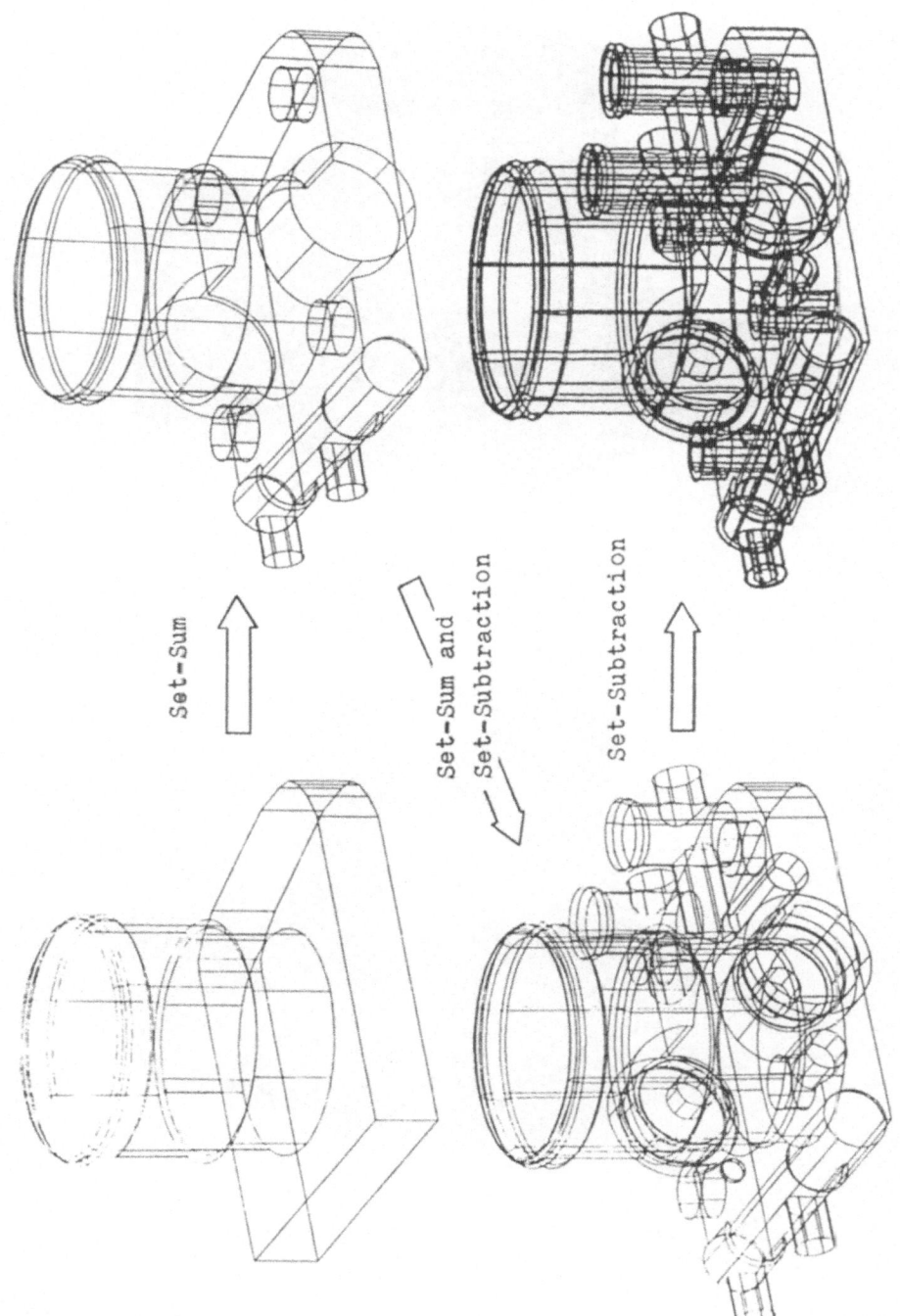

Fig.4. Solid modelling procedure for a die-cast part

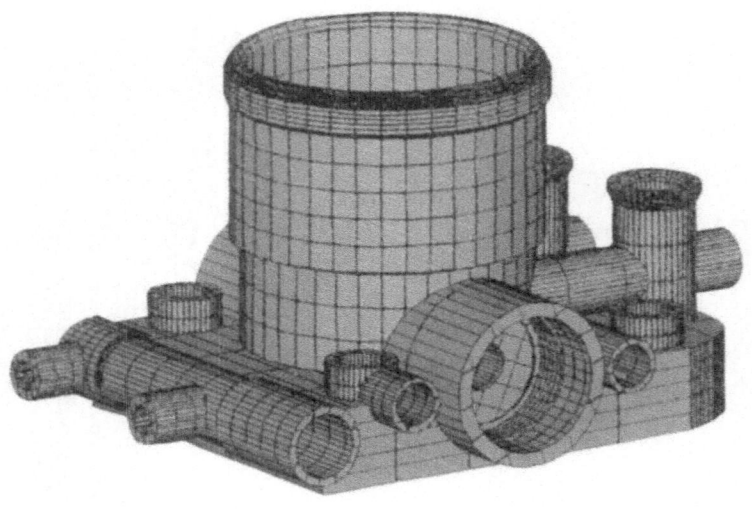

(a) Image with polygon boundary

(b) Image without polygon boundary

Fig.5. Die-cast part shaded after finite polygon division

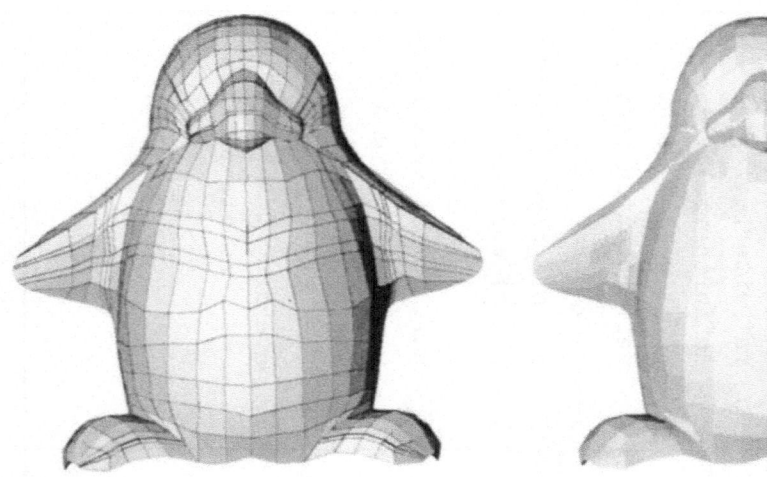

(a) Image with polygon boundary

(b) Image without polygon boundary

Fig.6. Penguin doll (Division ratio n=1)

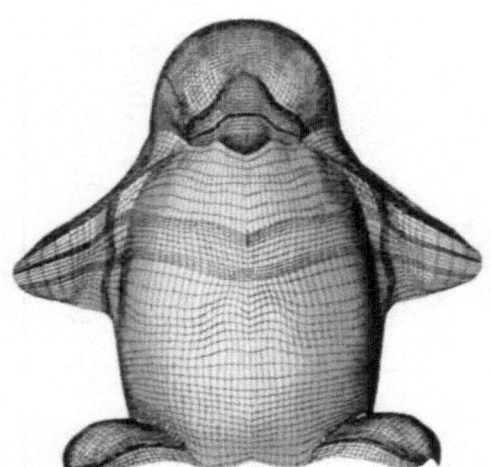 

(a) Image with polygon boundary

(b) Image without polygon boundary

Fig.7. Penguin doll (Division ratio n=4)

Table 1 Formulas of mass property

Property	Formula	Approximation(formula)	Comment
Area (S_M)	$\int_{\partial M} ds$	$\dfrac{1}{2}\sum_{i=1}^{K}\vec{n}_i \cdot \sum_{j=1}^{L}(\vec{r}_{ij}\times\vec{r}_{i,j+1})$	M 3D object ∂M surface of M ds infinitesimal area dv infinitesimal volume $\vec{r}$ point vector to dv $\vec{w}$ unit rotation vector
Volume(V_M)	$\int_M dv$	$\dfrac{1}{6}\sum_{i=1}^{K}\vec{r}_i \cdot \sum_{j=1}^{L}(\vec{r}_{ij}\times\vec{r}_{i,j+1})$	
Center of gravity ($\vec{G}_n$:Vector)	$\int_M \vec{r}\cdot dv / V_M$	$\dfrac{1}{24}\sum_{i=1}^{K}\sum_{j=1}^{L}(\vec{r}_i^2+\vec{r}_{ij}^2+\vec{r}_{i,j+1}^2+\vec{r}_i\cdot\vec{r}_{ij}+\vec{r}_{ij}\cdot\vec{r}_{i,j+1}$ $+\vec{r}_{i,j+1}\cdot\vec{r}_i)\{(\vec{r}_{ij}-\vec{r}_i)\times(\vec{r}_{i,j+1}-\vec{r}_{ij})\}/V_M$	K no. of polygon in ∂M L no. of corners in a polygon $\vec{n}_i$ unit normal vector of a polygon $\vec{r}_{ij}$ jth point vector of ith polygon $\vec{r}_i$ averaged point vector of ith polygon
2nd moment (I_M)	$\int_M (\vec{w}\times\vec{r})^2 dv$	$\dfrac{1}{60}\sum_{i=1}^{K}\sum_{j=1}^{L}\left[\vec{r}_i^2\cdot\vec{r}_i-\{(\vec{r}_i\cdot\vec{w})^2+(\vec{r}_{ij}\cdot\vec{w})^2+(\vec{r}_{i,j+1}\cdot\vec{w})^2\right.$ $+(\vec{r}_{i,j+1}\cdot\vec{r}_i)\vec{r}_i\cdot-\{(\vec{r}_i\cdot\vec{w})(\vec{r}_{ij}\cdot\vec{w})+(\vec{r}_{ij}\cdot\vec{w})(\vec{r}_{i,j+1}\cdot\vec{w})$ $\left.+(\vec{r}_{i,j+1}\cdot\vec{w})\cdot(\vec{r}_i\cdot\vec{w})\}\right]\vec{r}_i\cdot\{(\vec{r}_{ij}-\vec{r}_i)\times(\vec{r}_{i,j+1}-\vec{r}_{ij})\}$	

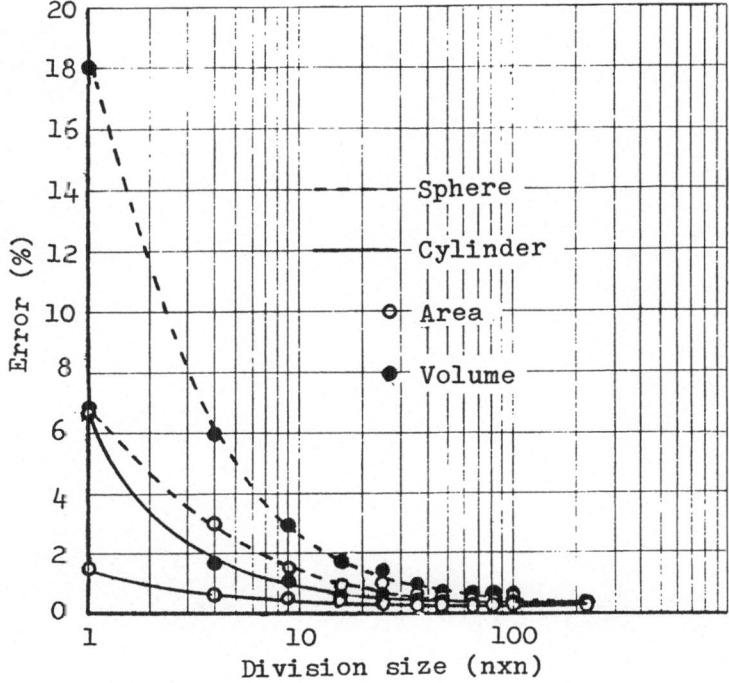

Fig.8. Numerical experiment on calculation of mass property

```
***    SOLID    ***
AREA  =   0.2791528E+07    VOLUME=   0.4246094E+08
              CENTER  OF  GRAVITY
      X                  Y                    Z
 -0.4882729E+02    0.1095833E+02      0.1352919E+03
                     MOMENT
      IX                 IY                   IZ
  0.2709394E+13    0.3234981E+13      0.3009736E+13
```

Fig.9. Mass property data displayed for the die-cast part shown in Fig.5

Chapter 2
Graphic Languages

A Data Flow Language for Intelligent Graphic Displays

Naota Inamoto, Kazunori Yamaguchi and Tosiyasu L. Kunii
Department of Information Science
Faculty of Science
The University of Tokyo
3-1, Hongo 7-chome, Bunkyo-ku
Tokyo 113, Japan

Abstract

We have designed and implemented a user-friendly data flow language for intelligent graphic displays. This language has a macro definition capability that includes both program and data, to make modular programming easier. We also discuss potential applications and extensions of this language.

I. Introduction

Today's graphic displays have the ability to perform various tasks locally, without bothering the host computer. This ability improves the performance of graphics applications, and speeds up user interaction.

User interaction is an essential part of interactive systems especially for computer aided design (CAD) and similar applications. For the user interface to be truly friendly, response to commands must be fast. If the user interaction is done through a host computer, quick response is impossible because of the limited speed of which data can be passed across communication lines, and the inability of the host computer to respond quickly in a typical time-sharing environment. To achieve quick response, the graphic display must be able to respond independently. To specify how the manipulation of interactive devices affects display data that is stored in the graphic display, application programs and display data must be distributed to the graphic display and host computer alike. Since application programs are user dependent, the graphic display must be programmable.

Most display systems provide a number of possibilities for interaction, such as control dials, data tablets and function keys. Users want to be able to use these devices without having to request the system to enable one. For the graphic display to respond to requests from multiple devices, programs must run concurrently.

Data flow programming provides one way of writing highly concurrent programs[1-4]. A data flow program can be represented by a directed graph. Nodes of the graph correspond to operators and arcs of the graph correspond to paths on which data flows. Execution of a data flow program is based on the availability of input data to operators. When all required input data to each operator is ready, an operator calculates what data will be required, and outputs the result of the calculation. Operators which have all the input data they need can operate concurrently. Synchronization in data flow programming is achieved by the flows of data, and no other dedicated control is provided or needed.

The problem with data flow programming is one of programming difficulty. A data flow program can be defined by declaring all operators, all paths and all initial input data in the directed graph. This method is not convenient for the typical user, however, because a lot of routine work is required, and all operators and paths must be declared explicitly, even if they are only used temporarily. We need a more convenient language for data flow programming.

We use the E&S PS300 graphics system as a typical example of a graphic display with programming capability for our discussion here. The

PS300 can be programmed in the data flow language but the user suffers from the low level of the language. To improve data flow programming productivity for graphics applications, we have designed a user-friendly data flow language called DFIG (Data Flow Language for Intelligent Graphic Displays). This language has the following features:

1. Inputs to an operator are written as arguments to a function.
2. It is not necessary to declare all operators explicitly.
3. A macro that includes both of a program and data can be defined.
4. A part of a macro definition can be shared to reduce the size of object programs.

Section II briefly explains the data flow language of the PS300. Section III aims the DFIG. Section IV describes some of the applications of the DFIG, and section V summarizes what was covered in this paper.

II. PS300 Programming

A data flow program in the PS300 is called a _function network_, and an operator of the data flow program is called a _function instance_. The PS300 has a predefined set of functions, such as add, eq and xrotate. Each function has a fixed number of inputs and outputs with predefined meaning. Data flow programming is accomplished by creating function instances and connecting inputs and outputs of those function instances.

The function network runs locally in the PS300 achieving the quick response to user interaction. Figure 1 is a sample function network. This function network specifies the action taken when a user rotates dials. The function instance "dials" is created at system initialization. "Dials" outputs a floating number to one of eight outputs, corresponding to the dial that have been rotated. The function "f:mulc" outputs a multiplication of input<1> and input<2> when data on input<1> is ready. Data needs to be sent to input<2> only once. That data is then used each time input<1> has new data. The function "f:xrotate" outputs a rotation matrix around the x axis.

In this example, a node "obj.rot" is an element of a display data structure. Here, the _display data structure_ is a hierarchical display data file stored in the PS300. The display data structure consists of three types of nodes: a _data node_, an _operation node_ and an _instance node_. A data node stores display primitives, such as vectors and characters. An operation node performs a display data transformation, such as rotation, translation, and perspective viewing. The operation is applied to data under this node when it is displayed. An instance node is used to group multiple nodes. Display data with a name can be referred to by the name from other display data structure elements.

Display data can be modified by commands and a function network. For example, a rotation angle is modified by sending a rotation matrix to the operation node. In Fig. 1, the rotation angle is modified by connecting the output of the function instance "rot" to the operation node "obj.rot" and sending a rotation matrix.

As this network shows, a function network is often connected to display data structure elements and interactive devices. For practical use, it is also connected to a host computer for up- and down- loading data.

The function network is created by the following three types of commands.

Type 1.   name := F:identifier;
Type 2.   CONNECT name<i>:<i'>name';
Type 3.   SEND constant TO <i>name;

A type 1 command creates a function instance with the specified name "name" of the function type "identifier". A type 2 command connects the i-th output of a function instance "name" and the i'-th input of a function instance "name'". A type 3 command sends a data specified "constant" to the i-th input of a function instance "name" once. Figure 2 (a) shows these commands. This program creates the function network in Fig. 1.

III. **DFIG**: A data flow language for intelligent graphic displays

This section explains DFIG, which provides a user-friendly data flow language for the PS300 graphics system. The PS300 presents the following programming difficulties:

(a) Relations among functions, inputs, and outputs are hard to understand because function declaration and its connections are done in different places.
(b) Each function must be declared explicitly and a name must be assigned to each function. This disguises the meaning of the program.
(c) A macro function composing several functions cannot be defined. A user must rewrite routine programs, even if they are often used.

We have done the following to overcome these problems.

1. A function and its arguments
To overcome the problem in (a), we use the following syntax and its interpretation in DFIG.
syntax:
    name := identifier(a_{11}| .. |a_{1s}, ... ,a_{n1}| .. |a_{nt});
interpretation:
    name := F:identifier;
    conn a_{11}:<1>name; ... conn a_{1s}:<1>name;
                      .
                        .
    conn a_{n1}:<n>name; ... conn a_{nt}:<n>name;

In this notation, a function instance which instances the function instance "identifier" is created by assigning the name "name". "a_{ij}" is an output of other function instances. "a_{ij}" is connected to the j-th input of the function instance "name". "a_{ij}" may be a data constant. In such a case, a data constant is sent to the specified input "<i>name". In DFIG, when a function instance is created, all the connections to inputs are specified as arguments to the function instance. When a single input has more than one connection, the connections are separated by the vertical bar "|" in DFIG notation.

Example: The function instance "rot" in Fig. 1 is connected to other function instances through its inputs and outputs. In the original language, the function declaration and connections are specified by

    rot := f:mulc;
    conn xrot<1>:<1>rot;
    conn yrot<1>:<1>rot;
    conn zrot<1>:<1>rot;
    conn rot<1>:<2>rot;
    send m3d(1,0,0 0,1,0 0,0,1) to <2>rot;

In DFIG, these are specified simply by

    rot := mulc(xrot| yrot| zrot, rot| m3d(1,0,0 0,1,0 0,0,1));

In DFIG, when a function has multiple outputs, each of the outputs is specified by a postfix output selector "<i>". The output selector "<1>" can be omitted because the output<1> is often used.

2. Temporary functions

The output<1> of a function can be specified as an argument. This notation eliminates the necessity to assign a name to a temporary function, overcoming the problem in (b). Example: The output of the function instance "xscl" in Fig. 1 is used temporarily. Two functions "f:xrotate" and "f:mulc" are declared explicitly by

    xrot := xrotate(xscl);
    xscl := mulc(dials<1>, 180);

It is not necessary to assign a name to the function "f:mulc" in the DFIG notation.

   xrot := xrotate(mulc(dials<1>, 180));

3. Outputs to display data structures

In addition to the DFIG command, which is explained above, we have a command in DFIG for connecting a function network to display data structures. This command has the format:

   $arg_0 | ... | arg_n$ -> <i>name;

"arg_i" is an output of a function instance. This command connects the outputs "arg_0"..."arg_n" to the i-th input of display data structures specified by the name "name". The input selector "<i>" can be omitted.

Example: In Fig. 1, the function instance "rot" is connected to the display data structure element "obj.rot" by

   rot -> obj.rot;

Fig. 2 (a) is a program in the original notation and Fig. 2 (b) is a program in DFIG notation.

4. A macro function definition

To overcome the problem in (c), a new function can be defined as a user defined macro in DFIG. A function network that refers to the user defined functions expands the macro at each reference location.

The following is the syntax of a macro function definition in DFIG.

   define identifier
      input ($arg_1,...,arg_n$)
      output ($sel_1,...,sel_n$) := (argument_list)
   parbegin
      .
      .
      commands
      .
      .
   parend;

This definition groups a function network by a new function identified by "identifier". In this definition, "arg_i" is the i-th input to the macro function. The output of the macro function specified by "sel_i" corresponds to an expression in the argument_list. We use the keywords "parbegin" and "parend" in place of "begin" and "end", because functions surrounded by them are executed in parallel.

Figure 3 shows an example of this definition. The "for loop" is made by using the macro function "for".

5. A macro definition including display data structures

Until now, we have discussed ways to improve data flow programming and how to define a macro for a function network. We now should think about application programs, without separating the function network and the display data structure, because the function network is usually created to modify the display data structure.

In DFIG, a macro definition can have local display data structures. The local display data structure can be modified only through the user specified macro definition. Local display data structures are specified using the same syntax as the PS300 commands.

A macro definition can refer to display data structure elements by specifying names of display data structure elements as arguments, and outputs of the macro definition can be treated as names of display data structure elements. By this treatment, a macro definition of a display data structure or a macro definition including both a function network and a display data structure are possible.

As an example, let's display the robot arm shown in Figure 4. This robot arm consists of five parts (base, body, bicep, forearm and hand) and has four joints. Figure 5 (a) shows a sample macro definition which corresponds to the part "base". This macro definition includes both a function network, which modifies the rotation angle of the joints, and display data structures, which has the geometrical data of the part "base" and the information of the joints. This macro definition refers to the display data structure specified by the first argument, output<1> of this macro definition represents a name of the display data structure that corresponds to the part "base". The display data structure of the robot arm is created by five macro definitions shown in Figure 5 (b).

When a user displays two robot arms, or displays various kinds of robot arms created by composing various parts, a conflict between names occurs in the original language because names of the display data structure elements are global. This conflict of names does not occur in DFIG because names in the macro definition are local. DFIG improves program modularity.

6. Shared functions and data structure elements

Duplicating function instances or the display data structure elements is not efficient, if the function instances do not run concurrently or the display data structure elements can be shared. In DFIG, we can suppress duplication by using the following notation.

```
   parbegin
      .
      .
      shared
         .
         .
         commands
         .
         .
      end_shared;
      .
      .
   parend;
```

The function instances or the display data structure elements surrounded by the keywords "shared" and "end_shared" are expanded only once, and are shared by multiple reference locations. Figure 5 (a) shows an example of the shared display data structure element.

The advantages of shared functions and data structure elements are as follows:
1. Required memory is reduced.
2. Modifications to shared data affect multiple reference locations.

We have implemented DFIG under the UNIX operating system[6] on the VAX 11/780. The program is written in the C Language[7] using the YACC compiler-compiler[8] and the LEX lexical analyzer[9].

IV. Applications of the DFIG

We have designed DFIG to improve data flow programming for intelligent graphic displays. Because a data flow program can be represented by a two dimensional directed graph, the tools which use graphic displays and a graphics editor appears to improve data flow programming more than DFIG. One thing is certain: a graphics figure is easier to read than a text string. But the language in which programs are written and the user interface through which a user writes programs are different concepts. A graphics editor is a user interface for writing application programs. DFIG is a statement oriented language, not a user interface. When we write programs in the statement oriented language, we use a text editor as the user interface.

When a user develops a function network in DFIG, it is convenient to have a more sophisticated user interface (probably graphic). Even a good user interface, however, requires the user to learn many function network patterns to perform a simple task. To relieve the user from having to learn routine patterns, we are now developing application oriented software tools to generate a function network automatically from a simple specification suitable to applications. DFIG provides a basis for such software tools. A simple example is a menu handling mechanism. The following is an example of a simple menu specification.

```
primitive
        block
        cylinder
        cone
        ball
        torus
transform
        translate
        rotate
        scale
setop
        union
        intersection
        minus
exit
```

Generating a menu handler from this specification is not difficult, but it takes a lot of time to write and rewrite routine function networks many times. A simple tool which generates a function network from this specification reduces the user programming time.

V. Conclusions and future research

Local intelligence is being employed more and more to improve performance and response. But we still do not have a good way to develop programs for local intelligent devices. We have adopted a data flow concept to specify local action, and DFIG improves productivity of a data flow program.

The part of the application program associated with local action resides in the graphic display, the other part of the application program resides in the host computer. In order to develop a whole program that includes both the program in the graphic display and the program in the host computer, it is necessary to determine the communication protocol between the graphic display and the host computer and to write a program for the host computer in addition to the one for the graphic display. Thus the distribution of application programs and the functional interface between a host computer and a graphic display must be taken into account. These two points remain as topics for future research.

Acknowledgement

This work has been supported in part by the Software Research Laboratory of RICOH Co., Ltd.

References

[1] J. B. Dennis, J. B. Fossen and J. P. Linderman, "Data flow schemas," Lecture Notes in Computer Science, Vol.5, Springer-Verlag, 1972, pp.187-216.

[2] K. P. Gostelow and R. E. Thomas, "A view of data flow," NCC, 1979, pp.629-636.

[3] W. B. Ackerman, "Data flow languages," NCC, 1979, pp.1087-1095.

[4] J. R. McGraw, "Data Flow Computing: Software Development," IEEE transaction on computers, Vol.C-29, No.12, Dec, 1980.

[5] "PS300 user's manual," Evans & Sutherland Computer Corporation.

[6] D. M. Ritchie and K. Thompson, "The UNIX Time-Sharing System," Comm. of ACM, 17, NO.7, July 1974, pp.365-375.

[7] B. W. Kernighan and D. M. Ritchie, "The C Programming Language," Prentice-Hall, 1978.

[8] S. C. Johnson, "YACC - Yet Another Compiler-Compiler," Computer Science Technical Report No. 32, Bell Laboratories, 1975.

[9] M. E. Lesk, "Lex - A Lexical Analyzer Generator," Computer Science Technical Report No. 39, Bell Laboratories, 1975.

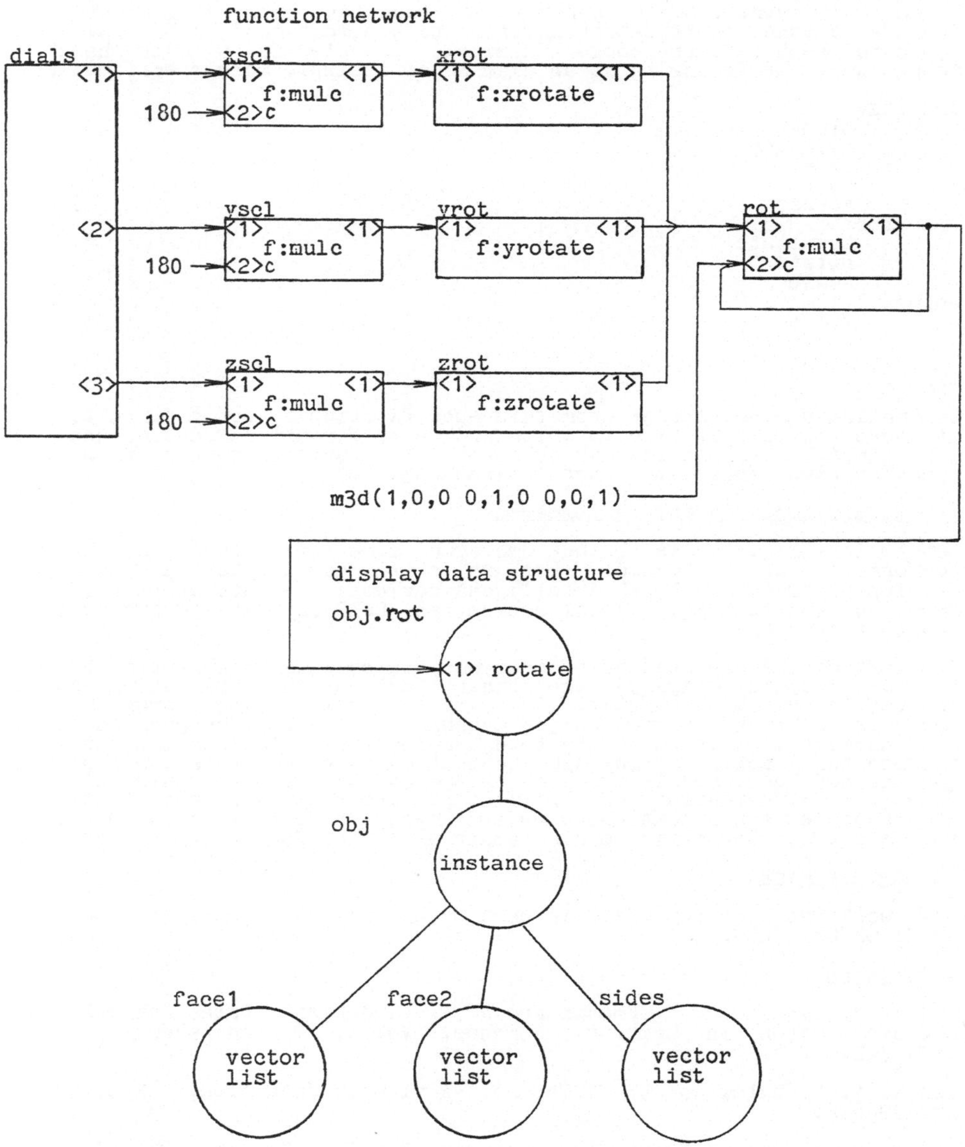

Figure 1. Sample function network for an object space rotation.

```
rot   := f:mulc;
xrot  := f:xrotate;
yrot  := f:yrotate;
zrot  := f:zrotate;
xscl  := f:mulc;
yscl  := f:mulc;
zscl  := f:mulc;

conn rot<1>:<1>obj.rot;

conn xrot<1>:<1>rot;
conn yrot<1>:<1>rot;
conn zrot<1>:<1>rot;
conn rot<1>:<2>rot;
send m3d(1,0,0 0,1,0 0,0,1) to <2>rot;

conn xscl<1>:<1>xrot;
conn yscl<1>:<1>yrot;
conn zscl<1>:<1>zrot;
conn dials<1>:<1>xscl;
conn dials<2>:<1>yscl;
conn dials<3>:<1>zscl;
send 180 to <2>xscl;
send 180 to <2>yscl;
send 180 to <2>zscl;
```

  (a) a program in the original notation

```
rot -> obj.rot;
rot  := mulc( xrot| yrot| zrot, rot| m3d(1,0,0 0,1,0 0,0,1));
xrot := xrotate( mulc( dials<1>, 180));
yrot := yrotate( mulc( dials<2>, 180));
zrot := zrotate( mulc( dials<3>, 180));
```

  (b) a program in DFIG notation

Figure 2. Programs for object space rotation
   corresponding to the function network in Figure 1.

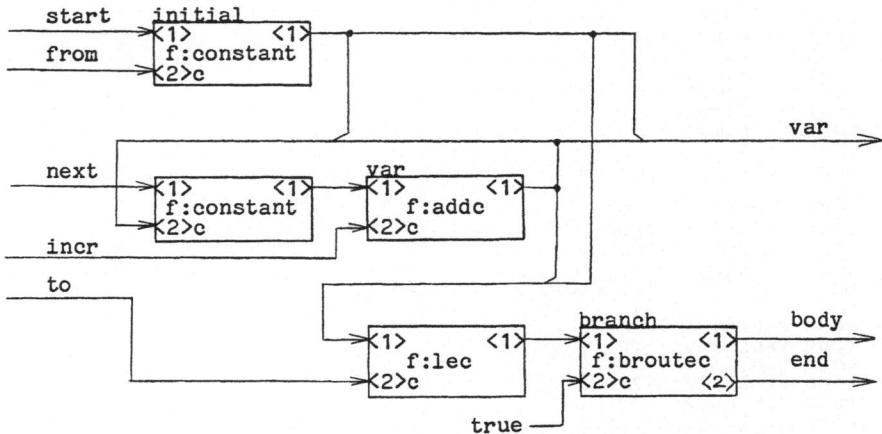

(a) the function network for making "for loop"

```
define for
    input   ( start, next, from, to, incr)
    output  ( end, body, var) :=
            ( branch<f>, branch<t>, initial| var)
parbegin
    initial := constant( start, from);
    branch  := broutec( lec( initial| var, to), true);
    var     := addc( constant( next, initial| var), incr);
parend;
```

(b) the macro definition corresponding to Figure 3 (a)

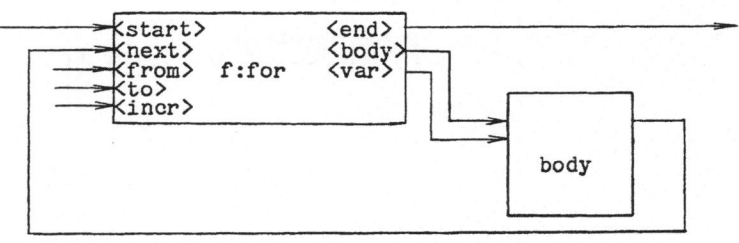

(c) the usage of a macro function "for"

Figure 3. Sample macro function definition.

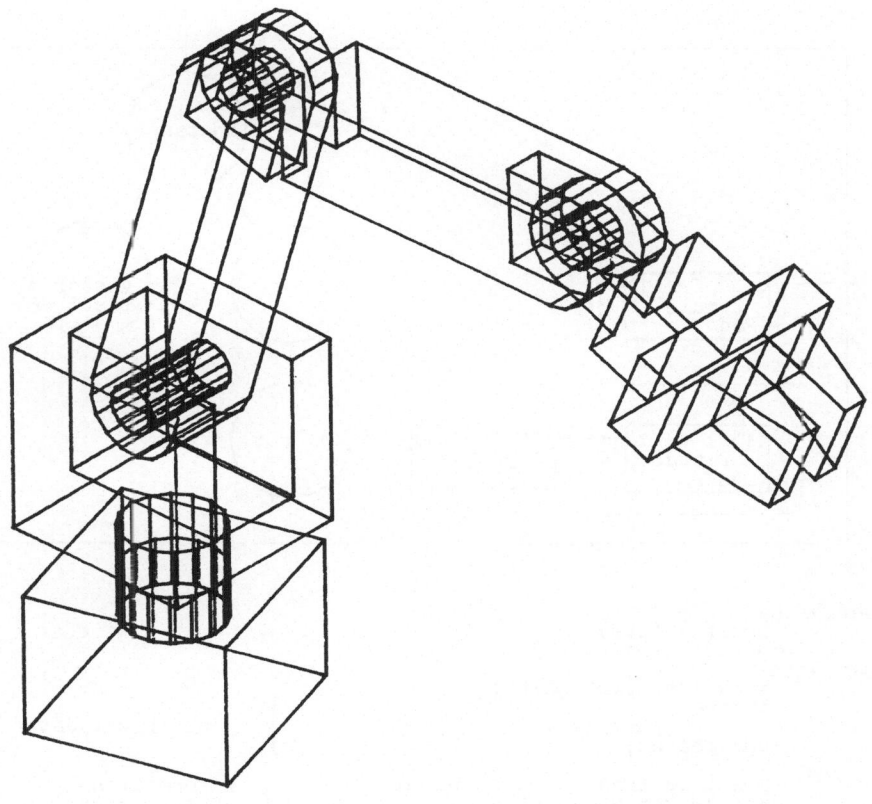

Figure 4. A robot arm.

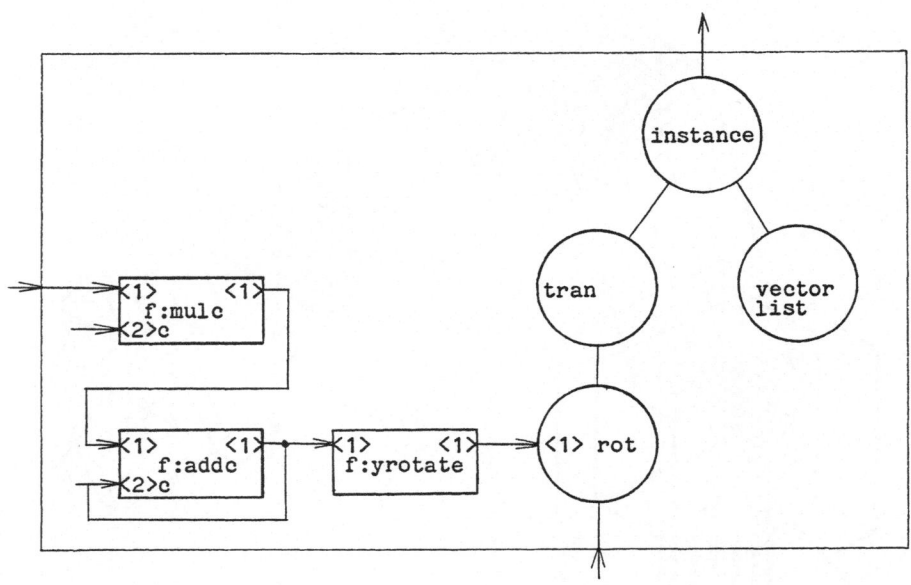

```
define base
        input   (o,a)
        output  (o) := (i)
parbegin
        i := inst part,joint;
        shared
                part := vec ... ;                } geometrical data
        end_shared;

        joint := tran ... appl to rot;           } information
        rot := rot y 0 appl to o;                } of the joint

        yrotate(angle) -> rot;                   } function network
        angle := addc( mulc(a,180), angle|0);    }
parend;
```

        (a) a sample macro definition
           which corresponds to a part of the robot arm


```
base    := base( body, dials<1>);
body    := body( bicep, dials<2>);
bicep   := bicep( forearm, dials<3>);
forearm := forearm( hand, dials<4>);
hand    := hand( finger );
```

        (b) the creation of the robot arm data

Figure 5. Macro definition that includes both a program and data

MIRA-Shading: A Structured Language for the Synthesis and the Animation of Realistic Images

Nadia Magnenat-Thalmann, Mario Fortin and **Louis Langlois**
Hautes Etudes Commerciales
Université de Montréal
Canada

Daniel Thalmann
Département d'Informatique
et de Recherche Opérationnelle
Université de Montréal
Canada

ABSTRACT

MIRA-SHADING is a structured graphics language that provides the programmer the way of specifying, manipulating and animating 3D shaded objects by the use of high level graphical types. The major application of MIRA-SHADING is a director-oriented 3D shaded computer animation system.

INTRODUCTION

Since several years, techniques have been quite successful in rendering realistic images of artificial objects. Detail like texture, reflections and shadow have been simulated by different algorithms (1-6). However, only little effort has been done for developing structured ways of defining these realistic characteristics in a programming language.

Based on our experience in designing and implementing the structured programming language MIRA-3D (7,8,9) for producing 3D wire-frames drawings, we have developed a new language called MIRA-SHADING. This language provides the programmer the way of specifying 3D shaded objects by the use of high level graphical types.

The major application of MIRA-SHADING is in the area of computer animation. A director-oriented 3D shaded computer animation system has been implemented in MIRA-SHADING.

HIGH-LEVEL 3D SHADED TYPES

Two types of entities are manipulated in MIRA-SHADING: <u>vectors</u> and <u>figures</u>.

A vector is defined by its three coordinates ≪E1,E2,E3≫. Vector constants, variables and functions can be defined and they are all of VECTOR type. Vectors may be read, written and compared, and the following operations are available: addition, external multiplication, dot product and cross product.

e.g.   var V1,V2,V3: vector;
         R: REAL;
        begin
          READ(V1,V2);
          V3:=V1 cross V2;
          R:= V1 * (V2+V3);
          WRITE (V3,R)
        end;

Standard functions are also defined such as DIST(V1,V2) which gives the distance between vectors V1 and V2, and NORM(V) that calculates the norm of the vector V.

Figures are high level graphical types that define the composition of a three-dimensional object. In MIRA-SHADING, an object is modelled as a combination of faces, vertices and edges. For example, a CUBE must be declared with the following specifications:

figure of 8 vertices, 6 faces, 12 edges

The syntax of the figure type is shown in Fig. 1

The characteristics of the figure are defined in a list of formal parameters that specify the object for the user. For example, to create a SPHERE, the user must give the center and the radius:

e.g.   type SPHERE = figure (CENTER:VECTOR; RADIUS:REAL)

These characteristics are the only ones that the user needs to know.

The user is not required to know that the SPHERE is actually constructed using 250 faces ! However, the construction of the object must be carried out in the type through statements using the parameters and any declarations that may be useful (constants, variables, types, procedures, functions). The specification section defines the name of the figure, the type of shading and the main characteristics: number of vertices, faces and edges. As these numbers may need to be calculated, statements are allowed in the specification section. For example:

        type STRANGE = figure (N: INTEGER;...);
                    var N2:INTEGER;
                    spec
                       N2:=N * N;
                       name 'STRANGE', shading PHONG
                       figure of N2 vertices, N faces, N+2 edges;
                    begin
                       ...
                    end;

The role of the statements in a figure type is to define the vertices, faces and edges. Vertices are specified in an assignment-like statement:

    e.g.   the statement
    vertices:= A, B+C, <<4,2,5>>

defines the values of the first three vertices of the figure
and the statement

>   vertices 4:= D,E cross F

defines the values of vertices 4 and 5.

The statement createface allows the programmer to specify the number of edges for a face and also optionally the color of the face in the RGB system.

>   e.g. createface 3 with 5 edges
>   createface 1 to 6 with 6 edges col <<0,0,1>>

The last statement creates six faces with 6 blue edges. The different faces are also built using an assignment-like statement where the vertices are given by their rank in the vertices statement.

>   e.g. face 1:= 3,4,5,7;

defines the first face with 4 edges 3-4, 4-5, 5-7 and 7-3.

For example, we present below a BOX type defining a parallellepiped object characterized by vertices as shown in Fig. 2

The figure type is as follows:

```
        type BOX = figure (A,B,C,D, COLO: VECTOR);
                   var CORI, BORI, DORI: VECTOR;
                   spec
                      name 'BOX', shading CONSTANT,
                      figure of 8 vertices, 6 faces, 12 edges;
                   begin
                      CORI:=C-A;
                      BORI:=B-A;
                      DORI:=D-A;
                      vertices:= A,C,B+CORI,B,D,C+DORI, D+BORI+CORI,D+BORI;
                      createface 1 to 6 with 4 edges;
                      face 1:=1,2,3,4;
                      face 2:=2,6,7,3;
                      face 3:=3,7,8,4;
                      face 4:=5,1,4,8;
                      face 5:=1,5,6,2;
                      face 6:=6,5,8,7;
                      COLOR(COLO);
                   end;
```

The whole object is coloured with the color COLO.

CREATION OF FIGURE VARIABLES

Graphical variables (or figure variables) are defined as variables of graphical type.

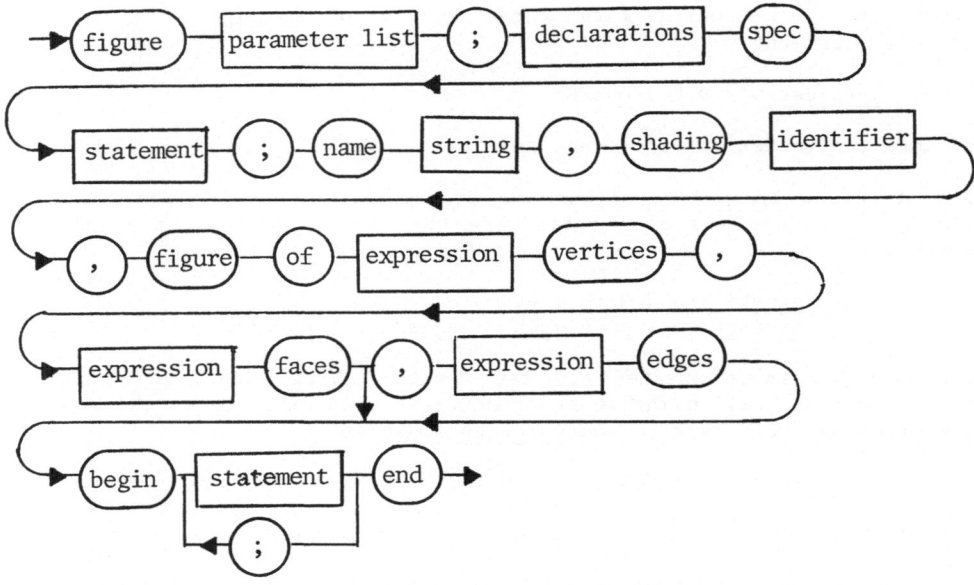

Fig.1 Syntax of the figure type

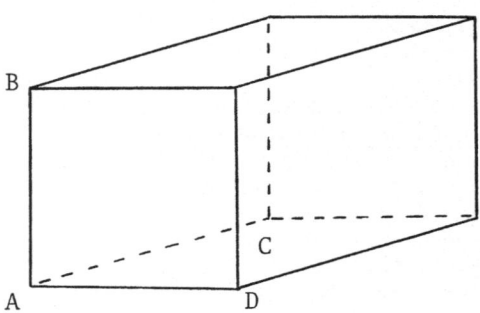

Fig.2 A box

```
        e.g.  var BO: BOX;
                   S: SPHERE;
```

The user characteristics of the variables are given with the statement <u>create</u> that requires the values of the actual parameters corresponding to the formal parameters in the graphical type. For example, the user must give the value of the center and the radius of a sphere.

```
        e.g.  create S(<<4,5,3>>, 12);
              - creates a sphere of center <<4,5,3>> and radius 12
              create BO(A, B+D, <<2,4,1>>, C, <<1,0,0>>);
              - creates a red colored box with vertices A, B+D, <<2,4,1>>
                and C
```

<u>SHADING</u>

In the definition of MIRA-SHADING, the term "shading" means the effect of the illumination of objects by one or several sources.

Several different shading methods exist, each being more cr less appropriate, depending on the object shape. We therefore provide all of the following kinds of shading:

1) constant shading
2) Gouraud's (10) shading
3) Phong's (1) shading

The kind of shading used is included in the specification of an object.

```
        e.g.  spec
              ...
                  name 'ELLIPSOID', shading PHONG,
                  figure of X vertices, Y faces, Z edges;
```

However, in order to give the user a way of specifying the type of shading when creating objects, we have introduced the data type TYPSHADE that is predefined as:

```
        type TYPSHADE = (CONSTANT,GOURAUD,PHONG);
```
A figure type can thus be defined as:

```
        type ELLIPSOID = figure (A,B:VECTOR;X,Y:REAL;SHA:TYPSHADE);
                  .
                  .
                  .
                  spec
                  .
                  .
                      name 'ELLIPSOID', shading SHA,
                      figure of X vertices, Y faces, Z edges;
                      .
                      .
                      .
```

Colors can be defined in different ways:

1) The object can be colored with a single color that is defined using the COLOR standard procedure.

2) Each face of the object can have a different color; this color must be specified in the <u>createface</u> statement; this is well adapted to constant and Phong's shadings, but is not convenient for Gouraud's shading.

3) A color is defined for each vertex of the figure; this color must be specified in the <u>vertices</u> statement. This procedure is only appropriate for Gouraud's shading.

    e.g. vertices:= A col <<1,0,0>>, B col <<0.8,0,0.2>>,
                 C col <<0.6,0,0.3>>, D col <<0.5, 0.1, 0.4>>;

3D SHADED TEXT

The text in MIRA-SHADING is of a very high quality suitable for titles and logos. To produce text, a variable of the type TEXT3D must be created. This is predefined as:

  TEXT3D = <u>figure</u> (TXT: STRING; ORIG,SIZE,SPACE,PLA,COL1,COL2,COL3:VECTOR)

TXT is the character string to be drawn; ORIG,SIZE,SPACE and PLA are vectors which respectively define the origin of the text, the character size (width, height and depth), the character space and the character plane.

COL1, COL2 and COL3 are respectively the colors of the front face of the characters, the back face and the lateral faces.

    e.g. <u>var</u> T:TEXT3D;

       <u>create</u> T('MIRA-SHADING', <<0,0,0>>, <<5,6,3>>, <<10,0,0>>,
            <<0,0,1>>, <<1,0,0>>, <<0,1,0>>, <<0,0,1>>);

creates the title MIRA-SHADING at the origin, with a width of 5, a height of 6 and a depth of 3; the character space is 10 along the X axis and the character plane is the XY plane. The colors of the faces of the text are red, green and blue. Shading is always constant. Fig.3 shows an example created with a perspective projection using the procedure PERCAM described below.

VIRTUAL CAMERAS

The viewing system in MIRA-SHADING is compatible with the ACM GSPC Core System (11). However to simplify the specification for the user, two procedures have been introduced in order to define a virtual camera. PERCAM(EYE,INTEREST,ZOOM,SPIN) locates a camera with the eye, the interest point, a zoom and a spin value. PARCAM(EYE,INTEREST,ZOOM,SPIN) is very similar, but the camera is defined using a parallel projection instead of a perspective projection.

MANIPULATION AND DISPLAY OF FIGURES

When a figure variable has been created, it can be placed in the list of figures to be displayed by the statement *draw*. It can be modified by an image transformation or by a *delete* statement. When all required figures have been put in the list, the scene can be displayed using the *image* statement.

    e.g. *var* S1,S2:SPHERE;
        .
        .
        .
    begin
        create S1(CENTER,RADIUS);
        TRANSLATION(S1,DIR,S2);
        delete S1;
        draw S2;
        image
    end;

TRANSLATION is a predefined image transformation defined in a similar way to other image transformations such as scaling, rotations, symmetries, homothesis. The user may also define his or her image transformation in two ways:

1) A 4x4 matrix M can be defined and passed as parameter to the predefined image transformation MATRAN (F1,M,F2).

2) An image transformation can be defined as a subprogram similar to a procedure.

    e.g. *transform* SCALE(FACT:REAL);
    begin
        NEWFIG:=FACT * OLDFIG
    end;

Image transformation statements define the transformation of a vertex (OLDFIG) of the original figure into a vertex (NEWFIG) of the new figure; OLDFIG and NEWFIG are predefined vectors. The transformation is implicitly applied to all figure vertices. A transformation call must correspond to the transformation definition; however, there are two extra parameters: the original and the new figures.

    e.g. SCALE(F1,S2,F2)

PREDEFINED SHADED FIGURE TYPES

A certain number of shaded figure types have been implemented:

1) CUBE, BOX, regular polyhedra with constant shading

2) SPHERE is defined with Phong's shading

3) cylinders are predefined by
   CYLINDER = figure (F:FIG; D:LINE; H:REAL)

   Where the cylindrical body is defined by the displacement of a line segment of direction D and length H along a curve F.

4) Cones are predefined by

   CONE = figure (F:FIG; S:VECTOR; FRACT:REAL)

   where the conical body is defined by the displacement of a segment line along the curve F passing through S; FRACT is a parameter that allows the representation of truncated cones.

5) Revolution bodies are defined by the rotation of a figure F around a line D and can be created using the following predefined type:

   REVOLUTION = figure (F:FIG; D:LINE; FRACT:REAL)

   The parameter FRACT can be used to limit the revolution to less than 360°.

6) Patch surfaces are also predefined using 3 figure types: parametric surfaces, Coons surfaces and Bezier surfaces.

   Examples of predefined figures are shown in Fig. 4-8.

ANIMATION PRIMITIVES

Several animation primitives are predefined in MIRA-SHADING. In particular, different motion primitives are available like Catmull laws, circular motion, pendulum motion, collisions ... There is also an INBETWEEN function to calculate the inbetweens when two 3D shaded objects are given. With this primitive, it is easy to develop programs that give analogous effects to those achieved with key-frame systems.

IMPLEMENTATION

MIRA-SHADING was implemented by developing a preprocessor. This consists of a 6500 source line program in ISO PASCAL developed on a DEC VAX 11/780. The output is an ISO PASCAL program. The runtime library is written partly in MIRA-SHADING, and partly in PASCAL. This library is device-independent except for a few routines that have been implemented on the AED 767 terminal. Hidden faces are processed using a scan-line algorithm and the shading is computed using the different algorithms.

Fig.3 Shaded text

Fig.4 Spheres

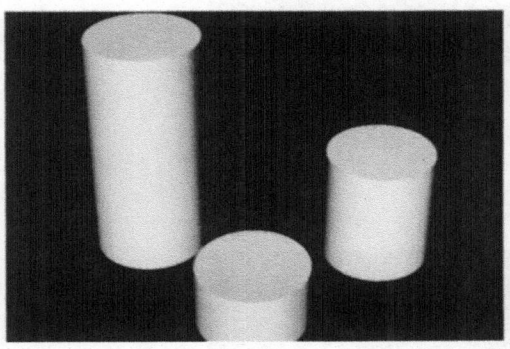
Fig.5 Cylinders

Fig.6 Revolution bodies

Fig.7 Regular polyhedra

Fig.8 Shaded Corvette on a box

APPLICATION: A 3D SHADED ANIMATION SYSTEM

The largest application program that was written in MIRA-SHADING is a 3D shaded computer animation system. This system allows the animator to completely specify a script without programming. The animator can create actors with their motions and transformations and virtual cameras with their motions and characteristics. Decors can be also interactively built. Multiple light sources can be defined and they can have any motion. Eight modes are defined in the system and there are specific commands in each mode:

1) <u>Variable mode</u>

   In this mode the animator can create constants and animated variables. Such variables are defined with an evolution law that describe how their values are changing in the time. Among the available laws, there are Catmull laws and the main physical motions.

2) <u>Object mode</u>

   This mode corresponds to a limited 3D graphics editor to create objects. In fact, basic objects must be built outside the animation system. But, they can be modified in this object mode by rotations, translations, scaling and coloring.

3) <u>Decor mode</u>

   In this mode, the animator can build a decor with objects and display it.

4) <u>Actor mode</u>

   This mode is the most important. The animator defines actors (animated objects) then he gives a list of transformations that are applied on each actor. 16 kinds of transformations are now available including rotation, sizing, translation, shears, torsion, traction, flexion, stochastic transformation, color changing. The parameters of a transformation can be animated variables and this is the normal way of specifying the time dependance. For example, in a rotation the angle can be an animated real number and the direction of the axis can be a animated vector.

5) <u>Camera mode</u>

   In this mode, the animator can define one or several virtual cameras. Each camera has an eye point and an interest point that can be animated vectors. Moreover, clipping, spin, viewport and zoom can be specified for a camera and they can be animated. The eye point or the interest point of a camera can also follow the motion of a specific actor. By using several cameras at the same time, special effects like wipes can be easily realized.

6) Light mode

   In this mode, the animator can define one or several light sources and their motion(s).

7) Animation mode

   This mode is the director's mode; starting times and durations of actors, cameras and decor are decided in this mode. It is also in this mode, that shooting or playback is activated.

8) Control mode

   This mode allows the animator to enter in other modes, to save or retrieve actors, cameras, decors or to obtain a list of the script under the form of a summary of all variables, laws, actors, transformations, cameras, lights and so on.

The following short example shows the user interface. A dodecahedron is rotated around the Y-axis with an animated angle. The eye of the virtual camera is also animated. The modes are indicated :

```
VA> VECTOR PT,C,0,0,0              - defines a constant vector PT.
VA> REAL ANG,A,0,90                - defines an animated real ANG.
VA> LAW MYLAW,UNIFORM,4            - defines a uniform law.
VA> EVOLUTION ANG,MYLAW,0,5        - applies the law to ANG.
VA> VECTOR EYE,A,0,0,-600,0,0,-100 - defines an animated vector EYE.
VA> LAW ACCDEC,CATMULL,1,1,1       - defines a Catmull law.
VA> EVOLUTION ACCDEC,EYE,0,5       - applies the law to EYE.
VA> VECTOR INT,C,0,0,10000         - defines a constant vector INT.
OB> READ DODECA,FILE               - reads a dodecahedron.
AC> ACTOR,DODE,DODECA              - defines an actor.
AC> ROTATION DODE,Y,PT,ANG         - applies the rotation.
CA> CAMERA CAM,EYE,INT             - defines the camera.
AN> ACTOR DODE,0,5,0               - activates the actor.
AN> CAMERA CAM,0,5,0               - activates the camera.
AN> SHOOT,0,5                      - shoots 5 seconds.
```

This animation system consists in 12000 source lines of MIRA-SHADING and we use it to produce animated scenes for entertainment and commercial films. Data structures consist in dynamic lists of objects, laws, actors, cameras and light sources. Each actor is defined by a list of objects and a list of transformations.

CONCLUSION

MIRA-SHADING is a structured language that allows the user to quickly implement systems for producing realistic images. The language offers all the advantages of the PASCAL language, an elegant way of defining realistic 3D shaded objects and operations for the manipulation and the animation of these objects. A very complex 3D computer animation system has been successfully developed with MIRA-SHADING and we use it extensively for the production of computer-animated films.

REFERENCES

(1) Bui-Tuong, Phong, "Illumination for Computer-generated Pictures", Comm. ACM, 18(6), 1975, pp. 311-317.

(2) Blinn, J.F. and Newell, M.E. "Texture and Reflection in Computer Generated Images", Comm. ACM, 19(10), 1976, pp. 542-547.

(3) Cook, R.L. and Torrance, K., "A Reflectance Model for Computer Graphics", Proc. SIGGRAPH'81, pp. 307-316.

(4) Crow, F., "Shadow Algorithms for Computer Graphics", Proc. SIGGRAPH'77, pp. 242-247.

(5) Whitted, T., "An Improved Illumination Model for Shaded Display", Comm. ACM, 23(6), 1980, pp. 343-349.

(6) Fournier, A., Fussel, D. and Carpenter, L., "Computer Rendering of Stochastic Models", Comm. ACM, 25(6), 1982, pp. 371-384.

(7) Magnenat-Thalmann, N. and Thalmann, D., "The Use of High-level Graphical Types in the MIRA Animation System", IEEE Computer Graphics and Applications, Vol. 3, No. 9, pp. 9-16.

(8) Magnenat-Thalmann, N. and Thalmann, D., "MIRA-3D: A Three-dimensional Graphical Extension of PASCAL", Software-Practice and Experience, Vol. 13, pp. 797.808, 1983.

(9) Magnenat-Thalmann, N. and Thalmann, D., "Some Unusual Primitives in the MIRA Graphical Extension of PASCAL", Computers and Graphics, Pergamon Press, Vol. 6, No. 3, 1982, pp. 127-139.

(10) Gouraud, H., "Continuous Shading of Curved Surfaces", IEEE Trans. on Computers, C-20(6), 1971, pp. 623-628.

(11) "Status Report of the Graphics Standards Committee", Computer Graphics, 13(3), August 71.

ACKNOWLEDGEMENTS

The authors are grateful to the referees for their helpful comments.

Chapter 3
Visualization Techniques

"Steam Plume" Simulation

Hirohiko Kishino and **Katsumi Tanaka**
JGC Corporation
14-1, Bessho 1-chome, Minami-ku
Yokohama 232, Japan

ABSTRACT

For evaluating atmospheric pollution, the method of depicting contour of waste gas isoconcentrations is generally adopted. However, such phenomena as impeded visibility and scenic degradation due to the formation of "Steam Plumes" associated with the condensation of water vapor contained in waste gases cannot be indicated by this method. Therefore, computer simulation has been employed to visually express the conditions accompanying the formation of "Steam Plumes".

1. INTRODUCTION

Concurrent with the rapid progress now being made in the realms of computer hardware and software, extensive efforts are also being made worldwide to develop visual methods of presenting computer outputs which are more realistic than their predecessors. Initially, there was the method of projecting the mesh covering the surface of simple three dimensional objects, so-called wire-frame modelling, followed by the surface or the solid modelling which can express more realistic images of objects. Furthermore, B. B. Mandelbrot presented many realistic images of natural scenes which are complex and have both of randomness and regularity. The realism of computerized imagery is thus being steadily improved.

Meanwhile, with the increasing gravity of environmental problems, diversification of personal sense of values, etc., it has become necessary to obtain the consensus of the inhabitants concerned based on prior assessment of the environmental impact of not only large-scale industrial development projects in a specific area but also with regard to the ordinary construction of buildings.
For this reason, simulations and imagery using computers are frequently employed as effective tools to enhance mutual understanding between construction contractors and their clients, for presenting specific cases to local inhabitants, and so forth.

In this paper, we deal with "Steam Plumes" as an environmental problem. These "Steam Plume" appear upon the condensation of steam contained in waste gas being emitted from stacks and normally do not constitute a major air pollution problem. They are, however, regarded at times as a type of visual or scenic pollution.

Of the various problems surrounding atmospheric pollution, it is generally the amount of toxic gas emitted into the atmosphere or the concentration thereof that ranks foremost. Hence, in conducting prior environmental assessment work, maps showing zones bounded by isoconcentration lines based on the applicable emission conditions are prepared to determine zones in which permissible concentrations will be exceeded. With "Steam Plumes", however, evaluations utilizing isoconcentration lines based on emitted water vapor is impracticable. This is because even if the concentration of water vapor with respect to dry air, namely absolute humidity, is the same in separate instances, the formation of "steam plumes" at specific temperatures or barometric pressures will depend on whether or not their relative humidities exceed 100%.

The mechanism relating to the formation of "Steam Plume" is first discussed, followed by dispersion calculations for waste gases. Secondly the method of calculating amount of steam condensate in "Steam Plume" and the method of displaying "Steam Plume" on a graphic display device. Finally, considering the turbulence of wind, the method of displaying more realistic image of plume is mensioned in accordance with FRACTAL theory.

2. GENERATION OF "STEAM PLUMES"

The combustion of heavy oil and the like forms steam of 10 to 15 vol% in the waste gas. In addition, the use of wet desulfurizing and denitrating units causes an increase in the concentration of steam. Wet waste gases are thus discharged to the air through stacks at ejection velocities ranging from 10 to 30 m/sec, at temperatures of 100 to 200°C. In some cases, to avoid the formation of "Steam Plume", waste gases are heated to high temperatures prior to discharge to the atmosphere.

Steam is a colorless and transparent gas and cannot generally be seen with the naked eyes. Waste gases discharged from stacks are cooled rapidly by the surrounding air, and steam contained in the waste gases condenses, forming small droplets of water. As a consequence, the steam becomes visible to the naked eyes. Such phenomenon, called "condensation", takes place at high relative humidities (400 to 500%) in the case of adiabatic expansion of clean air. Condensation, however, actually takes place under supersaturated condition i.e. at relative humidities of 105% or lower.
This is because dust, smoke, O_3, NOx, Cl^-, NH_4^+, etc., which are called "condensation nucleus", existing in the air facilitate the condensation of steam.

The kinetic energy and lifting power of a waste gas itself cause the combustion waste gas (discharged from stacks) to rise in the air. In this case, waste gas plumes are cooled rapidly by mixture with the surrounding air. Steam supersaturated through such processes condenses around the condensation nuclei and turns to droplets of water.

It should be noted, however, that the size of droplets of water thus formed actually differs according to the size of the condensation nucleus, lapse rate and other factors, and cannot be estimated roughly. In this study, the size of droplets of water is estimated based on the radiuses of droplets of water in clouds.

It is reported by East and Marchall that in the case of cloud, the size of the water droplet ranges from 2 to 20 μ. In this study, therefore, the radius of a droplet of water has been assumed to be 5 μ.

3. DIFFUSION CALCULATION

The original form of a "Steam Plume" is one of gases, i.e. steam. "Steam Plume", therefore, is diffused by molecular diffusion or air turbulence diffusion. In general, the diffusion of "Steam Plume" in the air arises chiefly from medium- and small-scale vortexes in the air. Various diffusion calculation formulas have so far been annuounced.
In this study, the following diffusion calculations are conducted using the calculation method developed by Ooms et al regarding jet streams formed by waste gases (discharged from stacks). The following assumptions are first established regarding general jet streams.

(1) The mean flow velocity perpendicular to the main flow in the length direction of the plume is small in comparison with this main flow velocity.

(2) The velocity profiles are similar in all sections normal to the plume axis. The density and pollutant concentration distribution in cross-sections, too, are assumed to retain their shape.

(3) Molecular transports are considered negligible in comparison with turbulent transports.

(4) Longitudinal turbulent transports are small compared with longitudinal convective transports.

On the basis of the above assumptions, the flow rate, density, concentration and the like of steam at the central axis of a plume are represented by the following simultaneous differential equation.

$$\frac{dx}{ds}=\cos\theta$$

$$\frac{dz}{ds}=\sin\theta$$

$$\frac{d}{ds}\int_0^{\sqrt{2}b}\rho u 2\pi r dr = 2\pi b \rho_a \{\alpha_1|u^*(s)|+\alpha_2 u_a|\sin\theta|\cos\theta+\alpha_3 u'\}$$

$$\frac{d}{ds}\int_0^{\sqrt{2}b} Cu 2\pi r dr = 0$$

$$\frac{d}{ds}\int_0^{\sqrt{2}b}\rho u^2\cos\theta 2\pi r dr = 2\pi b \rho_a u_a\{\alpha_1|u^*(s)|+\alpha_2 u_a|\sin\theta|\cos\theta+\alpha_3 u'\}+C_d\pi b \rho_a u_a^2|\sin^2\theta|$$

$$\frac{d}{ds}\int_0^{\sqrt{2}b}\rho u^2\sin\theta 2\pi r dr = \int_0^{\sqrt{2}b} g(\rho_a-\rho)2\pi r dr \pm C_d\pi b \rho_a u_a^2\sin^2\theta\cos\theta$$

$$\frac{d}{ds}\int_0^{\sqrt{2}b}\rho u C_p(T-T_{a,0})2\pi r dr = 2\pi b \rho_a C_{p,a}(T_a-T_{a,0})\{\alpha_1|u^*(s)|+\alpha_2 u_a|\sin\theta|\cos\theta+\alpha_3 u'\}$$

Where,

- C : Concentration of exhausted steam (kg/m³)
- C_p : Ratent heat of plume (J/kg.°K)
- $C_{p,a}$: Ratent heat of ambient air (J/kg.°K)
- C_d : Drag coefficient (-)
- g : Gravitational constant (m/sec²)
- r : Distance from plume axis (m)
- s : Distance along plume axis (m)
- T : Temperature of plume (°K)
- T_a : Temperature of ambient air (°K)
- $T_{a,o}$: Temperature of air near stack top (°K)
- u : Flow velocity of gas (m/sec)
- u^* : Difference between flow velocity at plume axis and wind velocity (m/sec)
- u_a : Wind velocity (m/sec)
- u' : Flow velocity of air from ambient air to plume (m/sec)
- x : Down wind distance from stack (m)
- z : Height from stack top (m)
- α_1 : Entrainment coefficient of free jet (-)
- α_2 : Entrainment coefficient of line thermal (-)
- α_3 : Entrainment coefficient by turbulence (-)
- θ : Gradient of plume axis (rod)
- ρ : Density of plume (kg/m³)
- ρ_a : Density of ambient air (kg/m³)

"r" represents the distance from the central axis and "b" the expanse of a plume. Where the standard deviation of distribution of gas flow rate is assumed to be σ_u, $\sqrt{2}b = 2\sigma_u$. Consequently, the extent of integration becomes $2\sigma_u$. To know the expanse of a steam plume in the radius direction, the distribution of flow rate, density and concentration in the radius direction is assumed as follows, based on Assumption (2) above.

$$u(s, r, \theta) = u_a \cos\theta + u^*(s) \exp\left[-\frac{r^2}{b(s)^2}\right]$$

$$\rho(s, r, \theta) = \rho_a + \rho^*(s) \exp\left[-\frac{r^2}{\lambda^2 b(s)^2}\right]$$

$$C(s, r, \theta) = C^*(s) \exp\left[-\frac{r^2}{\lambda^2 b(s)^2}\right]$$

Where, $\rho^*(s)$: Difference between the density of steam (at the central axis of a plume) and the surrounding air density

$C^*(s)$: Concentration of steam at the central axis of a plume

λ^2 which is so called "Turbulent Schmidt Number", is known to be approx. 1.35. This means that in the cross section of a plume, the distribution of density and concentration is greater in standard deviation to that of flow rate. In other words, where the standard deviation on density is assumed to be σ_ρ, $\sigma_\rho = \lambda \sigma_u$.

4. AMOUNT OF CONDENSED STEAM

Steam begins to condense at a relative humidity of approx. 105% (Chapter 2). It is considered that steam, the relative humidity of which exceeds 100%, turns to droplets of water.

The steam concentration, temperature, flow velocity and other conditions along the centerline of the plume can be clarified by conducting diffusion calculations mentioned in Chapter 3.

The conditions under which a "steam plume" forms, are as discussed below.
In Fig. 4.1, the waste gas emitting conditions are represented by Point A and the atmospheric conditions by Point B.
In other words, when the waste gas has a temperature of 100°C and a water vapor (steam) concentration of 0.1 kgH$_2$O/kg of dry air (16 vol%), the atmospheric temperature and water vapor (steam) concentration becomes 10°C and 0.004 kgH$_2$O/kg of dry air (relative humidity 50%) respectively.
The plume released through the stack is diffused, diluted and cooled: its conditions vary from Point A to Point B.
In this course, if the diffusion is relatively rapid and the cooling is relatively slow, the plume conditions vary as represented by Line (1): in this case as no steam condensate occurs, the plume is invisible.
Inversely, if the diffusion is slow and the cooling is rapid, the conditions vary as represented by Line (2): in this case, as the humidity exceeds the saturation point at the thick line point, the steam plume becomes visible.

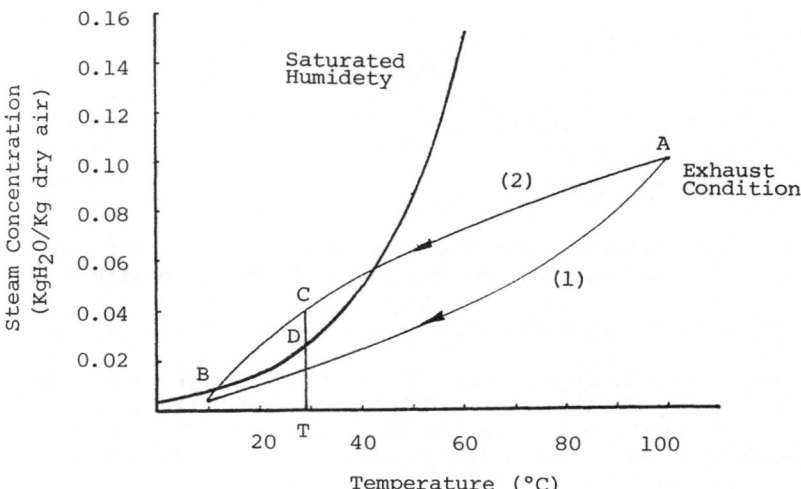

Fig. 4.1 Steam Concentration VS Temperature

The steam condensation rate in this case can be calculated as follows:
Select a small region in the plume.
Assume the weight of the dry air in the region to be Δa, kg and the temperature thereat to be T°C, and the water vapor (steam) concentration in the plume can be represented by Point D and the saturated humidity by Point C.
Therefore, the steam condensation rate can be formulated as shown below.

$$W \Delta a = (H_C - H_D) \Delta a \qquad \text{(kg)} \qquad \ldots\ldots (4.1)$$

5. INDICATION OF STEAM PLUME

The number (density) of water particles (droplets of water) in the actual space can be calculated by the following formula:

$$N(x,y,z) = \frac{W(x,y,z)}{4/3 \cdot \pi (5 \times 10^{-6})^3 \times 1{,}000} \qquad (1/cm^3) \qquad \ldots\ldots (5.1)$$

Thus, the water particles concentration in a 3-dimensional space in the "steam plume" can be calculated. To display the "steam plume" on a CRT, the 3-dimensional "steam plume" figure must be converted into a 2-dimensional figure. For this conversion, perspective projection and parallel projection are available. Herein, for simplicity, parallel projection onto a x-z plane is used.

The water particle concentration in the 3-dimensional space calculated by Formula (5.1) can be calculated by integration (toward the Y-direction) as a water-particle concentration projected onto the x-z plane as follows:

$$N_y(x,z) = \int_{-\infty}^{\infty} N(x,y,z) \, dy \qquad (1/m^2) \qquad \ldots\ldots (5.2)$$

(Refer to Fig. 5.1)

Now, all the water particles projected onto the x-z plane are not actually visible: since backward water particles are hidden by forward water particles, they are invisible. In other words, the number of water particles calculated by Equation (5.2) is not that of the water particles which are actually visible.

The location of each individual water particle is utterly random and it is probabilistic whether water particles appear or are hidden. However, as the number of water particles is astronomically large, for instance, 9.6×10^{10} particles per m^3 in the vicinity of the centerline in Fig. 5.8 the locations of such numerous water particles cannot be determined even if by using a computer.

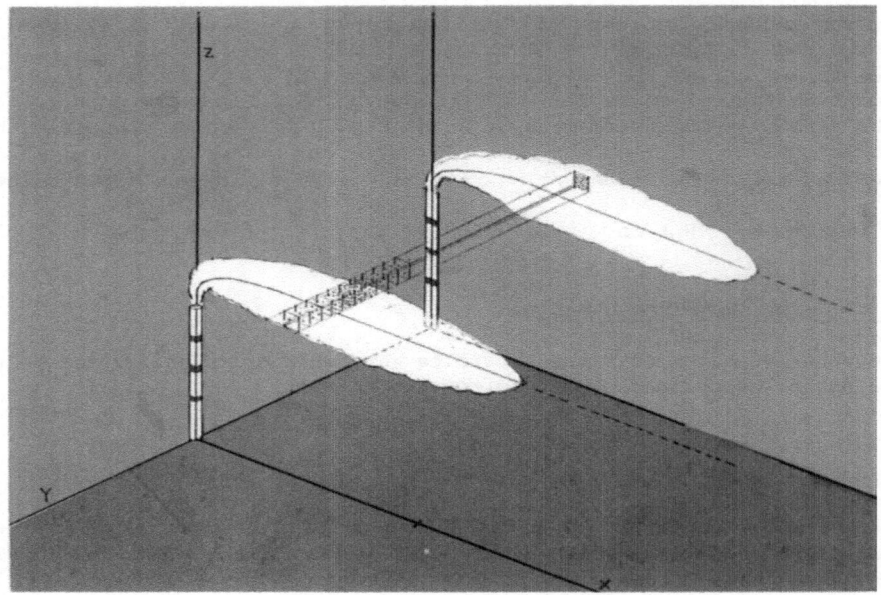

Fig. 5.1 Integration of Water Particle Concentration

Therefore, herein, the number of water particles is approximated by the following equation:

$$My(x,z) \triangle A = N_{\triangle}A \left(1 - \frac{1}{Ny(x,z)/N_{\triangle}A + 1}\right) \quad \cdots \quad (5.3)$$

Where $\triangle A$: Small region on x-z plane, (m^2)

$N_{\triangle}A$: Number of water particles over all $\triangle A$, namely,
$$N_{\triangle}A = \frac{\triangle A}{\pi \times (5 \times 10^{-6})^2}$$

$My(x,z)$: Number of visible water particles per unit area of x-z plane

The small region can be determined as discussed below.
One of the methods is to decide on a small region so as to correspond to a pixel(s). In this case, the water particle concentration (My) corresponds to the color of the pixel. If the water particle concentration (My) is large, the color of the pixel is white, but if it is sufficiently small, the color becomes the same as that of the background. The levels of the color graduations are within the range which can be shown by a display device. In this case of this method, as all the pixels that cover the smoke are colored at the depth of the color of the smoke, the display figure has an unnatural appearance as if the plume were a shaded solid.

Therefore, herein, the color graduation of "steam plume" is displayed as follows:
A 5 x 5 pixel square area is assigned to each small region on the x-z plane. Since one region contains 25 pixels, 0 to 25 color graduations can be displayed. In other words, a matrix as shown in Fig. 5.2 is prepared and white of a respective graduation level is given only to the pixels which are to be white at that graduation level. Since pixels other than those given white of some graduation level are not colored but are of the color of the backgruond, the figure appears to be white smoke.

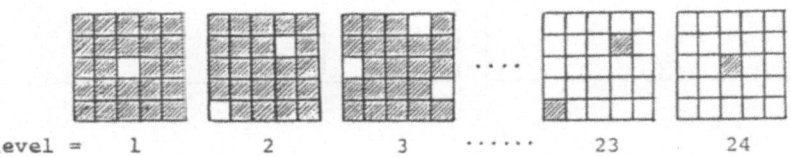

level =   1   2   3   23   24

Fig. 5.2 Pixel Matrix for Displaying each Graduation Level

Fig. 5.3 shows the relationships between the water particle concentrations and 26 color graduation levels which have been approximated by Equation (5.3).

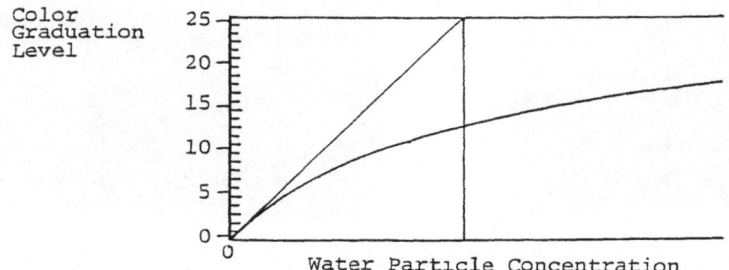

Fig. 5.3 Water Particle Concentration VS Color Graduation Level

The figure of "steam plume" discussed in Chapter 3 can be displayed as mentioned above.
The figures of "steam plume" have been calculated for some different meteorological conditions as shown below.

Meteorological Condition:
    Temperature   5 °C
    Relative Humidity (RH)   indicated in Figures
    Wind Velocity (V)   "

Exhaust Condition:
    MW of Exhausted Gas   29
    Outlet Temperature   200 °C
    Concentration of Steam   18 vol%
    Ejection Speed   30 m/sec
    Diameter of Stack   1 m

The contour lines of water vapor concentrations under the same conditions are shown in the uppermost portion for reference.

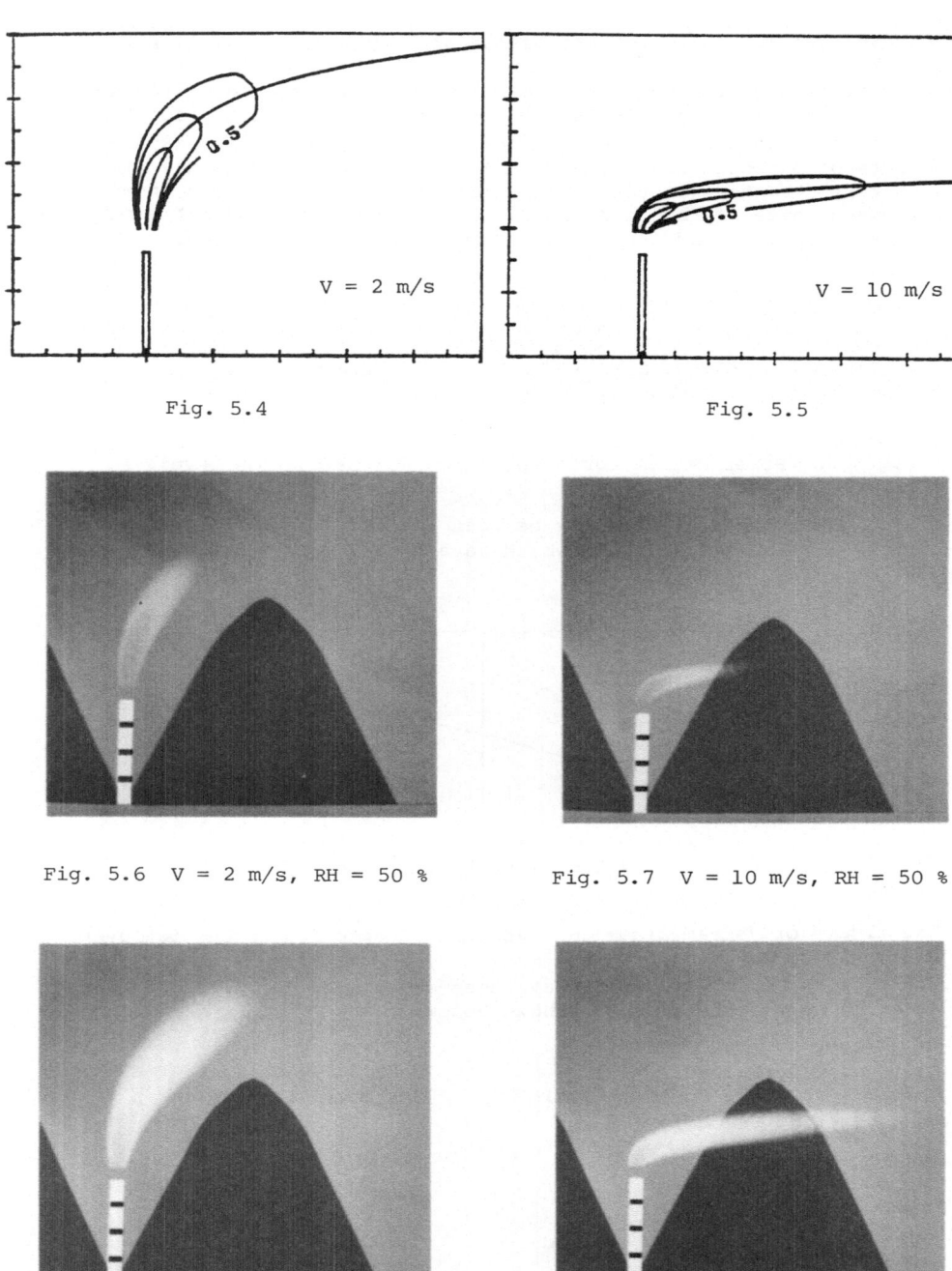

Fig. 5.4   V = 2 m/s

Fig. 5.5   V = 10 m/s

Fig. 5.6 V = 2 m/s, RH = 50 %

Fig. 5.7 V = 10 m/s, RH = 50 %

Fig. 5.8 V = 2 m/s, RH = 90 %

Fig. 5.9 V = 10 m/s, RH = 90 %

6. WIND VARIATIONS AND SHAPE OF PLUME

The shape of a plume is varying at all times: it is improbable that it will remain unchanged. The reason for this is that the shape of a plume is governed by the movement of the air, namely, wind: the direction and velocity of wind are always changing.

Each wind flow involves vortexes of various sizes and wave-motions. One of these wave-motions is a constant wave-motion called "internal gravity wave" which exists at a height of several dozen metes to several hundred meters from ground level. This wave-motion is due to te "vertical structure" of atmospheric temperature and wind velocity. This relative stable upward-downward movement of smoke as often seen are caused by this wave-motion.

Such upward and downward wave-motions are approximated by using a sine curve and applied to the centerline of the plume mentioned above, as shown below.

The trajectory of the plume centerline calculated by the differential equation mentioned in Chapter 3, can be represented as follows:

$$Z = f(x) \quad \quad \quad \quad \quad \quad (6.1)$$

The new centerline influenced by wind variation can be represented as follows:

$$Z = f(x) + a \sin\left(\frac{2\pi x}{b}\right) \quad \quad \quad (6.2)$$

Where a = amplitude of plume

            b = wave length of plume

The shape of the plume obtained by using the above equations are as shown in Figs. 6.1 and 6.2.

Fig. 6.1   a = 1.0, b = 20   Fig. 6.2   a = 1.5, b = 10

Next, the effects of smaller vortexes and wave-motions must be considered. Such small motions can be regarded as random motions by which the shape of a plume is disordered. The shapes of plumes are irregular but undergo repetition of similar shapes. Such phenomena are occasionally seen in the natural world, for example, coast lines, the rise and fall of land, such as mountain ranges, river branches and the patterns of insulation damaged by electric discharge.

B.B. Mandelbrot named figures having self-similarity as "Fractal" and described "Fractal" figures similar to those seen in the natural world by using a computer system. The fact that plume shapes and many other shapes present in the natural world which undergo repetition of irregular shapes, is largely related to the fact that natural phenomena are irregular (dissimilar) if observed from the micro standpoint but uniform if observed from the macro standpoint.

In this report, the simplest 2-dimensional pattern model is used to represent the flow of atmosphere which is an extremely irregular phenomenon. This model is prepared as follows:
First, 2-dimensional meshes are provided. The digit "1" is assigned to one of the meshes and zero to the adjacent meshes and the ditig "-1" to all the other meshes.
Next, one of the zero meshes is selected at random and the digit "1" is assigned thereto.
Zero is assigned to the meshes adjacent to the mesh (to which the digit "1" has been assigned).
In this case, the meshes to which the digit "1" has already been assigned, must be left untouched.

Random patterns obtained as mentioned above are put on the centerline of the plume at proper intervals.
As a result of this, a Fractal "steam plume" figure can be obtained. Some examples are given in Fig. 6.3.

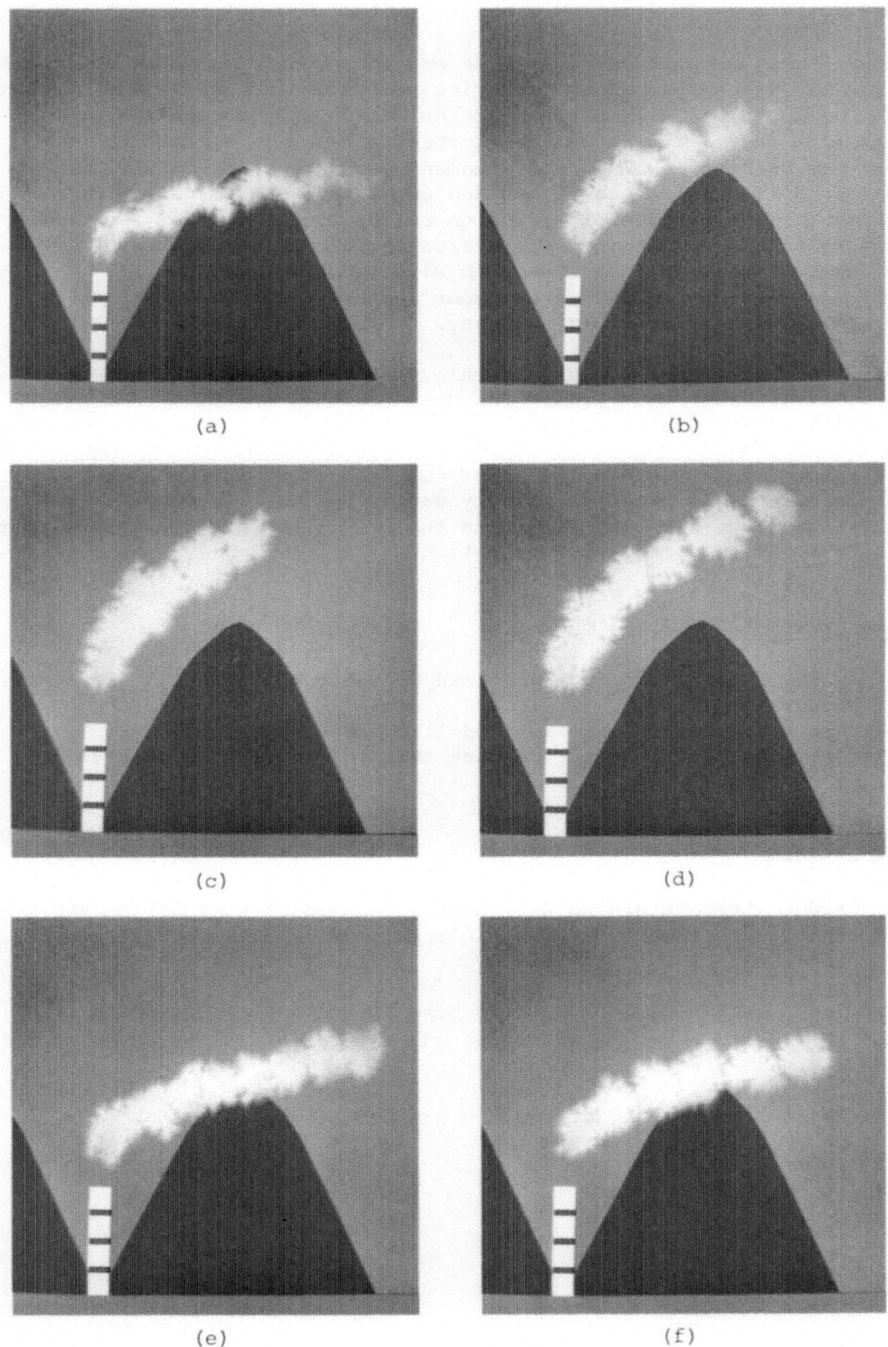

Fig. 6.3 Various "Steam Plume" Patterns Simulated by Computer

7. SUMMARY

In this report, we have discussed the procedure for displaying the shape of a visible "steam plume" by computing the diffusion conditions of waste gas in the turbulent air current and the water vapor concentration and condensation rate. The mechanism of the diffusion in a turbulent air current has been reviewed for environment assessment and many other purposes and theoretical equations and empirical equations have been developed for the purpose of diffusion calculation. Further, various parameters have been obtained for diffusion calculation by conducting actual measurement and experiments in wind tunnels.
In any case, as the object "water vapor (steam) concentration" is invisible, its measurement is not easy.

However, by the method discussed herein, it is possible to display the shape of a visible "steam plume" for comparison with that of the steam plume which will actually appear.

It is expected that the conditions of the atmosphere as the place of diffusion can be clarified relatively easily by visually comparing the actual steam plume with the figure on the CRT screen without measuring the actual water vapor (steam) concentration.

8. ACKNOWLEDGMENTS

The study reported herein was performed by the computer of JGC Information System Corporation.
The authors thank Kaoru Sakai for modelling the program part displaying the plume by FRACTAL theory. He made the program very quickly and properly.

9. REFERENCES

1. Y. Sawada, "Furakutaru no suri to nijigen patān"
   (Mathematical science for FRACTAL theory and 2-dimensional pattern), MATHEMATICAL SCIENCES, No.221, Nov. (1981).

2. G. Ooms, A.P. Mahieu & F. Zelis, "THE PLUME PATH OF VENT GASES HEAVIER THAN AIR", C.H. Bushmann, ed., Amsterdam, Elsevier Scientific Pub. Co. (1974).

3. "Kishogaku handbook" (Meteorology handbook), Gihodo (1954).

Computer Graphics Techniques for Three-Dimensional Flow Visualization

Kenneth A. Kroos
Mechanical Engineering
Villanova University
Villanova, PA 19085, USA

ABSTRACT

The objective of this research has been to develop techniques by which the flow characteristics of an incompressible, heated fluid could be displayed in three-dimensions using computer graphics. The numerical model used to analyze the flow characteristics is the Simplified Marker-and-Cell (SMAC) technique developed at Los Alamos. This technique uses a forward-time, center-space (FTCS) finite differencing scheme to solve for velocities, pressures, and temperatures at selected nodal locations in the flow field.

Two techniques were used to display flow characteristics. The first method constructs flow vectors at nodal locations utilizing Cartesian velocity components. Several vector arrow models were compared for their relative effectiveness in visualizing the flow. Perspective was applied to isometric drawings of the three-dimensional flow field to show multi-dimensional trends. The second method analyzed the path of motion of a neutrally buoyant "particle" of fluid. Again, perspective was used to emphasize the 3D motion.

If this paper is accepted for presentation at the Computer Graphics Tokyo '84 Conference, the author will present the paper. Financing for travel will be provided by the Mechanical Engineering professional development funds.

INTRODUCTION

With the development of high-speed computers, a great number of engineering problems that were either too complex or too timely to solve by conventional analytical techniques are now solveable by numerical techniques that have been developed within the past fifteen years. This is especially true in the fields of fluid mechanics and heat transfer. In the past, only one-dimensional and very simple two-dimensional problems could be solved by other than experimental techniques. Today a variety of numerical schemes exist that can be used to determine fluid flow characteristics and temperatures in two and three-dimensional flows of complex geometry.

A common drawback with numerical techniques applied to high-speed computers is the sheer bulk of simple numeric output generated and the difficulty in deriving meaningful results from this data. This is especially true when modeling three-dimensional problems. When numerical data is presented on two-dimensional paper, the effect of the third dimension cannot be ascertained.

One solution for presenting calculated data in a more meaningful manner is the use of graphical output. Graphs and pictures can often show meaningful insight into a problem that might not be recognized in simple numeric data. This application of graphic analysis to numerical data has opened up a whole new field of engineering design known as computer-aided design (CAD). Only within the past few years through has this technology been applied to thermofluid design. (1) These applications are essentially limited to two-dimensional models and as such are restriced in the number of practical problems they can be used to solve.

A very real need exists today for computer graphics techniques by which three-dimensional trends in thermofluid characteristics can be effectively displayed. Such information would be most effective in disseminating significant relationships in such flows. If this information could be displayed quickly, a true interactive, three-dimensional thermofluid design package could be developed. This type of thermofluid CAD system would significantly advance developmental research in fluid mechanics and heat transfer.

OBJECTIVES

The objective of this research was to develop simple computer graphics techniques by which the transient, three-dimensional thermofluid characteristics of a flowing, viscous, incompressible, heated fluid may be understandaly displayed. The principles behind the graphic procedures were kept simple so that they could be easily applied to different computers and graphics systems. For this same reason the drawings were done in monochrome using the PLOT 10 graphics language which is in common use and is supported on many types of graphics terminals.

METHODOLOGY

The major obstacle in visualizing three-dimensional flow fields is the fact that these patterns must be displayed and recorded on two-dimensional surfaces. To accomplish the objective of this research, a significant and understandable representation of flow and thermal conditions must be displayed on a computer terminal screen or hardcopy page.

The one effective method by which single three-dimensional drawings can be presented on a two-dimensional piece of paper with easily discernable results is the use of perspective. The difference between perspective drawing and conventional isometric or oblique drawing is the natural reduction of size with increasing distance implemented in perspective drawing as shown in Figure 1.

The production of perspective drawings by conventional drafting techniques is quite difficult and time consuming. Such drawings are simple to produce by computer graphics techniques. Translation, rotation, scaling, and perspective transformations of a standard isometric view are obtained using subroutines employing 4x4 matrix operations.(2)

Flow velocities are true three-dimensional vectors and as such will require a unique scheme for graphical representation. Most flow modeling techniques calculate the Cartesian components (Vx, Vy, and Vz) of the flow velocity vector at regularly spaced locations in the flow field. The graphic model developed in this study can be applied to regular or adaptive grid locations where true velocity vectors can be defined.

The vector components in the x, y, and z direction are transformed to a modified x', y', and z' system by a series of 4x4 matrix operations which rotate, translate, scale, and add perspective to the components. The vertical and horizontal screen coordinates are then calculated using the isometric coordinate Equations 1 and 2.

$$XPLOT = Vx*\cos(30°) - Vz*\cos(30°) \quad (1)$$
$$YPLOT = Vy - Vx*\sin(30°) - Vz*\sin(30°) \quad (2)$$

XPLOT and YPLOT represent the horizontal and vertical screen increments which define the direction and magnitude of the velocity vector on the screen.

To draw the vector, the graphics cursor is "moved" to the location of the velocity vector in the flow field. This base location has also been transformed to include rotation, translation, scaling and perspective. The vector is then drawn to a relative vector end at coordinates (XPLOT, YPLOT). Since velocities can vary widely in the flow field, a separate scaling factor can be used to magnify or shrink the entire field of vector magnitudes according to the following equations:

$$XPLOT = XPLOT*S$$
$$YPLOT = YPLOT*S \quad (3)$$

The main thrust of this project was to develop a graphics program package by which these vectors can be drawn to show the three-dimensional nature of the flow field. The first objective was to compare various arrow-type vector representations for their quality in displaying the flow vector at each node. The various arrows tested are shown in Figure 2. The vector type is arbitrarily chosen by the user to allow a comparative evaluation.

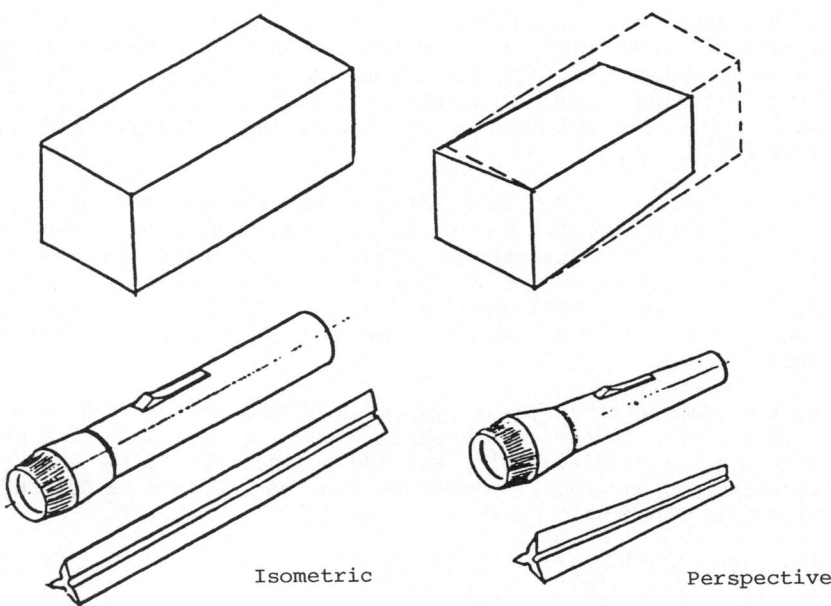

Figure 1
A Comparison of Isometric and Perspective Drawings

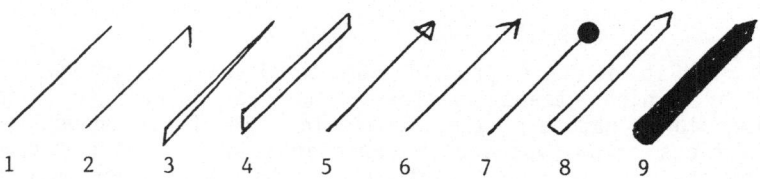

Figure 2
Vector Configurations

The following factors were used to ascertain the effectiveness of each vector model:

1) Quality of image - Is it clear and precise?
2) Effect of Perspective image - Does it show a true three-dimensional vector?
3) CPU time required for drawing the vector.

A viable alternative to using flow vectors to visualize a flow field is to show the path of motion of one or more "particles of fluid through the field". This can be accomplished by locating a neutrally buoyant marker somewhere in the flow field and allowing it to be moved by the velocities affecting that region. The Cartesian components of the flow velocity at the marker can be approximated by interpolation from known velocities at nearby nodal locations. When these components are multiplied by the time increment used in the numerical solution; the three translational displacement components are obtained and the marker can be relocated. By redrawing a marker symbol at each location corresponding to incrementing time steps, a transient path of motion is obtained. The use of perspective with this technique is essential. As the marker symbol nears the viewer, it will become larger to show this relative motion. The markers used in this study were opaque circles whose radii were altered to take perspective into consideration.

These visualization techniques were applied to several fluid flow problems that were numerically modeled in a Cartesian coordinate system. The basic technique used in the numerical analyses is the Marker-and-Cell (MAC) technique developed at Los Alamos (3). The MAC technique is a forward-time, center space (FTCS) solution of the transient continuity, Navier-Stokes, and energy equations. This technique solves these equations in the primative variables (velocity, pressure, temperature). It is conditionally stable for the nodal system shown in Figure 3. Velocities are not defined at the same nodes as the pressures.

Both the laminar and turbulent equations may be applied to this three-dimensional nodal mesh. The laminar governing equations have the form:
Continuity Equation:

$$\frac{\partial u}{\partial x} + \frac{\partial v}{\partial y} + \frac{\partial w}{\partial z} = 0 \tag{4}$$

where u, v, and w are velocity components in the x, y, and z Cartesian Coordinates Navier Stokes Equations

$$\frac{\partial u}{\partial t} = -(\frac{\partial(uu)}{\partial x} + \frac{\partial(uv)}{\partial y} + \frac{\partial(uw)}{\partial z}) - \frac{1}{\rho}\frac{\partial p}{\partial x} + \nu(\frac{\partial^2 u}{\partial x^2} + \frac{\partial^2 u}{\partial y^2} + \frac{\partial^2 u}{\partial z^2}) \tag{5}$$

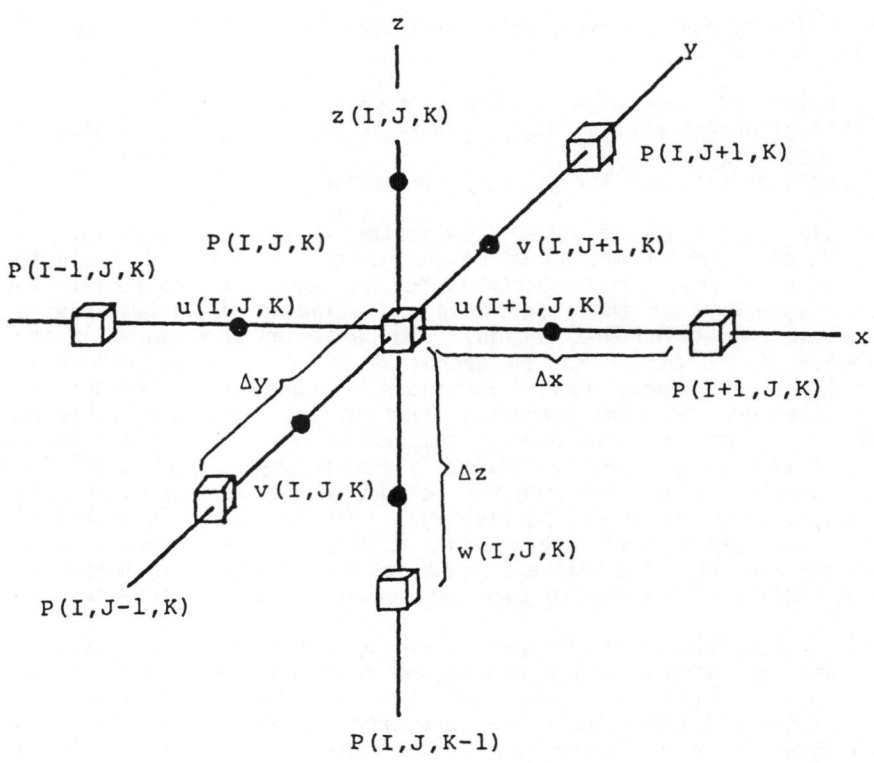

Figure 3
MAC Nodal System

$$\frac{\partial v}{\partial t} = -(\frac{\partial (vu)}{\partial x} + \frac{\partial (vv)}{\partial y} + \frac{\partial (vw)}{\partial z}) - \frac{1}{\rho}\frac{\partial p}{\partial y}$$
$$+ \nu (\frac{\partial^2 v}{\partial x^2} + \frac{\partial^2 v}{\partial y^2} + \frac{\partial^2 v}{\partial z^2}) \tag{6}$$

$$\frac{\partial w}{\partial t} = -(\frac{\partial (wu)}{\partial x} + \frac{\partial (wv)}{\partial y} + \frac{\partial (ww)}{\partial z}) - \frac{1}{\rho}\frac{\partial p}{\partial z}$$
$$+ \nu (\frac{\partial^2 w}{\partial x^2} + \frac{\partial^2 w}{\partial y^2} + \frac{\partial^2 w}{\partial z^2}) - \beta g(T - T_e) \tag{7}$$

where P = pressure
 ρ = density of the fluid
 ν = fluid kinematic viscosity
 d = coefficient of volumetric expansion
 g = gravitation acceleration
 T = temperature
 Te = reference temperature

Energy Equation

$$\frac{\partial T}{\partial t} = -(\frac{\partial (uT)}{\partial x} + \frac{\partial (vT)}{\partial y} + \frac{\partial (wT)}{\partial z}) + \frac{k}{\rho c} \cdot$$
$$(\frac{\partial^2 T}{\partial x^2} + \frac{\partial^2 T}{\partial y^2} + \frac{\partial^2 T}{\partial z^2}) \tag{8}$$

where k = fluid thermal conductivity
 c = fluid heat capacity

The stability criterion for this technique are as follows:

$$2\nu\delta t < \frac{\delta x^2 \delta y^2 \delta z^2}{\delta x^2 \delta y^2 \delta z^2} \quad \text{and} \quad \nu > \delta x^2 \frac{du}{dx} \tag{9,10}$$

The MAC technique has four advantages over other numerical techniques. They are:
1) The solution is obtained in the primative variables.
2) Boundary conditions are easy to apply.
3) The MAC technique adapts well to graphical display.

4) If desired, a free surface can be modeled.
Both free-slip and no-slip fluid boundary conditions are easy to apply. The options of thermal boundary conditions consist of insulated and conductive conditions beneath the surface, and a wide range of convective, evaporative, and radiative conditions which can be applied to the surface.

RESULTS

The flow vector method was applied to three flow problems:
1) A uniform flow field
2) A diverted uniform flow field
3) A three-dimensional driven cavity

The following is a list of the characteristics of each vector type and how each performed.

1) Vector type 1 is a simple line based at the node whose radius is proportional to the average flow velocity at that node. This line points in the flow direction. The advantages of this vector type are that it is quickly drawn and gives an uncluttered view of the flow field as shown in Figure 4. The main disadvantage to vector type 1 is that the base and end are identical, thus leading to confusion as to the exact direction of flow.

2) Vector type 2 is a modification of number 1 in that a vertical tail is applied to the end of the vector. This clearly shows directioon without sacrificing simplicity as shown in Figure 5.

3) Vector type 3 is another modification of number 1. Here a small tail is dropped from the vector base (node) and then connected to the end of the vector forming a long triangle that points in the flow direction. This technique was found to be just as effective as vector type 2 as shown in Figure 6.

4) Vector type 4 constructs a parallelogram angled into the direction of flow. This technique suffers from the same directional uncertainty as type 1 with no additional benefits.

5) Vector type 5 is an extension of type 1. Here a triangular arrowhead is added to the end of the vector. This improves the directional clarity of the flow field, as shown in Figure 7, but also requires triple the run time to draw the vectors.

6) Vector type 6 is similar to 5; but instead of drawing a triangular arrowhead, type 6 utilizes a "V" shaped arrowhead. The performance is essentially the same.

7) Vector type 7 applies an opaque circle to the end of the vector. This circle is easy to recognize and its size can vary with perspective distance as shown in Figure 8. The major drawback of this scheme is that several seconds of elapsed time are required to draw the opaque circle.

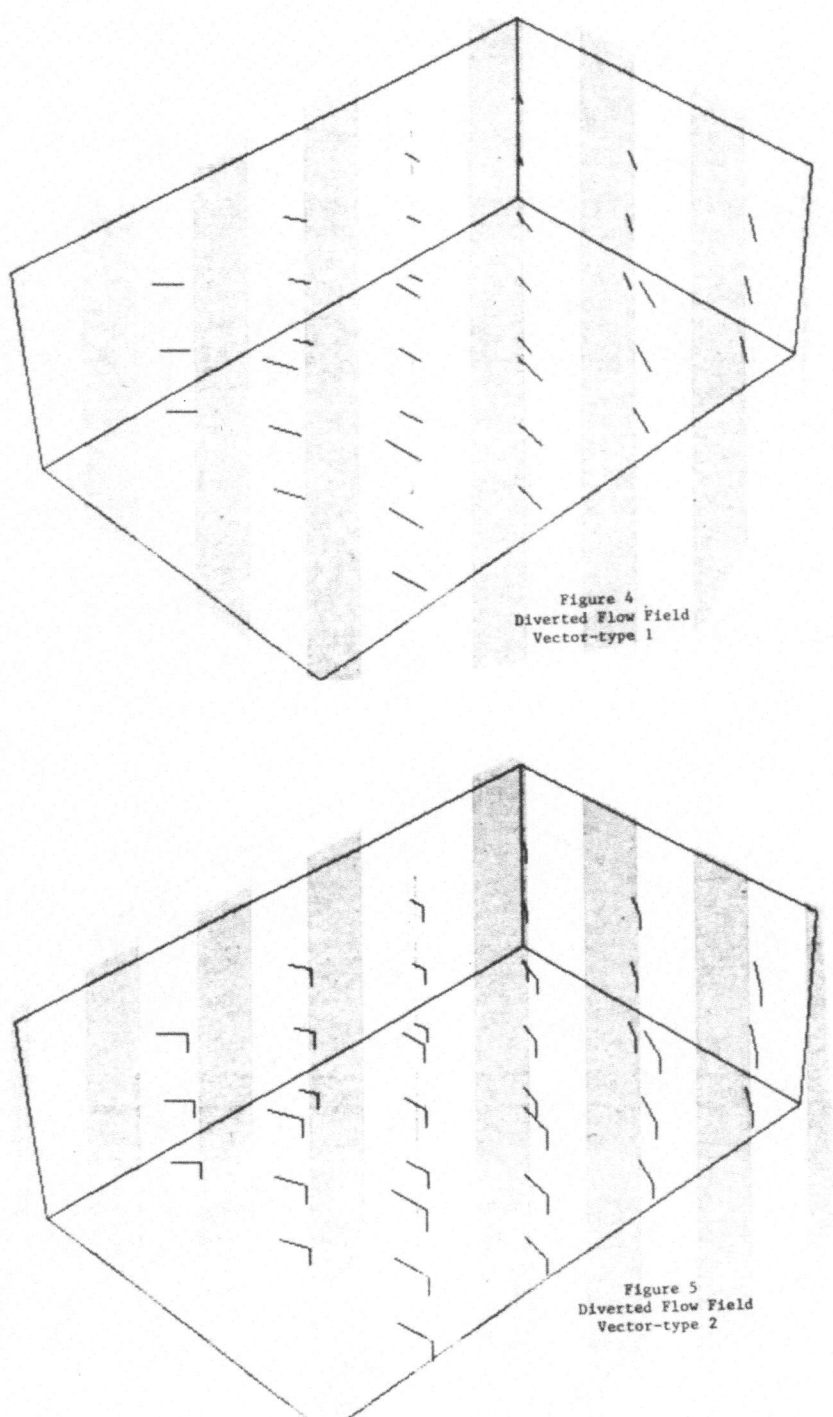

Figure 4
Diverted Flow Field
Vector-type 1

Figure 5
Diverted Flow Field
Vector-type 2

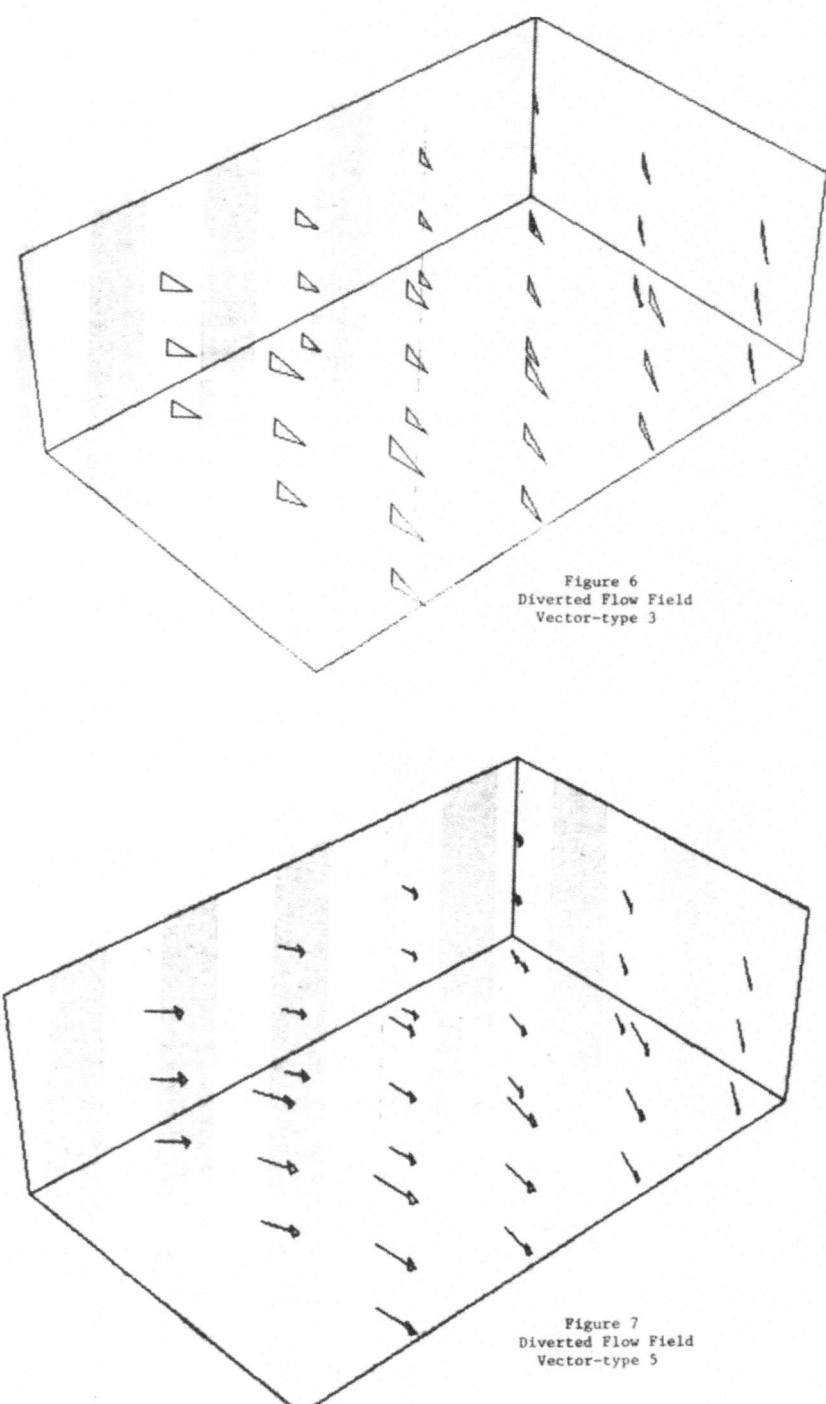

Figure 6
Diverted Flow Field
Vector-type 3

Figure 7
Diverted Flow Field
Vector-type 5

8) Vector type 8 is a much more sophisticated type of drawing. A rectangular box is developed extending from the centered base point (node) to the vector end. This box is capped with a "V" shape arrowhead as shown in Figure 9. The calculations required to determine this shape extend the run time only slightly over the simpler shapes.

9) Vector type 9 represents an attempt to produce a solid, three-dimensional vector. For this configuration, vector type 8 is rotated about its central axis to produce a missile-shaped surface of revolution. The two major problems with this vector type are the enormous run time needed to develop the vectors and the fact that these bulkier vectors obscure detail behind them as shown in Figure 10.

The effectiveness of the vector method was demonstrated by applying it to the problem of the transient driven cavity. A three-dimensional cavity measuring 160 by 100 by 60 unit high was given a surface velocity with the horizontal (x) components of velocity given a value of -1.0. The sides and bottom of the cavity were given a noslip boundary condition.

The development of flow in the driven cavity is shown in Figures 11 through 16 which show the flow field in vector type 7 for times of 1 sec, 5 sec, 10 sec, 20 sec, 50 sec, and 100 sec. The flow is static for the first 5 seconds. At 10 seconds viscous flows develop along the driven surface. By a time of 50 seconds, circulating flow in the cavity begins to develop.

The flow path visualization method was applied to the problem of a uniform flow field diverted $45°$ from its original path. Markers were located at equal intervals along the bottom left side of the flow field as shown in Figure 17. The neutrally buoyant particles move toward the upper far right corner as time progresses. The effect of perspective for this technique is clearly not as pronounced as with the vector approaches shown in Figure 18.

As a means of evaluating the effectiveness of each of the nine vector types, 20 advanced heat transfer students were asked to examine samples of flow regimes modeled with each vector type. Each vector type was rated from poor quality (1) to high quality (10). The results of this survey are shown in Table 1.

The first three categories characterize the vector as a single entity. These figures represent the potential of a vector type to transmit information. The last category represents the effectiveness of each vector type in representing an entire flow field.

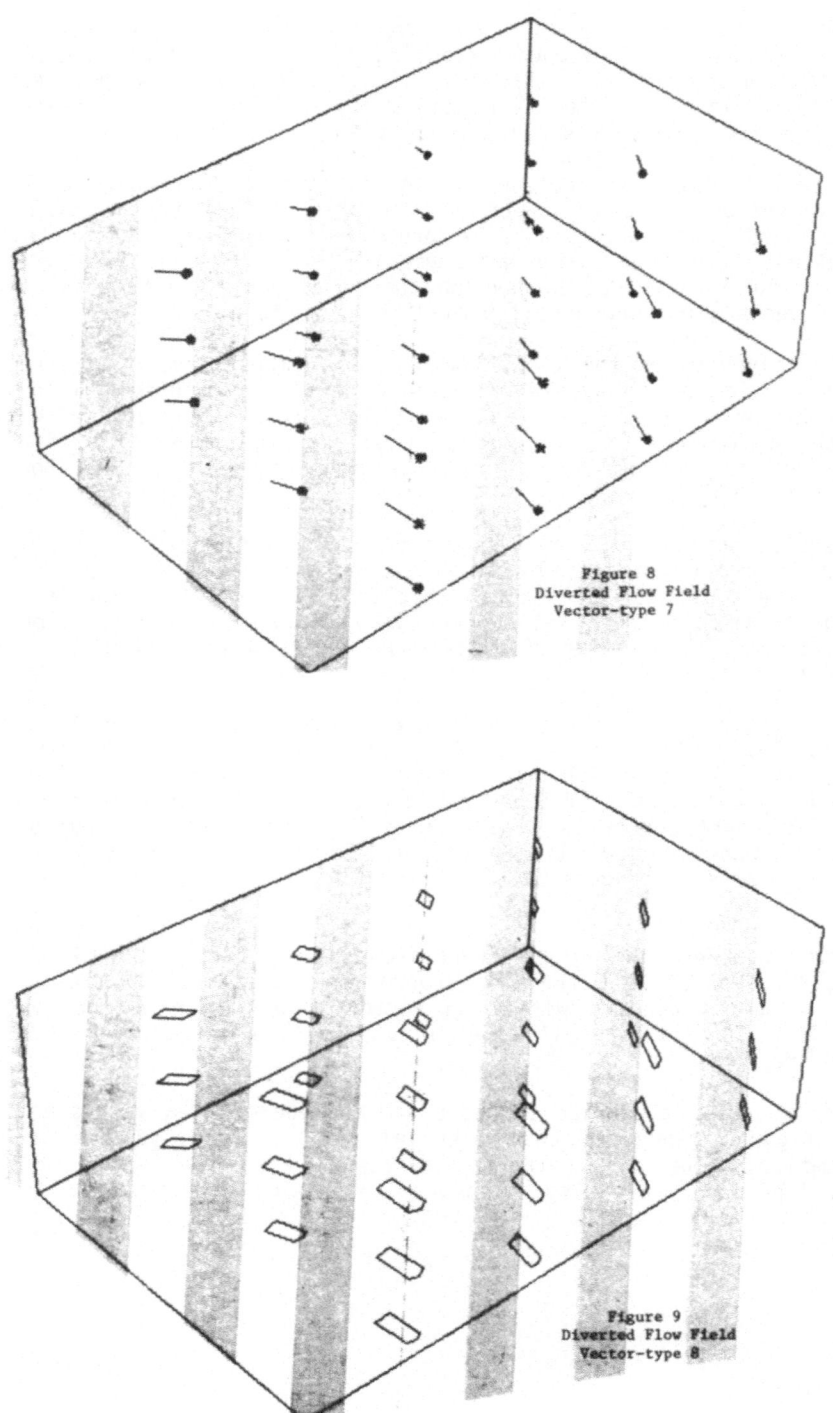

Figure 8
Diverted Flow Field
Vector-type 7

Figure 9
Diverted Flow Field
Vector-type 8

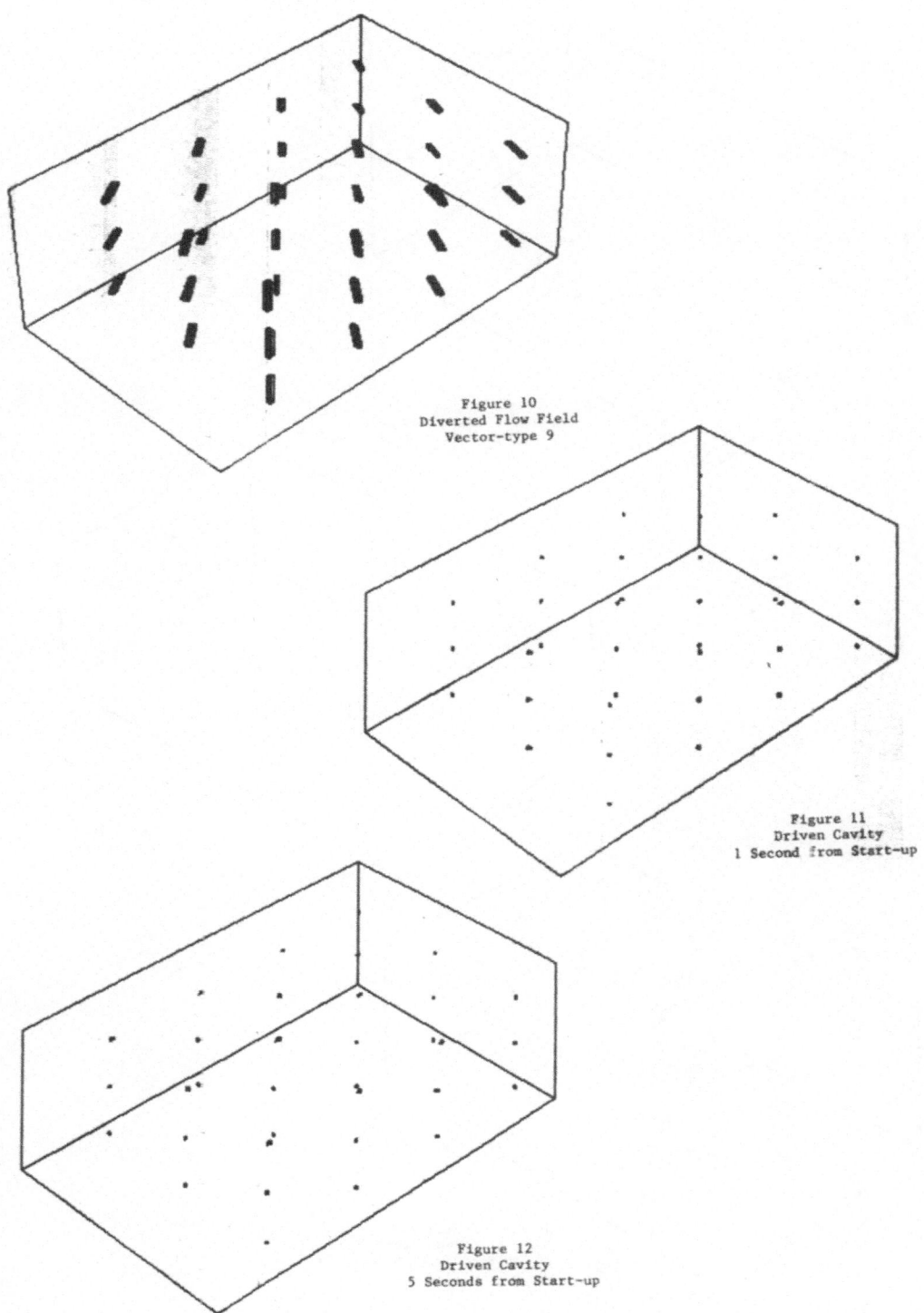

Figure 10
Diverted Flow Field
Vector-type 9

Figure 11
Driven Cavity
1 Second from Start-up

Figure 12
Driven Cavity
5 Seconds from Start-up

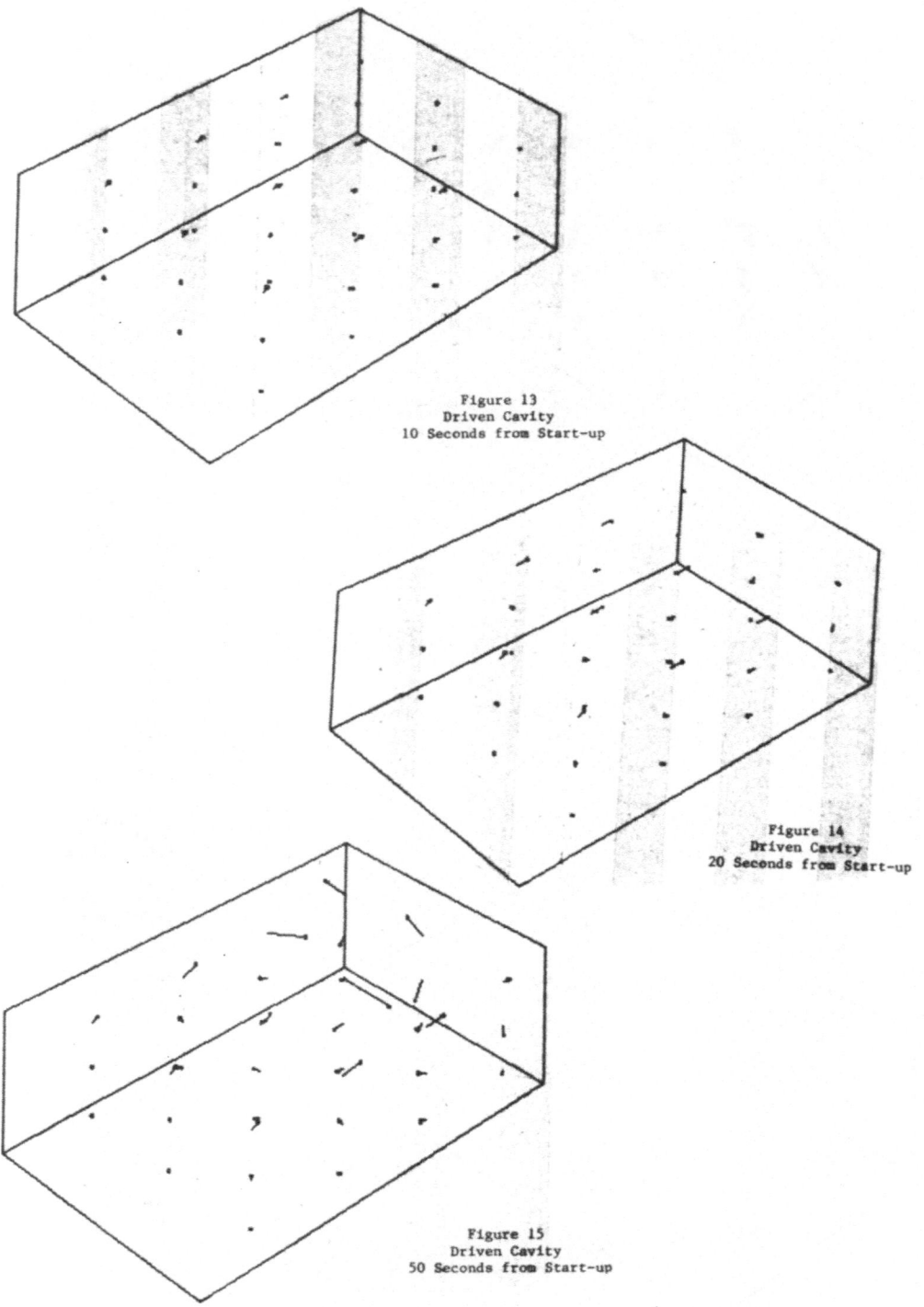

Figure 13
Driven Cavity
10 Seconds from Start-up

Figure 14
Driven Cavity
20 Seconds from Start-up

Figure 15
Driven Cavity
50 Seconds from Start-up

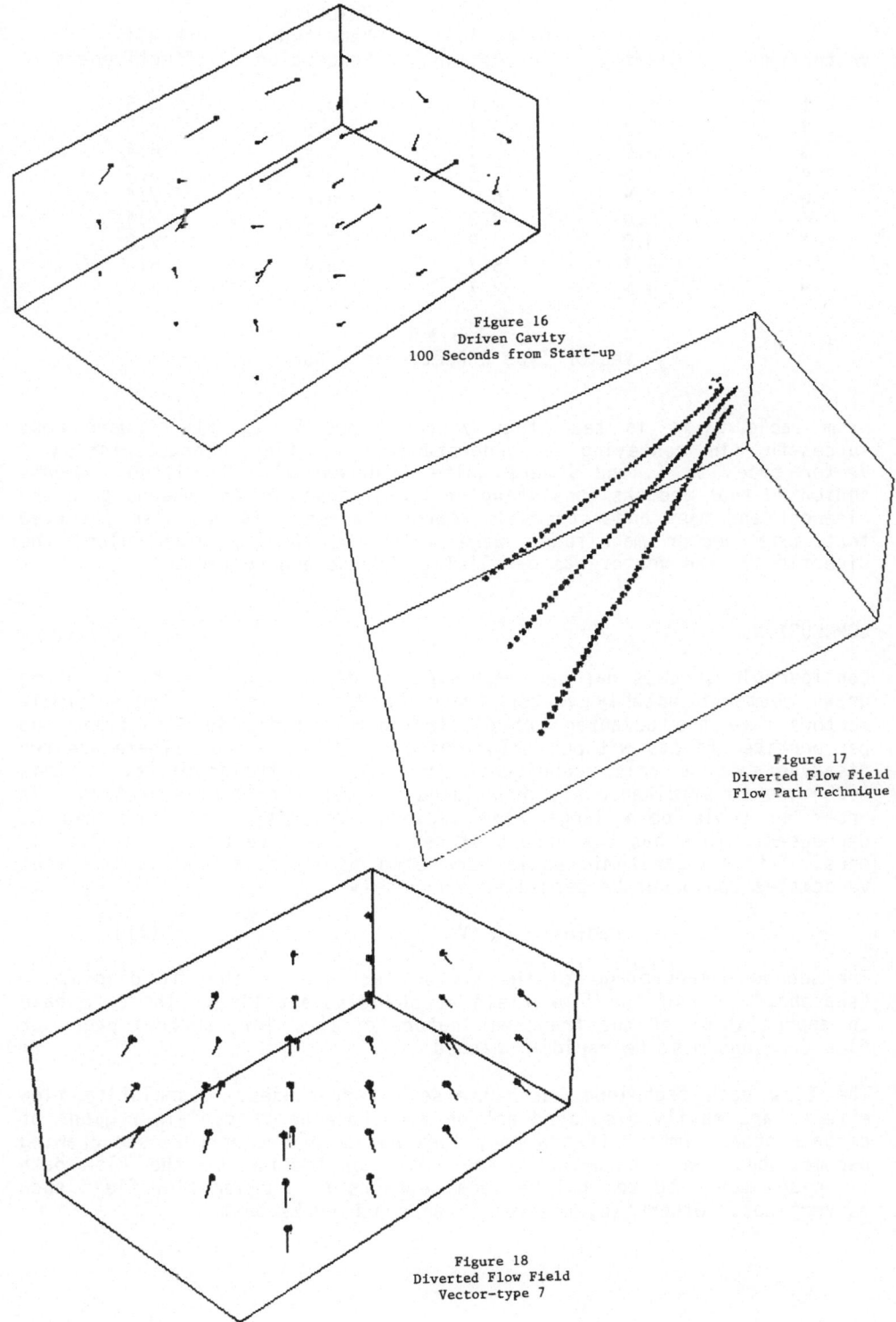

Figure 16
Driven Cavity
100 Seconds from Start-up

Figure 17
Diverted Flow Field
Flow Path Technique

Figure 18
Diverted Flow Field
Vector-type 7

Vector type	Clarity	Direction Perception	Velocity Magnitude Perception	Overall Effectiveness
1	4.9	2.1	4.2	3.5
2	5.7	5.4	4.9	4.5
3	6.9	7.4	6.5	6.4
4	4.3	3.5	4.7	3.9
5	7.8	8.0	6.2	7.4
6	8.0	8.2	7.3	7.4
7	8.0	7.9	7.1	7.8
8	5.7	5.7	6.4	5.4
9	4.6	2.7	2.4	2.9

Table 1
Vector Type Effectiveness Survey

From Table 1 it is seen that vector types 5, 6, and 7 were most successful in conveying an understanding of flow characteristics. Vector types 1, 4, and 9 were quite unsuccessful. Submitted comments indicated that vectors consisting of lines capped by arrowheads gave the clearest and most understandable representation. It was also reported that some vector magnitudes were difficult to determine unless the direction of the vector was parallel to the screen surface.

CONCLUSIONS

Considerable success has been achieved in displaying flow fields using drawn vectors; notably vector types 2, 3, 5, and 7. These simple vectors have the advantage of displaying magnitude, 3D direction, and perspective effects without "cluttering up" the drawing. There are two disadvantages to this technique. The first is the inability of this technique to simultaneously draw large and very small flow vectors. In order to scale down large flow vectors, velocity magnitudes can be decreased. This has the effect on reducing small vectors to negligible ones. If a logarithmic scale were used as in equation 11, the true velocities could not be perceived accurately.

$$radius = \ln(V) \qquad (11)$$

The second disadvantage to the vector techique is that it displays a "snapshot" view of the flow field at one discreet time. Thus, to gain an appreciation of the transient nature of the flow, several pages of flow drawings must be rapidly scanned.

The flow path technique has converse disadvantages. Cumulative flow effects are easily displayed but only pertaining to certain regions of certain other times. If too many flow paths are generated, the drawing becomes busy and confusing. The best application of the flow path technique would be to analyze local effects in a major flow field such as vortices. Otherwise, the vector approach works best.

RECOMMENDATIONS

Further study in this area might benefit from the use of color in displaying both flow vectors and flow paths. Color could be used to indicate temperature, pressure, or shear stress, thus adding to the information presented in the drawing. Color could also be used to distinguish between markers if several were used in the flow path technique.

The simple flow vectors used in this study had the advantage of requiring little CPU time and memory to draw. A much more effective flow vector might be constructed as a solid like vector type 9. Illumination graphics on a black-white-gray or color terminal could be applied to show a true three-dimensional vector under various lighting condition. It is believed that this would greatly enhance the display but at the sacrifice of considerable, even prohibitive run time and memory.

BIBLIOGRAPHY

1) "Getting the Picture Through Computer Graphics" by Thomas Gregory and Ralph Carmichael, Astronautics and Aeronautics, Vol. 21, No. 4, April 1983.

2) I. O. Angell, A Practical Introduction to Computer Graphics, Halstead Press, New York, 1981.

3) J. E. Welch, F. H. Harlow, J. P. Shannon, and B. J. Daly, The MAC Method: A Computing Technique for Solving Viscous, Incompressible, Transient Fluid Flow Problems Involving Free Surfaces, (Los Alamos Scientific Laboratory, November, 1976).

Geomatic: A 3-D Graphic Relief Simulation System

Serge Motet[1] and **Daniel Laurent**[2]
Institut Géographique National (LGN)[1]
ITODYS[2], Université Paris VII
CNRS LA34, 1, rue Guy de la Brosse
75005 Paris, France

ABSTRACT

A general command system for the simulation and display of 3-D views of relief maps is presented. This sytem is implemented on an Evans and Sutherland MPS connected to a VAX 11/780. This (3-D) Geomatic Graphic Relief Simulation System can be adapted and inserted as a software tool in a wide range of treatments (creating cartographic documents, optimizing an entity implant on a relief map with multiple constraints,...) ; it also provides the user with an opportunity for genuine interaction with the system in the choice and display of representations.

The 3-D Geomatic Graphic Relief Simulation System provides the user with an array of creation procedures which let the user obtain and display different realistic depictions of the relief of a terrain. These different realistic displays constitute, in practice, the basic tool for qualitative and dynamic use of a geographic data base, because the other entities (vegetation, hydrography,...) are supported by the relief. The system is interactive ; it lets the user define a call sequence from a menu. A task-scheduler precompiles the call sequence and establishes the correspondence between the menu and the sequence of operations for which he controls the execution.

INTRODUCTION

In the 70's many cartographic data systems were developed to meet specific needs. Some are intended for energy-related applications, others for thematic maps.

Yet, many mapping agencies are planning more comprehensive studies for computer-aided map production. Topographic data bases are scheduled in the U.S., Japan, France and Canada. The data they contain will be as diverse as that shown on standard topographic maps. This diversity requires what J. Borrel calls "a new kind of information retrieval".[1]

Computer graphics is a key element for the design or use of geographic information systems. Many authors point out that "the amazing capability that computer graphics affords is that of combining and displaying geographical data from diverse sources (maps, statistics, photographs, satellite imagery)". G. Nagy and S. Wagle say that "graphic input and output components often play a dominant role in and shape the architecture of the remainder of the system".[2]

Many cartographic institutions have developed geomatic or raised relief data bases.[3] In France, the "Institut Géographique National" (IGN) maintains such a data base.[4] These data can be handled by a variety of simulation processes ; thanks to computer graphics, such data bases can be endowed with qualitative research capabilities heretofore unreached.

Simulation generally calls for the realistic display of geographic entities in their geometric, spatial and metric context and for the display of the corresponding non-metric attributes. By their very nature, these objects are inherently 3-D, while their depiction on a 2-D map is only a particular representation convention. The context to which the objects are frequently returned is a topographical (3-D) environment defined by the relief.

At Paris VII University, we have devised a general command system for the simulation and display of 3-D views of relief maps. This system is implemented on an Evans and Sutherland MPS connected to a VAX 11/780. This Geomatic Graphic Relief Simulation System can be adapted and inserted as a software tool in a wide range of treatments (creating cartographic documents, optimizing an entity implant on a relief map with multiple constraints,...) ; it also provides the user with an opportunity for genuine interaction with the system in the choice and display of representations.

The 3-D Geomatic Relief Graphic Simulation System provides the user with an array of creation procedures which let the user obtain and display different realistic depictions of the relief of a terrain. These different realistic displays constitute, in practice, the basic tool for qualitative and dynamic use of a geographic data base, because the other entities (vegetation, hydrography,...) are supported by the relief. To situate and display information related to these other entities, a mastery of altimetry is indispensable. The system is interactive ; it lets the user define a call sequence from a menu. A task-scheduler precompiles the call sequence and establishes the correspondence between the menu and the sequence of operations for which he controls the execution.

Discussion of the system is divided into two parts :
- Relief-mapping representation modes and display procedures
- Interactive modes and task-scheduling.

I - RELIEF-MAPPING REPRESENTATION AND DISPLAY (3-D)

The display (3-D) of the relief of a terrain really involves drawing an undeformable solid from a particular numerical representation of the relief. This is a two-step process entailing :
- a creation procedure that generates a 3-D display list containing only constants representing coordinates where the solid lies,
- a display procedure which transforms this list into a screen image ; through man-machine interaction, different realistic views of the object can be obtained from data provided by the user.

Two types of representation, a digital terrain model and a contour drawing, can activate these procedures.

a) Digital Terrain Model (DTM)

A DTM is a matrix whose coefficients are altitudes. The coordinates of index ij are $x = i * \Delta_x$ and $y = j * \Delta_y$, in which Δ_x and Δ_y are the horizontal discretization steps.

In geomatics, the DTM is the basic data structure. It is represented as a block diagram, i.e. a gridwork in which the node coordinates are (i, j, MNT_{ij}) (fig. 1).

b) Contour drawing

This structure is more flexible than the DTM and is related to sequential storing of coordinates with a sparse index. There are three levels of abstraction : the point which is described by two or three coordinates, the contour which is a series of points and which represents curves, and the object composed of all the contours.

The points are stored in a stack. A contour is represented by a filing containing the address in the stack with the first point, the number of points and color-related information. The elements in the stack are ordered for each contour from the first to the last point. So there is no ambiguity.

There are two types of contours, depending on whether they are defined by 3-D or 2-D curves. The entire object is described by the chain of contour filings. Access to this object is gained via a "first" pointer on the first contour.

Access and start procedures are specific to this representation, particularly :
- Initialization of the object with initialization of the current color. This color will be assigned to all forthcoming contours.
- Initialization of a contour with possible modification of the current color. This new contour becomes the current contour. It is the only one which can be modified.
- Update of the level for 2-D contours.
- Insertion of a point at the top of the stack.
- Display of a contour. When construction of a contour has ended, it can be displayed immediately without waiting for the end of the creation procedure. The user is thus informed of the stage of progress of a treatment.
- Standardization of the object. This procedure transforms the contour structure into a 3-D display list. It is therefore the last instruction in the creation of an object.

Basic Output Procedures

- *Shading*

This procedure, classical in display of spatial data,[5,6] aims at determining shaded zones created by an imaginary sun. Lines located in these zones are therefore darkened. The operator can interactively choose the position of the sun defined by the angle of the horizon and the zenithal distance. This procedure makes it possible to shade the block diagrams or the curve contour levels (fig. 2).

The lighting of a surface at a point is the scalar product between $\vec{n}$, the normal of this surface at this point, and the direction of the sun $(\vec{s})$ (angle Θ).

$$L = \cos\Theta = \vec{s}.\vec{n} = \vec{s}.(\vec{u} \wedge \vec{v}) = \det(\vec{s},\vec{u},\vec{v})$$

with $\vec{u}$ and $\vec{v}$ as vectorial bases of the tangent plane at this point.

The surface is lighted if L is positive, i.e. if $\det(\vec{s},\vec{u},\vec{v}) > 0$. Let MNT_{ij} represent an element of DTM and P_{ij} a point associated with MNT_{ij}. By approximation, the tangent planar to the surface at point P_{ij} (with coordinates $i \Delta x$, $j \Delta y$, MNT_{ij}) is defined by the two directions $P_{i,j} P_{i+1,j}$ and $P_{i,j} P_{i,j+1}$. Shading starts by calculating the sign of L, which is the sign of

$$\det(\vec{s}, P_{i,j}P_{i+1,j}, P_{i,j}P_{i,j+1})$$

One thus obtains a boolean table designated "shade" which ties P_{ij} with the sign of L. So it is natural to associate that portion of terrain T_{ij} located between P_{ij}, $P_{i+1,j}$, $P_{i+1,j+1}$ and $P_{i,j+1}$ with point P_{ij} and to consider that 'shade'$_{ij}$ determines whether T_{ij} lies in the shade.

- *Hidden faces*

The procedure for eliminating hidden faces uses the transformation parameters, i.e. the configuration of the terrain with respect to the plane of the screen. This procedure is an adaptation of standard procedures ;[5] it aims at a sharper picture by retaining only those pieces of the grid which are wholly visible, while discarding all the others. This results in creation of a "solid" plane. However, it is a creation procedure insofar as the object displayed cannot be deformed.

Another procedure detects hidden faces from a contour drawing or from a Digital Terrain Model ; so it can be applied to curves denoting altitude.

This algorithm is along the same lines as the shading algorithm. It determines whether the element of terrain T_{ij} is visible or not. The first step is therefore the calculation of the boolean table of visible faces ; then the object is restructured by replacing each contour by the list of contours formed by pieces of line passing through all visible T_{ij}'s.

Determining the visible elements of the terrain uses the mask method. Since DTM is a rectangular lattice, four corners can be defined. The two corners nearest the viewer, together with the vertical to the rectangle, form the foreground. The planes parallel to the foreground containing points from the DTM are called cross-sections. The horizontal direction included in a cross-section and going towards the background is labelled u, and the orthogonal line towards the back is labelled v. The indices k and l designate discretization according to u and v.

A mask is a surface included in the plane of the screen and whose upper edge is a line joining DTM point projections. It is associated with an index l and represents the outline of cross-sections indexed from 1 to l-1. An element from surface T_{kl} is said to be visible if the projection of P_{kl} onto the screen lies beyond the l-order mask (fig. 3).

When an 1-order mask is available, one can determine whether elements from T_{kl} are visible. The next step is to construct mask l+1, i.e. to insert the visible points.

A mask is achieved by a list of filings containing the coordinates of the upper line. Point P_{11} is always visible. Hence, mask modification starts with the insertion of the coordinates of P_{11} at the head of the list. For each P_{kl}, the mask is scanned until the points framing P_{kl} are found. If P_{kl} lies above the segment joining the two points of the mask, P_{kl} is inserted into the list.

The next step is smoothing : if P_{k-11} also lies on the mask, the points on the mask between P_{k-11} and P_{kl} are deleted.

- Contour levels

The aim of this procedure is the generation and display of constant altitude curves. During the treatment, each curve is displayed immediately after its creation, thereby making it possible to assess progress in calculations (fig. 4).

The initial data are the values of the DTM. The curves are drawn on the surface of the terrain depicted by a block diagram. However, this block diagram does not define a single surface. Indeed, there is no simple surface passing through the four corners of a grid (fig. 5). Hence the inside of a grid is considered as being formed by two sections of a plane :[5] the first goes through $P_{i,j}$, $P_{i+1,j}$, $P_{i,j+1}$ and the second through $P_{i+1,j+1}$, $P_{i+1,j}$ and $P_{i,j+1}$.

Any part of a plane reconstituting the terrain is called a facet. For each level z, the set of facets is scanned in search of those facets intersecting the horizontal plane at altitude z. If a facet meets this requisite, a curve is initialized, then lengthened. When this lengthening is over, one returns to the starting point and continues the search for other curves.

In the search and lengthening phases, the visible phases are marked. They can no longer be chosen to initialize a curve.

So the problem scales down to lengthening the start of a curve. The algorithm used for this treatment is recursive. For a given facet containing a curve, the following facet is determined. When the sequence of facets is known, calculating the curve coordinates contained in these facets is no more than an interpolation problem.

For a facet containing a curve, the configuration is defined as the set of the edges or summits through which the curve passes. To avoid pathological cases, the next facet necessarily has a two-element configuration. Hence, facets meeting this requisite are sought among the adjacent facets. It can be shown that by means of a few specifications about the configuration concept, this constraint ensures the uniqueness of the next facet.

If this next facet is marked, i.e. if it has already been studied, the curve is closed. Otherwise, it becomes the current facet and the recursive process is applied. When two successive facets are known, the point of their shared section crossed by the curve is calculated.

Circling the DTM with negative altitude points resolves the problem of unclosed curves and thereby constitutes a bigger gridwork where all curves are closed.

It should be noted that the curves are oriented, i.e. if they are scanned in order of storage, the highest points are to the left. This is achieved by orienting the two initial points of a curve.

The problems posed by the realization of this algorithm lie in the topology and in specific cases (cf. fig. 5). Curves must be prevented from getting lost in plane zones or from backtracking once they have crossed a horizontal edge (by entering in one facet and leaving in the adjacent facet).

II - INTERACTION AND THE TASK-SCHEDULER

Interaction is ensured by the user of a menu. This choice is not original, but it fully suits complex command languages. However, menus are generally static. Indeed, the task-scheduler, i.e. the module devised to manage interruptions, depends on the texts enclosed in the menu boxes and on the tasks associated with each box. Actually, this conflicts with and limits the adopted extension possibilities.

This is why we have elaborated a task dispatching generator. This generator, which results from precompilation of the call sequence uses a simple language to describe menus and actions. It generates a distributor specific to the command language. In particular, it creates menu display orders and instructions for plugging into the various tasks.

a) Simple example

The following text is the description of the simplest language :

    {Definition}
    menu 0 FORMAT TEXTE A GAUCHE
    1 = 'box 1'
    2 = 'box 2'
    3 = 'box'/'3'
    {Call}
    1   proc1
    2   proc2.

Obtaining the corresponding commands is a two-step process. First of all, the above text is compiled by the generator which creates the distributor code. Then the distributor code is linked with procedures proc1 and proc2 and the image appearing on the screen shall be

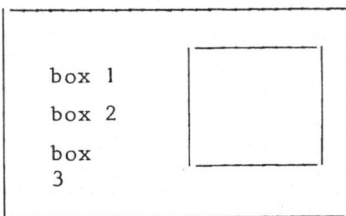

Pointing to 'box 1' will activate the execution of creation procedure proc1.

b) **Conditional instructions**

The command language can contain conditional instructions. If so, the choice of actions depends not only on the menu box but on already called procedures as well.

Taking the above-cited simple example and adding

>   3 after proc1 gives proc31
>   3 after proc2 gives proc32.

Pointing to box 2 and then to box 3 gives rise to the execution of proc32.

c) **Complex tasks**

Pointing to a box activates the execution of a task. In the above the tasks amount to execution of a creation procedure. However, it is also possible to call a new menu or another display procedure.

The task scheduler is unrelated to the mode of image production, so it can command a call to any library where creation procedures are distinct from display procedures. These features account for the general and open nature of the Graphic Relief Simulation System.

CONCLUSION

The Graphic Relief Simulation System is an open one that is flexible and anticipates foreseeable developments. The task-scheduler generator is general. The system can be enriched by considering new creation procedures which are both broader (to cover the generality of problems) and more specific (to adapt to certain applications).

Two fields of application where such an interactive and flexible system will be of considerable interest are data base creation and map layouts.

Indeed, geographic information systems have unique features for access methods and defining conceptual schemes. The proposed simulation system could contribute to defining and assessing DBMS components. Moreover, texts contained in a map are relatively important ; some can be shifted, but not onto essential map features. Application of the existing set of ill-defined rules regarding map outlays could be handled by computer to deal with problems such as the search for an expert map-making system.

These are only two examples based on current cartography needs. Other applications in a wide variety of fields could also be envisioned, since the task-scheduler applies to the handling and display of any solid whatsoever.

REFERENCES

1. Computer Graphics : The Next Step in On-Line Retrieval. Jerry Borrel, 4th International On-Line Information Meeting, London 9-11 December 1980.

2. G. Nagy and S. Wagle, Geographic Data Processing, ACM Computing Surveys, 11, 2, 139, 1979.

3. "The Use of 'Digital National Land Information' : Present State and Future Possibilities",T. Kanakubo and K. Nonomura, Data for Science and Technology, Proceedings of the Seventh International CODATA Conference, Kyoto, Japan, 8-11 October, 1980.

4. A. Bernard, Digitization of Relief Data and Exploitation of Digital Terrain Model at IGNF, Actes d'Auto-Carto V, 1982.

5. J.C. Davis, M.J.Mc Cullagh, Display and Analysis of Spatial Data (NATO Advanced Study Institute), John Wiley & Sons, 1973.

6. J.D. Foley and A. Van Dam, Fundamentals of Interactive Computer Graphics, Addison Wesley, 1982.

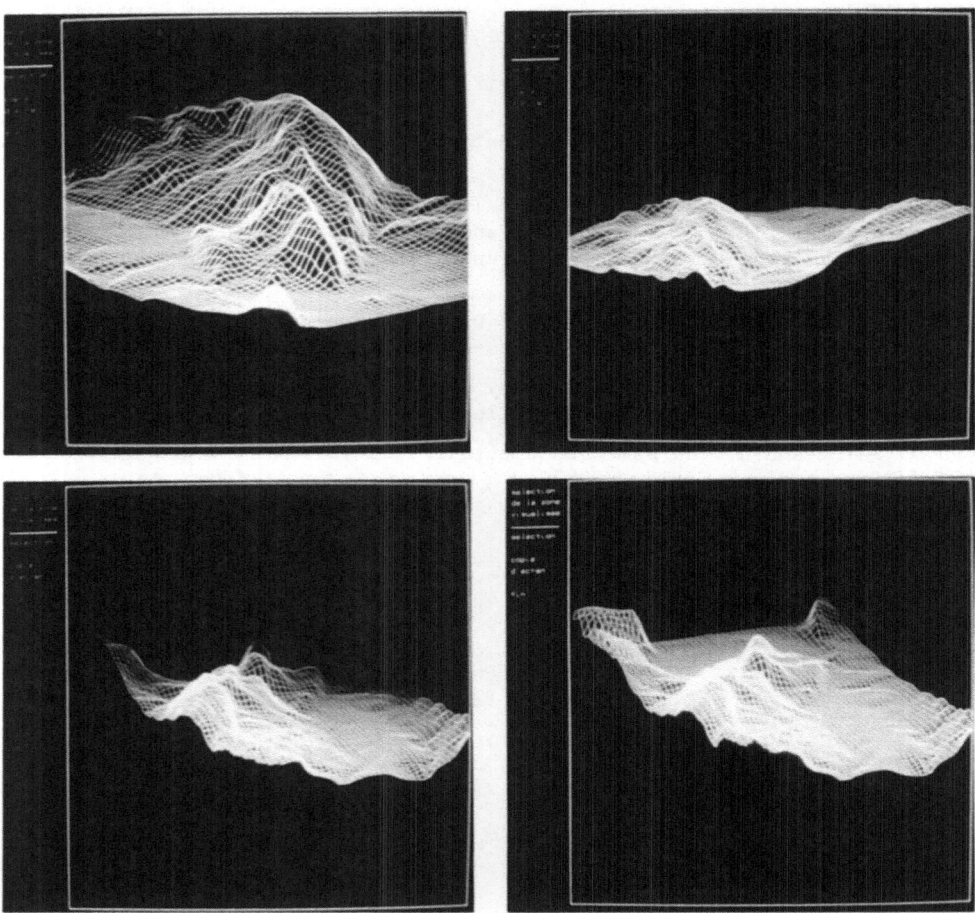

Figure 1 : A *block diagram representing a Digital Terrain Model (DTM) is a matrix whose coefficients are altitudes.*
Said block diagram is depicted as a gridwork in which the nodes are related to the DTM elements and to the vantage point of the viewer (static or dynamic).

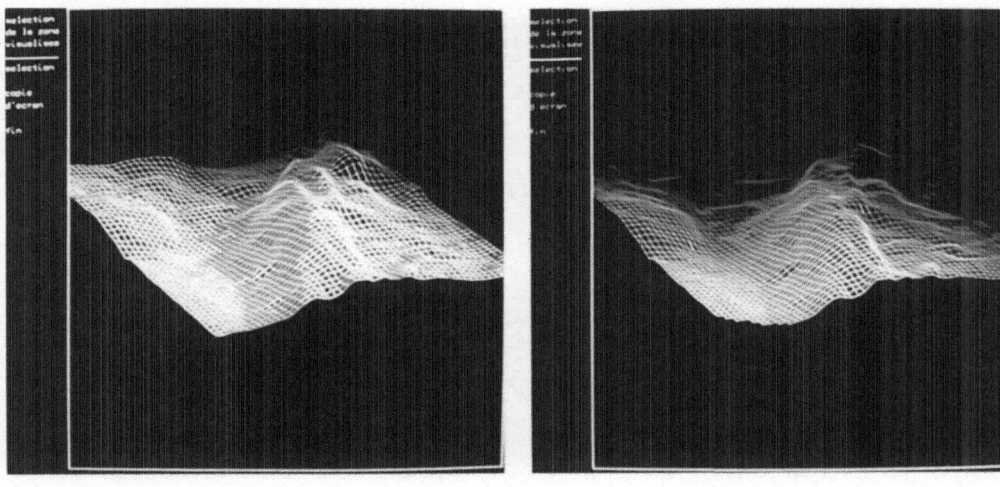
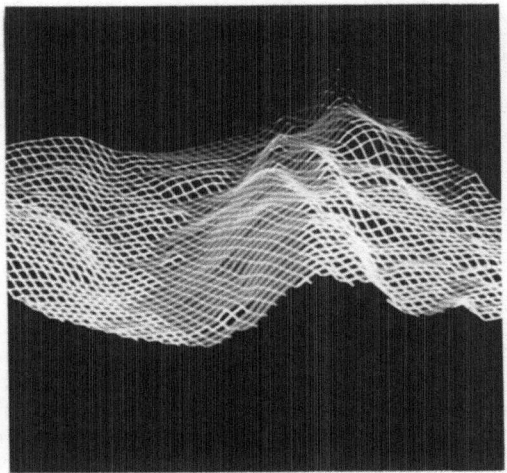

Figure 2 : *Shading*.
Shaded zones created by an imaginary sun are calculated. Lines lying in these zones are darkened. The user can interactively choose the position of the sun defined by the angle of the horizon and the zenithal distance.

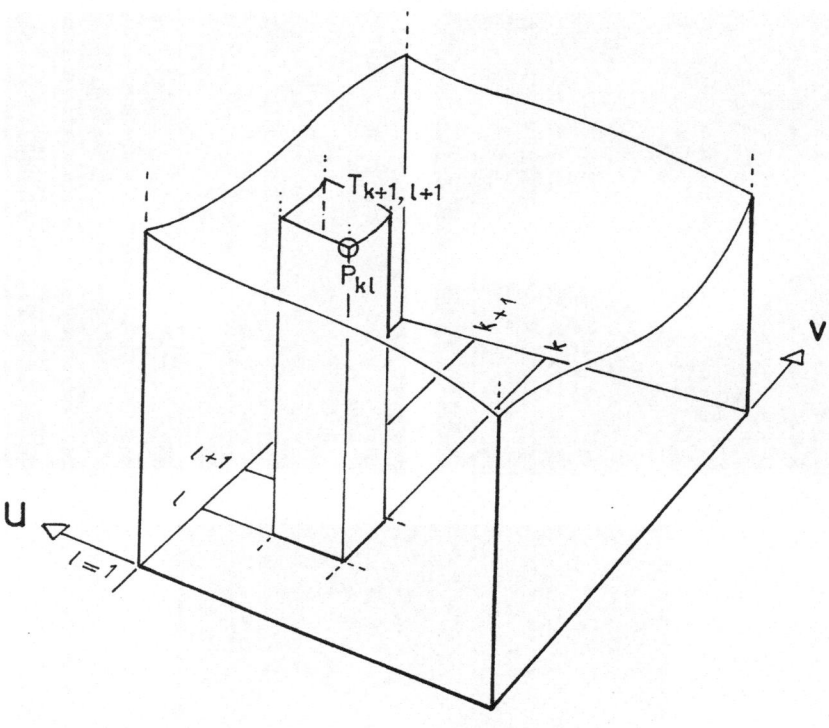

Figure 3 : *Hidden faces - geometric notation.*
The object is restructured by replacing each contour by the list of contours formed by pieces of line passing though all visible portions of terrain (T_{ij}). Indices k and l designate discretization according to horizontal direction u going towards the background and the orthogonal direction v towards the back. An element from surface T_{kl} is said to be visible if the projection of P_{kl} onto the screen lies beyond the l-order mask.

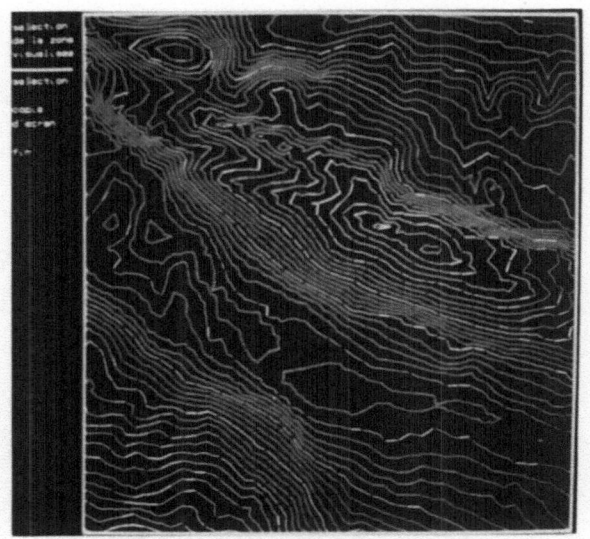

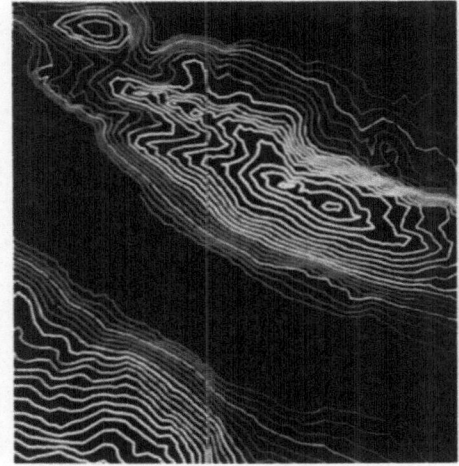
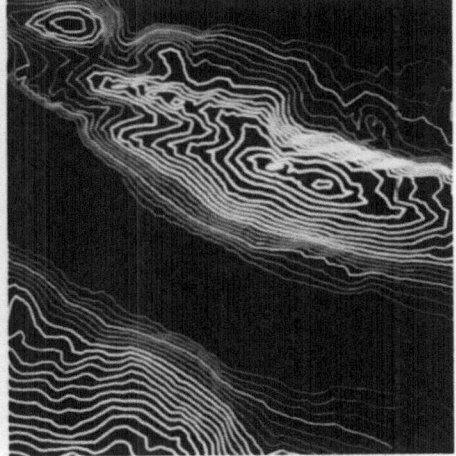

Figure 4 : *Contour levels*.
Constant altitude curves are displayed. During the treatment, each curve is displayed immediately after its creation, thereby making it possible to assess progress in calculation.

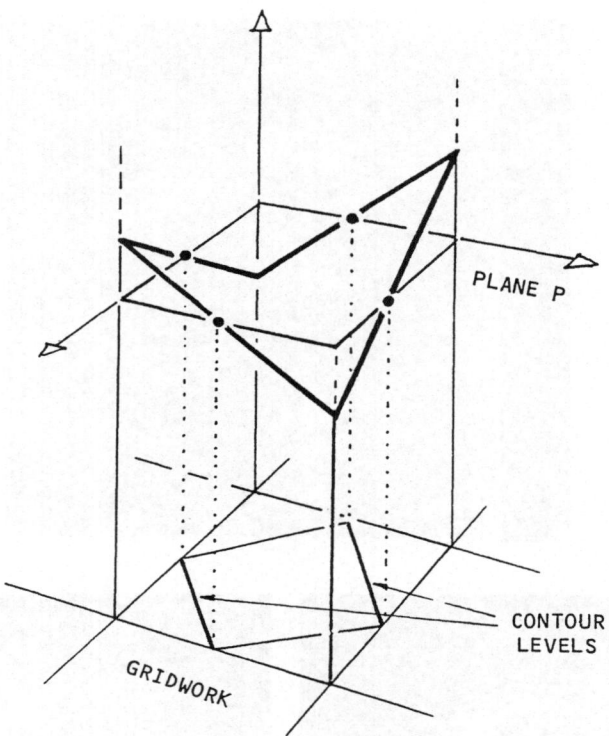

Figure 5 : *Contour level generation.*
This is one of the particular problems which should be resolved with a contour level algorithm : dark thick lines depict a grid with four points of intersection (•) with horizontal plane P. Four contour levels can be made to cross the grid ; however, only two of them are valid.

Realistic Effects with Rodin

Hervé Huitric
Département d'Informatique
Université Paris VIII
2 rue de la Liberté
93526 Saint Denis, France

Monique Nahas
U.E.R. de Physique
Université Paris VII
2 place Jussieu
75005 Paris, France

ABSTRACT
In our program RODIN, objects are formed through the use of bicubic B-Splines. We will describe aspects of this program that allows us to generate realistic scenes and special effects that are characteristic of B-Splines.

INTRODUCTION
In this article we introduce aspects of our program RODIN, that enable us to construct scenes and specials effects particularly characteristic of B-Splines. We will also describe how we have expanded J. BLINN's texture in order to generate rocky and grass covered landscapes, leafy environments, and attempts at human hair (1).

1. DESCRIPTION OF THE PROGRAM : GENERATION OF SHADOWED SURFACES
We form objects by using bicubic B-Splines surfaces because these are well suited for constructing smooth 3-D objects. The surface is defined by a set of "control points" $P_{i,j}$, with each point represented by its x,y,z coordinates. B-Splines are not interpolating surfaces, i.e. they do not pass exactly through their defining control points; but they can be locally controlled and lie within the convex hull of their control points. RODIN calculates visible surfaces and shadows by using algorithms based on depth buffering which are similar to those described in (14). Visibility calculations are performed as follows. We step along the u,v parameters which define the surface in equal increments and generate the corresponding points P(x,y,z) on the surface. Each point P is projected onto a discretized "screen" to determine the corresponding pixel. The depth (i.e., the distance VP, where V is the viewpoint) is computed and compared to the depth stored in a Z-Buffer for the appropriate pixel. If P'Depth is smaller than that in the Z-Buffer, then P'depth is stored in the buffer.
Shadow calculation is similar to the visibility calculation. We use an S-Buffer in which we store distances SP between the punctual light source S and the surface point P. The S-Buffer corresponds to an auxiliary screen approximately orthogonal to the "average" light direction, and is constructed in the same way than the Z-Buffer. The Z-Buffer and the S-Buffer are computed in a single u,v scan of the surface. To produce a display with shadows we proceed as follows. We traverse the surface again. For each point P we determine visibility by comparing the depth VP with the appropriate entry in the Z-Buffer. If P is visible, we project it onto the auxiliary screen and determine if P is illuminated by comparing the distance SP with the contents of the S-Buffer. If SP is greater than the

corresponding value of the S-Buffer, then P belongs to a shadow. If P is illuminated then we compute its intensity by using LAMBERT's law or different formulas as described in (11). Surface normals are computed by finding the partial derivatives with respect to u and v by using DE BOOR's formulas (3), and then evaluating the cross product of these derivatives.
The final display is obtained by using an bi-linear interpolation. First we compute the points of the surface corresponding to two sucessive values of v and to all the values of u. After projection on the "screen", two sequences of 2-D points are thus obtained. Then we interpolate each polygon of four points. To each corner of the 2-D polygon being considered, we associate a set of values to be interpolated simultaneously: (a) brightness value, (b) the content of the Z-Buffer, (c) the values of the two indices of the S-Buffer, (d) the content of the S-Buffer itself, (e) the depth, (f) the S-Depth, i.e., the distance between the point and the light source, (g) the color R,G,B. During the interpolation the shadow and the hidden part are evaluated for each point. Note that a GOURAUD shading (6) is included automatically.
A scene can be generated sequentially, one object after another. Upon viewing the display after the addition of each object it is possible to modify the parameters of the next object to be added. Furthermore, use of the Z and S-Buffers provides the avantage of conserving all necessary information for a scene. Thus new objects can be added to the display with correct shadowing and positioning by applying an "UNION" program that utilizes the Z and S-Buffers as well as those of the new objects. In this way, calculation is economized even if the objects are not placed in the foreground of the scene. Note that this procedure does not apply to scenes with reflection or refraction, in which case all objects must be calculated simultaneously.

2. TEXTURE

RODIN uses ideas from (1). Texture is produced by modifying a point in the direction of its' surface normal and then re-estimating the normal of the deformed point. In order to generate the texture of an image, we use a two dimensional array, TEX(I,J), whose size is determined in initiating the program. Besides the modes describes by J. BLINN for filling in this array, we use the following mode:
$$TEX(I,J) = MAX(I,J) * RDN(I,J)$$
RDN is a random function with an average value of zero, and a maximum amplitude one. The function TEX(I,J) depends on I and J in differents ways, for example it can have a constant value on certain level lines determined by a relation between I and J. This function must be calculated before running the program.
The function MAX(I,J) determines the maximum variations possible for the texture. It can be: constant, which means that the entire texture of the surface will be homogenous, image 1; or can vary according to I and J. In the latter case, we determine the control values for some points I and J of the array and we calculate the values in all points through a B-Spline function, making sure of smooth transitions between the control values, images 3,4. The use of an array during calculation of the surface is described in (1). Each point of the display is determined by the two values of the u and v parameters and has a corresponding point in the texture array.

This allows us to compute the new position of the considered point, and estimate its' new surface normal, thus its' lighting. The scanning described above interpolates the values calculated for the four corners of the polygon but does not re-calculate texture for each point scanned. This assures continuity useful in creating landscapes or mountainous scenes, images 1,2. The density of points calculated on a surface is therefore related to the density of the texture. For certain effects it can be necessary to generate a texture for each pixel. In such cases an interpolation of surface normals within the scanning is required image 13.
Texture can be used to create movement by varying the value of $MAX(I,J)$ image by image in a sequence. For example, increasing its' value for each image. In this case the array $RND(I,J)$ is determined for the complete sequence in order to avoid temporal aliasing. At the same time as the amplitude, the texture can vary in size. We used this technique to produce effects of wind blowing on sand dunes, images 3,4. Now we are working to add particles of sand to this image in order to create dust. Stochastic properties of texture also seem to be useful tools for realizing irregular, natural shapes (13).

3. SURFACES TRANSFORMATIONS

The uses of B-Splines allows us to work with form similar to the way in which a sculptor models clay. We call this method modulation.
Effects for animation are particularly characteristic of the properties of B-Spline surfaces. At this time we will describe two types of applications: surface modulations, and interpolation of control points.

3.1. Localized Surface Modulation

Modulation is a change in form obtained by varying control points according to a modulation function:
$$P_{i,j} = P_{i,j} + T_{i,j}$$
The modulation function $T_{i,j}$ can be:
- a mathematical function, for example, a sinusoidal function can be used to create waves or wrinkles.
- an array defined by a set of control values $T_{l,m}$, chosen for designated points $P_{l,m}$. The numeric contents of the array are calculated by a B-Spline function, or interpolation functions.
- a random variation with given average and amplitude. In any case, the OSLO algorithm (1), (2), proves to be very useful. This algorithm permits control points to be added in any region of the surface without changing its form. The density of control points is directly related to the possible modulations. Since moving a control point influences its surrounding points, the extent of its influence depends on the density of its environment. Therefore very localized deformations of a surface are possible.

An example of modulation: the construction of a faun's head, image 5, from the modulation of a smooth head itself visible on image 6. Control points were added around the smooth head at place where hair was to be placed. Then, in modifying the amplitude of movement of these points over the period of several images, we constructed a sequence of the film "9600 bauds", where the modulations around the head are clearly seen.

3.2. Control Points Interpolation

By interpolating the control points of two B-Spline surfaces, we obtain a 3-D interpolation. The OSLO algorithm is very useful here, as it allows us to equalize the number of control points of the surfaces to be interpolated, and to introduce new control points in selected places. Two sets of control points, $P_{i,j}$, $P_{i,j}$, can thus be transformed into a new set by a blending function.

All function F which is continous with respect to its parameters and variables will produce continuous sequences.

An example is the linear interpolation, (the new set $P_{i,j}$ of control points is defined by the following equation:
$$P_{i,j} = a_{i,j}(n) \; P_{i,j} + (1 - a_{i,j}(n)) \; P_{i,j} \;.$$
This example shows an interpolation between objects 1 and 2 when coefficients $a_{i,j}$ are equal to one before the transformation and equal to zero at the end. If these coefficients are dependent on the values of i,j, mixed images will result at each stage of transformation. The head emerging from a mountain in the film "9600 bauds" (7), and the statue rising from the water in the film "synthetique O'synthetique" are two examples of this kind of interpolation. In both cases the coefficients $a_{i,j}$ were equal to one in the beginning stages of the transformation. They keep the value of one for some values i,j in order to conserve the initial scene; then they vary continuously, decreasing till they reach zero. At this point the second object dominates the screen. Images 7, 8.

4. CONCATENATION AND SUBDIVISION OF SURFACES

Blending two B-Spline surfaces together is required to obtain complex shapes, such as bodies with arms, or trees with branches. The problem is to adjust the different parts so that they fit together as smoothly as possible (with continuity of derivatives), image 12.

We use the OSLO algorithm to cut the B-Spline in two or four subdivisions. To concatenate two B-Splines we concatenate their control points by giving a multiplicity (three in our case) to the boundaries control points, and computing the new surface with a standard knot vector. For example, we add a "branch" surface to a "trunk" surface in the following way: we cut the "trunk" in two at a chosen spot. The "branch" is then added to the part of the trunk we have chosen, and displayed as one object, along with the other part of the trunk. The trees in image 9 were realized in that way.

The process of cutting the trunk and attaching the branch is recursive, and the branch was automatically translated and transformed before each concatenation.

In image 9 a tree is shown that was constructed from two basic surfaces. Other surfaces, such as leaves, fruits or nuts could also be added (8).

5. BRIGHTNESS AND COLORATION

In order to remain as simple as possible, RODIN uses the following relation between the brightness and color components of a pixel:
$$L = (R + V + B)/3$$
normalizing L between 0 and 255. The hue H is an angle between 0 and 360 degrees, and the saturation S, a number between 0 and a maximum value less or equal to one, depending on L. We use the formulas of (12) to compute the corresponding values of the three components R, G, B. The brightness of a

point can be computed using LAMBERT's law or other formulas (5).
Each pixel's corresponding value of R, G, B are then obtained by interpolation during the scanning of each polygon. Hue and saturation can be calculated in different ways:
- by a B-Spline variation computed before running the main program. In this case they are defined by a set of control values corresponding to a choice of coloration of some given points of the surface. The results are stored in an array used in the same way that the texture array.
- or, during the program, in fuction of the parameters u,v of the surface and using interpolating polynomials.
We have added coloration functions in order to modify the computed values of brightness, hue and saturation in accordance to some esthetic requirements. Until now, these three caracteristic components of the color were computed independently: by an a priori determination for hue and saturation, and by usual formulas giving the brightness from LAMBERT's law and hightlight computation. We have added modifying functions in the following way:
- first setting maximum and minimum limits to the brightness of an object in order to avoid black and white in the picture.
- providing the possibility of modifying the computed hues in function of brightness of an object, for example giving a yellow coloration to the clearest part of the picture. This can be controlled by some parameters: a hue parameter that has to be mixed with the computed hue, a saturation parameter that is mixed with the computed saturation in the same way, a distance parameter giving the distance to the maximum brightness and defining the interval of brightness on which the mixture is made, and finally a mixture parameter defining the proportion of the mixture is then effectuated in decreasing proportion along the given brightness interval, in order to insure a smooth transition between the computed hue and saturation at the beginning of the interval and the modified values at the end, image 10.
- the shadows are colored in a similar way, by giving brightness, hue, saturation as well as a blending parameter used to mix the shadow in given proportion with the rest of the image.
- finally we also use a texture of colors made by random variations around the computed values and depending on the values of brightness, hue and positions. Such pointillistic effects were used in image 9.

CONCLUSION
We are investigating the problem of defining input data which are convenient for object movement or expression. For an object can be described in an infinite number of ways depending on the control points used, and each type of description effects the potential transformations of the object. This problem has been posed by F. PARKE, who developed a structured set of parameters to realize facial movements (9). We believe that this type of formalization is possible based on key control points of any surface, using regrouping or bonds between the key points. Expressive structure could therefore be given by a graph of control points with defined flexible or muscular (not rigid) relations between them (10). We have already tried some expressive possibilities, such as smile and smirks, through control points transformations. The different faces of the image 11 were obtained by a FOURIER transformation of the control points of the initial face,

filtering of the coefficients and inversing the FOURIER transformation. The continuity and local properties of B-Spline surfaces provides an appropriate base for all these variations.

ACKNOWLEDGMENTS

The first version of RODIN was implemented on a VAX 11/780 under VMS at the University of Rochester, N.Y., U.S.A. We are grateful to the Production Automation Project of the University of Rochester for facilitationg our artistic research by hosting us during 1981-1982. We would especially like to thank Dr. Herbert Voelcker, Professor and Director of the P.A.P., and Dr. Aristides Requicha, Associate Director.

REFERENCES

(1) BLINN J.F, "Simulation of wrinkled surfaces", ACM Computer Graphics, vol.12, n°3, pp.286-292, August 1978.
(2) BOEHM W, "Inserting new knots into B-Spline curves", Computer Aided Design, vol.12, n°4, pp.199-201, July 1980.
(3) DE BOOR C, "On calculating with B-Splines", J. Approximation Theory, vol.6, n°1, pp.50-62, July 1972.
(4) COHEN E., LYCHE T., RIESENFELD R., "Discrete B-Splines and subdivision techniques in computer-aided geometric design and computer graphics", Computer Graphics and Image Processing, n°14, pp.87-111, 1980.
(5) COOK R.L., TORRANCE K.E., "A reflectance model for computer graphics", Computer Graphics, vol.15, n°3, pp.307-316, August 1981.
(6) GOURAUD J., "Continuous shading of curved surfaces", IEEE Transactions on Computers, vol.C-20, n°6, pp.623-628, June 1971.
(7) HUITRIC H., NAHAS M., "Computer Art with Rodin", Information Processing 83, R.E.A. Mason (ed.), pp.275-282, IFIP 1983.
(8) MARSHALL R., WILSON R., CARLSON W., "Procedure Models for generating three dimensional terrain", Computer Graphics, vol.14, n°3, pp.154-162, 1980.
(9) PARKE F.I., "Parameterizd Models for Facial Animation", IEEE CG&A, vol.2, n°9, pp;61-68, Nov. 1982.
(10) PLATT S.M., BADLER N.I., "Animating gacial expressions", Computer Graphics, vol.15, n°3, pp.245-252, August 1981.
(11) NEWMAN W.M., SPROULL R.F., "Principles of Interactive Computer Graphics", New-York:McGraw-Hill Book Co., 2nd edition, 1979.
(12) SMITH A.R., "Color gamut transform pair", Proceedings of the Fifth Annual Conference on Computer Graphics and Interactive Techniques, Siggraph 1978, pp.12-19, August 1978.
(13) VOSS R.F., "Fourier Synthesis of Gaussian Fractals:1/f noises, landscapes, and flakes.", Seminar on state of the art image synthesis at Siggraph '83, July 1983.
(14) WILLIAMS L., "Casting curved shadows on curved surfaces", ACM Computer Graphics, vol.12, n°3, pp.270-274, August 1978.

IMAGE 1
Textured Mountain.

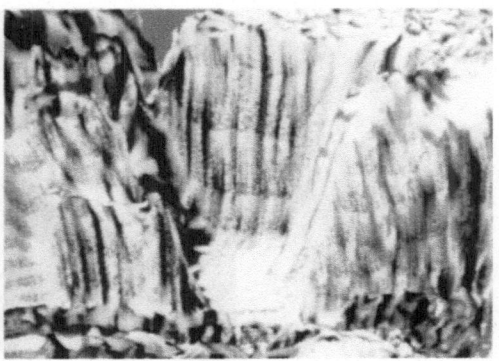

IMAGE 2
Homogeneous Texture.

IMAGE 3
Variable Texture.

IMAGE 4
Variable Texture.

IMAGE 5
Faun's Head.

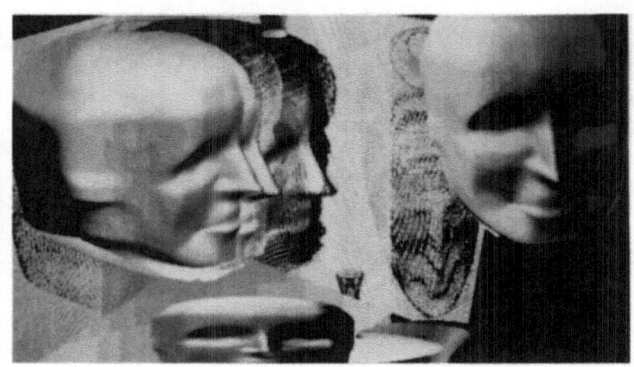

IMAGE 6
Heads.

IMAGE 7
Interpolation of control points.

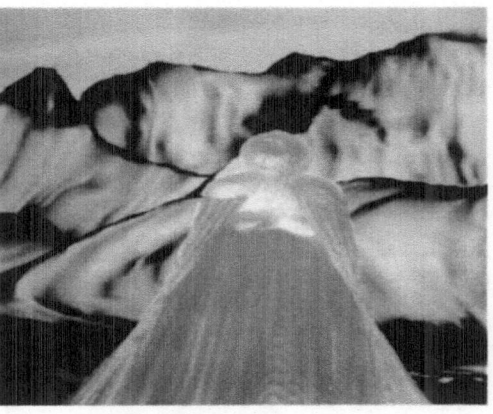

IMAGE 8
Interpolation of control points.
Image from the movie:
"Synthétique, O'synthétique"

IMAGE 9
Effect of pointillistic color texture.

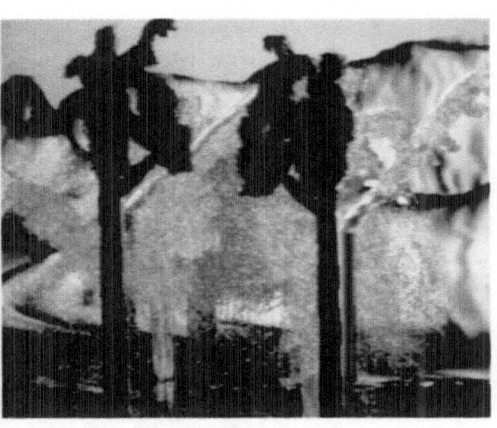

IMAGE 10
Forest

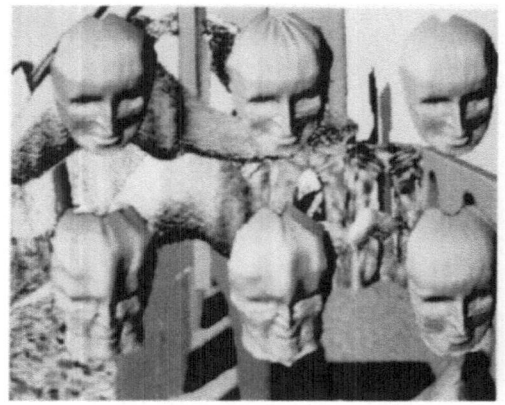

IMAGE 11
Fourier : Transformation of control points.

IMAGE 12
Dinosaur.

IMAGE 13
Effects of texture.

Chapter 4
Human Factors

Human Factors Redesign and Test of a Graphics System

Phyllis Reisner and **Glen G. Langdon, Jr.**
IBM Research Laboratory
5600 Cottle Road
San Jose, CA 95193, USA

ABSTRACT

This paper describes two versions of a small interactive graphics system. The two versions have essentially the same function, but differ in the design of the man-machine interface. The first version was designed from the "inside out", without explicit consideration given to ease-of-use. The second version was redesigned specifically from the "outside in" with major emphasis on human factors considerations. Behavioral experiments comparing the two versions showed significant differences in ease of learning the two systems. The intent of the paper is 1) to make explicit in a small, easily understandable example, the rationale behind some of the human factors design decisions, and 2) to show that differences in human interface design can result in measurable differences in ease of use.

INTRODUCTION

The increasing emphasis on providing computers for those who are unwilling or unable to learn computer concepts motivates the design of systems which are easy to use. But how does one accomplish this goal? With luck, one may rely on the intuition of a good interface designer. But intuition can not form the basis of a discipline. We can see the result of a design based on intuition, but not the reasons for the effectiveness of such a design.

On the other hand, one may rely on more structured approaches such as design reviews (10), human factors testing (see, for example, (4,8)), use of analytic tools (1,7), or the use of human factors guidelines or principles (2,9). In particular, the use of guidelines appears to be increasing. However, the path from guidelines to design is far from clear. For example, what situations require which guidelines? How does one choose between conflicting guidelines? This paper provides a "case study", relating specific items of an interface design to human factors guidelines, and showing why specific design tradeoffs were made.

Several years ago a psychologist (PR) and a computer scientist/engineer (GGL) collaborated to redesign a small experimental color graphics system. The psychologist concentrated on redesign for ease-of-use, and the computer scientist on functional use of the available hardware and internal program structure. The psychologist then ran behavioral tests to see whether the human factors redesign did actually improve ease-of-use. This paper describes the human factors redesign. The internal program design has been described in (3). A related paper describes use of formal grammar to describe a users action language and to predict ease-of-use (6). The current paper focuses specifically on the details and rationale of the redesign.

The paper describes: 1) the human interface of the original system, ROBART I, 2) the method used for identifying flaws in design that made ROBART I hard to use, 3) the revised system, ROBART II, 4) some rationale and principles underlying the design, with particular emphasis on tradeoffs between conflicting guidelines, and 5) the behavioral comparison of ROBART I and ROBART II. The final discussion contains some personal reflections on human factors redesign.

ROBART I

ROBART I was an interactive program used for creating slides for technical presentations and artwork. Pictures consisting of various combinations of primitive shapes were created on a color TV monitor. The emphasis in this paper is not on the function or the interface ideas, but on clarifying the principles underlying the human factors redesign. Only portions of the redesign are described.

The ROBART I program was written from the "inside out", with primary consideration given to debugging an experimental hardware system with minimal programming effort. The human interface is described in terms of the following arbitrarily defined components:

1. Hardware and displays
2. Picture creation "language"
3. Storage and display "language"
4. Photography subsystem
5. Documentation, teaching and help subsystems

Hardware and Displays

Hardware: Major components of the user interface are shown in Figure 1. It consisted of: a color TV monitor, an IBM 3277 keyboard, a joystick with a turnable knob on top and a switchbox with various switches and buttons. Also available were: a camera and a tripod for photography; a closed circuit TV monitor, camera, and separate box with turnable knob for superposing pictures on the screen ("image mixing").

TV monitor display: The TV monitor display can be seen in Figure 1. The display was partitioned into three areas: a paintbox of colors (colored rectangles) permanently displayed on the screen during the picture creation stage; a menu area with prompts for saving and displaying pictures directly above the paintbox, and a drawing area above that, consisting of the remainder of the screen.

Switchbox: The switchbox consisted of various switches and buttons, as shown in Figure 2. Buttons labelled GO were interrupt buttons. The rationale for the two sets of START, END and GO buttons was to accomodate right and left handed people.

Picture Creation Language

The primitive shapes were the basic <u>discrete shapes:</u> line, open circle, solid rectangle, horizontal line and vertical line; the basic "continuous" or <u>sketching shapes:</u> continuous line, continuous open circle, and continuous solid rectangle, and two sizes of <u>text.</u> The continuous shapes were sequences of lines, circles or rectangles that could be drawn freeform on the screen by moving the cursor (see Figure 3). In addition to the basic shapes, the following <u>derived shapes</u> could be created from the basic ones: solid circle, open rectangle, and sketch line. To create a primitive shape, the user selected the color and the shape, then created the shape on the screen with the desired size, location, and orientation. A picture or object could also be projected on the screen from the closed circuit TV camera. The user could then create his picture with the projected picture as background.

<u>Selecting colors:</u> To select a color the user dipped a cursor, via the joystick, into the desired color of the paintbox. <u>Feedback:</u> A small, barely visible color and shape indicator directly above the paintbox changed color and shape to serve as feedback to the user about the color and shape selected.

<u>Selecting shapes:</u> To select a shape, the user first verified the position of the switches to see if any previously set switches needed to be reset to the off (DOWN) position. He then set the desired switches to the on (UP) position, then pressed the GO (interrupt) button to cause the computer to read the position of the switches. Various combinations of switches controlled the shapes selected, as shown in Table 1. <u>Feedback:</u> The position of the switches was visible by inspection of the box. The color and shape indicator mentioned above changed to the shape selected. There was a sound engineering rationale for using several switches per shape (minimize the number of switches). There was also a sound human factors rationale for having text always available. It was felt that since text entry would be a frequent activity, eliminating the switch setting activity would decrease the amount of user action required.

<u>Creating basic discrete shapes:</u> Once the basic discrete shape had been selected, the user had to indicate the location, size and/or orientation of the shape by two points on the screen (e.g. center and a circumference point for circle). The user positioned the cursor at the first point, simultaneously pressed the START and GO buttons, then positioned the cursor at the second point and simultaneously pressed END and GO. (Either set of START-GO and END-GO buttons could be used.) <u>Feedback:</u> A small dot was left on the screen to mark the position of the first point. After selection of the second point, the figure created was visible on the TV monitor.

<u>Creating derived discrete shapes:</u> Neither solid circles nor open boxes were directly available as options in ROBART I. The solid circle was created by carefully rotating a continuous line. The open box was created by placing a smaller box of the background color inside a larger box of the desired color.

Creating basic continuous shapes: To create a continuous shape, the user marked the starting position, set parameters for size or orientation, "drew" the cursor across the screen, then marked the end position. Marking the start and end positions, and indicating the size or orientation parameters, was controlled in a complex fashion by the ROTATE/WIDTH switch.

Creating derived continuous shapes. ROBART I had no sketching line. To create such a line, the user carefully created a continuous line of very small width (a dot), using the ROTATE/WIDTH switch. This dot, when continuously swept out by the joystick, served as a sketching line.

Erasing the picture area: To erase the picture area, the user set the RESET switch to the UP position, then pressed GO. To get ready for a new picture, he set RESET to the DOWN position and pressed GO.

Image Mixing: To project an external picture on the screen, the user positioned the picture in front of the closed circuit TV camera, then turned on the IMAGE MIX knob.

Storage and Display Language

To store a picture for later redisplay, the user had to first initialize the file (we ignore this step). He then had to open a file, draw his picture, then close the file. The user procedure was:

1. Press a function key on the keyboard labelled SEGS (for segments)
2. Type "o" (for open), then a number between 1 and 150
3. Press ENTER
4. Create picture as desired
5. Press SEGS
6. Type "c" (for close)
7. Press ENTER

To display pictures an analogous procedure was followed.

Photography Subsystem

To take a picture, the user set up a 35 mm camera on a tripod and then photographed directly from the screen.

Documentation, Teaching and Help Subsystems

An illustrated user's manual described how to use the system. There was no explicit teaching or help subsystem. The manual could, however, be used in this capacity.

ANALYSIS OF ROBART I

Anecdotal evidence, the psychologist's own perceptions, observation of users, and exploratory behavioral tests were used to determine 1) whether ROBART 1 was easy to learn and 2) where the problems were.

Anecdotal Evidence

ROBART I was not suitable for computer-naive, and especially computer-fearful users. One intelligent, well-educated artist used the system, with great joy, for about one week. However, an assistant sat beside her for the entire week to change the position of the switches. Towards the end of the week, the artist tentatively began to try to control the switches herself. Her comment: "I am a college graduate and consider myself reasonably intelligent, but this thing makes me feel dumb". Later behavioral tests of ROBART I substantiated the psychologist's feeling that the system was indeed not easy to learn to use.

Exploratory Tests: Ease of Learning

An obvious way to measure ease of learning a system is to teach subjects how to use it and measure either the time required or the level of performance achieved. These both require that a particular learning method be available as part of the system. However, there was no learning method incorporated in the ROBART I system, so a "progressive" method of teaching was used. We feel the best kind of system is "exploring", requiring no teaching at all. Next would come self-instruction from the manual, and last, a human tutor. How much of the system the users could learn with each of these methods was taken as an indicator of its ease of learning.

METHOD

Subjects were first given a 15 minute demonstration of the system. Then they were given a list of basic functions to perform (e.g. select a color, draw a box, erase the screen and draw anything on it). They were asked to learn as much as they could with the given method, then demonstrate it to the experimenter. Then they were asked to proceed with the next method. An upper time limit was set for each method.

SUBJECTS

There were four experimental subjects, none color-blind, all able to type 40-60 wpm.

RESULTS

"Explore" Method: By the "play around, see what you can learn method", subjects could learn almost nothing. They were all able to select colors, but nothing else. It was thus clear that the system was definitely not self-explanatory.

"Read the Manual" Method: By using the manual, half the subjects could learn all the functions. Looking at the functions rather than the subjects, roughly 58% of the functions could be learned by all subjects. For example, all subjects could pick a color, draw a line, erase and reset the screen. However, only 50% of the the subjects could draw connected horizontal and vertical lines. Although there were only 4 subjects in this exploratory test, these numbers indicate that they could not understand ROBART I easily from the manual.

"Teacher" Method: All subjects were able to "understand" all functions when a teacher was involved, where the ability to "demonstrate the function immediately after it has been taught" constitutes understanding. However, later tests showed that even though they "understood", subjects quickly forget many of the functions.

Ease of Use Problems

To determine where subjects were having problems, and why (if possible) the learning session was followed by practice and performance sessions, during which subjects were asked to make various slides and to comment on their problems as they were working. The experimenter also observed which functions seemed to cause problems, when reference to the manual was made, and common user errors. Only the picture creation language was formally tested. In addition, questionnaires probed for users' subjective responses. A few of the detailed problems are described below to give a sense of the kind and variety of interface design problems.

SOME PROBLEMS

Forgetting GO: All subjects forgot the GO button. One subject was still forgetting it in another part of the experiment 3 1/2 hours later. They also inserted GO where it was not needed. This appears like a small problem, and indeed it is. However, such "small" problems can lead to total user frustration. For example, one subject, trying to draw a line, forgot GO. Since she had previously drawn a box, when she attempted to draw the line, a box appeared! Checking the position of the switches revealed that line, not box, was, correctly, in the ON position, but the computer still was drawing a box! (The new position of the switches had not been read and the previous setting was stored in the computer).

START: Subjects unnecessarily pressed START-GO when in continuous mode.

Setting the width of a continuous function: Immediately after the learning session, with the manual available for reference, some subjects were unable to set the width of a continuous function.

Refering to the manual: A number of functions required reference to the manual (shortly after they had been demonstrated correctly)! Among them were drawing continuous shapes and changing the length continuous shapes.

Forgetting SEGS: Users very frequently forgot to type SEGS.

Forgetting to "open": Users frequently forgot to open a file before drawing a picture. Since they sometimes decided that a picture was worth saving after it was drawn, this was unpleasant.

Overlay: It was not possible to incorporate one picture in another. This made it impossible to set up a template to be used in several pictures. Complete redrawing was required.

Making changes: It was not possible to make changes to redisplayed pictures.

USER'S SUBJECTIVE COMMENTS

Subjects generally found the system "fun", "colorful", "fascinating" etc., but also found many problems. The range and variety of problems in such a simple system was both startling and instructive. There were problems with the meaning of the functions in user terms (e.g."continuous lines were strange"), problems with the labelling of the switches, problems with the user procedures, problems with the expected result (e.g. I can't tell how large a circle will be), and problems with the physical hardware (e.g. "the box moves").

Here are a few comments about the interaction. Notice how prominently remembering comes up - and ROBART I was a very simple system! The first two comments are particularly telling. Even when subjects <u>understood</u> how to use the system, they found actually using it far from easy.

* It seemed so easy, but I kept making the same mistakes.
* (What was hard was) not doing things in the right sequence, not knowing what you missed, having to repeat and repeat.
* Combining switches (was hard). One switch would be easier.
* It is difficult to remember what to do, when
* Selecting shapes was harder than colors.
* I can look up circle, but it is hard to do when combined (i.e. circle, then box).
* You need a reminder to hit GO.

DESIGN OF ROBART II

The redesign of ROBART I had several purposes. The first was to improve its ease of use. However, it had also been decided to shift from the old hardware to an IBM 5100 desktop computer. The 5100 was required. Another goal was to keep the function constant so that two equivalent systems would then be available for behavioral testing.

Method

The redesign of the human interface was the responsibility of the psychologist. The computer scientist provided comment on ease of implementation and feasibility. Based on the psychologist's own intuition, observations, and behavioral tests she produced a preliminary redesign. The redesign was circulated for review and comment to ROBART I users. Some comments were then incorporated into a revised design and the process iterated.

Overview

Design of ROBART II involved a basic rethinking of the human interface, not merely "cosmetic" changes. The user interface for ROBART II is shown in Figure 4. Although not a major goal, some additional function was incorporated. Major changes were made to the hardware, the assignment of function to hardware, and the screen format. Changes to the interactive language for creating pictures and the language for storing and displaying pictures were substantial. The documentation was rewritten and an on-line help subsystem added.

The Redesign

ADDITIONAL FUNCTION

The following functions were added to ROBART II.

Explicit function: The derived functions in ROBART I (solid circle, open box, sketch line) were added as explicit functions in ROBART II.

Error Correction: Error correcting functions were added. One was an explicit UNDO function. Another was an explicit method for creating a colored background for text background to simplify correcting typing errors when using a colored text background.

Photoclear: A PHOTOCLEAR function, which removed everything but the drawing area from the screen was added to avoid photographing extraneous material.

Changing previously created pictures: With the new picture storage and display language it was always possible to save the picture on the screen. It was also possible to make changes to a redisplayed picture, to superimpose several pictures and save the result; to save intermediate stages of a picture, to use a picture as a template for several pictures (copy it into several files). None of these features were possible in the more difficult to use ROBART I language.

On-line help: An on-line help-function (REMINDER) was also added (see below).

HARDWARE AND ASSIGNMENT OF FUNCTION TO HARDWARE

The keyboard belonged to the IBM 5100. Function keys were assigned for image mixing, for erasing, and for picture storage and retrieval operations. The external switchbox for shape selection was replaced by a menu of icons on the screen.

SCREEN FORMAT

The screen format for ROBART II can be seen in Figure 4. The screen now included areas for selecting the shape, the WIDTH and ANGLE of continuous functions (not shown) and for optional REMINDER messages. The shape selection area contained icons of the shapes, as seen in Figure 5. The menu for picture storage functions was no longer displayed on the screen.

PICTURE CREATION LANGUAGE

Color selection: The color selection process (dip cursor into color) was retained. The color feedback was changed to a white rectangle surrounding the selected color.

Shape selection: Two changes in the method for selecting shapes were central to the redesign. The switches and GO buttons were replaced with icons on the screen, as mentioned. A second change was very important. The design used one icon per shape instead of several icons. These two changes made shape selection <u>consistent</u> with color selection (dip cursor in icon, press EXECUTE). Feedback for shape selection, like that for color, was a white rectangle around the shape selected.

<u>Creating discrete shapes:</u> Discrete shapes were still created by two points as in ROBART I, but the EXECUTE key on the 5100 replaced the START-GO and END-GO buttons.

<u>Creating continuous shapes:</u> Continuous shapes were created in a manner consistent with discrete shapes. In addition, the ROTATE/WIDTH switch was replaced by a menu of icons on the screen. This supplementary menu, which appeared only after a continuous shape had been chosen, permitted separate control of the width and angle of continuous shapes (a source of confusion in ROBART I).

STORAGE AND RETRIEVAL LANGUAGE

Two function keys called SAVE and DISPLAY were defined for storing and redisplaying pictures. To save a picture, the syntax was SAVE <n> EXECUTE, where n was the file number. The DISPLAY syntax was analogous. The ERASE key erased both the screen and a stored picture area in memory. The user did not have to remember to open or close a file. It was, furthermore, possible to superimpose pictures on the screen, and in memory, simply by displaying a second picture from the file without an intervening ERASE. Superimposed (and subsequently edited) pictures could be stored if desired.

DOCUMENTATION

A new manual was written for ROBART II. It was considerably shorter than the ROBART I manual.

ON-LINE TUTORIAL

An optional on-line tutorial/help component was added (REMINDER). This facility was invoked by a function key. With the tutorial/help function on, instructions were coupled to individual shape selections. Once a shape was selected for drawing, instructions on how to proceed with drawing that particular shape were shown in the REMINDER area. For example, once "circle" had been selected, the user was told to put the cursor at the center of the circle, press EXECUTE, put the cursor at any point on the circumference, and press EXECUTE again.

PRINCIPLES AND RATIONALE FOR ROBART II DESIGN

What were some of the principles underlying the design? Some of them were:

1. Minimize manual motion
2. Minimize visual alternations
3. Minimize the number of keystrokes. (More generally, minimize the number of user physical actions)
4. Minimize the amount of information on the screen ("clutter"),
5. Be consistent

6. Minimize what the user has to remember

In this part, we discuss how these principles were implemented, how they interrelate, and finally, how decisions involving conflicting principles or guidelines were resolved.

Some Principles and Related Design Decisions

<u>Minimize manual motion:</u> The use of icons on the screen decreased the back-and-forth motion of the user's hand for drawing pictures. In ROBART I, to draw a discrete shape, for example, the motion was: joystick, switches, GO, joystick, START-GO, END-GO. In ROBART II it was: joystick EXECUTE, joystick, EXECUTE.

<u>Minimize visual alternations:</u> The use of icons also decreased the number of different places the user had to look. With ROBART I, the sequence was: SCREEN (for color), switchbox (for shape), SCREEN (for selecting first point), switchbox (for entering first point), etc. For ROBART II, it was joystick to EXECUTE, etc.

<u>Minimize the number of keystrokes (generally, minimize user actions):</u> The use of icons removed the need to reset the previous shape and then press GO. The one shape per icon principle reduced the number of selection steps to one. Consequently, the number of steps to select a continuous line, for example, was reduced from four in ROBART I (undo, continuous up, line up, GO) to one in ROBART II (dip cursor in icon). In the file system, replacing the typing of SEGS, "o" (for open), etc. by a single key depression and a file number also decreased the number of user actions.

<u>Minimize the amount of information on the screen:</u> While the one shape per icon rule decreased the number of steps, it increased the amount of menu information on the screen. If an analogous rule had been applied in ROBART I, it would have increased the number of switches.

<u>Be consistent:</u> The decision to select the first point of continuous shapes (i.e. "lift" the paintbrush) by placing the cursor at the start, then pressing EXECUTE, was made on the basis of consistency. The syntax was now the same as that for selecting the first point of discrete shapes. Consistency also motivated the decision to require an explicit selection step for text, rather than having text always available. Note, however, that the first decision increased, rather than decreased, the amount of manual motion. Instead of keeping his or her hand on the joystick, for the sequence KNOB OFF, move cursor, KNOB ON, the user now had to alternate between joystick and EXECUTE on the keyboard. The second decision, too, has its disadvantages. With text always available, as in ROBART I, the user was not required to explicitly select it.

<u>Minimize the number of user actions to be remembered:</u> This is the key principle behind ease of learning. It motivated a number of design decisions. First, with icons, unlike switches, it was not necessary to <u>remember</u> to reset the switches. It was also not necessary to remember to press GO. The one shape per icon rule also made it unnecessary to remember that continuous line was CONTINUOUS and LINE. Adding the on-line

REMINDER function, coupled to each shape, reduced the need to refer to a manual. The user did not have to remember that the two points for circle were the center and a point on the circumference.

Some other principles require brief mention. The list is not complete.

* Frequently desired functions should be easily available (e.g. sketching line, erase).
* Feedback for user actions should be available - and visible (e.g. feedback box).
* Functions should relate to user needs, not program requirements (e.g. users should not be required to open a file).
* Vocabulary should be familiar to the user (e.g. SEGS had meaning to a programmer, not a user).
* Documentation and tutorials should be accessible when needed (e.g. REMINDER).
* It should be possible to correct errors (e.g. UNDO).
* Avoid unnecessary clutter (e.g. The supplementary ROTATE/WIDTH icons were only available when needed).
* What you see is (should be) what you get (e.g. the user should not see the LINE switch on when the computer is reading BOX). This principle is commonly known as WYSIWYG.

How are the Principles Related

Decreasing manual motion also, in this case, decreased visual alternations. Replacing the switchbox by icons decreased the amount of gross manual action. The one shape per icon principle decreased the number of steps and the amount of fine manual action. The principle "be consistent" clearly decreases what the user has to remember. Instead of several syntactic "patterns" to remember, only one pattern need be remembered.

However, some of the principles conflict. Regarding text selection, "reduce the number of actions" conflicted with "be consistent". In the paintbrush lifting problem, "minimize manual motion" also conflicted with "be consistent". In both cases the decision was made in favor of "be consistent". In the one shape per icon rule, "reduce the number of actions" conflicted with "minimize the amount of information on the screen". Here however, the decision favored "reduce the number of actions". There was clearly an implicit priority ordering of principles, even though such ordering does not in general exist in published lists of guidelines and principles.

What Prompted the Particular Priority Ordering of the Principles

Where guidelines conflict, a prioritization cannot be avoided. The choices made for ROBART do not imply a universal priority ordering of guidelines independent of problem context. The choices were based on: the particular kinds of users involved (computer naive), the particular facet of ease-of-use emphasized (ease of learning), and a personal judgement about relative sizes of the effects (how bad would the clutter on the screen be, compared to the difficulty of remembering extra steps).

In the context of computer naive subjects learning a system, it was felt
that decreasing memory load was paramount. Thus although the REMINDER
option increased the information on the screen, it was judged to be
vital. The amount of clutter did not seriously hamper the users ability
to perform his tasks (and REMINDER could always be turned off). These
decisions were based on judgement regarding tradeoffs, not on any
detailed cost-benefit analysis. In principle, one can run experiments to
determine the "cost" (in time, errors, user frustration) of a particular
amount of clutter on a screen, for example, and compare it to the cost of
extra steps. For the most part, such experiments have not been done.
For a discussion of some tradeoff analysis, see (5).

BEHAVIORAL COMPARISON OF ROBART I AND ROBART II

The results of behavioral tests of ROBART I and of ROBART II (6) are
summarized here. Ten office workers learned both versions of ROBART,
primarily from the manual and other tutorial materials. The experimenter
supplemented the self-teaching when absolutely necessary. A maximum of 2
hours was allotted to the self-teaching so that the entire sequence of
learn-test could be completed in one day per subject. To structure the
learning process, subjects were given a list of simple tasks to perform
(e.g. draw a green line). Then were then given an immediate memory test.
Manuals were removed and they were asked to demonstrate the same tasks
using the same list. A maximum time per item (2 minutes) was set to
preclude excessive trial and error). Success or failure on each item was
noted.

Results - overall learning: While learning time was not a major focus of
the experiment, the relative time required to learn the two systems is
interesting. For ROBART I, the average was 76 minutes. For ROBART II, it
was 51 minutes. This is roughly a 50% difference. These are not total
times required for self teaching, since a maximum time was set; some
subjects did not complete the entire learning process; and some required
experimenter help. Since the methods were consistent and there was no
obvious tendency to "give up and ask for help" sooner in ROBART II than
in ROBART I, the comparison is sensible. Nine of the ten subjects
learned ROBART II faster than ROBART I. (Nine out of ten is statistically
significant with a sign test, $p<.05$, one- tailed).

Results - errors and subjective opinions: Subjects also made fewer
errors in ROBART II than ROBART I (an average of 6.4 and 8.6, respectively, out of a maximum of 57). Nine of the ten also made fewer errors with
ROBART II than ROBART I. All subjects, when questioned, said that they
found the "SCREEN ROBART" easier to learn and remember than the "BOX
ROBART", although one surprisingly preferred the latter. (She felt more
"in control").

Results - shape selection: In general, shape selection was easier in
ROBART II than in ROBART I. There was also a wide difference, by shape,
in the number of subjects unable to select the shape in ROBART I. (In
general, the more switches required, the more subjects had trouble with
the shape, although there were other factors involved). The differences
between shapes tended to disappear in ROBART II. Selecting a line was not
difficult in either system, for example (LINE required). However,

selecting circle was difficult for 8 of the 10 subjects in ROBART I, but for none in ROBART II. (LINE and BOX was required in ROBART I). Selecting continuous shapes in ROBART I was, in general, harder than selecting discrete shapes, while there was no apparent difference in ROBART II. The fact that the function was the same in both cases, but the interface design was different, is important. If only ROBART I existed, it would not be possible to tell whether the increased difficulty of the continuous functions was attributable to the interface design or to some difficulty inherent in the function itself.

DISCUSSION

This section contains some subjective comments on the redesign.

Missing function vs interface redesign: One method of evaluating an interface is to distribute it to potential users and ask for their comments, which frequently take the form of comments on missing function. We found in the case of ROBART that identifying missing function was relatively easy. Identifying problems with the interface design was not as easy. Developing a coherent interface design to solve those problems was considerably more difficult.

Increasing function implies decreasing ease of use: It is sometimes felt that "the more function, the harder to use". The two versions of ROBART are a clear counterexample. ROBART II had both more function and was easier to use. An underlying, sometimes forgotten assumption in the "more function, therefore harder" statement is "all else being equal". In the two ROBART systems, the interface design was NOT equal.

Design reviews: A procedure sometimes used to improve ease of use is a design review (10). In redesigning ROBART we used an informal "design review" (comments by various users of the early system). Comments of various reviewers were sometimes contradictory. Furthermore, while most reviewers had a great deal to say, the coverage of each one, individually, was sparse (some reviewers commented on some points, some on others). The process of design review is worth considerable study in its own right.

User perception of the source of usability problems: We noted a tendency on the part of subjects to blame the manual, rather than the interface design, for their problems. They treated the equipment as unchangeable, but realized that documentation could be good or bad. However, the problems that they attributed to the manual were frequently inherent in the interface design. While a good manual can mitigate problems, it can not solve them.

Components of the user interface: One of the most important factors in redesigning ROBART was that we thought of the user interface in a larger sense than just hardware and code. Documentation and training were considered an integral part of the System. Design decisions about more traditional parts of the interface, such as the user language, were made with regard to how these components could be integrated. (For example, we rejected one possible kind of command language - e.g. type "p" (for point), then type "c" (for circle) because reminders for each shape could not be provided with the first point).

SUMMARY

This paper describes and contrasts two versions of an interactive graphics system. The first version was designed without major attention to ease of use. Users unfamiliar with computers found the first system "fun", but difficult and frustrating to use. A number of detailed causes for their problems are identified. The second version was designed with ease of use as a major goal. Some specific principles of human factors design are described and related to the redesign, and to each other. Behavioral experiments showed that there were measurable differences in the ease of learning the two systems.

ACKNOWLEDGEMENTS

The original design of ROBART was due to R. Williams. The following people contributed to the design and/or development of ROBART I or ROBART II: M. Breternitz (ITA, Sao Paulo, Brazil), A. Fan (Mills College), G.M. Giddings, F.P. Palermo, D. Raimondi, R.M. Revelle, D. Silberberg (MIT), D. L. Weller.

REFERENCES

1. Card, S. K., Moran, T. P. and Newell, A., The Psychology of Human-Computer Interaction. Hillsdale, N. J.: Lawrence Erlbaum Associates, 1983.
2. Engel, S.E. and Granda, R.E. Guidelines for Man/Display Interface, Technical Report TR 00.2720, Poughkeepsie, New York: IBM, December, 1975.
3. Langdon, G.G. Jr., Reisner, P. and Silberberg, D., ROBART 2: A Stand-alone Graphics Terminal System for Color Slides, Technical Report RJ2871, San Jose, California: IBM, July 17, 1980.
4. Moran, T. P. (ed.), Special Issue: The Psychology of Human-Computer Interaction, ACM Computing Surveys, March, 1981.
5. Norman, D. A., "Design Principles for Human-Computer Interaction", in Proceedings of Human Factors in Computer Systems Conference, Boston, Dec 12-15, 1983.
6. Reisner, P., "Formal Grammar and Human Factors Design of an Interactive Graphics System", IEEE Transactions on Software Engineering, vol. SE-7, No.2, March, 1981.
7. Reisner, P., "Analytic Tools for Human Factors of Software" Research Report RJ 3808, IBM, San Jose, CA, March 3, 1983, also in Lecture Notes in Computer Science: Enduser Systems and Their Human Factors (Ed. Blaser, A. and Zoeppritz, M.), Springer-Verlag, Berlin, 1983.
8. Shneiderman, B., Software Psychology, Winthrop Publishers: Cambridge, Mass., 1980.
9. Smith, S. L. and Aucella, A. F., "Design Guidelines for the User Interface to Computer-Based Information Systems" MTR-8857, Mitre Corporation, Bedford, Massachusetts, March, 1983.
10. Weinberg, G. M. and Freedman, D. P., "Reviews, Walkthroughs and Inspections, IEEE Transactions on Software Engineering, vol.SE-10, No.1, Jan. 1984.

LOCATION OF ILLUSTRATIONS

Figure 1:   after the paragraph labelled "TV monitor display" on page 171.

Figure 2:   after the paragraph labelled "Switchbox" on page 171.

Figure 3:   after the first paragraph on page 172.

Figure 4:   after the last paragraph on page 176.

Figure 5:   after the section labelled "SCREEN FORMAT" on page 177.

Table 1:   after the paragraph labelled "Selecting shapes" on page 172.

Figure 1. ROBART I user interface

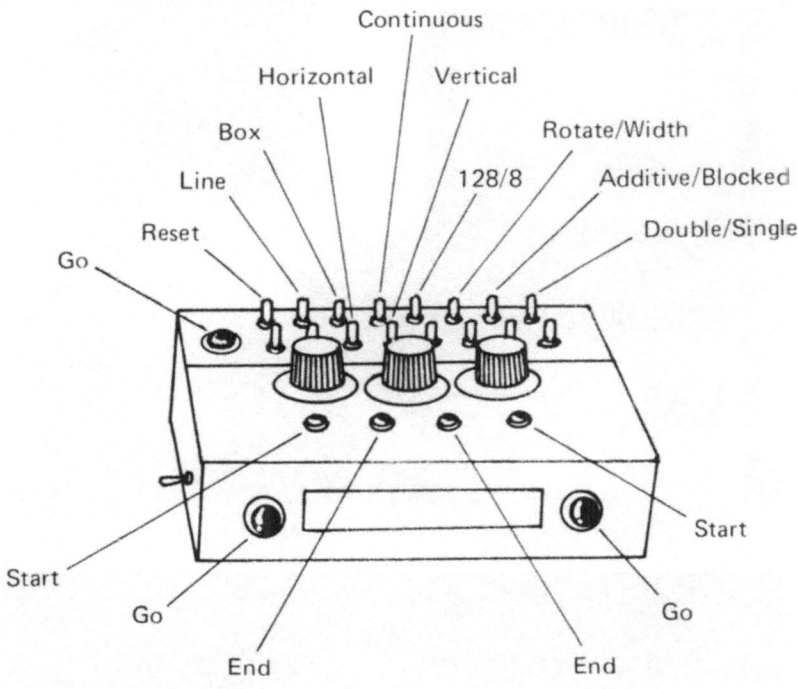

Figure 2. ROBART I switchbox

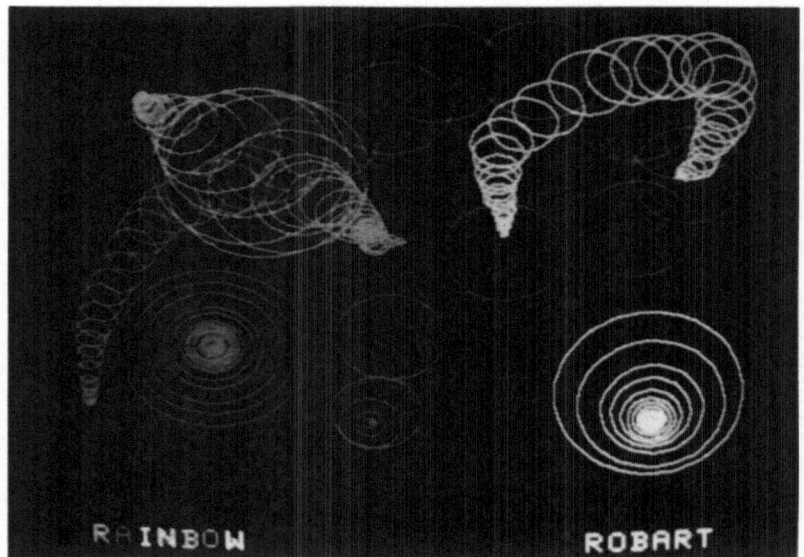
Figure 3. An example of sketching of continuous circles

Figure 4. ROBART II user interface

Figure 5. ROBART II paintbox and icons

Table 1: Switch settings for shape selection in ROBART 1.

shape selection	switch setting
line	LINE
horizontal line	HORIZONTAL
vertical line	VERTICAL
rectangle	BOX
circle	LINE and BOX
continuous line	CONTINUOUS and LINE
continuous rect.	CONTINUOUS and BOX
continuous circle	CONTINUOUS and LINE and BOX
text	No switch was required

Toward the Standardization of Input Peripherals in the Urbanistic Design Process and Person-Machine Interaction

Mauro Salvemini*
Facolta' di Ingegneria
Universita' dell' Aquila
67100 L'Aquila, Italy

ABSTRACT

Input peripherals are the first medium of communication between a person and a computer. In computer graphics in particular they are essential. This paper will focus on the effectiveness of the relationship between input devices and the physical ,i.e. anatomical characteristics of the user .Since various standards are still being developed for computer graphics work stations,it is important to have qualified information for making decisions about input peripherals.

The paper is based on several years' experience in the field of computer graphics applied to urbanistic design and the communication of numerical and iconic information for decision making to non-specialized users. The conclusions of this paper and the design idea of the WHOLE STATION for the interactive computer graphics spring from direct experiments conducted on professionals in urbanistics and graduate students of design courses. The conclusions are part of a major project which is supported by the C.N.R. (Consiglio Nazionale delle Ricerche , in Italy) whose effort is to define the hardware and software characteristics of an interactive work-station for design purposes in the engineering and architectural field.

It is paper's main goal to analyze the relationship between the human being and the interactive input devices for computer graphics. Three categories of typical users have been selected and examined in terms of impact with input peripherals.

(*) He is in charge of the Laboratorio di Computer Grafica of the Istituto di Architettura ed Urbanistica - L'Aquila University (I) and is adjunct assistant professor in the School of Architecture of R P I ,(N.Y.,USA).

INPUT PERIPHERALS AND COMPUTER SYSTEMS

When considering the requirements of input devices and their use , the following parameters have to be taken into account :
1- to clean the data entry;
2- facilitation of interaction with the computer;
3- decrease or the elimination of noise and surplus data entry;
4- to make the graphic software more powerful;
5- to avoid preprocessing input drawings.

Cleaning the data entry: this can be measured by examining both the quantity and quality of input and/or interaction errors performed by the user.
A typical reason why these problems arise is that the wrong peripheral device is used for data input,e.g.,to digitize some contour lines it is more convenient to use a cursor digitizer instead of a stylus digitizer.Use of the former peripheral device would increase the capability of the operator to digitize the input and therefore reduce errors significantly.

The facilitation of the input devices' interaction with the computer : since the beginning of the computer graphics ,when the TX-2 computer and the sketchpad were fixed at MIT , the aim was to make interaction with the computer easier.Not all peripherals facilitate in the same way interaction between the person and the computer. The choice of the peripheral has to be shaped to the host computer system and has to match the needs of the user .It is not always true that a device which is easy to use will perform the necessary work.

The decrease or elimination of both noise and surplus data entry : the problem of handling the high quality of data necessary for computer graphics has been almost overcome by the use of large-core computers and large mass storage capabilities although in small computers, and generally speaking for computation economy, the minimization of data to be processed is an essential aim. The parameter related to this problem can be measured by the time saved in data-processing inputting. The peripheral device must be shaped for the improvement of this saving in time and memory so that only essential data are input.

To make graphic software more powerful: the power of standard software is substantially upgraded by the input and interactive devices most appropriate to it.

To avoid the preprocessing of input drawings: very often additional costs and technical gaps arise in the preprocessing of the inputs which are to be processed by input peripheral devices. Problems will arise about size ,shape ,colors,etc..To calibrate the choice of input device ,the input supports to be used (maps,human drawings,machine drawings,etc.),and the input operations which have to be performed ,all have to be known in advance.

INPUT PERIPHERALS AND USER

The table shows the physical parts of the user involved in the use of each input device and the part of the computer system and/or working station to which the user has to pay attention during the use of the input peripheral.

The table shows the devices in ascending order in terms of interaction. The 12 of the 13 devices is the 3D digitizer, followed by the automatic scanner which does not involve the user in terms of inputs and can be used in robot applications. Each peripheral in the table has explanatory notes.

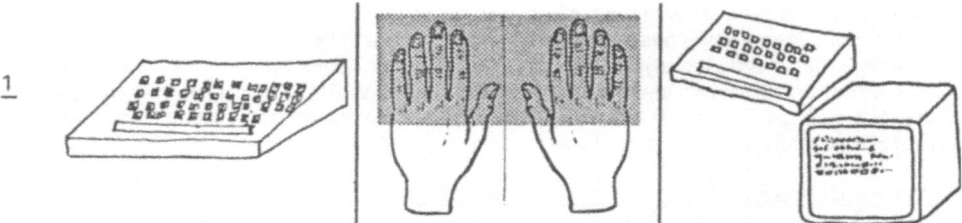

1

The keyboard is the ancestral tool for data entry, the fingers of both hands are involved in its use. In the interaction process the user has to pay attention simultaneously to the CRT or printer and to the keyboard especially if he does not have skills in typewritting.

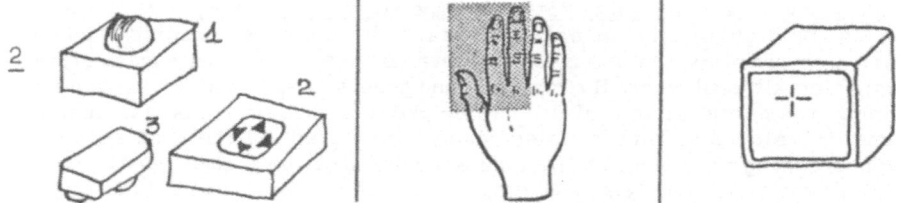

2

To use the trackball(1) the paddle(2) and the mouse(3) only the palm of the hand has to be employed for gross adjustments and/or two three fingers for fine adjustments. The user does not pay attention to the input device but must follow on the CRT the pointer which is monitoring the peripheral's movement.

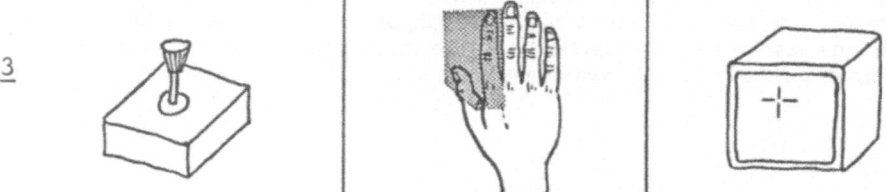

3

To operate the joysticks, depeding on their degrees of spatial freedom (1,2 or 3), involves 2 or 3 fingers of one hand while the attention of the user is devoted to the display.

 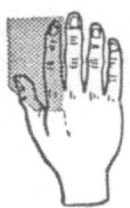 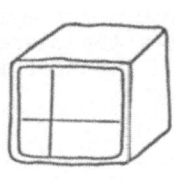

An unique type of joystick can be operated by only two fingers of one hand. It allows very accurate pointing through two displayed crossing lines.

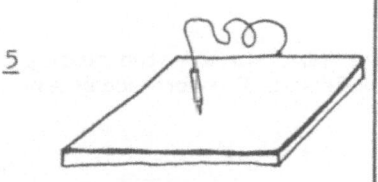 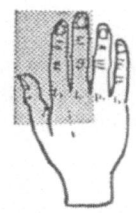 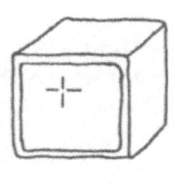

The digitizer is becoming a widely-used device for menu selection and for inputting operations. Equipped with a stylus (useful to operate on menus) it is used by only one hand. Attention must be focussed also on the display in order to control the input operations.

 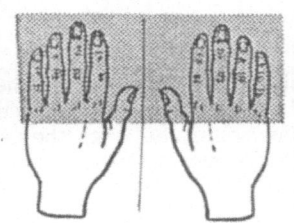 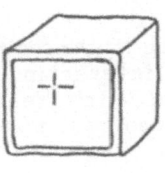

The use of the cross reference cursor for digitizing generally requires the operator to use two hands in order to avoid problems from accident and to input through the key data and commands to the system.
Interaction with the output of the system is performed simply by the operator's paying attention to the display.

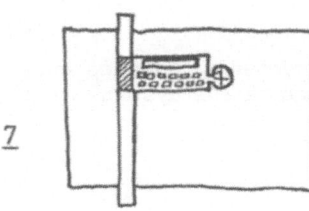 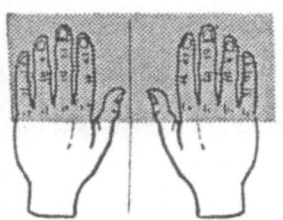 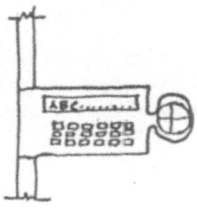

In activities where the operator's attention must be focussed continually on the digitalization area it is useful to use a cursor with incorporated display. This allows the interaction with the system to be confined to the same small area where the input is performed. Generally two hands are required to perform this operation.

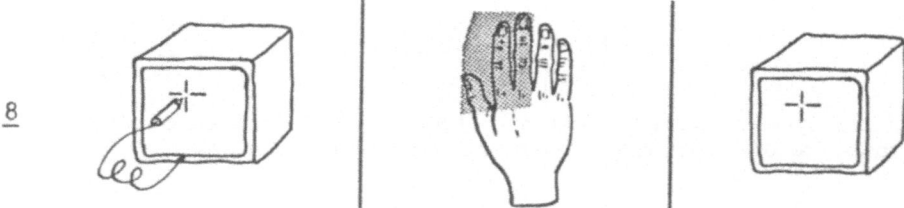

8

The light pen is operated by only one hand on the same surface (the display screen) where the output takes place. The operation is as well understood by any draftsman as using pencil on paper.

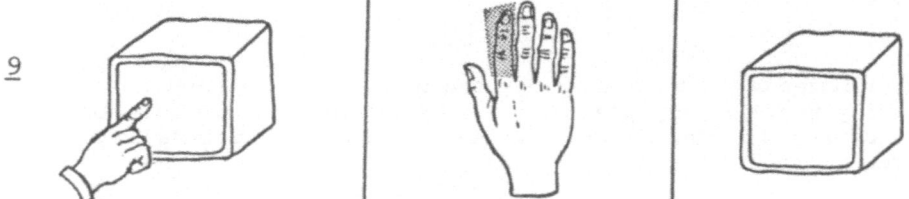

9

In the touch sensitive panel only one finger of one hand is used.
The interaction takes place on the same surface where the output is shown without the presence of any medium between the user and the device. The gesture is used by the operator to communicate with the machine. The precision is sacrificed.

10

The interaction between person and machine can be performed by inputting voice and eventually getting the voice output from the machine. The system is not widely used for computer graphics but some workstations use it.

Advanced projects are making the livable 3D space as a 3D digitizer able to monitor the movements of the human body and undersatnding human gestures. In this case the input device will match with the 3D space, there is no physical filtering between man and machine.

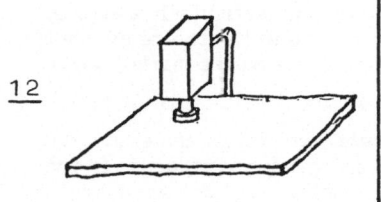

There is no interaction between person and machine in the automatic digitizing through scanners, television camera, laser scanners, etc.. The device is self operating and the user will be called to operate on the image or data in the processing.

USERS IN CREATIVE ENVIRONMENT

The users analyzed have been divided into three categories :
- artists and designers;
- technical designers and draftspersons;
- non specialized users;

Artists and designers are those people who use computer graphics to produce images and forms for volatile support (colour monitors , etc.) and physical support paper , mylar , etc.. These users have particular problems in using the present day tools of computer graphics input peripherals , which can be summarized in the problem of space inconsistence and in the lack of personalized tools.

The space inconsistence is the problem deriving from the non-use of electronic-sheet. Though the electronic pencil is widely used , the support medium on which the input operation is performed is not the same medium on which the processed information are displayed. Design action and display are not therefore performed on the same medium as they were thousands of years ago. And this means that the user' eyes go back and forth from the input peripheral to the output peripheral and viceversa. This generally does not happen during normal design activity.

The personalized tool or medium is the typical skill of whom is operating in a creative environment. Each artist and designer likes to decide about the tool to use so he can have a completely free relationship with his pen, pencil, brush etc.. At the moment the input peripherals on the other hand require to the user a large amount of adjustment. As these users have very few ideas about the ergonomy of the work station, they generally become easy victims of the work station components which have to be mobile to follow the requirements of the user in terms of space architecture.

The technical designers and draftspersons are the best oriented for using input peripherals in interactive workstations. In this group the problems are mostly related to fatigue in using input devices and involve recurrent errors which are often difficult to detect and depending from ergonomy.

The non-specialized users are mostly interested in learning quikly and in the play element of interaction operations. Great popularity of iconics in office workstations is an example of this characteristic. These users are particularly aware of the ergonomics of workstations, but they are not discerning in the choice of input peripherals and often prefer the simplest devices available on the market which resemble previous less complicated equipment.

In examining input equipment three specific parameters were taken and evaluated qualitatively through experiments on professionals and graduate students in the design courses. These parameters are : intrinsic complexity of the equipment, how far the human body was involved directly in input operations and the possibility of checking graphic output during input operations. The following graphs represent these three parameters in function of twelve input devices studied.

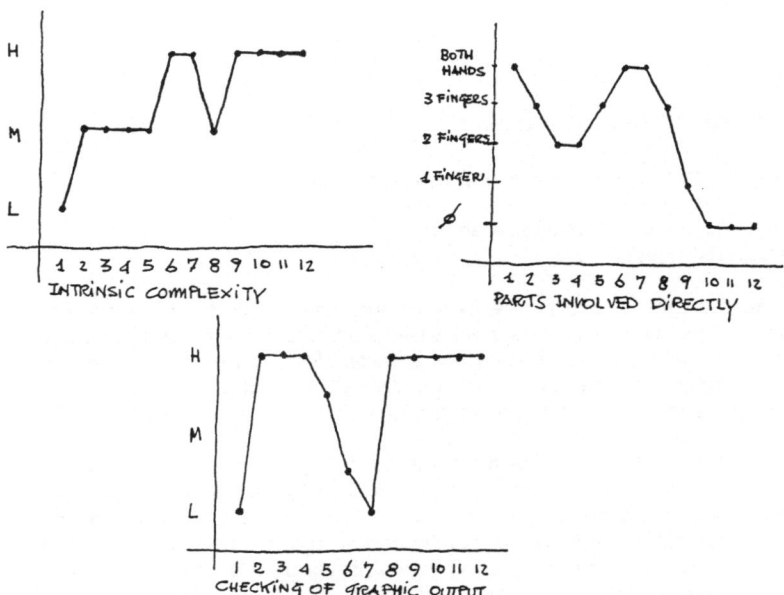

The complexity of the equipment increases noticeably from the keyboard onwards, the cursor present slight complication , light pen and touch panel are particularly easy in terms of intrinsic complexity.
The above illustration of each input device showes clearly how far the human body is directly involved in the use of each peripheral.In this examen only parts which directly touch the equipment were considered.

Most input peripherals allow graphic output to be checked during digitalization which means that there is the tendency for the operator to avoid concentrating on input alone. This is typical for the use of pen device on digitize tablet which is highly interactive in the menu selection and is less interactive in pure digitalization operation. The cursor behaves in the same way.

Three diagrams show the extent to which the three group of users accept and became familiar with input peripherals.
There are strong differences in the behavior of three groups : technical oprators prefer the peripherals where large parts of human body is involved expecially the hands even though they have no immediate control of the output.

The non-specialized users prefer equipment with low technological content involving the widest use of human body (both hands). They prefer the 3D digitize environment , the touch panel and the video digitizer since they are the most simple to operate. Since these tendency is easly to forecast how tremendous will be the impact of these peripherals on the next years house and personal shelter environment.

The artists and designers are quite uninterested in input peripherals which are too simple and immediate at least from the user's point of view. The peripherals they prefer are mostly those which resemble in function and form the instrument in common use such as pen , pencil , brush , etc. They particularly appreciate the video digitizer since it supplies the canvas on which they can display the artistic skills.

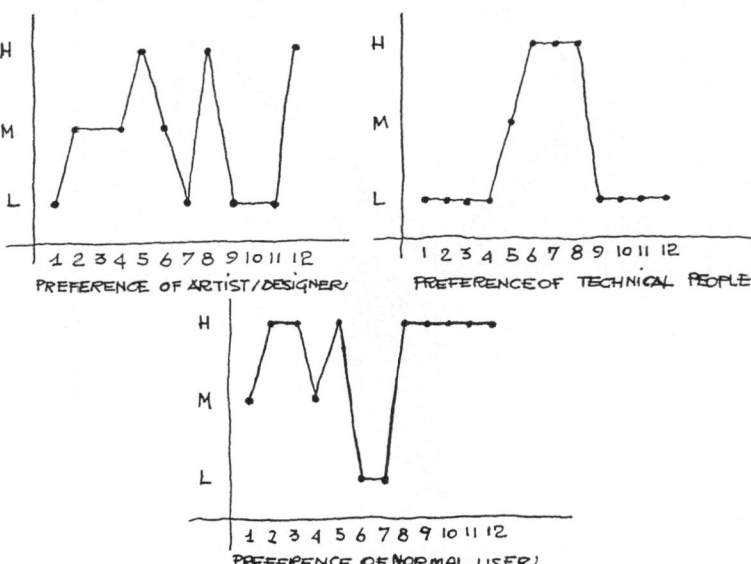

THE WHOLE-STATION

In different ways the work stations for computer graphics from the qualitative and quantitative point of view, disturb communication between the source (computer or person) and the recipient (person or computer) regarding the filter of operations and sense (see figure).

The whole station should satisfy the following requirements :
- the spatial cosistence between input and output peripheral (electronic pencil versus electronic sheet and viceversa);
- immediate and visual compatibility between input and output;

- personalization of the input tool ;

- naturalness in the user/machine approach and use.

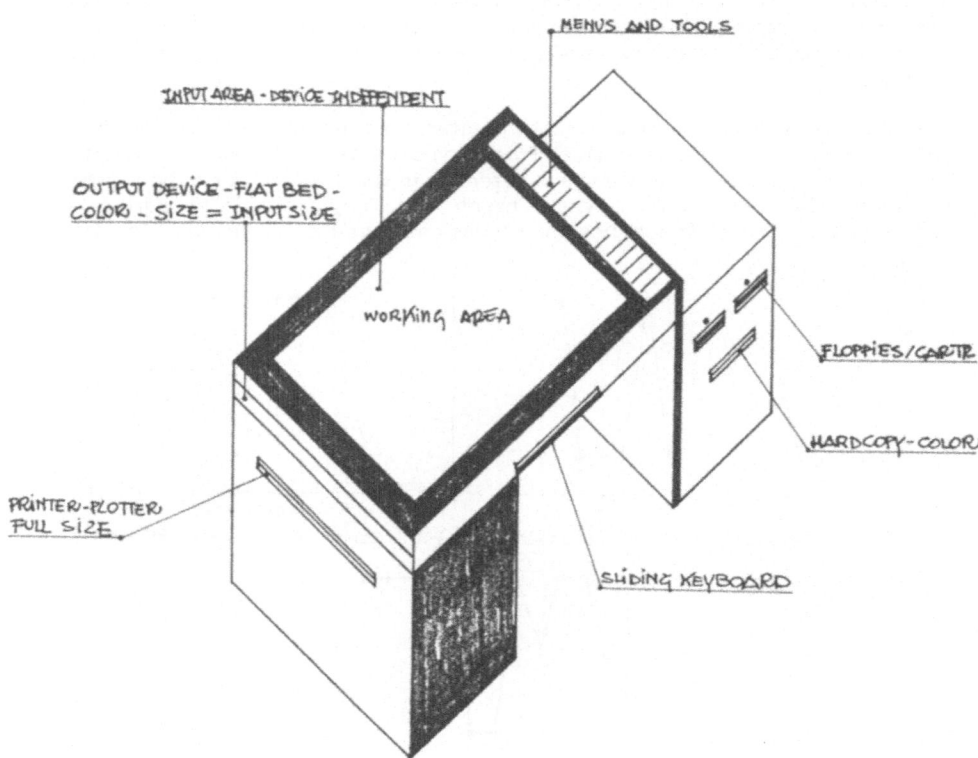

THE WHOLE STATION

The whole station can be designed as in given figure, the flat operational plane is simultaneously the input and the output device as the drafting table.The user is operating on the input device , drafting on the input surface and using the normal drafting tools. He can call specific functions from a design container on ore side of the table .

On the bottom of the input device , which is the same size of as a drafting table , there is the output device which is a flat bed colour monitor of the same dimensions and the same nominal resolution of the top of the input plane. A sliding keyboard helps to perform non-iconic input operations.The hard copy devices lie on the lowest part of the station and allow outputs to be obtained on different media and in different sizes.

The project was supported by the Italian C.N.R. (Consiglio Nazionale delle Ricerche) under contract N.82.01851.07 and carried out at the Laboratorio di Computer Grafica - Istituto di Architettura ed Urbanistica - Universita' L'Aquila -Italy.

REFERENCES

Munari, B. - Design e comunicazione visiva - Editori Laterza , Bari (i), 1976 , pp.80-90

Salvemini ,M - Computer grafica - Introduzione alle tecniche automatiche di rappresentazione - Gruppo Editoriale Jackson , Milano (i) dicembre 1982

Schmandt ,C. - Spatial input/display correspondence in a stereoscopic computer graphic work station - Computer Graphics Vol.17 N.3 - SIGGRAPH '83 Confrence proc.

Swezey W.R and Davis E.g. - A case study of human factors guidelines in computer graphics - IEEE Computer Graphics and Applications , Vol.3 N.8 (ISSN0272-1716),pp.21,30

Weinzapfel G. - Mapping by yourself - A multimedia paradigm for computer based geographics - Interactive techniques in computer aided design , ACM Italian Chapter ,Bologna (i) 1978 (78ch1289-8c) ,pp.211,215

User Interface Management System with Geometric Modeling Capability: A CAD System's Framework

Tapio Takala
Laboratory of Information Processing Science
Helsinki University of Technology
SF-02150 Espoo 15, Finland

ABSTRACT

The interactive construction and design (CAD) of geometric models is considered. It is found that the user interface manager (UIMS) in such situations could and should include a geometric or even more general modeler, besides its graphics interaction capability. The main task of UIMS is the management of models - how to update them and to operate different tool algorithms on them. A testbed environment (AGX) is programmed to meet these requirements, and used for practical application experiments.

INTRODUCTION

Today the generation of high quality images based on a geometric model is quite well understood. There are many experimental systems [1-5], where a model can be visualized in different ways: as a wire frame, line figure with hidden lines removed, a colored raster image, or a shaded picture with illumination taking account to reflection and transparency of materials.

Standardization of graphics program packages, beginning some ten years ago and culminating at an international standard [6-9], based on the assumption that modeling and drawing (viewing) should be separated. Then the output pipeline, with graphical primitives (drawing operations) and windowing, was well defined.

Problems, however, arose on the input side. The proposed input primitives were soon found to be much too primitive, and to have no direct correspondence with the output primitive functions [10]. Also it was realized that input actions often refer to the existing picture on the screen (the 'pick' device), which of course then has to be stored. This data structure, called segment storage, is essentially a model of the picture.

In the development of standard graphics, portability and device independency were the main criteria, but the user-friendliness was sacrified. In fact, however, ergonomy has to be very device dependent! For example, an application may use a tablet 'locator' for digitizing drawings. If it is replaced with the logically similar mouse device in another system, the task becomes very unprecise, or even impossible.

This discrepancy lead to a new concept called User Interface Management System (UIMS), well surveyed in [11]. The general idea of UIMS is to encapsulate computer's communication with the user into a module. This is done either by combining input primitives to higher level functions callable by the application ("internal control"), or by modularizing the application to subprograms, each executable by just one user's command action ("external control").

In a recent conference [12] it was also pointed out that the UIMS will not be interfaced to a standard graphics system, but it rather will include graphics as a part of it. The tradeoff between device dependency and portability can be optimized, if logical input devices are not statically implemented with particular physical devices, but their association is controllable by the UIMS.

Interesting aspect of a UIMS is its communication with applications. In a typical implementation of "mainstream" standard graphics [13], both UIMS and the application are linked into a single program, where control and other data are flowing through procedure calls. A more flexible variation is an operating-system-like structure, where UIMS and application (or possibly many in parallel) reside in separate processes, resulting in a "windowing" system. In such a system the user can communicate with multiple applications, each having its own window on the screen [13,14]. Parallel processes communicate via messages, which can be interrupt signals and/or shared data structures. As the ultimate case of parallelism, UIMS has its own workstation processor separated from the applications.

The author's opinion is that most effective construction of geometric (and other) models will be facilitated, if the UIMS contains a modeler in it [15]. Then the common data structure shared by UIMS and applications would be the model itself, and the "modeler" is just a collection of routines to manipulate it. In fact, a potential geometric modeler already exists in the segment storage of graphics systems, which could be used after minor modifications [16]. However, an even more general modeler might be more useful, as will be explained in the next chapter.

DESIGNING A MODEL

Perhaps the simplest way to design is to combine objects from a predefined collection of building blocks. This "bottom-up" approach closely corresponds to that how an object may be constructed or assembled. For example a house may be designed by combining factory-made building elements. In geometric modeling this is reflected most purely in the Constructive Solid Geometry (CSG) methodology [17], where every solid object is defined as a logical combination (binary tree with set operations) of primitive objects. In the original form of CSG, the primitives are half-spaces defined by a mathematical inequality.

The results of bottom-up design, however, are not always very pleasing, as can regrettably often be seen in modern city architecture. The reasons for this are two-fold: First, the set of primitive parts may be too restrictive. As an example from CSG, even a very simple object may require cumbersome constructions (Fig.1), if the individual operations do not correspond to the real manufacturing operations of the object. Many kinds of objects may even be impossible to construct this way.

The second reason is that the result as a whole (its "gestalt") cannot be seen before the object is fully constructed. This makes the design process very difficult in many cases, because the result can only be imagined by the designer.

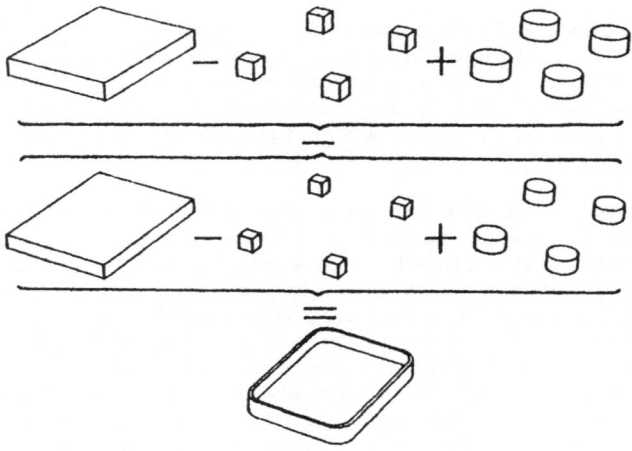

Fig.1: CSG definition of an ashtray.

Top-down design

What actually is done in the designer's mind and imagination, is a "top-down" decomposition process. The first step of design is usually a fuzzy sketch, which will later be detailed and decomposed. In a good CAD system, this phase of design should also be supported. The need of computer support to top-down approach is realized as well in architecture [18] and VLSI electronic design [19], as in programming methodology.

The key idea in top-down design is that function precedes form - structure precedes details. In highly regular application areas, like VLSI design, this means that once the required function is defined, then the geometric results can be found automatically, either algorithmically or by using expert systems [19]. In other areas this conversion from function to form still needs human intervention, but it seems that very widely applicable concepts, like metamodels or "Pai-numbers" [20], could help a lot in the future.

A special case of exception in this key principle is artistic design, where the form of an object also is part of its (aesthetic) function.

From the CAD system's point of view, top-down design means that the object is at the beginning not defined by geometric primitives, but with very different terms. The initial design concept may be for example a mathematical formula, a free-hand graphical sketch, or even a couple of textual sentences. The system should be able to cope with all these types of data, besides the representation of the full results at the end of design.

What is a model?

Design is, by definition, formation of a model of an object. A "model" is any entity showing the same properties as the (real or imagined) entity to be modeled. We may define that a model is just a collection of properties, or attributes. Any attributes that either are explicitly included to the model (defined by the designer), or can be derived or inferred from them, are attributes of the model.

As can be shown [21], the set of all attributes defines a topology on the set of all possible entities, and the design process consists of a convergent sequence of elements in this topological space. These elements are the metamodels. The more attributes there are defined, the smaller becomes the set of entities satisfying these attributes. Once all the relevant attributes of the model are known, the design process is finished, and a complete model results.

It is possible that only a subset of all relevant attributes is defined. Then the (meta)model represents a whole family of objects, which have these attributes in common. The missing, undefined attributes serve as parameters for selecting particular members of the family. For example, we may first define a family of otherwise similar bolts, but with variable length. The designer can then choose the right one by this length parameter. However, he may also want to first define the length, and then choose a particular bolt type. In such a case the set of all bolts of that length form another family.

As another example of partially finished designs, three different approaches at the goal "table and chair" are shown in figure 2. The first (drawn by a 7-years old) is most fuzzy. However this iconic representation shows some relevant attributes: the table is about round with four legs, the chair has straight legs and a lean. The second example is a (professional's) drawing with details, showing construction aspects of the chair. The third, although with most realistic representation (real objects in an exhibition), shows only schematic functional properties of the furniture.

No one of the above designs is complete. Despite of their different representations (simple sketch, precise drawing, real object), they all require some additional attributes to be defined.

We conclude that a modeling system should be capable of storing and managing diverse representations of objects, with manyfold properties that can be changed and refined by the designer. No designer's information should be discarded by the system, regardless of the order or time it is given. Instead, the history how an object was designed, is extremely valuable when the design is revised, and should be also modeled by the system.

SYSTEM STRUCTURE

The user communicates with the model by adding new information, displaying it, referring to its contents, changing some attributes and evaluating others - shortly: by editing it.

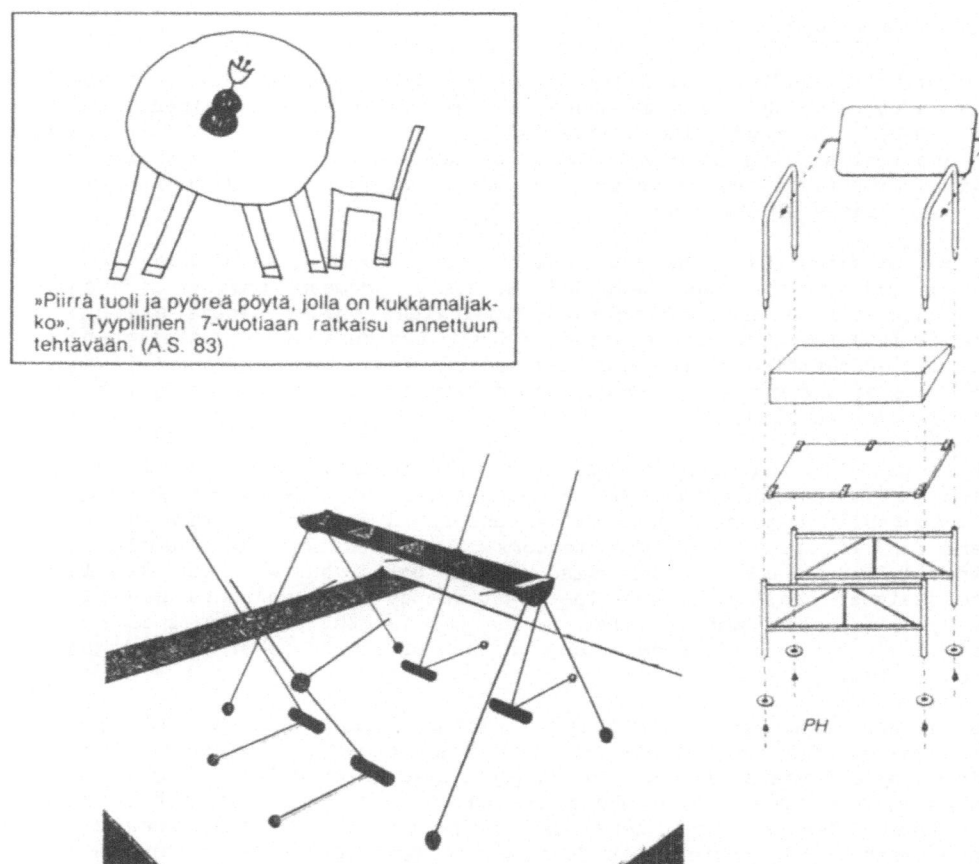

Fig.2: Three different designs of a chair (from [25]).

The model consists of a set of attributes, which are any partial aspects of the modeled object. Actually these attributes are also models themselves, which may in turn be decomposable into a set of simpler attributes. Thus the model is a hierarchy where each subpart is individually manipulatable. The parts may be distinct properties of the model, or perhaps alternative representations of the same aspect, like there are in some advanced rendering systems [2,22].

Because most important attributes of the model are either those given by the user or those directly shown to the user (most effectively a graphical picture), it is evident that the model should reside within UIMS, most near the user. UIMS should be a modeler which is general enough to manage any kind of data that the user wants.

On the other hand, in order to be portable and expandable, the UIMS should not contain much of the specialized application functions as an integral part. Rather the application functions should be independent tool programs callable by the modeler. So there should exist an agreed interface format for data transfer between UIMS modeler and the application tools. This brings us to the schematic structure of figure 3, which is well suited for present day distributed computing.

Compared to a standard graphics system, the structure has some similarities: the geometric model of the object displayed to the user corresponds to the segment storage, and the model structure containing the history of input and output (an "audit trail") corresponds to the metafile. The difference is that in a UIMS both data structures are fully editable.

Manipulation operations on the model are two-fold: either performed by the user (editing) or by the application tools (automatic operations). For user the difference is evident, but from the point of view of design process it may be irrelevant: In both cases the model or a part of it is sent from UIMS (either to display device or to background channel), and some new information is received, which can then be added to the model. Input to and output from the UIMS go on both sides of it.

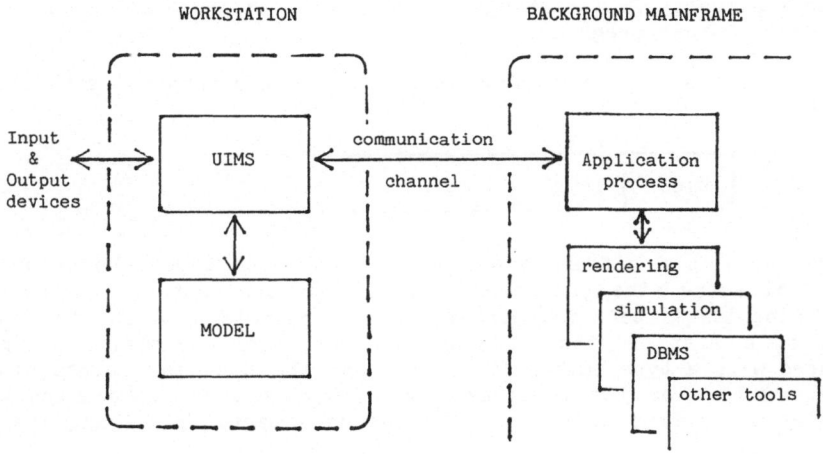

Fig.3: System structure of a modeler UIMS with application tools.

This feature makes the structure flexible and extendible. If there exists an algorithm to perform an operation on the model (say, measuring its dimensions), then an execution request will be sent to the background application together with the relevant part of the model as input for the tool. Otherwise, if the operation cannot be automated, the user's help is asked by outputting on display and reading input devices. The division of labour depends only on the sophistication of application tools, not on the system itself. It doesn't cause any changes, if a tool is replaced with a new algorithm, or even with special hardware.

The most important issues in implementing this kind of system are:

(1) an agreed format of communication between UIMS and applications,

(2) the management of files and concurrent processes, and

(3) efficient (preferably graphical) tools for interaction.

AN EXPERIMENTAL ENVIRONMENT

A system, called AGX (Advanced GeometriX) is implemented by the author, having the above mentioned objectives in mind. The models are represented as hierarchical list structures (logically trees), linearized into a contiguous sequence of computer words. This "stream" form makes them suitable for file transmission without any conversions.

Because every list element can be handled simply as a block of words, it is easy to program general list manipulation functions, which do not care of the contents and internal structure of the elements. Specific data types (text, lines, areas, solids, lists, etc.) are identified with a tag word at the beginning of each element. This feature makes the data structures "self-declarative", facilitating their right interpretation also when transferred to other programs.

The general form of a list element is similar to the proposed metafile format in GKS:

type	length	data...	

The 'type' word is a different number for each data type, the second word 'length' tells the size (in computer words) of the contents (data) of the element. The 'data' part may contain either specific data for the type of element, or a list of other similar elements. For example, a polygon is represented with a type number 'POLYGON', and the data part containing the coordinate values of its vertices. A solid object is represented with a tag 'SOLID' and a list of polygons as the data part, specifying its boundary.

The basic object types used for geometric modeling in AGX are lines and areas: POLYLINE and POLYGON, both in 2- and 3-dimensional space. In 3D there is also the volumic type SOLID, consisting of a set of polygons that pairwise meet at their edges. In AGX there is no topological connectivity information stored in the models of solids. Whenever such information is needed, it is found by comparing coordinates of the vertices of polygons. So the methodology is different from another modeling system developed at the same laboratory, called GWB [23-24].

New object types can easily be added to the system. A new tag number is reserved, and the needed generation and manipulation functions written for that type. These functions can largely reuse the existing general manipulation functions for list elements. The new type does not interfere with others, because all tools are written to recognize the relevant types of their operands, and to leave others untouched. This way many tools can use a general recursive tree walker within the list hierarchy.

An interactive editor program serves as an experimental UIMS. It contains the basic manipulation functions (insert, delete, replace) of elements in the model data structure, and navigation within the hierarchy of lists. It always keeps track of the 'current element', telling the user its location in the structure. Each operation takes that element as its operand.

Interaction facilities consist of request-type input handling, output of pictures on different displays, and the common graphical operations: transformation, clipping, conversions of representation. They each operate directly on the model and are repeatable at will. So they are more useful than the output functions in standard graphics packages where they only affect the primitives within a predefined output pipeline.

The tools can be classified into different types:

(1)   generators of objects (resulting in new list elements),

(2)   transformators (affecting the coordinates of existing elements),

(3)   intersections (taking two objects and resulting a new one), and

(4)   evaluators (calculating new attributes of elements).

The input functions are understood as special generators, and graphical output as evaluator of visual attributes.

Important functions are also reading and writing of models into files, and execution of external application tool programs ("daemons") as concurrent processes, with these files as input and output. Generally useful daemons are for example a hidden-line-program, set operations in 2D space, graphical text formatter, and a pen plotter device driver.

The system is written in C-language under UNIX bsd 4.1 running on a VAX 11/750 computer. It has also been used for practical applications (a prototype of mining design system) in a SUN Microsystems' workstation computer. Future plans include moving it into a SEILLAC-7 workstation.

A design example

As an example of AGX editor functions, hypothetical design of a chair is worked out in figure 4. First the three legs of the chair are defined by the command sequence:

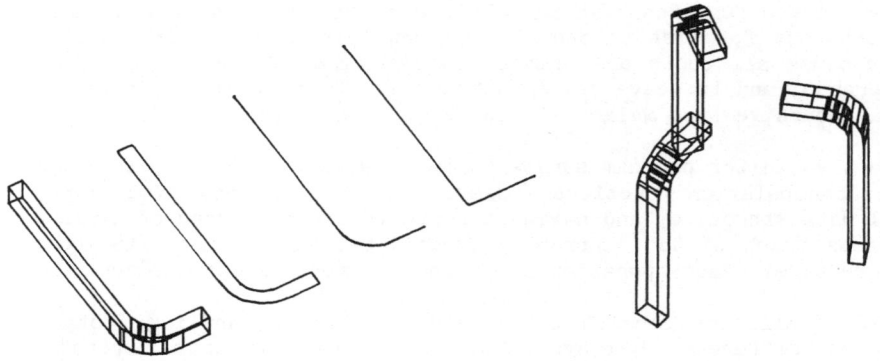

1) CLEAR WORKSPACE
2) APPEND 2D POINTS
3) x,y (mm)= 120 0
4) x,y (mm)= 120 380
5) x,y (mm)= 0 380
6) TYPE IS POLYLINE
7) EXECUTE TOOL: round by radius of 60 mm
8) INPUT RESULTS
9) EXECUTE TOOL: grow polyline by 13 mm, resulting in a POLYGON
10) INPUT RESULTS
11) SWEEP POLYGON in 3D by 44 mm along z-axis, resulting in a SOLID
12) ROTATE 90 degrees around x-axis
13) TRANSLATE 80 mm at x-axis
14) COPY
15) ROTATE 120 degrees around z-axis
16) REDO 14-15
17) DRAW A PICTURE ON PLOTTER

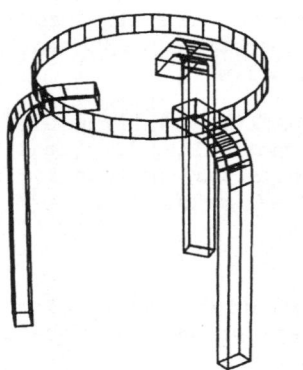
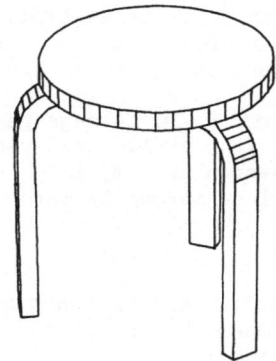

Fig.4: Possible steps defining a chair (original design by A.Aalto).

The commands are abstractions of real ones, whose exact form of course is device dependent. For example, the coordinates could have been given either numerically from the keyboard, or by pointing with a cross-hair cursor. However, this kind of differences are of "cosmetic" or "pragmatic" nature, and don't affect the abstract syntax of commands. For standard-like viewing and other common operations, default values can be used as parameters, which are thus not mentioned in the commands.

By similar commands the top of the chair is constructed using a rotational sweep operation on an input point, and appended to the structure containing the legs.

If we want to design a variation of the same chair, the conventional way would be to start from scratch and use similar commands again. However, if we take the command sequence above as a model of its own stored in the UIMS, then we can slightly modify it and execute again:

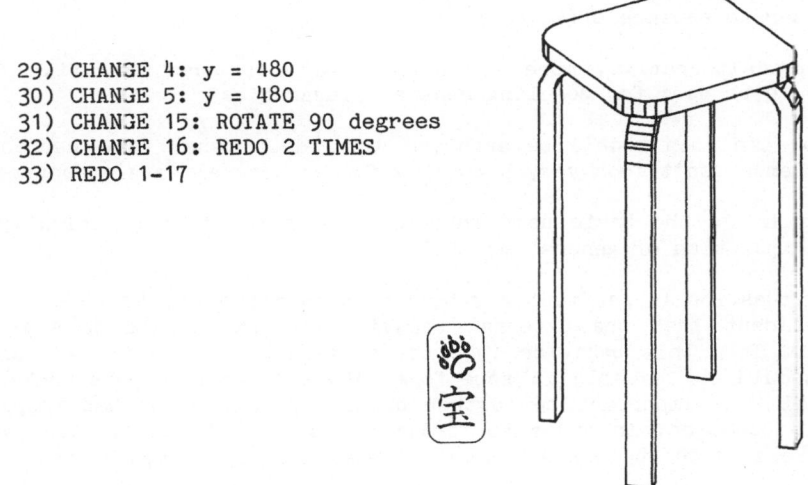

```
29) CHANGE 4: y = 480
30) CHANGE 5: y = 480
31) CHANGE 15: ROTATE 90 degrees
32) CHANGE 16: REDO 2 TIMES
33) REDO 1-17
```

Fig.5: A variation of chair in similar style.

Similarly changing the definition of the top of the chair results in another variation, shown in figure 5.

Also non-constructive, restrictive design is possible. The user may state assertions on the model, defining for example the width and height of a chair. This information is also a geometric (meta)model, although it might be difficult to evaluate its outlook. Its usefulness is in checking validity of later design proposals. The system can tell the user if his model satisfies the assertions in a stage of design, and the appropriate parameters of the history model can then be changed (like in the example above).

CONCLUSIONS AND FUTURE RESEARCH

It is found that a more general modeler than the conventional geometric modelers is really needed in design applications. It should be possible to handle different representations of objects within a UIMS, one of the most valuable being the history trail of design operations.

The described, very general modeling workbench structure of UIMS has the potential of being the kernel of a distributed CAD system. The local capability of a workstation UIMS to handle different data types may largely vary with the intended application area - a non-design application has of course less demands. However, any such system can be expanded with tool programs in other (background) computers.

The most important and interesting questions for future development of such systems are:

(1) How much of the local workstation functions could be hardwired, in order to enhance efficiency?

(2) What alternative, more efficient data structures and file formats could be used for modeling general hierarchies?

(3) How can such models be archived in a data base? The current DBMS schemes don't look very promising for so general data structures.

(4) Which are the basic user interface functions that efficiently allow manipulation of general models?

The last question is particularly important from the user's point of view. It is evident that the external behavior of UIMS should be application dependent. Then this behavior (how the workstation responds to user's actions) should be loadable in some form into a general purpose workstation. Also it will be important to further develop a mechanism that keeps track of user's behavior, in order to facilitate personalization. This will be closely related to the history model of commands, described above.

REFERENCES

[1]   Whitted, Weimer: A software test-bed for the development of 3-D raster graphics systems, ACM Computer Graphics, Aug 1981

[2]   Crow: A more flexible image generation environment, ACM Computer Graphics, Jul 1982

[3]   Sequin, Strauss: Unigraphix, 20th Design Automation Conference, IEEE 1983

[4]   Hall, Greenberg: A testbed for realistic image synthesis, IEEE Computer Graphics & Applications, Nov 1983

[5]   Sabella, Wozny: Towards fast color-shaded images of CAD/CAM geometry, IEEE Computer Graphics & Applications, Nov 1983

[6]   Newman, van Dam: Recent efforts towards graphics standardization, Computing Surveys, Dec 1978

[7]   Guedj, Tucker (eds.): Methodology in computer graphics, IFIP Workshop at Seillac, May 1976 (North-Holland 1979)

[8]   Status report of the graphic standard planning committee, ACM Computer Graphics, Vol.13 No.3 (Aug 1979)

[9]   ISO TC97/SC5/WG2 N117, Graphical Kernel System (GKS), Version 7.0 (Jan 1982)

[10]   Guedj, et al.: Methodology of interaction, IFIP Workshop at Seillac, May 1979 (North-Holland 1980)

[11]   Graphical input interaction technique (GIIT) workshop summary, ACM Computer Graphics, Jan 1983

[12]   IFIP/Eurographics workshop on user interface management at Seeheim, Nov 1983 (to be published 1984)

[13]   Rosenthal: Managing graphical resources, ACM Computer Graphics, Jan 1983

[14]   Goldberg, Robson: Smalltalk-80 the language and its implementation, Xerox 1983

[15]   Takala: Communication mediator - a structure for UIMS, (in [12]) 1983

[16]   Takala: Standard graphics as a geometric modelling device, Eurographics'83 Conference, North-Holland 1983

[17]   Requicha: Representation of rigid solid objects, (in Encarnacao: Computer Aided Design), Lecture Notes in Computer Science 89, Springer 1980

[18]   Sambura, Gero: Framework for a computer integrated design environment, (in IFIP workshop on CAD systems framework at Roros, Jun 1982)

[19]   Gajski, Kuhn: New VLSI tools, IEEE Computer, Dec 1983

[20]   Yoshikawa: CAD framework guided by general design theory, (in IFIP workshop on CAD systems framework at Roros, Jun 1982)

[21]   Yoshikawa: General design theory and a CAD system, (in Sata, Warman: Man-Machine Communication in CAD/CAM, IFIP Workshop in Tokyo, Oct 1980), North-Holland 1981

[22]   Clark: Hierarchical geometric models for visible surface algorithms, Comm. ACM, Vol.19 No.10 (Oct 1976)

[23]   Mantyla,Takala: The geometric workbench (GWB) - an experimental geometric modeling system, Eurographics'81 Conference, North-Holland 1981

[24]   Mantyla,Sulonen: GWB: a solid modeler with Euler operators, IEEE Computer Graphics & Applications, Sep 1982

[25]   Muoto (Journal of Finnish Association of Designers), Mar 1983

Chapter 5
Interactive Graphics Design

Critical Issues in Computer Graphics Education for Graphics Design

Robin G. King
Sheridan Computer Graphics Laboratory
1430 Trafalgar Road, Oakville
Ontario, Canada L6H 2L1

Abstract

With the recent introduction of sophisticated computer graphics design systems into the marketplace, design educators must now come to terms with radical changes in design methodology and stylistic content. The advantages and limitations of these new technologies will force significant departures from current curricula and will demand the development of novel program designs, and new teaching strategies.

Some of the immediate concerns which must be addressed include such diverse yet interrelated problems as; the effect of interface design on teaching design methodology, the influence of software limitations on stylistic content, the transitional changes in organizational behaviour which surface in response to the introduction of computer-based technology, and the positive and negative influences of these technologies on creative behaviour and productivity.

This paper will explore the above issues, discuss the design curriculum changes which must be considered, relate the experiences of a case study at Sheridan, and make specific recommendations to those institutions which must now respond to these challenges by developing educational frameworks that are appropriate, responsive, and evolutionary.

A Current Perspective

Two distinct educational issues surface with the emergence of both inexpensive microcomputer-based graphics technology, and sophisticated, minicomputer-based, dedicated graphics design and animation systems. The first concerns the degree to which this technology is appropriate and useful as a tool for facilitating, enhancing, and improving the process of teaching the basic principles of design and visual language. The second concerns the development of appropriate educational frameworks and curricula for advanced design education. The former will not be discussed here as these issues are the subject of a separate study currently under review.

While there are many contemporary examples of the traumatic repercussions caused by the sudden introduction of sophisticated technology within different disciplines, graphic designers and visual arts educators have never, until today, faced such a radical shift in the nature of their basic image-making tools.

The flexibility and precision of computer graphics systems are generally unequalled by manual techniques, and in many cases, speed and productivity are dramatically increased, especially where repetitive tasks are required. In addition, these systems encourage and facilitate the development of wide varieties of design alternatives which can be easily manipulated, combined and recorded. One particular characteristic which makes them attractive is the (almost) real-time response to creative thinking and ideation, allowing the artist to experiment with a larger variety of potential solutions to a visual problem.

However, these tools possess inherent design and technical constraints which may seriously limit the characteristics of the product. They may constrain the expression of ideas because of poor interface design (the procedural dialogue used to communicate between artist and machine), a restricted variety of primitive descriptions (only certain shapes can be illustrated or certain manipulations performed), a lack of textural qualities in most systems, and often poorly defined typefaces with limited or non-existent letter spacing (except by slow and laborious techniques).

Each of the factors considered above may have serious and long lasting effects on one of four aspects of creative visual production. First, they dramatically alter the traditional design methodology and creative processes which characterize artistic activity. Second, they affect the creative individuals who use them because the user must come to terms with the virtual elimination of traditional manual skills, a problem which is often perceived by the neophite user as a serious threat (frequently the 'mystique' of manual dexterity is replaced by the mystique of the technology). Third, the characteristics of the technology (software design, display system and hardcopy) have distinct properties which tend to restrict the types of products and images produced. And last, the introduction of computer graphics into a visual arts environment will affect all members of the institution, in some cases stimulating new directions, in others causing a 'return to basics' movement.

The development of new program designs, teaching techniques and appropriate curricula demand a thorough grasp of these problems In fact, experience has shown [1] that considerable experimentation and innovation are neccesary if we are to successfully introduce specialized computer graphics courses at the graduate level. Because of the rapid changes of technology and the evolution of new computational and production techniques, substancial reevaluation of curricula must take place on a regular basis. Programs must be sufficiently flexible to accomodate changes as soon as they appear, and probably **significant changes need to be made each time the program is run.**

Interface Design

In order to produce graphic images, each computer system is controlled by a software program which has been designed to provide a dialogue between the operator/artist and the hardware. The design of the interface (that part of the program through which the operator has direct control of the image) and of the supporting software, regulates the types of graphic primitives available (e.g. line, circle, pie), their attributes (e.g. colour, size, texture) and the range of manipulations through which they may be changed (e.g. rotation, scaling, movement or interpolation).

Whether a facility is equipped with low or high-resolution equipment, an individual system or a variety of different systems, commercial turnkey design workstations or institutionally developed technology, the design of the software which mediates the man-machine interface is a critical factor in courseware design and development.

For example, if a high-resolution system capable of, say, eight to sixteen million colours and 3000+ line resolution are used, the technology must include curricula which details the specific attributes and design methodologies supported by its particular interface design. The strategies used for designing graphic images are a function of the interface commands and therefore must be well understood and documented by the instructor. Unfortunately, in most cases, these methodologies are often different from, and not consistent with, the strategies and techniques most familar to visual artists, although the software has been 'designed' to mirror them to some extent.

Usually, the development of interface designs have been the responsibilty of engineers and systems designers who have a limited understanding of graphic design methodologies or artistic processes. They are typically developed for specific applications such as slide preparation, chart making or speaker support, with productivity and easy of use the formost criteria of performance. In recent years, the graphic design community using these systems has started to demand revisions to the interface designs in an attempt to make them more appropriate to the design processes commonly in use. Students and educators should be active participants in this process. A few systems developers are finally employing graphic designers and artists as part of the design team.

For an example of the thoughtful response of a graphic designer to this issue, the reader is encouraged to reference the work of Aaron Marcus, an internationally recognized visual artist who has written extensively about this problem. In his article 'Designing the Face of an Interface' [2] he points out that:

> The design of interfaces is not a science, nor is it solely an art. It is an activity of design, a mixture

of articulated analytical methods, intuition, and creative insight. (p29)

The design and implementation of graphics interfaces are therefore of central concern to the computer graphics educator. They mediate design processes, demand specialized methodologies and significantly affect the stylistic and conceptual content of the images which result from their use. A curriculum which responds to these problems must do so by ensuring that the student thoroughly understand these issues from both practical and theoretical viewpoints. Teaching graphics system use without serious and in-depth analysis, criticism, and evaluation of the influence of the technology on design methods and the human-computer interface, simply serves to further mystify and confuse its practical application. The use of different types of input system (mouse, keyboard, tablet) has dramatic influence on interactivity and so design methodology.

With these comments in mind, the curriculum development process should strive to obtain a balance between courses which teach theory, technology, systems skills, and applications, and those which foster critical analysis of design methodology issues, independent of the specific graphics systems used in the program.

System Design and Stylistic Content

The characteristics of computer graphics technology influence stylistic content and conceptual direction to a remarkable degree. Of primary concern are the characteristics of the display system. The usual graphics display consists of a video monitor with resolution in the range of 600 x 400. Typical systems can display anywhere from 16 to 16 million colours, but normally from 16 to 256 simultaneously. In addition, the artist is working with transmitted rather than reflected light, and with a limited range of graphic primitives and manipulations.

Clearly, designing with computer graphic technology means decision-making which differs greatly from traditional methods. Designing on a screen with limited resolution involves approximations, and is particularly problematic when accurate letter and line spacing are required. The images created are seldom reproducable with the colours (and sometimes contrast) of the display and therefore the designer must relate screen colours to a separate 'palate' in slide form.

Design decisions are significantly different when one is dealing with images intended for transmitted light systems (slide, film amd video) than they are for reflected light, such as print. For example, black text on a white background is the accepted form of print reproduction, but neither this arrangement, nor the reverse (white type on a black field), are acceptable for slide, film or video production.

It is therefore critical that the curricula which support computer graphics programs for experienced designers bring the issues of technological limitations and design strategies for non-traditional reproduction into clear perspective.

During the past few years, a computer image 'style' has developed, characterized by the use of space grids (Figure 1), wireframe objects, science fiction imagery (Figure 2) and three-dimensional effects. The contemporary influence of science fiction films and surrealistic imagery, and the popular demand for them by the media, have caused this stylistic trend. The commercial application of computer graphics is largely influenced by the demand for images which are clean, simple, precise, and easy to reproduce, or have the obvious characteristics of low resolution computer games. Speed of production is important, as well as the requirement for images which communicate ideas clearly and with precision (Figure 3). Most commercial computer graphics design houses develop simplified strategies and formats for this purpose and support them with libraries of standardized images in order to be competitive.

In contrast, graduate students should be encouraged to question the nature of current stylistic trends and to explore, experiment with, and develop new stylistic and conceptual approaches to computer graphics, especially where advantage may be made of the new imaging potentials of the technology (Figures 4,5 & 6). The limits of representational imagery should be explored (Figures 7 and 8). At the same time, novel ways should be found to deal with information graphics, the design of imagery which reduces complex ideas and systems to illustrations which communicate the underlying and essential aspects of a problem. This should be supported with instruction and practical exercises dealing with the temporal nature and use of these images; their context within a presentation, the design of supporting databases (e.g.videotex), and the basics of animation.

As new systems are developed, additional facilities within the software and hardware will extend the capabilities of the artist. Larger computer memories will allow images of greater complexity, advances in software will increase the variety of graphics primities to include increased numbers of user-definable 'brushes' and texturing, and improved three-dimensional software will aid in the development, rendering and display of complex images with 'organic' characteristics.

A Note on Programming Expertise

A difficulty faced by all computer graphics educators is the degree to which the student should become involved with computer programming. This is a simple decision for engineering and computing schools, the requirement is obvious. But the problem of applications to graphic design, animation and fine art are more problematic. In general, at least in North America, most fine art students program their own microcomputers or, when working with advanced systems, develop their own advanced programs.

For the professional designer and graduate design student however, the problem is slightly different. All students need to know the overall design characteristics of two and three-dimensional software in some detail. If only commercial turnkey systems are used by the institution, the amount of programming skill required may be minimal. On the other hand, if the student is already knowledgable in this area and wishes to pursue programming and interface design issues, uses systems which require direct control of the frame buffer, or expects to enter the field in areas which require programming ability, then facilities must be available to develop this expertise.

Organizational Structure

A significant departure from traditional program structures is essential. The nature of new technologies, and in particular the increasing complexity and variety of connections among them, have resulted in a wide range of constantly changing developments and applications. Also, the complexity of the technology and the need for frequent revision of program content (coupled with a rapidly changing information and technology environment) make it practically impossible for a small number of specialized staff to provide the full range of expertise required.

Serious consideration should be given to the development of a program structure which permits the widest variety of instructional skills and philosophies as well as to the notion of networking. Networking, communicating with others of similar interest and of divergent specializations, is rapidly becoming the most appropriate form of sharing specialized information, technical development, and common problems. Whether through electronic channels or by conventional communications systems, constant exchange of updated knowledge among institutions, commercial users, and system manufacturers and suppliers is of substantial, mutual benefit to all concerned. The networking concept should be an essential component of any program if its structure is to be viable over a long period and evolutionary in its response to the information environment.

Creative Behaviour

Computer graphics workstations alter and influence the most basic of creative activities associated with image development. No other tool for graphic communication has the dynamic flexibilty to change part or whole of the image characteristics as quickly, or with such dexterity, while at the same time maintaining image quality. The colour, shape and proportions of figures, groups and backgrounds can be changed, almost in realtime, making it possible to respond to visual stimuli in a different temporal and mental framework. Imagery made be developed which would not be possible or would be extremely difficult with traditional techniques. Decisions can be made more frequently and mental blocks appear more often.

If there is a novel characteristic of this new technology, it will not be clarified simply by studying the characteristics of the images which are produced. **Its emergent property, that which sets it apart from any previous image-making tool, is the new form of interactivity between man and machine, a new set of dynamic conditions for the creative process.**

This fundamental concept is one on which the curricula for computer graphics, especially at the graduate level, should be founded. Previous research has shown that the development and use of models of creative behaviour can be achieved within a single structural framework [3] which may be used as the basis for both the study of interactive interface design [4] and the development of program structure and curricula for a computer graphics program [5]. In the later case its manifestation is the current graduate program at Sheridan Computer Graphics Labs.

A Case Study in Computer Graphics Program Design: Sheridan Computer Graphics Laboratory

The structure of the Graduate Program in Computer Graphics at Sheridan is a direct result of several years research in the areas of creative behaviour [6] and interdisciplinary education. Its structural framework is rooted in the notion that all aspects of the creative activity (person, process, product and environment) must be considered as a whole; a dynamic, evolutionary, open system. It is from this perspective that the observations noted in the first part of this paper have emerged.

Sheridan Computer Graphics Laboratory is a publicly-funded department in a School of Visual Arts which has undergraduate programs in graphic design, animation, illustration and photography. With over eleven hundred students, the School has a well-established reputation for visual arts education and a solid base for a specialized program of this type. Two separate programs are taught in each year, a one-year (eight month) in-depth program, and a 14 week condensed 'Summer School'.

We have found that, in order to ensure a creative environment, students with a post-secondary background in one or more of five specific specialties provide the ideal 'mix' for the program. Graphic designers, illustrators, animators, fine artists and media (film amd video) specialists are chosen on the basis of professionalism and innovative capability. Previous computer experience is not a pre-requisite, although some exposure has been observed as an advantage. The group is chosen carefully as positive group dynamics and cooperation have been found essential.

The program philosophy, structure and curricula were formulated to reflect an emphasis on creative visual problem-solving and creativity, with the major emphasis on design methodology, animation dynamics, and stylistic content.

The program consists of an integrated group of core courses
designed to cover a wide variety of computer graphics
technology and applications.

As we have found the initial period of instruction to be critical, the first several weeks are devoted entirely to hands-on
experience with a single turnkey graphics system. The psychological environment is designed to be one in which the technology is introduced as a new tool for visual problem-solving
with an emphasis on the relationship between traditional design
methodologies and those appropriate to computer-based systems.
Small group instruction ensures each individual can be helped
through the difficult transition from 'manual' techniques to
computer-based image construction. Group discussions and 'debriefing' sessions develop group cohesiveness and help students
through this difficult period. The rest of the first and
second semester consists of a series of courses based on the
following subjects. Some courses are considered core, others
depend on the specific student's background.

Computer Graphics Technology

All students study a curriculum of basic concepts in computer
graphics covering the fundamentals of graphics technology,
terminology, systems and applications. Topics covered include
basic terminology, computer hardware and architecture, raster
and vector display systems, frame buffer and colour look-up
table systems, input and output devices and their characteristics, and a variety of hard copy devices and systems.

Computer Programming

While computer programming is not a major emphasis, a labbased, hands-on course is given. The direction is towards
skills and vocabulary which the graduate may need for communicating with computer professionals. The elements of structured programming are reenforced with practical applications in
animation and graphics programming. Special consideration is
given to frame buffer control for videotex. The second semester consists of invited guest lecturers who deal primarily
with interface design, together with a short workshop in Unix
and C. In the latter part of the year, some students may
undertake independent study in 3-D software development on a
minicomputer.

Graphics Systems (Lab)

Continued hands-on training is conducted in small groups on a
variety of medium and high-resolution turnkey computer graphics
systems. A Genigraphics 100C and Dicomed D38 provide skills
for direct commercial applications such as speaker presentation
slides and graphics. Three Norpak IPS 2 workstations are used
to give practical experience in data-base design and graphics
for videotex applications. An N.Y.I.T. Images 2 paint system
with full colour scanning and triple frame buffers, provides

an excellent tool for illustration, fine art and audio visual applications.

Three-dimensional graphics and animation are taught using a VAX 11/750 with Jupiter 7+ terminals and frame buffers. The software support for this is a unique package developed in Canada and marketed by Neo-Visuals; this software supports the development of graphics primitives from cartesian coordinates and surface of revolution information with the facility to extrude, rotate and explode solids from any viewpoint and with various user-definable angles of view. The resolution-independent software supports low resolution, real-time preview of animation. Complex objects may be illuminated with up to nine point-light sources with control over ambiant light. Further refinements available include surface shading and ray tracing.

Two dimensional animation is achieved using the Genigraphics 100C or the Dicomed. The Genigraphics is equipped with a video interface for recording, and a single-frame Bolex and Matrix 3000 are used for film and slide recording.

Computer Graphics Methodology

The central issues of concept development and stylistic content are explored through mutually-selected research and development projects supported by courses and consultation in three areas; graphic design (design methodology, stylistic content and visual problem-solving), animation (animation fundamentals, story boarding and animation dynamics) and creative behaviour (psychology of creative process, general systems theory, systems analysis, and informational design).

Research Thesis

A weekly production seminar serves to coordinate activities, provide program feedback, explore new developments in the field and, during the second semester, focuses on independent practical research and applications of computer graphics, together with a suporting thesis.

The central core and guiding spirit of the program is the application of this technology to the development of solutions to visual problems. Each student has unique skills and areas of interest and are carefully selected to give a balance of specialties as mentioned above. It is this dynamic blend of interests and t he exchange of interdisciplinary ideas and perspectives which provide the program with a creative and evolutionary environment.

There are no full-time faculty other than the Program Coordinator. Computer graphics methodology is taught by practicing professionals, hands-on training is provided by graduates who are working in the field or in some cases by the students themselves (their average age is twenty-six and many have practiced professionally). A full-time technologist provides technical support and programming instruction, and additional coordination is provided by a part-time administrative support staff member. One faculty member's salary is sufficient to cover all faculty costs including a broad program of guest lecturers invited from all parts of North America.

In addition to the regular program, the staff and students are involved in a program of college-wide research and development funded by the College's R and D Division. Students have provided data-base design and graphics images for computer-aided-learning systems, microprocessor-controlled interactive video-tape instruction systems, videotex data base design and graphics, 2-D and 3-D animation feasibility studies, sound synthesis technology evaluation and have developed instructional support slides for conferences such as SIGGRAPH'83 and '84. This program of active research and development is essential in providing an atmosphere of dynamic involvement with other high technology specialists as well as external professional organizations.

Conclusions and Recomendations

The program structure and curricula outlined above have not been clarified without trial and error. In the absence of any prototypical model, at least two iterations of the program were necessary before many issues could be understood and program corrections made. Of special concern are the difficulties associated with when, how quickly, and in what context, complex technical information should be introduced. For students without a background in computers, there can be some initial trauma involved with the first working sessions with a graphics system. Frustrations with interface design and software surface, especially among professional designers and illustrators whose initial expectations may be greater than the technology can support.

At first, an interdisciplinary environment may be a new experience for many visual artists who have trained primarily in one area for many years. The hurdles of technical information and keyboard training must be overcome. Priorities of access must be fairly administered, and schedules organized to ensure maximum use of the equipment. Curricula must be designed with a set of core concepts but must also be flexible and responsive to technological change, especially with the introduction of new workstations, communications systems, frequent software updates, additional image recording facilities and a changing 'information environment'. Program designers should anticipate that this type of program will require adjustment and change probably several times a year.

It is crucial that a well-defined Program Philosophy is clearly specified **before a program is designed.** Virtually all decisions regarding program structure and design should depend on a strong structural and philosophical base. The conceptual foundation should not be just a _response_ to technology, it should reflect a desire to solve specific types of visual problems. Equipment and software should be purchased _after_ the program has been organized, otherwise there is a danger of adjusting the program philosophy to fit the technology (although test situations can provide important experiences on which to make final decisions). A significant part of the curricula should be technology-independent, that is, provide a core of information and perspectives which do not depend on the particular systems the students are currently using.

Another important consideration relates to the introduction of computer graphics systems into the traditional visual arts school. Care should be taken to select faculty and staff who are clearly interested in the problems and issues associated with new approaches to image generation. Forcing involvement on those who are clearly nervous at best and cyberphobic at worst should be avoided, and open discussion of the long term effects of the technology on traditional visual arts disciplines should be encouraged.

References

[1] King, Robin G. **A Graduate Program in Computer Graphics for Graphic Design,** in 'Panel:Computer Graphics in Higher Education', Chair - Dr James D Foley, SIGGRAPH'83 Conference Proceedings, Association for Computing Machinery, Vol.17, No.3, 1983, pp 31-34.

[2] Marcus, Aaron. **Designing the Face of an Interface,** I.E.E.E Computer Graphics and Applications, Vol.2, No.1, January 1982, pp 23-29.

[3] King, Robin G.. **A General Systems Model of the Creative Process,** in 'General Systems Research and Design: Precursors and Futures', Proceedings of the Twenty-Fifth Annual North American Meeting of the Society for General Systems Research with the American Association for the Advancement of Science, Toronto, January 6-9, 1981, pp 121-130.

[4] _____. **A Structural Model of Creative Process for Improved Graphics Interface Design,** in 'Advances in CAD/CAM: Case Studies', Kluwer Academic Press, March 1984.

[5] _____. **A Graduate Level Program in Computer Graphics for the Visual Arts.** Proceedings of the 'Computers in Art, Design, Research and Education Conference', San Jose State University, Jan. 1984, pp105-110.

[6] _____. **A General Systems Analysis of the Creative Process in Visual Art.** Unpublished M.A. Thesis. York University, Downsview, 1979.

New Office Automation Environment: In-House Graphics and Publishing Capabilities

Alice Bernhard
Bernhand Design
RD 1 Hillcrest Lane, Box 242
Rhinebeck, NY 12572, USA

ABSTRACT:

The development of In-House Graphics capability is becoming a key function of Business and Management and in some instances in-house publishing becomes a feasible complement or extension. Based on case studies, the author suggests an integration of Graphic Designer with Business and Management for efficient computerized visual communication.
To achieve cost-effective solutions for business graphics needs the computerized office effects changes. Adjustments in roles and responsibilities of Designer, Programmer and Business Professionals are necessary to fully utilize these new electronic tools. It is not uncommon, however, to take the new tools and try to continue to work in the previous or usual manner. Being wasteful of resources, both human and machine, is a reason why Office Automation, in many instances, has not succeeded.

INTRODUCTION:

The development of In-House Graphic capability is increasingly becoming a function of Business and Management resulting from the computerized office. This creates unique demands and possibilities for today's Graphic Designer.

It is interesting that often computer graphics capability, design, and development is initially in the hands of individuals not trained in Graphic Art/Design. Most business people are involved in either the preparation and/or delivery of communication. However, awareness and successful use of the components of effective graphic communication is not common.

The computer graphics workstation is a most powerful communication tool often poorly utilized. The lack of understanding of Communication Design and the potential use of this technology make it difficult for those who are expected to incorporate it into their work and meet business graphic needs. The DP Professional needs to learn about computer graphics and be given adequate information to appreciate the power and place of Visual Language. The need for non-art/design persons to have an understanding of the elements of graphic design and basic visual communication is more important than ever, since they have access to the computer terminal which is a tool for today's graphic communications.

USING AND UNDERSTANDING COMPUTER GRAPHICS

To utilize the computer graphics workstation the User needs design information and knowledge of the techniques necessary to produce effective presentation visuals. Since for the most part, design information, capability or techniques are not yet embodied in the actual graphics software (some business graphics may be an exception) and not an integral part of the firmware or hardware, the person at the terminal in most cases must provide design decisions and input. The Manager or Secretary are seldom, if ever, trained in the area of graphic design, either in the understanding of the subject itself or the development of needed skills. As a result, the User takes a new tool and tries to use it with information learned when using old tools.

The Secretary who is asked to make visuals (slides or overheads) usually brings those skills acquired at the typewriter. For example, underlining for emphasis, which can make it less readable; also the use of black type on a white background, which is the most harsh contrast and most fatiguing for the audience to read (1). Technology opens a new world allowing choices which usually result in the overuse and abuse of color and the misuse of font selections and combinations. The Manager similarly resorts to making the best of a variety of communication skills acquired during a career, which are not necessarily effectively adaptable to Computer Graphics communication.

There is a need for proper training on an introductory level of Computer Graphics Design information and techniques. This might include not only the technical know-how of 'how-to' operate, but efficient, cost-effective use of this new tool. DP Professionals need to understand which Computer Graphics should be used, when, by whom, and how. The answers to much of this depends on the Business needs, existing technology and capabilities of the User. The presentation visuals used today in business, industry, and education and many of the slides viewed at lectures during Computer Graphics conferences and seminars are ample evidence of the need for an understanding and use of visual communication concepts.

The Designer-Educator may point to the power of the visual (language) emphasizing how we communicate readily and easily in picture or graphic form (2). Remembering in the visual language, something is always communicated, good or bad, clear or confusing. Before a User sits down at the graphics terminal, an understanding of Visual Communication as a product of Computer Graphics is recommended. The concepts of Visual/ Graphic Language should be studied along with examples of good use of the graphic Elements and Principles of Design (3). Considering the information explosion environment and the hectic pace in which many Managers, Staff and Secretaries find themselves, special in-house lectures/ seminars could be structured with time and content meeting specific and special needs which include:

1. An understanding of the efficient, effective and successful use of the Computer Graphics office terminal;

2. Deciding on the production requirements of all types of visual (slides) presentations and the selection of a Designer if and when needed; and

3. The ability to communicate more clearly with a Designer as to content and concept of visual presentations.

IN-HOUSE GRAPHICS AND PUBLISHING

With the introduction of word processing and other computer techniques to office practice, typesetting is a natural addition. In turn, the use of typesetting may lead to an in-house art department. A further development of reprographics and phone services with the use of the computer leads to communications in general. But even without sizable development, the communications concept relates to the use of word processing and the division of administrative, editorial, and graphic responsibility (4). The use of computer technology brings change and opportunity.

Mainly practices of commercial art and graphics can now be brought into the office as the use of communications is brought to a professional level with the development of in-house graphic capability. Such a development, followed with in-house publishing capability, where appropriate, is the logical extension of the equipment and technology being put into place.

Here the Author discusses from personal experience a particularly innovative and successful method of creating a visual presentation utilizing computer graphics with a team structure and role/responsibility alterations.

During a meeting with upper level managers responsible for input into the presentation the Consultant/Designer listens, asking pertinent questions regarding the purpose of the presentation, the nature of the audience, the intended message and desired effect. An initial idea of the presentation is roughed out by the Designer/Consultant. A second meeting covers verification, clarification and further questioning. The Designer/Consultant returns to home based studio location where layouts are "drawn" at the computer graphics workstation and then sent electronically in seconds to the Manager's location, rather than driving a few hours. A combination of phone and computer graphics terminal communications allows approvals and electronic changes to be made efficiently. It should be noted this is only possible if in the initial meetings communication goals are geared for this process and a good foundation and rapport is set up. After electronic approval of layouts, the Designer constructs format sheets on the system and again forwards them electronically. When they are received at the Manager's location, they are brought up on the system. Hard-copy is made and distributed to the Staff members who begin to follow the format instructions and actually produce the visuals on the terminal. The visuals may be sent back to the Designer for design corrections if needed. However, this is usually at a minimum, since the Designer conducts necessary sessions with the staff members beforehand, giving instructions on how-to-do computer graphics and emphasizing following format sheets.

What is to be avoided is using the new tools but continuing to work with them in nearly the same manner as before. The potential of these machines needs to be understood and fully utilized.

Although many of the design principles for technical documentation and publication are similar to those in presentation graphics, the Designer should instruct on these similarities and differences making both people and machines more productive. Now writing, storing, revising, formatting and composing technical documents which may include graphics can all be accomplished within one electronic master copy. In addition to technical documentation, newsletters, publications, manuals and guides may be produced in-house. The impact of such innovation alters traditional roles and requires individuals to function within a team structure.

The following considerations are aspects of technical documentation, but for the most part also refer to business presentation graphics:

TIME, ERRORS.
With one electronic master copy of a document, numerous revisions and/or additions may be made without the expected type errors from the usual several versions or retyped copies. Material is not misplaced when it exists as one copy on file electronically and is retrieved quickly and efficiently. The normal time loss from the previous confusion, extensive proof-reading and paper shuffling, which at one time seemed necessary, becomes part of the past.

CREATIVITY, PRODUCTIVITY.
The natural flow of working on the document, not being interrupted by previously extraneous steps, permits the author greater creativity and productivity. The ideas, thoughts,

and organizing may be maintained by the author's ability and
creativity and not interfered with or controlled by outside
services or influences. The balance of structure/discipline
and freedom within the creative process and the design
process involves having all the variables and information
available, choosing/selecting at random, yet with order, the
appropriate pieces. Then at the same time fitting and
organizing these pieces into a whole which will embody the
design solution after it tests successfully at various
stages (5). The Designer/Author in optimum surroundings,
given a particular level of expertise, may produce work of a
quality which far exceeds that of what was possible in the
past without electronic capabilities. Accomplishing this in
less time permits the Author, alone or as part of a team, to
be more productive and make each project considerably more
cost-effective. That team usually includes an Author (Writer)
a Designer and Illustrator who each know and use the
appropriate electronic graphic/alphanumeric tools.

In this situation examples of role adjustments the Author
learns the mark-up language and also learns the graphics
"drawing" tool. Instead of roughing out in pencil the
Author now can rough out on the system and if desired, may
do the complete drawing on the system. The Author enters
the mark-up which merges the illustration with text, position
and size. The Author may work with the illustrator who learns
the computer graphics workstation for both drawing and the
merge function.

The Designer may work with the Programmer, offering programmable layouts to make the various CRT screens more readable, facilitating the ease and effectiveness of the computer
graphic application program. Also the Designer is part of a
team (6) meeting with the Author and Businessperson on
technical publication requirements, develops design decisions
and standards, i.e. number of columns, column width, font
selections, etc. The Designer then works with the Programmer
to achieve design standard defaults in the graphics application program for document creation, including the merging
of text with graphics.

GRAPHICS: ILLUSTRATIONS, DIAGRAMS.
It is common in producing technical publications to have
difficulty with the illustrations and diagrams provided.
Quite often the diagrams submitted are generations removed,
with weak, not clean, sharp and dense lines. They are,
perhaps, copies of copies and thought of as good enough.
However, this has to be questioned; "good enough for what? "
Many times illustrations and diagrams are of little or no
use, serving to fill a space and possibly add some frustration to the reader, who glances over the illegible material
and picks up a residual feeling of irritation or fatigue.
The expense of doing these illustrations over cannot be

justified. However, can the cost of an only somewhat useable
manual be justified? The "cutting corners" may have to be
examined more closely. What is the cost effectiveness of
such a common practice when the manual collects dust in the
corner and the User seeks out an experienced User to explain?
When a diagram is drawn and stored electronically, every copy
is an original. In other words, it is a useable illustration,
functioning as it should, to give information or clarify
printed word information. This is true cost effectiveness.
The attitude of the Reader/User is more positive and with
that, is encouraged to continue with a higher level of
concentration, retention and productivity and lowered error-
rate, fatigue and negativity.

CHANGES, REDUCTION.
Changes are common in diagrammatic material and the cost to
re-do drawings seems sometimes close to prohibitive. The
time spent traditionally patching up, given the often less
than desirable results and usually slower reproduction process, is seldom economical. The changes made to an electronic
drawing are clean, precise, easy and fast, all of which reflect cost effectiveness, especially since the information
is truly in useable form. In addition to needing revision,
graphic materials submitted for publication are seldom the
correct size for the column width. The decision may be to
use the diagram as is, taking up too much room on the page,
or cropping or making photostat reductions. None of these
methods compare with the efficiencey of an electronic reduction, which results in an original drawing of finest quality
for reproduction and therefore useability. The reduction
or enlargement of an area may be made in minutes as opposed
to hours or days. Time is money. In terms of out-right
cost, what is the value of time loss and delayed or
interrupted production schedules?

MERGING GRAPHICS AND TEXT
With the corrected electronic illustration or diagram and the
capability of merging the text with graphics, the author may
make the publication much more coherent and readable. Each
illustration may be "dropped in" appropriately, integrating
with descriptive or associated text. This may end the common
but frustrating situation of having to hunt for given figures
when referred to in the text. It is not unusual to have to
search facing pages for the graphic explanation referred to
as Fig. 1, 2, 3, etc.. Often the reader must turn the page
and finds a group of "figures". The layout Designer may
claim the page looks aesthetic or is economical, but it is
not functional in that if the graphic illustrations are part
of the descriptive text they should be read within that text.
Graphics and text should be integrated on the page and the
new tools make this possible, improving the readability and
useability of the technical publication.

DESIGN STANDARDS

User standards in graphics help to establish and maintain the image of the company. Standards are also desirable to eliminate confusion for an author in laying out the page, whether it be text, a form, or any one of many business publications. The purposes of image, consistency and convenience are valid. However, new emphasis must come from perhaps the design world, questioning the basis for some of the already established standards in use by businesses. The terms "aesthetic" or "aesthetically pleasing", heard often from both Designer and Executive, may be reflecting poor design or lack clarification of purpose. "Because we always did it this way" is another invalid excuse for not producing printed technical material that is comparable to the caliber of the machines it describes and the level of cost-effective work expected to be produced. Putting aesthetics aside, the concept of function needs the spotlight. Perhaps a reason designers come up with so many non-functioning designs is due to the acceptance of "buzz words" such as aesthetics. A closer look is needed at the concepts of architect Louis Sullivan who capsulized his thoughts on design with the statement, "form follows function". Unfortunately too often this has either been forgotton or reversed. The establishing of standards and revived interest is good. The clarification must come from many areas. Designers might re-examine their role and begin to emphasize the process of design, the definition of design and design guidelines (7).

GRAPHICS APPLICATION PROGRAM

The application program for composing documents and merging graphics into the text should be structured in a way as to permit the user to focus on creating and entering document material and have defaults design the layout of the page. To produce such a successful application program, a team of Programmer, Designer, Author, Publications Professional, etc. is required to discuss a variety of needs and issues. This is part of designing a productive and cost-effective application package (8). It might also be noted here that bringing this information and attitude into the curriculum of design students may help to better prepare them for the electronic graphics design world.

EDUCATION, COMMUNICATION.

Although major effort is needed to develop tutorials and seminars to instruct the User on the How-to's of the technical equipment, an understanding of design is pertinent. It is necessary, for example, when producing or updating a technical manual to ask: "what is it for?", "why is it being produced?", "who is to use it?", "under what conditions?", and "for how long?" Many questions should be answered before anything is considered for typesetting, drawing or photographics. Today we see documents with small type and little or no white space. The argument is that there is a lot of information to impart so therefore, how else is it to be put together? The cost of paper must be considered.

Similarly in the early days of printing books the cheaper books were set in italic type only because that was more economical. More (9) words could fit per page. We know, encouraged by the interest of human factors and ergonomics, that cheap costs can be very expensive. In some publications we see the opposite which is an overabundance of white space. In spite of it the information is none the easier to read. This is due to a lack of use or functioning of white space. The graphic element of space should be used to make the text and graphics more readable. It is part of the visual communication that takes place and has either a positive or negative effect on the Reader/User. This needed clarification of using the design process and elements may be communicated to the business/management community through the Designer as Educator.

DESIGN, FUNCTION.
The integration of function and form is needed today in document publication design if users are to have truly useable manuals in their hands. The function of the piece must be questioned so fully that all of the variables follow in an easy flow. The process of design is needed also when putting educational materials together for users of these electronic tools. The function of these machines and their intended purpose should be known and what is expected of the User.

Design may be defined as problem solving: finding the best solution to a given problem, with certain guidelines and limitations (10). The first step in the process of design is "to state the problem clearly".(11). How often is this done? Looking at available publications offers an answer. Unfortunately the extremes of solid packed typed, overly decorative use of type, color and graphics, results in documents which frustrate instead of inform or educate. Beginning with the correct use of the element of space, an increase of useability may result (12).

DESIGNER:

TRAINING AND FEARS.
Training programs which address the problem of people reverting back to old patterns of behavior when under extreme stress, are needed. It is of utmost importance to prevent situations which encourage a confused or unsure User to figure out how things should work by relating back and doing things the way they had been done before the new equipment had been installed. In using machines productively, cost effectiveness is the expected result. Nothing less should be anticipated or designed; both people and machine fully functioning with clarity, speed, harmony and efficiency. However, for the Designer/Artist, the computer graphics terminal has perhaps all too frequently been wrapped in apprehension. It is not uncommom to hear Designers express the fear of being taken over or replaced by a computer. Like the ancient cartographers

whose quote "beyond this lies dragons", the unknown or uncharted may be laced with fears. The stress of a new encounter needs to be made a positive energy force with the attitude of "here is a new design tool, let's see what I can do with it!"

NEEDS AND RESPONSIBILITIES
The Designer/Artist needs to learn how to use a new design tool and appreciate today's business demands and design requirements. Just as the Designer learns to use paint, markers, templates, tapes and the endless variety of color-ink pens, felt-tip, nylon, etc., the computer graphics workstation can be learned. The Designer needs time to experiment and discover what are the possibilities of the graphics terminal (13). The technology potential should also be considered with the Designer requesting additional capability that would enhance, expand and more fully utilize the design tool. The negative stress accompanying the Designer's view of the computer graphics workstation at present can be turned around. Given the design expertise and experience of the Designer, computer graphics can mean an exciting adventure with a new and powerful design tool.

The use of word processing for in-house graphics implies the need for typographic art skills to design and produce the graphic product. Certainly the same skills are required as for professional commercial graphic studios. Office skills do not include art skills, because the extent of office graphics has traditionally ended with the business letter. The design of a graphic product and the inclusion of visual material are the point at which art skills become a necessary part of a communication complex. With greater skills in design and visuals, in-house graphics becomes an art department that is part of a communications complex serving business and management graphics needs.

However, there is no automated substitute for art skills. The ability to visualize and to draw in relation to an individual and unpredictable need is not automated (14). What is available today is storage of predesigned formats, a catalog of visuals, and the capacity to produce a chart from formatted statistical input. The non-art DP Professional with some design guidance may well utilize these for presentation graphics. Having stored pictures available on the system is similar to the clip-art used in the traditional graphic studio to create illustrated graphics.

To create a catalog of illustrations and fully utilize the drawing and color potential of today's computer graphic workstation the artist should be an excellent draftsman, colorist, and the level of working in abstract visualization of concepts should be of the highest caliber (15). This negates the fear of learning to use the tool as being the most important consideration.

Graphic Design is the only field of pictorial creation concerned with the formal design of all visual signs in so far as they serve the purpose of communication. Hence today's Graphic Designer has to collaborate with technicians and scientists wherever programs leave scope for the formal design of signs. There are still misunderstandings between free artists and graphic designers on the one hand and technologists and graphic designers on the other. Graphic designers are expected to supply the skills needed before harmony can be established between aesthetic criteria and the utilitarian functions of communication. We have Designers with expertise and experience in visual communication design and graphics but with little or no computer knowledge or skills; experienced computer users lacking graphic design and visual communication understanding and/or technique and the business person who has neither computer or design background information.

SPECIALIST TO GENERALIST.
The designer cannot hold out in the non-computerized studio and the business person should not be continually frustrated as the creator or receiver of computer graphics information that is neither successful nor cost effective communication. In every field today it becomes more apparent that it is necessary to work as a team, interacting, communicating and cooperating.....technical, business, and management professionals with artists and designers. There is a need now for specialists to become generalists. Scientists have known for a long time that their work keeps spilling over its traditional boundaries. Architects are no longer only designing buildings but interiors, graphics, large-scale planning and some into entrepreneurial ventures. Industrial designers in addition to products have expanded to exhibits, market surveys, commercial interiors and building systems.

There is a shift from specialist to generalist as the connections between things take on an importance formerly reserved for the isolated things themselves. This goes on in all fields of endeavor. Specialists with curiosity and energy are unable to resist looking up from their work from time to time, becoming more aware of complex wholes, the connections that hold them together, and some of the dynamics of the systems.

Working as a business/design team generates ideas as well as expressing and communicating them. Designers/Artists may need to re-think their role as it applies to today's business needs (16). Vast amounts of information which is both current and timely must be presented with speed, clarity and accuracy. Although this is not a new problem, it has intensified and requires more designer awareness in technology and social changes. Concise and precise information needed at a rate which has never before existed puts new demands on the Designer. In times of rapid change, when new social configurations are being only dimly perceived, the person who sees them as a whole is the urgently needed clarifier and intellectual leader.

UNDERSTANDING BUSINESS MANAGEMENT.
With the amount of business communication which must be put into graphic form increasing, the Designer must communicate with the Businessman to understand the needs and help make judgments as to the graphic requirements. Graphic projects and production methods must be evaluated, playing the quality of the finished product against the amount of labor involved and its costs in relation to the product being produced. Information and instruction regarding Computer Graphics is important and helpful to non-design/art professionals giving them an understanding and appreciateion of visual communication. It does not mean they will become designers or establish expertise in this field. It can, however, result in the increased ability to effectively communicate with a Designer on the concepts and substance of the presentation or document which is to be produced.

Considering that word and title slides still comprise approximately seventy percent of the slides produced today, technology limitations could account for this(17)However, communication and understanding may contribute far more than technology limitation to the high percentage of "text only" visuals.

What appears to be a better way to meet business and management graphic needs is an experienced Graphic Designer who finds the computer graphics terminal an exciting new graphics tool for extending creative possibilities in visual communication and information design. However, in certain production situations, it may be feasible to have the Designer instruct apprentice Artists, Secretaries or Data Processing Staff at particular workstation(s). The creator/producer uses the tool.

COMPUTER GRAPHICS AS A KEY FUNCTION OF BUSINESS AND MANAGEMENT.

Immediate benefits of computer graphics appear to be that business and management utilize the clarity, simplicity and immediacy of charts and graphs to read data, analyze and make decisions as opposed to pouring through stacks of printouts. During meetings which make use of data, managers again find graphic visuals highly effective in communicating information to a group. This would not be possible using printouts or any other forms of data requiring an individual to sit and read the information alone. Filing or storing the graphic data/information electronically means knowing exactly where to find it immediately. The completed visuals are stored easily; wrinkled or soiled graphics are no longer a frustration. This aspect is also appreciated when changes are made electronically; always fresh, clean originals; usually in minutes or hours, not days and delays.

For high level presentations the Manager may use a Designer's assistance to turn a very large amount of information into simplified visuals that function, i.e. communicate only the necessary information and not confuse the listener with superflous points which either do not help to clarify or are not in a sequence which permits the audience to follow and understand the speaker's message or train of thought.

If the Designer works closely with business and management as a Consultant, Guide, Educator and Designer a successful presentation may be more quickly assembled by the Designer and with a thorough understanding of the nature and content of the presentation. In the past a Designer might only reproduce what the Speaker requested. It is now apparent that the Designer must accept the role and concerns of Information Design with attention given to the appropriate use and flow of all charts, diagrams, text, illustration and concepts. Usually top Management prefers a teamwork and Designer as Consultant, Guide and Educator method. There is an awareness that the advertising notion, "don't rely on artists, save $$$, create your own visuals" does not produce truly effective visual communication. Ads for some presentation graphics hardware/software suggest an idea that sitting at the terminal makes the User into an Artist/Designer, resulting in huge savings. The computer graphics workstation is only as good or talented as its User/Operator.

The Author as Designer/Educator/Consultant cites, from personal case studies, desirable features of computer graphics as expressed by Business and Management:

1. A more efficient way to prepare data/information and a more effective way to communicate business information.

2. Since this permits the Designer to know the particular system(s), used to create the business and presentation graphics, the most effective and economical presentation may be designed using full capability of the system.

3. The presentation is created in-house on the Manager's system permitting control, access and security at all times.

4. A time-saving storing and filing system for electronic visuals means they are always in the same predictable place with clean original quality.

5. The expertise of the Designer is available as needed in the role of consultant, designer, instructor and guide.

6. The Designer may teach the Manager, Staff and Secretaries how to use the computer graphics system adding to the useability of in-house computer graphics for business and management.

7. With successful integration and teamwork, changes and updates may be made by the Manager and/or Staff. In addition to benefits mentioned, this permits unexpected last minute changes in the presentation data, deadlines being met, and without geographical limitations.

Graphic Designers may well examine their role and see where the questioning should be focused...the question of new technology and the computer taking over seems inconsequential in view of understanding the visual communication of information needs and demands of today, especially in the area of Business and Management Graphics in the Automated Office.

REFERENCES:

1. Sargent, Walter. The Enjoyment and Use of Color. Dover Publications, Inc. 180 Varick Street, New York, N.Y. U.S.A. 1964

2. Anderson, Donald M. The Art of Written Forms: The Theory and Practice of Calligraphy. Holt, Rinehart and Winston, Inc. 383 Madison Avenue, New York, N.Y. 10017. 1969

3. Ocvirk, Otto G. and Bone, Robert O. and Stinson, Robert E. and Wigg, Philip R. Art Fundamentals: Theory and Practice. Wm. C. Brown Company, Publishers, Dubuque, Iowa. 1978

4. Van Uchulen, Rod. Word Processing: A Guide to Typography, Taste, and In-House Graphics. Van Nostrand Reinhold Company, 135 West 50 Street, New York, N.Y. 10020, U.S.A. 1980

5. Pile, John F. Design: Purpose, Form and Meahing. W.W. Norton & Company, Inc. 500 Fifth Ave. New York, N.Y. 10036. 1979

6. Bernhard, Alice. Involve Your Graphic Artist/Designer. Business Graphics: Systems Implementation, U.S.A. case studies. Computer Graphics '83: International Conference. London, UK. October 1983.

7. Ellingson, David G. Niels Diffrient: Free to Test the Design Profession. Industrial Design Magazine's 28th Annual Review, Designer's Choice '82.

8. Bernhard, Alice. Involve Your Graphic Artist/Designer. Business Graphics: Systems Implementation, U.S.A. case studies. Computer Graphics '83: International Conference. London, UK. October 1983

9. Gates, David. Type. Watson-Guptill Publications, New York, N.Y. U.S.A. 1973

10. Hanks, Kurt and Belliston, Larry and Edwards, Dave. Design Yourself! William Kaufmann, Inc. One First Street, Los Altos, California 94022. 1978

11. Pile, John F. Design: Purpose, Form and Meaning. W.W. Norton & Company, Inc. 500 Fifth Avenue, New York 10036. 1979

12. Ocvirk, Otto G. and Bone, Robert O. and Stinson, Robert E. and Wigg, Philip R. Art Fundamentals: Theory and Practice. Wm. C. Brown Company, Publishers, Dubuque, Iowa. 1978.

13. Frye, Norma. Computer Slide Making in a Media Service Department. IEEE Computer Graphics and Applications. Vol. 3, No. 4 (ISSN 0272-1716), Jul. 1983. p.47.

14. Van Uchelen, Rod. Word Processing: A Guide to Typography, Taste, and In-House Graphics. Van Nostrand Reinhold Company, 135 West 50 Street, New York, N.Y. 10020, U.S.A. 1980

15. Stankowski, Anton. Visual Presentation of Invisible Processes: How to illustrate invisible processes in graphic design. Arthur Niggli Ltd. Teufen AR (Switzerland).

16. Ellingson, David G. Niels Diffrient: Free to Test the Design Profession. Industrial Design Magazine's 28th Annual Review, Designer's Choice '82.

17. Huelskoetter, Wayne R. The Evolution of Computerized Presentation Graphics at Dicomed. IEEEComputer Graphics and Applications. Vol. 3, No. 4 (ISSN 0272-1716), Jul. 1983. pp. 15-23.

Chapter 6
CAD/CAM

A Practical Application of a Computer to Industrial Design

Kenji Hatakenaka, Motokuni Yano, Akio Kotani,
Kazuo Yamada, Manabu Ishibashi, Yuichi Shibui,
Yutaka Kugai, Kenneth M. Jones, Kenichi Kobori[1]
and **Kiyoshi Sakashita**
Corporate Design Center, CAD Center[1]
Sharp Corporation
22-22 Nagaike-cho, Abeno-ku
Osaka 545, Japan

ABSTRACT
Computer graphics has found many applications in various fields in recent years. Industrial Design is an important task in the development process of many manufactured products. However, in the opinion of the authors many CAD/CAM systems have ignored or left unsolved such problems of emotion and sensitivity which are the stock in trade of artistically based activities such as Industrial Design. This paper describes a part of the CAD/CAM system introduced at the Sharp Corporation which is designed to satisfy the needs of the Industrial Designer in the specific task of design and production of graphics for product design. The CAPGraph (Computer Aided Product Graphics)system contains in its data base words,logos,graphic symbols,patterns and forms of designers 'know how', such as the spacing of the graphic elements commonly used in product designs. The system allows the designer to create graphic designs interactively using a graphic display and tablet, and then outputs automatically the finished artwork in a camera ready form suitable for use as a master for various printing processes.

INTRODUCTION
Ever increasing competition in manufacturing industry has resulted in the need to reduce product development time, increase productivity and improve the quality of products.
The application of CAD/CAM techniques to industry has offered one solution to some of these problems.Many CAD/CAM systems introduced into industry over recent years were intended for, and are used in,engineering based activities. These systems have had limited if any success when applied to art based activities such as Industrial Design

Previous CAD/CAM system development has placed an emphasis on algorithms for creating storing and manipulating such basic elements as points, lines, curves, surfaces and so on. The CAPGraph system takes this one step further by reproducing the accumulated 'know how' and specialised processes of the designers into the data base and interactive procedures of the system.This was achieved by researching and assimilating the graphic design techniques and knowledge of the designers within the company and incorporating it into the CAPGraph system. This makes it easy for the designers who must use the system to learn and accept it.
In this paper we will describe the principles behind,and the functions of, the CAPGraph system.

BACKGROUND
Today there are 183 designers working in the design department of the

Sharp Corporation on the Industrial Design of various products.
When the decision was taken at the top management level to exploit CAD/CAM technology within all sections of the manufacturing process, a study group was formed within the design center. This group was to look into the design practices with a view to finding the most effective ways to begin the introduction of CAD/CAM to the Industrial Design task.

Research into the daily work of the designers revealed that a disproportioate amount of time was being spent on the relatively noncreative task of drawing and finalising artwork for the printing of graphics onto products. This was found to be an average of 15% of a man year, rising to a maximum of 24% of a man year in some sections. This was seen by management to be too large an amount of time to be spent on such a task. Closer investigation found that this work was the result of minor changes required during the development of a product and was mostly noncreative and repetative in nature. Most designers disliked this work and wished to reduce the time spent doing it. The time saved could then be better spent doing more creative and interesting design tasks. It was decided that this area was the best candidate for the introduction of CAD/CAM into the design process of this company.

At the outset of the development of the CAPGraph system the following two principles were considered to be important:

1: The system should have a high level of interactivity.

2: The system should incorporate designers knowledge.

In order to create a CAD system to satisfy the needs of the graphic design task it was necessary to identify areas where rules and rationalisations could be applied. On investigation the following five areas for possible rationalisation were discovered:

1: If one ignores special alphabets, fashionable logotypes or marks, then most typography used on products was some form of the helvetica typeface in the case of English and NAR typeface in the case of Japanese.

2: All designers were basically using the same principles to determine the spacing between letters words and symbols. In actual practice however the spacing would vary according to the individual experience and aesthetic sense of each designer. This posed a problem for the quality control of the design and thus the overall corporate identity. Using the computer offered the possibility of standardising all spacing and thus overcome this problem.

3: The same words and phrases were being used over and over again on many different types of products with perhaps only minor changes. Using a CAD system words could be standardised and minor variations eliminated.

4: The minor modification of a piece of artwork was often required for different printing processes. This was being passed to external contractors resulting in quality control difficulties.

5: Model variations for OEM business and export markets requires making many versions of basically the same artwork with minor changes. This could be made considerably easier using a CAD system.

From these five areas the following principles were derived for the development of the CAPGraph system.

1: A new typeface original to Sharp based on the Helvetica Regular typeface should be developed for use in the system. In the case of Japanese the NAR typeface would be used.

2: The typeface data used in the system should be designed with regard for the special requirements of the different printing processes used by the company, eg. enlargement of reentrant corners in letter shapes for better ink flow in the silk screen process.

3: Letter and symbol spacing should be standardised and incorporated into the CAPGraph system allowing spacing to be done automatically by the computer.

4: The data base of the system should be designed to allow for organisation on the basis of the separate manufacturing divisions of the company.

5: The system should incorporate a facility which makes it possible to convert from one language to another or from one type style to another automatically.

6: The data base of the CAPGraph system should be compatible with the company's 3D CAD/CAM system for mechanical design (KERNEL 3D) which covers the total design process from conceptual design to tooling design and production. Fig.1 shows the relationship between the two systems.

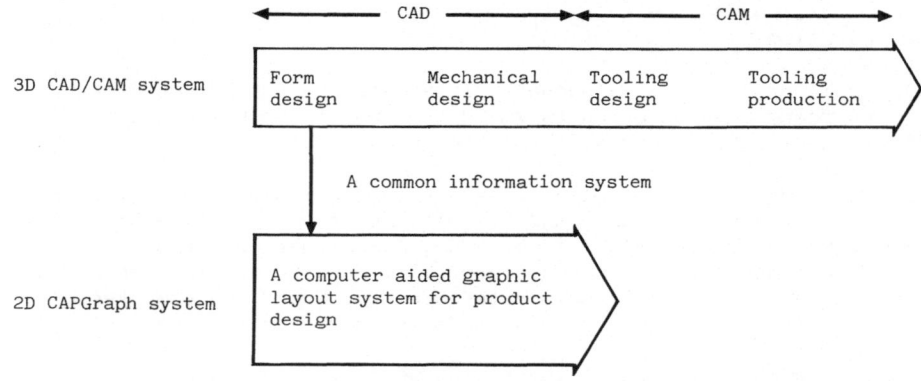

fig.1. The relationship between th 2D CAPGraph system and the 3D CAD/CAM system.

DESIGN KNOWLEDGE
The most important consideration when designing the CAPGraph system was the design of the actual letter forms and symbols and the system of spacing between them. This is one way in which designers knowledge was introduced to the system.
It was important to ensure that the artwork output by the system should not be illegible or open to misinterpretation when printed onto products. For

this reason all of the letters, characters and symbols in the system were individually designed with full regard for such things as aesthetics, clarity and the limitations of the computer and plotting machines. These points will now be considered in further detail.

TYPEFACES

So that the typefaces should have a uniform appearance when printed by different printing processes two versions of each letter were designed, one type suitable for the offset printing process and the other suitable for the silk screen printing process. One example of the differences between the two is the practice of enlarging corners to allow for the viscosity of printing inks. In the case of the silk screen process the ink is more viscous than that of the offset printing process and this is allowed for by making the corners proportionately larger, this can be seen illustrated in fig.2.

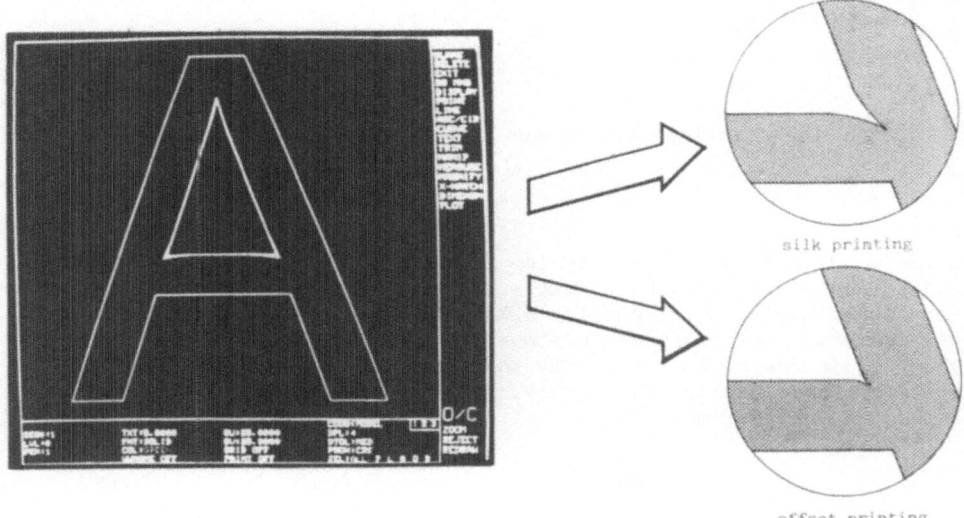

fig.2. The differences between typefaces for silk screen and offset printing.

SPACING

The principles of the spacing system are shown in fig.3. All letters, characters and symbols used in the system were based on a hypothetical uniform body size. The actual visual forms being visually balanced within this body. This ensures that any combination of Japanese characters, English letters, numbers or symbols of the same height will all appear visually correct.

The spacing system is worked out on the basis of the body size and the correct visual spacing for all necessary combinations are retained in the data base. Japanese characters are used vertically and horizontally which requires that spacing for both cases must be retained.

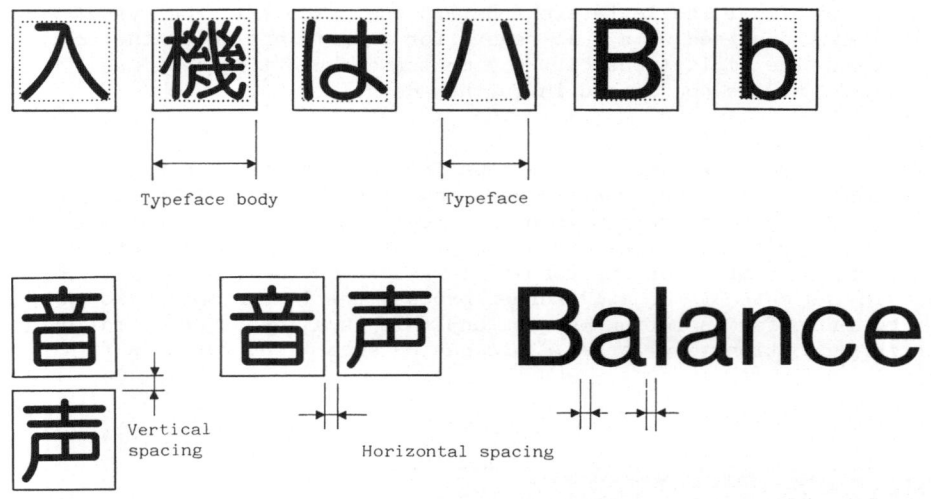

fig.3. The relationship between body size type size and spacing.

TRANSLATION
All the words and labels used on the control panels of products have been standardised and it must be possible to recall and include these in a piece of art work. Model variations for OEM business and for export means that these words must be retained in a number of different languages and type styles, it is desirable to be able to convert artwork output from one to another of these easily and quickly. Fig. 4 shows some of the variations required of the system.

Japanese	Capitals	Capital+small	Small
黒レベル	BRIGHTNESS	Brightness	brightness
バランス	BALANCE	Balance	balance
音声	AUDIO	Audio	audio
補助入力	AUX-IN	Aux-In	aux-in

fig.4. Variations of language and type styles.

HARDWARE CONFIGURATION
The hardware configuration of the CAPGraph system is outlined in fig.5. The current implimentation uses a VAX 11/780 32 bit super mini computer with a disc drive and 2MB of memory. The design work station is comprised

of a colour raster graphic display and tablet for interactive input. A character display and keyboard for alpha numeric input and output and parts listing etc.. Output devices supported include a pen/cutter plotter, electrostatic plotter, photo plotter etc. this work station is shown in photo.1.

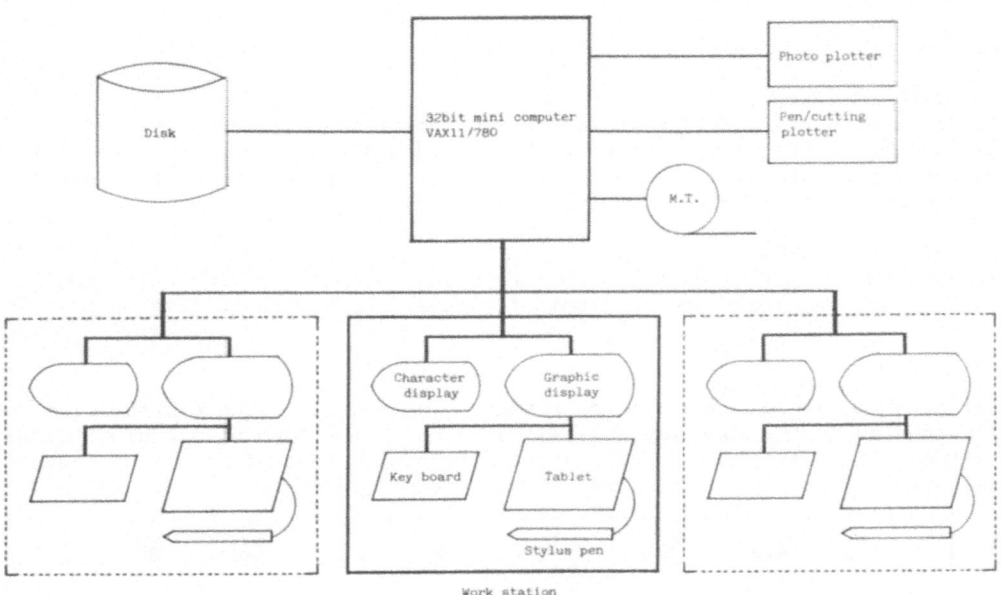

fig.5. The hardware configuration.

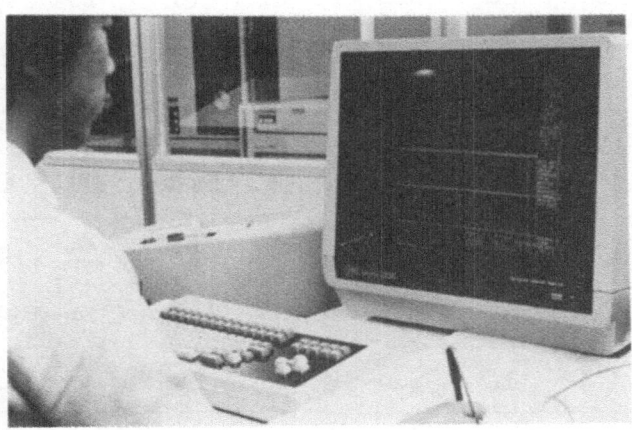

photo.1. The design work station.

DATA BASE STRUCTURE
The data base of the CAPGraph system is based on five disc files (see fig. 8), these are as follows:

1: Typeface File
2: Spacing Data File
3: Graphic Symbol File
4: Word Management File
5: Word Library File

1: TYPEFACE FILE
These files contain the basic letters and characters in the form of two dimensional patterns consisting of basic lines,circles and arcs. Letter forms suitable for both silk screen printing and offset printing are retained in a a form suitable for direct output on artwork.

2: SPACING DATA FILE
The spacing data file contains data representing the most suitable spacing between all necessary combinations of the letters and characters in the system.

3: GRAPHIC SYMBOL FILE
All graphic used on products are retained in this file. These symbols are represented in the same way as the typefaces in the form of two dimensional patterns. The size of the symbols is uniform with that of the typefaces. A selection of the symbols in the system is shown in fig.6.

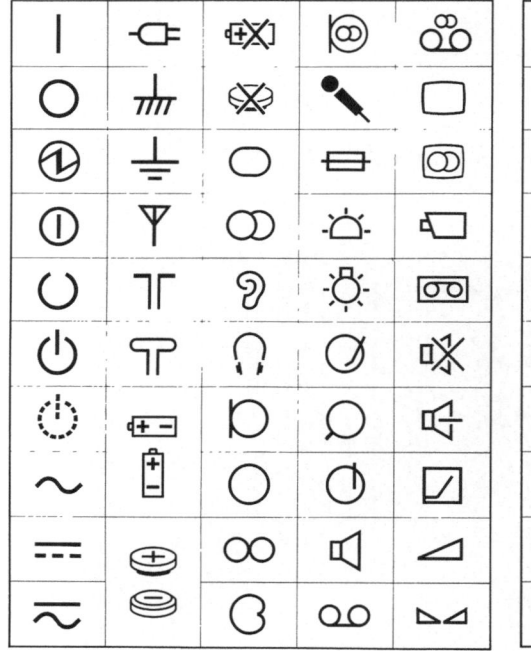 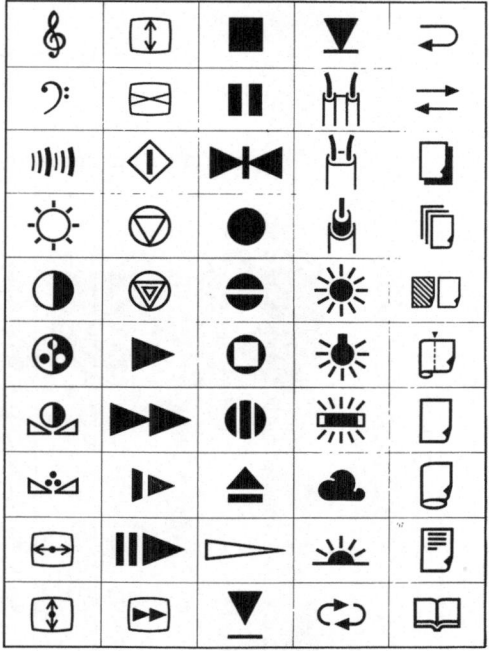

fig.6. Typical graphic symbols.

4: WORD MANAGEMENT FILE
This file contains the data necessary for the management of the word files
in the system. This data is needed for listing,translation sorting,searching
and creation of word files. Also retained in this file is a count of the
number of times a particular word is used, this facilitates the culling of
old and infrequently used words thus economising on disc space.

5: WORD LIBRARY FILE
Words most frequently used on products have been standardised and stored
in the library files on the basis of product type. Words are combinations
of basic typeface data combined with spacing data stored as patterns,the use
of word files is controlled by the data in the word management file.

SOFTWARE CONFIGURATION
An important factor in the acceptability of any CAD/CAM system by users is
wether it is easy to use, that is to say the level of interactivity of the
system.The CAPGraph system attempts to solve the problem of repeated input
of the same data,common to many CAD systems, by using preprepared patterns
in the form of typefaces and words.

The basic letter forms and symbols are first created by input of the
individual geometric data elements of lines and arcs etc. using the interactive 2D geometric editor these being stored in the form of patterns. Words
are automatically assembled and combined with spacing data and again stored
as patterns. The work of creating artwork consists of calling up these
patterns any placing them on the layout.

The system is divided into two programs; the word management program (WDMNG)
which is used with a keyboard and character display, and manages the word
library files; and the **artwork production** program which uses the interactive
graphic display for layout of the artwork in two dimensional space.

WORD MANAGEMENT PROGRAM (WDMNG)   fig.7
In the design of electronic goods the rate of innovation of new products
is very fast and new symbols and words are being created all the time for
use on these new products. The CAPGraph system has been designed to make it
possible to update the symbols and words in the data base quickly and easily.
The creation and maintenance of new words is carried out with the word management program. When a new word is created it is input from the keyboard in
either Japanese or English, the word is then stored in character form in
the word management file, the word is stored in alphabetical order. In the
next step the program takes the geometric data for each letter or character
from the typeface files and combines this with the correct spacing data and
inserts the new pattern onto the word library file. This program also enables
the use frequency of words to be examined so that obsolete and infreqently
used words can be deleted if necessary. In this way word library files can
be created and maintained by persons in authority such as a system manager.

ARTWORK PRODUCTION PROGRAM (AWP)   fig.8
The CAPGraph system can receive 2D data converted from 3D models created with
the company's 3D CAD/CAM system or 2D models can be created directly with
the system. AWP is a menu driven interactive program and has, as well as
basic drawing commands, the specialised commands required for graphic design
and art work production.These special commands include the following five

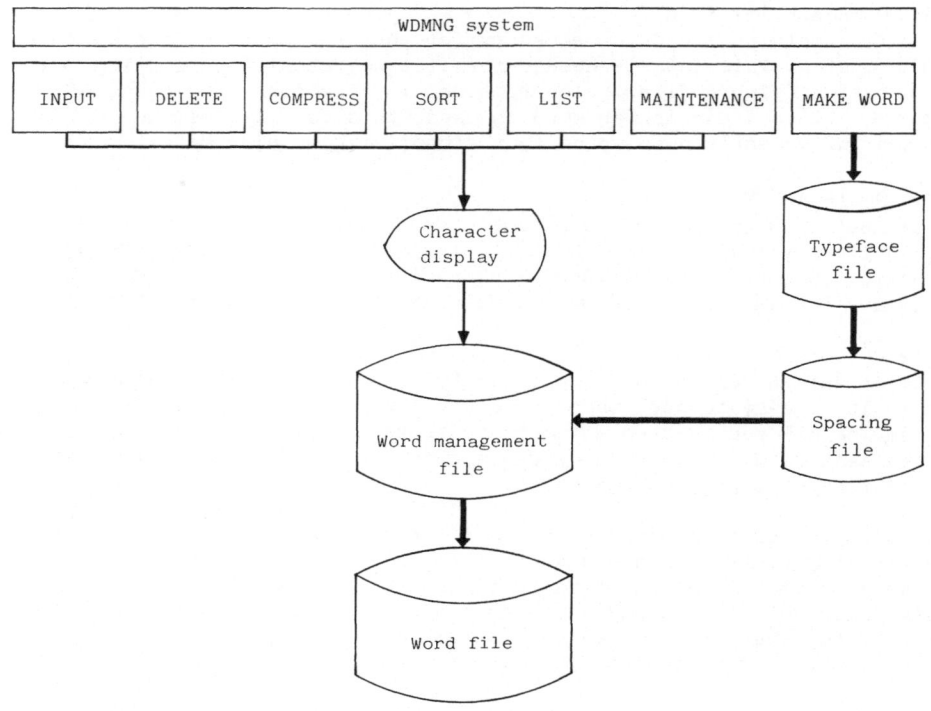

fig.7. Diagram of the word management program.

functions; WDLYOT, WDTRNS, MAKWRD, PICLYOT, MAKTMB.
The designer selects the functions from a menue and creates the art work on
the graphic display. Each function will now explained in detail.

WORD LAYOUT (WDLYOT)
English and Japanese words in the library file in pattern form are selected
and placed onto the artwork with this function. Artwork for both languages
or alternative styles can be created at the same time by selecting the
desired data. When patterns are retreved the designer can specify type size,
rotation angle and origin point by keying in the values at the keyboard. The
word is then displayed on the graphic display in the appropiate position on
the layout and, word lists and data related to the selected word can be
presented on the character display.

WORD TRANSLATION (WDTRNS)
Previously created artwork files can be converted to other languages or type
styles with the word translation function. The artwork is translated at the
graphic display automatically by the program and the file is then available
for visual checking and editing by the designer. WDLYOT and WDTRNS operate

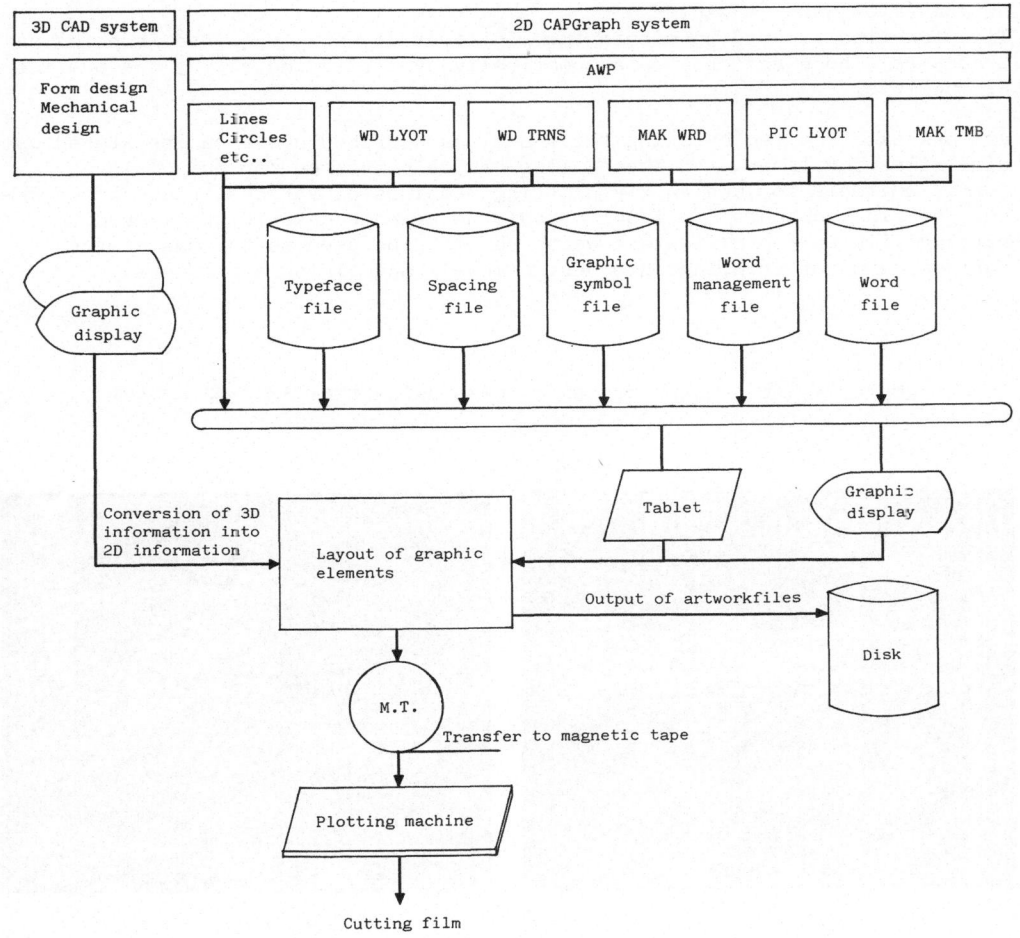

fig.8. Diagram of the artwork production program.

only on those words contained in the word library file less frequently used words are handled by the next function.

MAKE WORD (MAKWRD)
Infrequently used or other special words such as model numbers can be temporarily created at the keyboard and placed on the artwork with this function. The procedure is the same as that for WDLYOT.

PICTURE LAYOUT (PICLYOT)
Symbols, logos and other nonword graphics can be selected and placed in the same way as words with the PICLYOT function.

REGISTRATION MARKS (MAKTMB)
This function is used to create the registration marks required in printing processes. These are created automatically by merely indicating the outline of the model.

Artwork data created by using the functions decribed above can be stored on disc files for later use. These files can be converted for output in a format suitable for use on x-y plotting machines of various types for checking and final output. For final output the graphic data is transfered to cutting film or photo plotters which can then be used as the master for various forms of printing onto design models and finished products.

photo.2. The artwork design process using the CAPGraph system (a)-(k).

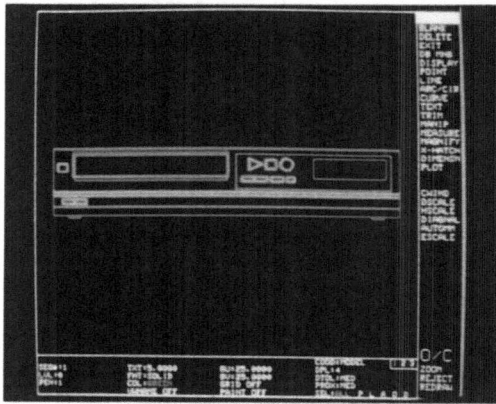
(a) 3D geometric model,

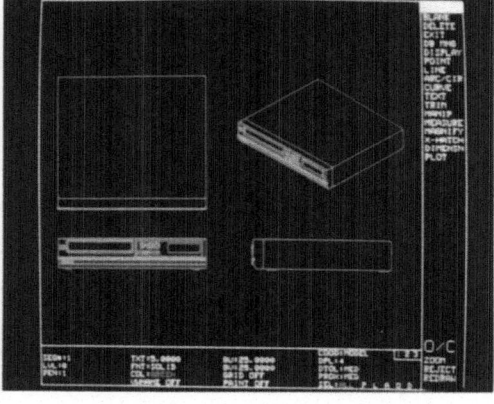
(b) conversion to 2D,

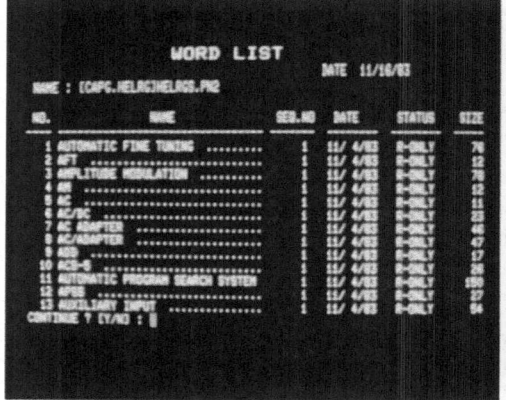
(c) selection of word from list,

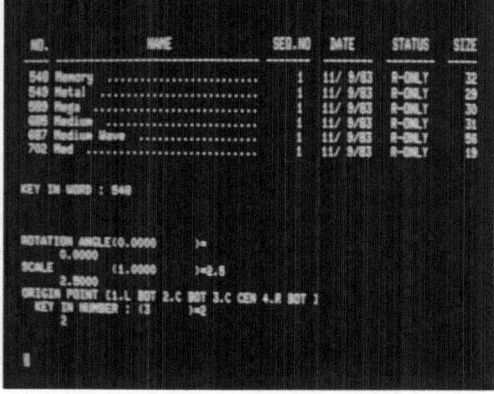
(d) input of size, angle and origin of word,

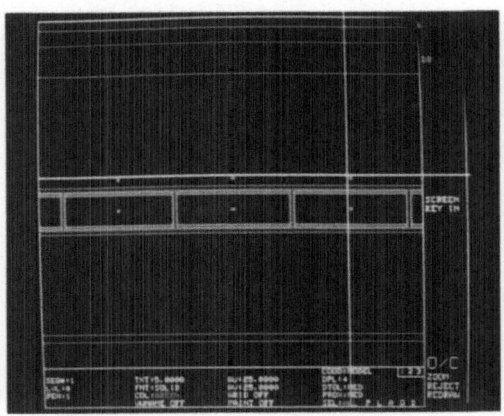
(e) selection of origin on layout,

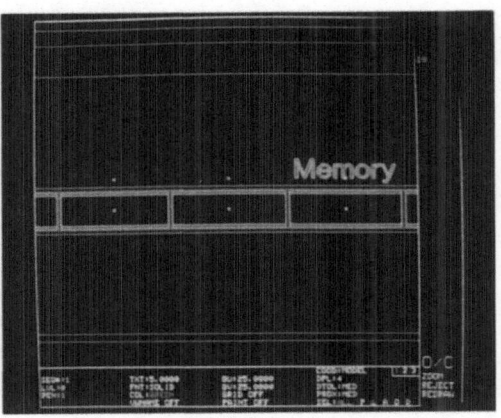
(f) retrieval of the word,

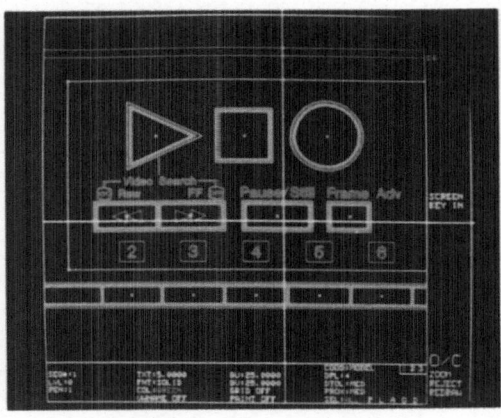
(g) examples of symbols,

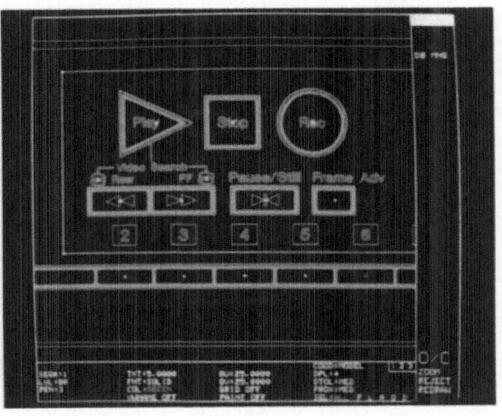
(h) the completed layout,

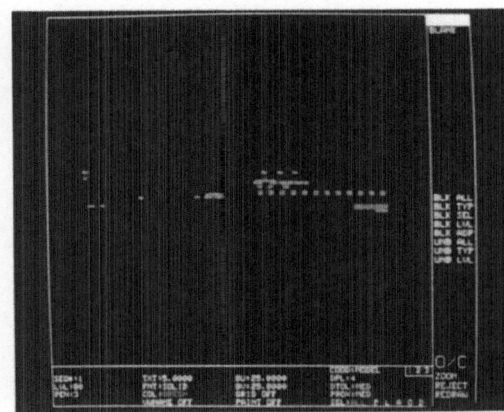
(i) removal of unnecessary data,

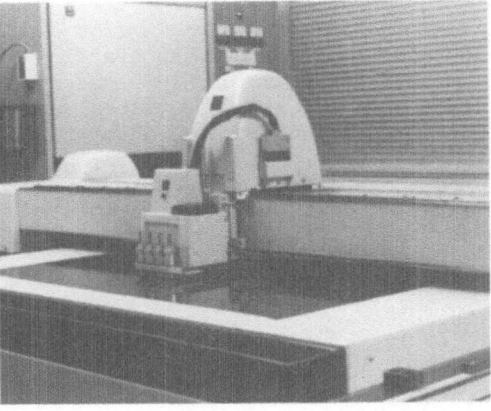
(k) the final output onto cutting film.

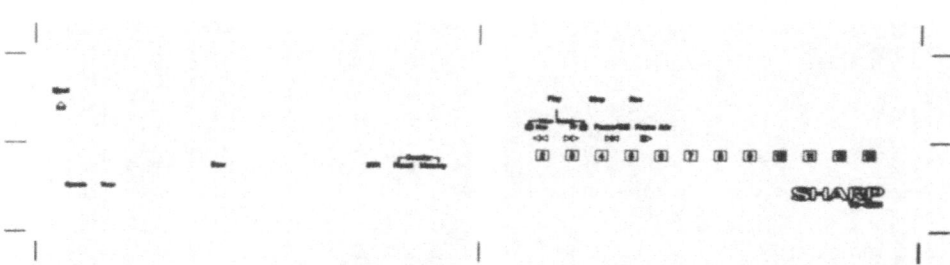

fig.9. An example of artwork with registration marks shown.

photo.3. An example showing the graphics on a video tape recorder.

CONCLUSION
An interactive system for the production of graphic artwork has been described. This system is intended for use by professional designers in the product design field and contains such artistic based knowledge as the size and spacing retationship between words and symbols. Various functions derived from actual company practices such as conversion between languages and type styles are incorporated into the system.
Further developments such as, the automatic selection of type size based on the usage of the product being designed and user eye distances and more legible typefaces are contemplated for future implementation.
This system has been introduced and is contributing to the productivity of the designers and allows them to spend their time on more creative tasks.

The CAPGraph system represents the starting point for the introduction of CAD/CAM to the Industrial Design process in the Sharp Corporation. We hope to be able to develop a total CAD/CAM system for Industrial Designers in the future.

ACKNOWLEDGMENTS
The authors would like to thank all the members the design center and the CAD center of the company, without whose help and hard work the CAPGraph project would would not have been possible.

REFERENCES
1: Kenchiku Sekkei Shusei,Architectural Institute of Japan 1983.

2: Istu Hirasawa and Kenji Hatakenaka: Perspective of Human Space - Experiment of Electronic Cottage, Sharp Technical Journal, pp.67-74.(1982)

3: Kenichi Kobori, Yoshinobu Sato, Yoshihiro Nagata, Kenneth M. Jones and Ikuo Nishioka: Development of a Total 3D CAD/CAM System for Electronic Appliances, MICAD'84,1984.

Development of a Total 3D CAD/CAM System for Electric Appliances

Kenichi Kobori, Yoshihiro Nagata,
Yoshinobu Sato, Kenneth M. Jones
and Ikuo Nishioka
CAD Center, Sharp Corporation
2613-1 Ichinomoto, Tenri
Nara 632, Japan

Abstract

This paper presents an overview of a 3D CAD/CAM system for electric appliances. The distinctive features of the system are as follows;
1) The system supports a wide range of design activities, conceptual design, engineering design and production design.
2) The system enables a conceptual designer to evaluate design options based on realistic representations of objects.
3) Various kinematic simulation functions enable engineers to analyze mechanisms.

Introduction

There has been a growing interest in CAD/CAM systems for mechanical design, and there are many systems in use throughout the world. However, because these systems are general purpose in nature, we found that they did not satisfy our needs. As a result of such findings, we started the development of an original system several years ago. At this present time, we have put this system, which supports not only drawing functions, but also various simulation functions, to practical use. We have developed the system based on the following four principles.
   1) Producing a drawing is not necessarily design.
   2) The system must aid the designer in mutually effective ways, that is to say, by using the computer for tasks at which it is most efficient and at which the human being is least efficient.
   3) The system must be a total design tool, which cover all processes of design, from conceptual design to N/C processes in tooling design.
   4) At the conceptual design stage, it should realize effective presentation of the designed object.
This system is unique in its emphasis on the implementation of principles 2) and 4) outlined above. In the case of principle 2), an interactive kinematic simulation facility helps engineers create more accurate designs. In case of principle 4), the difficulty of applying CAD systems to the industrial design task has been solved by the use of realistic presentation of models with surface definition, shading and texture simulation techniques.

Hardware configuration

The hardware configuration is illustrated in Fig. 1. The system operates on a VAX 11 computer coupled with a color graphic display for line drawing. This color display coupled with a tablet forms the basic workstation of the system.

The color raster display(1) has 24 bits per pixel, and can present realistic images of objects created at the line drawing device during the conceptual design stage. At this stage, the designer merely inputs several surface detail parameters of the object, such as material, color, etc. As a result he can get a sophisticated shaded image on this display.
The color display(2) has a simple shading capability implemented in hardware. The user can get greater understanding than that provided by 3D wire frame pictures at interactive speed.
The scanner and TV camera reads 2 dimensional textures and patterns which are used in electric appliance design, and the system simulates the appearance of the object with the texture applied to the surface (TEXTURE MAPPING).
The machining center, which is directly connected to the computer, mills a model by using cutter path information generated by the N/C module. This plays an important part in the generation of a physical prototype or the production of molds.

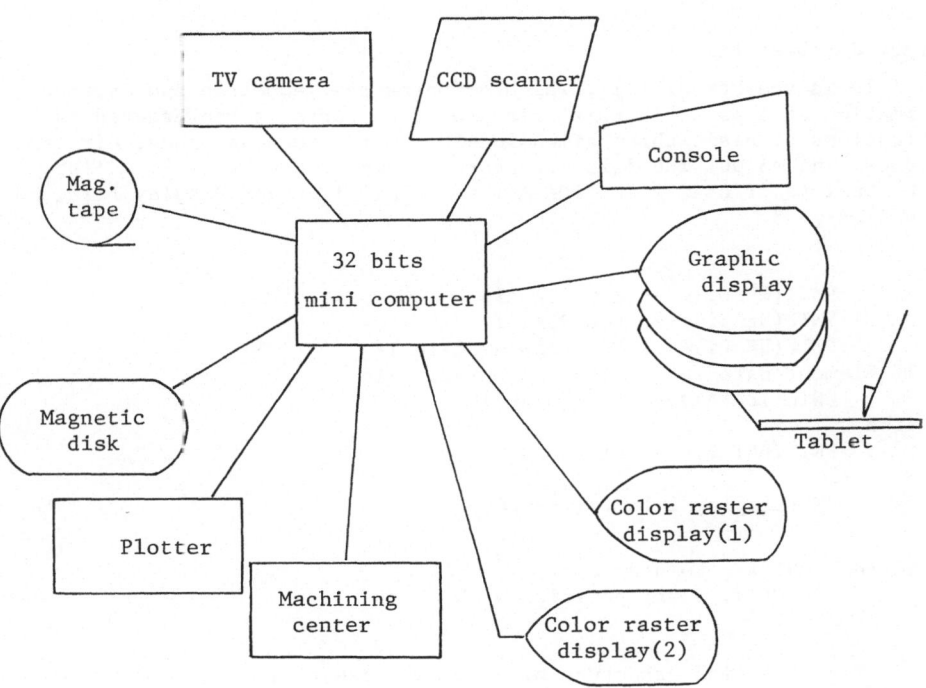

Fig. 1 Hardware configuration

Data structure

In this system, the part data base file is the main file, which can be converted into formats suitable for other modules and applications, as shown in Fig. 2.

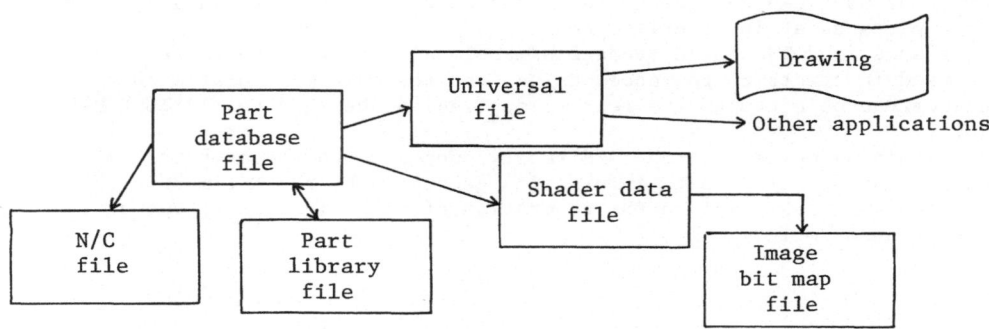

Fig. 2 Data structure

A) Part database file

This file is the kernel file, which contains the geometric and attribute information of a part. In this file a part or parts is represented by combinations of basic three dimensional elements such as lines, circles, surfaces, and so on. The file structure is constructed by a link list, which consists of HEAD list, IDATA list, RDATA list and Display file, as shown in Fig. 3.

```
        PNT1(HEADi)←--- LOC(IDATAi)
        PNT2(HEADi)←--- LOC(RDATAi)
        PNT3(HEADi)←--- LOC(Display file i)
If element data .eq. surface or group then
        PNTn(IDATAi)←--- LOC(HEADj)
else
        PNT(IDATAi)←--- empty
end if
        PNT(Display file i)←--- LOC(HEADi)


where   PNT(X): Pointer of X
        LOC(X): Start position of X
```

Fig. 3 A link structure of part database file

The IDATA list, the RDATA list and Display file are managed and maintained by HEAD list. This HEAD list contains various information such as a select flag for editing use and a visibility flag for windowing, which are intended to realize faster interactivity (see Fig. 4).

```
1) Data type
2) Attribute data
3) Select flag
4) Visibility flag
5) Group flag
6) Library flag
7) Pointers to IDATA, RDATA and Display file
```

Fig. 4 Contents of record in HEAD list

IDATA list contains detailed relational information concerning an element and several pointers by which groups of elements and surfaces are formed. RDATA list is composed of blocks, each in the form of variable length records containing the geometric information necessary to specify an element.
Display file data is divided into two parts, head record and data record. The head record contains a visible flag and a select flag for fast editing. The data record consists of two dimensional screen coordinate data, as shown in Fig. 5. Lines are represented by 'SET POSITION' and 'VECTOR'. In order to reduce the Display file data size, points are represented by 'SET POINT' only.

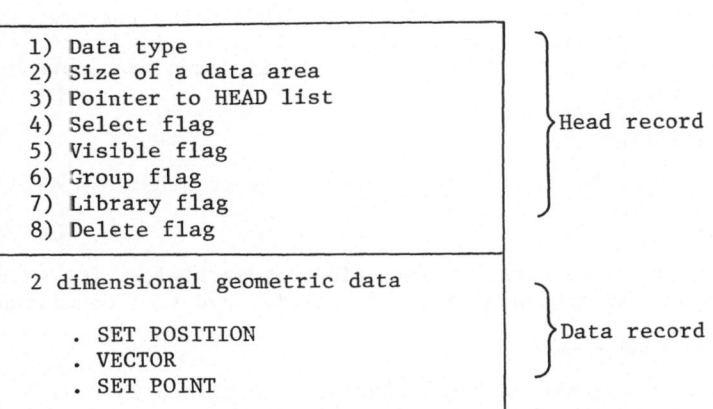

Fig. 5 Contents of record in Display file data

B) Part library file

A part library file is a common file which provides an efficient way to store collections of many standard parts which all users of the system can access. This file has the same structure as the part database file, and in addition contains informations related to security and data management.

C) Shader data file

This file is used by the Design simulation module and contains geometric and attribute data necessary for the generation of sophisticated shaded images. Such data includes surface data, normal vector, color, reflection properties, surface textures and so forth.
The shade data file structure is also constructed by a link list as shown in Fig. 6.

```
PNT1(Parts head i)←--- LOC(Polygon data i)
PNT(Polygon data i)←---LOC(Geometric data i)
PNT(Geometric data i)←---LOC(Parts head i)

PNT2(Parts head i)←---LOC(Shade data i)

PNT3(Parts head i)←---LOC(Texture head i)
PNT(Texture head i)←---LOC(Texture data i)
```

where PNT(X): Pointer of X
      LOC(X): Start position of X

Fig. 6 A link structure of shader data file

Parts head list contains parts names, parts types and pointers to the polygon data, shade data and texture data lists.
Polygon data list contains various polygon attributes used when generating the scene such as texture mapping status, shading style, etc. This list also contains the pointers to the geometric data of the polygon.
Shade data list includes the color data, reflection and transparency attributes of the parts in the 'scene'.
Texture head list contains pointers to texture data, texture names, texture type and other information used during texture mapping.
Texture data consists of color data, reflection and transparency attributes for each texture.

D) Universal file

This file is used for plotting or interfacing to other system.

E) N/C file

The N/C file contains detail information for machining, for example, characteristics of the N/C machines, and material and tool conditions.

<u>Software configuration</u>

The software configuration of the system is outlined in Fig. 7. The present implementation of the system consists of nine modules which are outlined below.

A) 3D Interactive modeler

The interactive modeler of this system has a high level of interactivity in the human interface. Fig. 8 shows the screen layout of the 3D Interactive modeler. The menu on the right hand side has a hierarchical structure in order to protect against an operation miss. The lower section

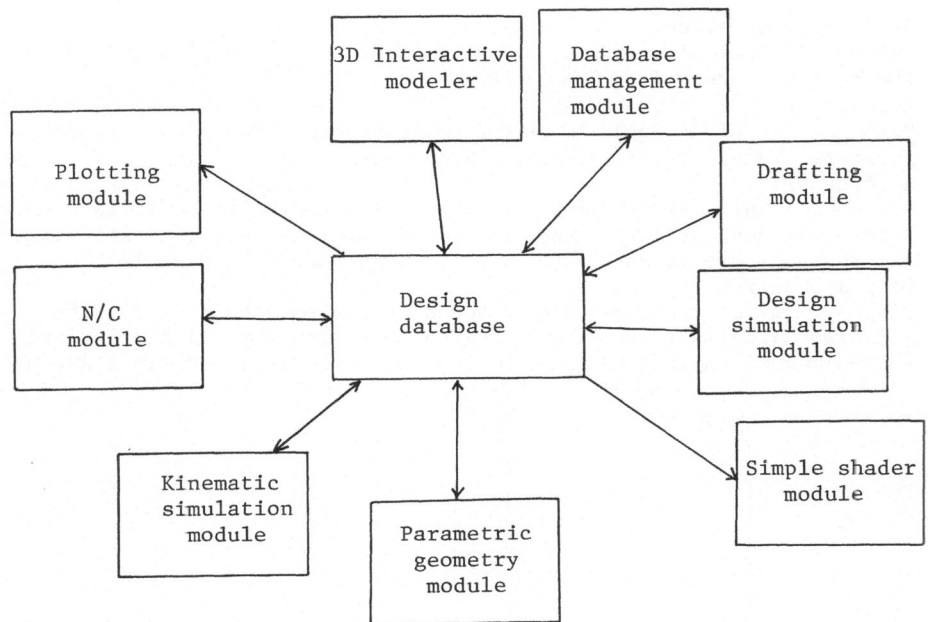

Fig. 7 Software configuration

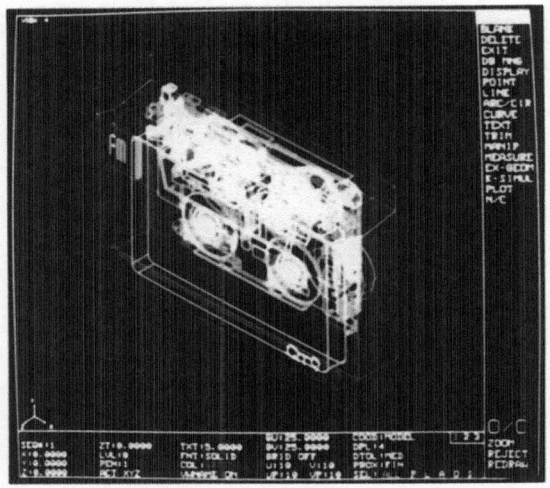

Fig. 8 The screen layout of the modeler

contains information on the status of the system including such things as line font, color, text size, grid scale and so on. These values can be changed at any time during the codeling process. The model consists of a collection of basic elements, such as points, lines, circles, arcs, ellipses, splines and texts. The modeler provides the following functions.

- Generation of basic elements.
- Deletion of basic elements.
- Data manipulation. Move, rotation, mirror, array, group, trim, fillet, scale, stretch (see Fig. 9), etc.
- Assembly function. The function assembles several parts quickly into a unit by indicating a face on each part.

. Cross section slice.
  Automatic sectioning allows the details of a part to be examined during the design process (see Fig. 10).
. Mesurement.
  Verification of a single element, relationship between two elements, perimeter, area, ruler, 3D grid, etc.
. Surfaces[1].
  A range of surfaces including planes, ruled, revolution, fillet, curve driven and mesh surfaces can be created interactively (see Fig. 11). All surfaces are trimmed with any other surface (see Fig. 12).
. Display control.
  Display control routines can be speedily implemented by using the efficient display file. Models can be seen from any orientation and at any magnification, with up to four windows displayed simultaneously.

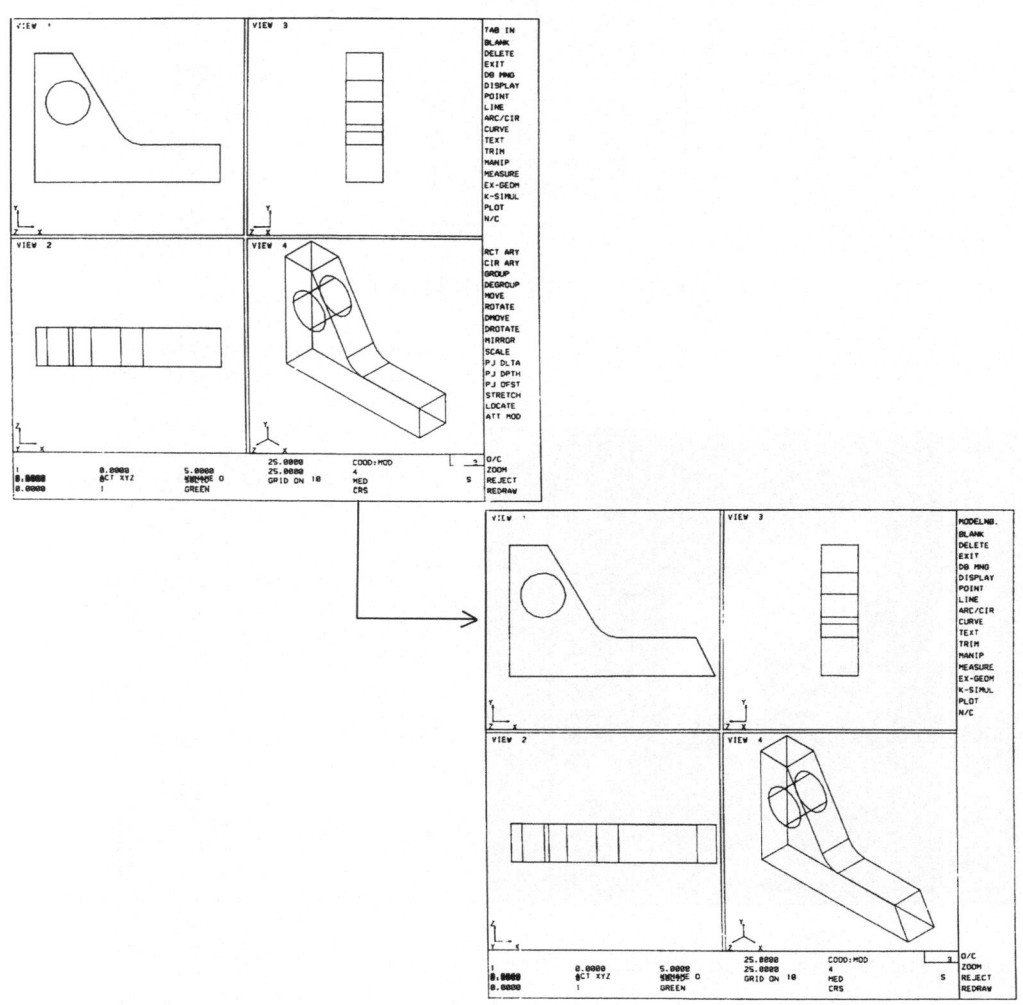

Fig. 9 An example of the 'stretch' command

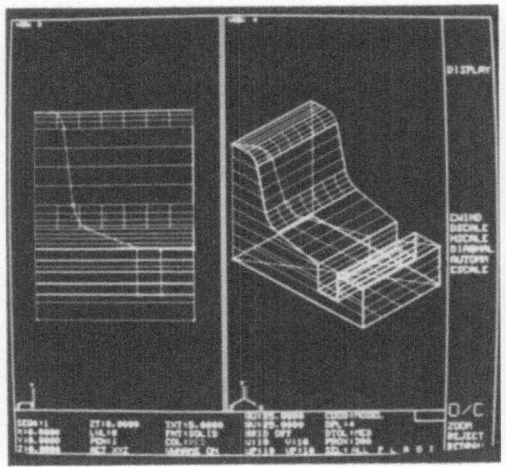

Fig. 10 An example of a cross section slice

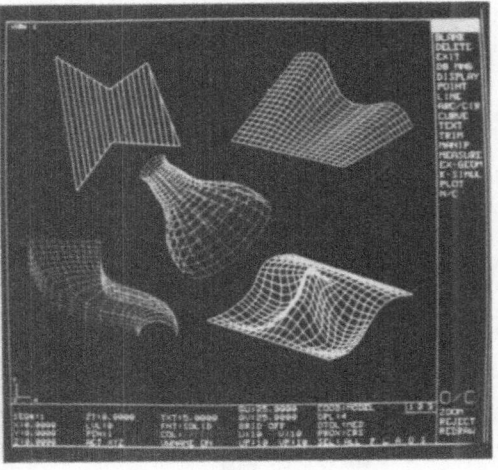

Fig. 11 An example of various surfaces

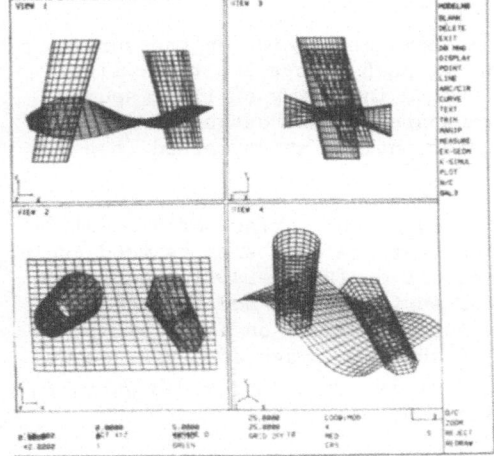

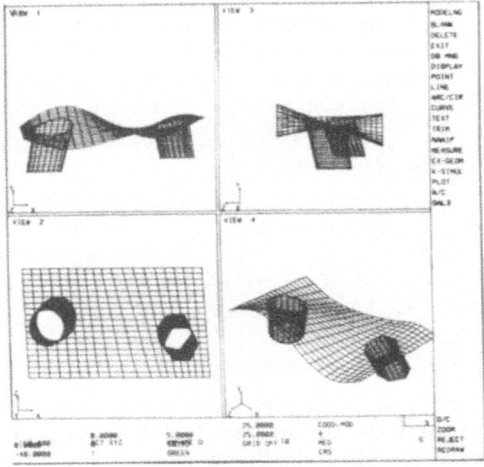

Fig. 12 An example of the 'surface trim' function

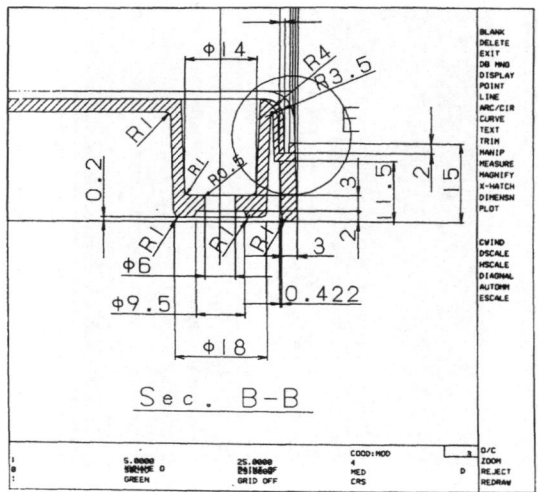

Fig. 13 An example of dimensioning

B) Drafting module

This module is capable of creating high quality drawings to the JIS standard.
Features include;
- Automatic dimensioning of elements inside a specific area.
- Easy modification of dimensioning.
- Automatic generation of a magnified copy of data within a circular region.

Fig. 13 shows an example of dimensioning.

C) Design simulation module

This module is a design tool which is intended to emulate the designer's thought process, and includeds the following features.

- Generation of a shaded image[2],[3].
  The shading routines determine the shade of a point on the surface of a model in term of several attributes such as eye position, light source position, reflective properties, intensity of light source, intensity of ambient lighting, transparency, and outputs a shaded image using the polygon normal vector interpolation method (see Fig. 14).
- Representation of texture.
  Two dimensional textures can be mapped on the surface of a model[4], [5]. The system uses two dimensional texture data such as wood grain, which has been digitized with a scanner or TV camera. Subsequently this data is tranformed on selected surfaces in a model space and sampled for display. The stone pattern is mapped on each wall of a castle as shown in Fig. 15. Fig. 16 shows an image of a rice cooker with a painted gradation around it. It is possible for designers to evaluate such effects in a realistic way.

D) Simple shader module

A color shaded image can be automatically displayed during the construction process by utilizing the intelligence of the graphic terminal. These images are displayed rapidly, allowing the engineer to work at interactive speed. The algorithm is based on the Gouraud intensity interpolation method (see Fig. 17) [6].

E) Parametric geometry module

There are two approaches to define a model, one way is to use the 3D Interactive modeler as mentioned above, the other is to use the parametric geometry module. There are many parts with a similar shape used in electric appliances, such as standard parts like screws, keypads, etc. This module provides an algorithmic language which contains Fortran statements, and

Fig. 14 An example of a shaded image

Fig. 15 An example of texture mapping

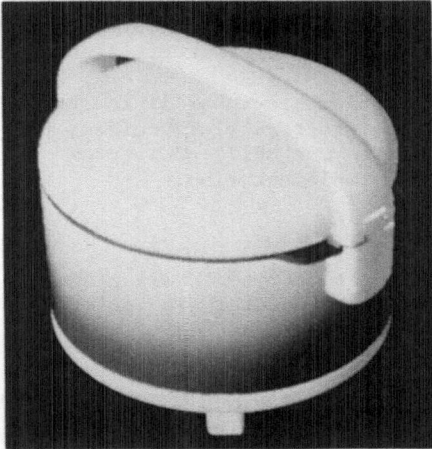

Fig. 16 An image of a rice cooker

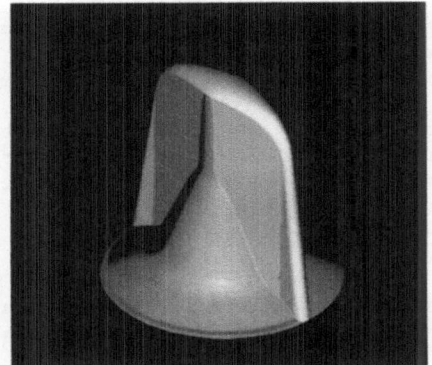

Fig. 17 An example of simple shading

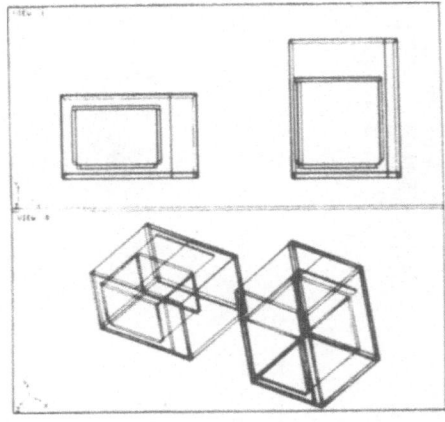

Fig. 18 Parametric geometry parts

geometry defined with   algorithmic programming provides a powerful tool for the generation of families of parts.

For instance, when this technique is applied to a micro wave oven design, if the dimensions of the oven's bottom plate are decided then the overall size and necessary wall and door clearance can be found according to a simple formula. Thus a three dimensional model can be recreated by the parametric language (see Fig. 18). When this process was applied to the actual design of an oven, design time was reduced to one third and design error was significantly reduced.

F) Kinematic simulation module

The authors have found that previous systems for kinematic simulation were difficult to use, with in most cases, off-line data creation and lacking in interactivity. As a result, we have developed an interactive kinematic simulation function which can be invoked at any point during the model creation process. Furthermore, hither to difficult simulation problems have been made possible by the inclusion of the following capabilities.
  . Spline curves can be used for slide lines (see Fig. 19).
  . Interference with arbitrary elements can be used as limits of motion
    for connector links as well as driver links.
With previous link simulation systems if link mechanisms with more than four bar links are to be analyzed a convergence technique is utilized with its associated inaccuracy and slowness.
The authors have found that in most design problems four bar links or combinations of four bar links can be used satisfactorily. Therefore, this system uses the instantaneous center of rotation method[7] and vector algebra resulting in a fast and more accurate implementation.

G) Database management module

The database management module is a manager's tool for controlling and organizing parts and libraries of parts. The module contains a variety of commands for modifying a model's attributes.

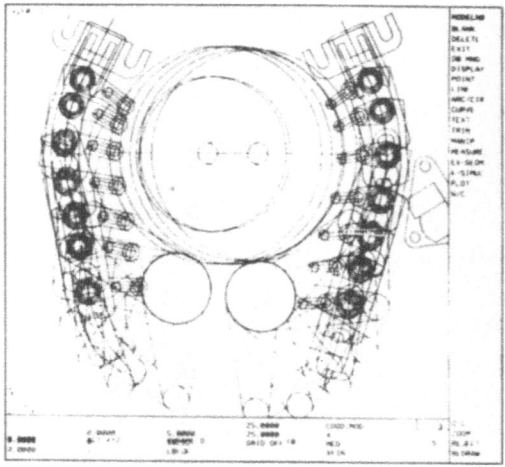
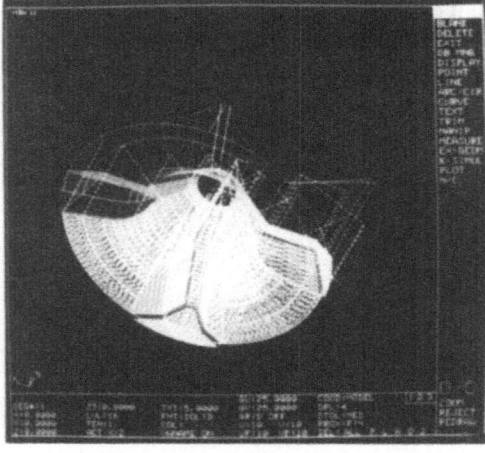

Fig. 19 The result of link simulation   Fig. 20 An example of N/C cutter path

H) N/C module

In this module, cutter paths for the N/C machine tools can be generated directly from a computer model, as shown in Fig. 20, and physical model is machined by this cutter path information. This capability allows the creation of prototypes accurately and speedily. The module generates cutter path information from tangent vectors along the surface, and the use of check surfaces prevents under or over milling by the tool.

Conclusion

We have described an outline of a CAD/CAM system, which supports a wide range of design activities from industrial design to the manufacturing. This system has contributed much to reducing design errors and optimizing product performance and quality. Development is continuing on more complex simulation packages, expanded interactivity and enhanced design tools for the industrial designer.

Reference

[1] D.F. Rogers and J.A. Adams: Mathematical Element for Computer Graphics, McGraw-Hill, 1976
[2] Blinn, J.F.: " Models of light reflection for computer synthesized pictures", Computer Graphics, Vol. 11, No 2, Summer 1977
[3] Bui-Tuong, Phong: "Illumination for Computer-Generated Images," CACM, 18(6):311-317, June 1975
[4] Blinn, J.F. and Newell, M.E.:"Texture and reflection in computer generated images," CACM, 19(10):542-547, Oct. 1976
[5] Eliot A. Feibush, Marc Levoy, Robert L. Cook: "Synthetic texturing using digital filters," Computer Graphics, Vol. 14, No. 3 July 1980, pp. 294-301.
[6] Gouraud, H: "Continuous Shading of Curved Surfaces," IEEE Trans. on computer, June 1971, pp. 623-629
[7] J.E.Shigley: Theory of Machines, pp. 104, McGraw-Hill, 1961

Bottle Design Arts System

Yoshio Sato and **Makoto Akeo**
Applications Software Development
Nippon Univac Kaisha, Ltd.
17-51, Akasaka 2-chome, Minato-ku
Tokyo 107, Japan

ABSTRACT

BDAS is a CAD system developed for the purposes of bottle design. It was developed with the primary requirement that it be a practical system, and as such its development required a full analysis of bottle characteristics. The results of this analysis were employed to produce a system designed to permit dramatic improbement in the efficiency of design work and require only simple operation for such operations as shape definition, shape modification, design calculation, precision rendering, output of 3-view drawings, output of mesh data, and output of data to NC programs.

1. INTRODUCTION

New product development of detergents, shampoos, and cosmetics etc. is a field subject to fierce competition. It is therefore vitally important that development times are reduced to the minimum in order to ensure that no opportunities are lost in placing new products on the market.

Shape of bottles used for these products has an important effect on their customer appeal, usability etc. so that these factors must be given considerable thought by the conceptual designer. These shapes commonly involve complex curves and are rarely duplicated in another product.

The CAD system described in this paper was developed at the request of Lion Corporation for the purposes of bottle design in consideration of the points mentioned above.

A quick glance at bottle design commonly leaves the impression that it is a field easily applicable to use with a CAD system. This impression stems from that fact that bottles frequently consist of free curves which need only be defined and rotated on the vertical axis to produce a bottle shape, the rotated shape being modified as required to produce infinite variation. This impression, combined with the numerable photographs of bottle shapes output on graphic terminal screens have lead to a rather oversimplified view of the field.

While a large number of these photographs have been published, only a small number of the designs have ever reached the stage of being developed into a final product. This is primarily due to considerations of bottle volume and ease of molding etc., as well the difficulties involved in modelling shapes exactly as conceived by the conceptual designer.

The following sections are centered on descriptions of the functions of the BDAS system.

2. BASIC DEVELOPMENT PHIOLOSOPHY

The following requirements were established before development began in order to ensure BDAS as a practical and easily operated system.

(i)   Well developed functions to support product design.

(ii) Ease of operation.

(iii) No knowlecge of geometrical theory required to operate the system.

(iv) Short processing times to permit completed design of approximately one bottle per cay.

In order to satisfy these requirements the following work was performed prior to programming.

(i)   Approximately 1000 design drawings were statistically analyzed to obtain information as to line and surface characteristics, and commands and parameters determined accordingly.

(ii) The opinions of product designers, as well as conceptual designers and die designers were collected to establish sufficient levels of accuracy and functions.

(iii) Thorough cesk simulation was conducted in relation to the determined commands and parameters. This resulted in a dramatic improvement over the requirements of the original specifications in terms of ease of use even before programming began.

3. BDAS FUNCTIONS (Fig. 3)

Although design drawings (Fig. 4) express the conceptual designer's original concept in considerabel practical detail in the form of 3-view drawings, consideration of design matters relates only to rough calculations of volume. Further examination of drawings often reveals geometrical contradictions and vague aspects in the design. Product design employs these design drawings as the basis for a consideration of various design points (bottle capacity, strength, ease of molding etc.) and repeated modification of the original shape to produce the shape of the final product. The BDAS system uses the following functions to aid this work.

3.1 Shape Definition

Modelling involves the following procedures.

- Definition of lines in front, side, and section drawings in order.

- Use of defined lines to define surfaces.

- Deletion of unnecessary portions of defined surfaces.

- Definition of surfaces joining defined surfaces.

To check the shape of the bottle as a whole, horizontal sections are taken at a suitable pitch and all sections displayed simultaneously on the screen.

- Connected lines (Fig. 5, 6)

Design drawings are combinations of arcs and straight lines, different arcs commonly being joined together to form extreme changes in curvature. Forcing approximations of these curvatures with free curves may result in difficulties in operation as well as with internal processing.

Connected lines are lines formed by the combination of arcs and straight lines into a single line without further modification. These lines are such that they are easily understood by the user and are easily manipulated during shape modification as described later.

- Basic surfaces (fig. 7, 8)

Surfaces having the same gradient are commonly considered as being the same surface. A feature unique to the surfaces found on bottles is the presence of an excessive number of restraining lines for these individual surfaces.

Basic surfaces define these surfaces. To improve ease of operation, all restraining lines are input together to define these basic surfaces. Internal processing involves proportional division of the tangent vectors and position vectors of the restraining lines in order to reduce the frequency of discontinuities between surfaces as much as possible. Surface data employs the Coons patch format.

3.2 Shape Modification (Fig. 9)

Shape modicication involves the manipulation of connecting line elements defined on the basis of the design drawings. It employs the following two methods.

(i) Modification of graphic elements

Modification of the arcs and lines forming connected lines. The radius, center, and start and end points of arcs, and the start and end points of lines, may be modified.

(ii) Modification by translation

This method involves the parallel movement of connected line elements. A minimum of one element may be moved, and multiple elements are adjusted to ensure continuity.

Elements adjacent to those subject to modification are adjusted automatically (except in cases where a graphic element is deleted) to maintain the mutually continuous relationship established when the connected lines were defined.

Modification of a line is accompanied by automatic regeneration of all other related lines in accordance with the commands and parameters input at definition. When modification of all lines is completed, input of a surface regeneration command results in automatic regeneration of all surfaces involved in line modification.

Provided that only the required elements are modified, the complete bottle shape is regenerated automatically.

3.3 Design Calculations (Fig. 10)

BDAS also supports functions for the calculation of capacity, cross sectional area, and surface area. As a simple calculation of the volume of the bottle itself is of little value to the designer, the internal capacity of the bottle is calculated taking into account wall thickness. Capacity calculations employ the average wall thickness of the bottle to calculate the following three items.

(i)   Bottle capacity

(ii) The level in the bottle for a specified contained volume of fluid.

(iii) The contained volume for a specified level of fluid.

As these calculations incorporate wall thickness, input parameters must include thicknesses at the opening, the base of the neck, and the bottom of the bottle, the volume of the bottom, and the weight and density of resin.

3.4 Display (Fig. 11-14)

Simultaneous display of horizontal sections taken at the desired pitch permits a check of the final shape of the bottle and replaces the conventional need for renderings and wooden models.

Arrival at this display format during the development of BDAS required a certain amount of trial and error. The following describes other methods of display based on this experience.

(i)   Wire frame display

Wire frame displays suffer from the disadvantage of being unable to display subtle changes in shape. The many lines extending from the neck to the bottom of the bottle are also not considered favorable by designers.

(ii) Display of individual surfaces

This method suffers from the same disadvantage as the wire frame dispaly, together with the fact that designers do not view favorably the joining together of the surfaces.

(iii) Solid display

In terms of ease of operation and processing time required etc., the use of this method to display collections of free surfaces such as those found in bottles is not considered practical at this time and is a subject for future development.

3.5 Plotter Output (Fig. 15-17)

The graphic designs on the display are output to a plotter to obtain higher accuracy and a clear indication of the detailed shape of the final product. This process is termed "precision rendering."

Output of 3-view drawings on the plotter is accompanied by automatic output of basic dimension lines and values, and various design values, on the same sheet.

Final product drawings are output separately with one of two methods. The first requires manual entry of dimensions while referencing a list of graphic attribute values, and the other involves the drafting and editing work with UNICAD[*1] via the use of graphic data files.

3.6 Generation of Mesh Data (Fig. 18)

Mesh data is generated for use with the BOP[*2] system. (Fig. 19, 20)

4. SYSTEM OPERATION

Ease of operation is a function of the ease with which basic data, connected lines in the case of the BDAS system, may be accurately input. The method used for input of these lines was determined as follows in order to ensure that input is in accordance with the concepts of both conceptual designers and product designers.

(i) Definition of each graphic element with the provision that input be continuous between the start and end points.

(ii) Temporary definition of graphic elements whose tangents and arc center cannot initially be defined clearly. When the rest of the graphic elements have been determined these temporarily defined elements are then defined accurately by internal processing.

(iii) Definition of the graphic elements without the use of local points or lines.

(iv) A minimum of commands and parameters.

Attention to these requirements has produced an easily operated system with provision for definition of connected lines while providing a line

---

*1. Universal Integrated Computer Aided Design system
*2. Bottle wall thickness Optimization Program

evaluation routine for evaluation of bottle line properties as a solution to the frequent problem of geometrical lines which cannot be mathmatically defined. This routine automatically determines the optimum solution in these cases.

Definition of section lines is achieved by specifying connected lines in front and side views as start and end lines, rather than by specification of start and end points. The start and end points are determined by the intersections of definition planes of sections, start lines, and end lines. As the relationship between section lines and connected lines in front and side views are determined, automatic modification of lines is considerably simplified.

5. USE OF THE BDAS SYSTEM

The BDAS system is currently used in product design and permits relative ease of input of both detailed and rough design drawings.

The system may also be used by the conceptual designer to finalize the shape of the bottle after he has determined its initial shape. Use of the system by conceptual designers to determine the shape from the beginning of the process will become possible by increasing the number of methods for input of line data.

The system may be used by die design sections for desgin of die cavities. Design of the die as a whole involves the use of UNICAD.

The use of SCULPTOR[*3] involves the use of BDAS graphic files to output punched tape for control of the NC machining process. (Fig. 21)

6. SUMMARY

As the development and maintenance costs of a CAD system are considerable, the use of a general purpose system is the most effective solution to this problem if at all possible. Development of the BDAS system stemmed primarily from the fact that a system which satisfied the requirements of both conceptual designers and product designers was not available for bottle design.

On the other hand, the use of as many functions of a general purpose system as possible is highly desirable. In this sense, the use of the UNICAD and SCULPTOR systems improves the benefits obtained from the BDAS system.

In conclusion, the authors wish to thank all those personnel listed below, as well as many others, who participated and cooperated in the development of the BDAS system.

---

*3. Surface CUtting tooL Path generaTOR
    Soft ware employed for machining of compound surfaces.

Lion Corporation: Yasufumi Yamaguchi, Osamu Aizawa

Nippon Univac Kaisha, Ltd.: Osamu Yanobu, Sachiko Shukuzawa, Tsukasa Bando

REFERENCES

1) F. Yamaguchi: Computer Graphics (ZUKEI SHYORI KOGAKU): NIKKAN KOGYO SHINBUNSYA, TOKYO, (1983)
2) F. Yamaguchi: Geometric Modelling [I], [II] (KEIJYO SYORI KOGAKU [I], [II]): NIKKAN KOGYO SHINBUNSHA, TOKYO, (1982)
3) M. Ake$_0$: Bottle Design CAD 'BDAS': Image Technology & Information Display, Vol. 16, No. 4, P.49-P.53, (1984)
4) Y. Sato & Y. Yamaguchi: BDAS-Bottle Design Arts System: PIXEL No. 15, P.144-P.148, (1983)

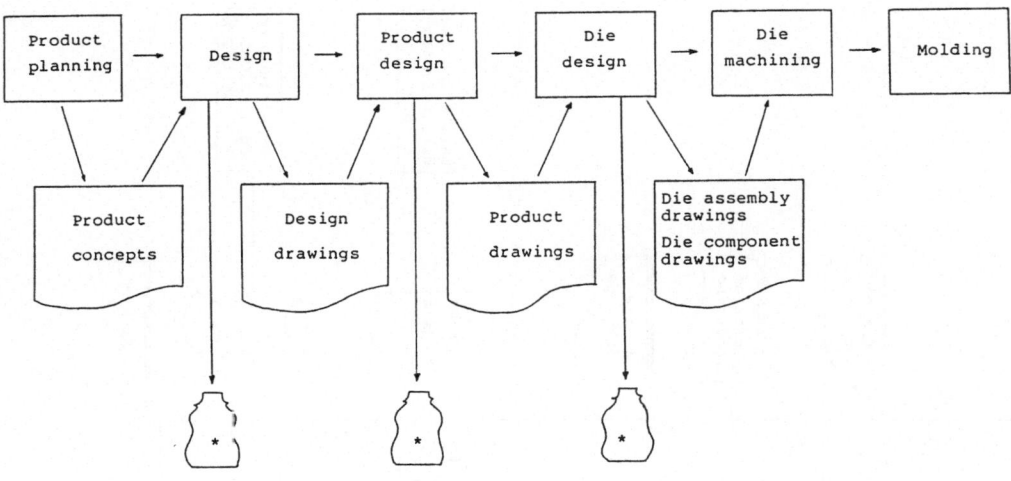

* Wooden model

Fig.1 Bottle Design and Manufacture

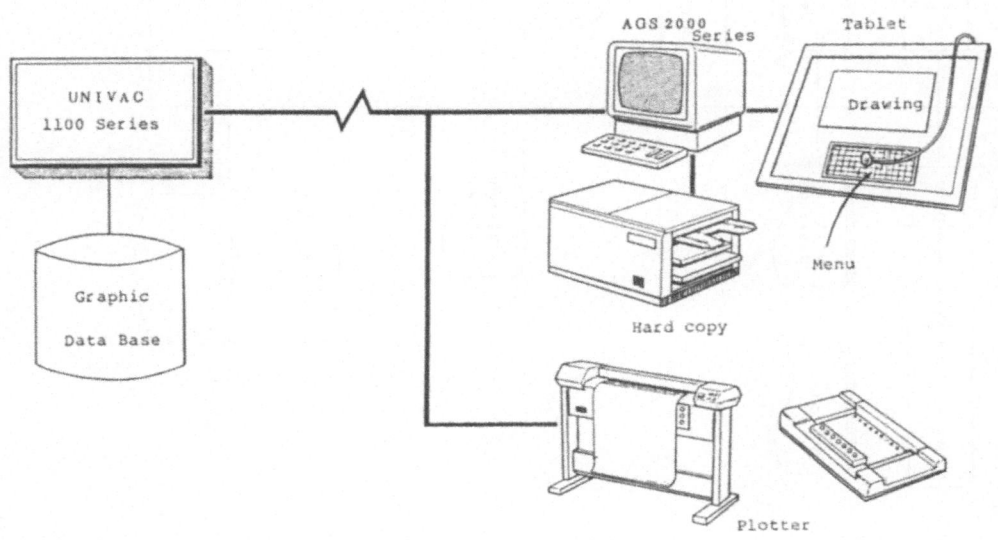

Fig.2 Equipment

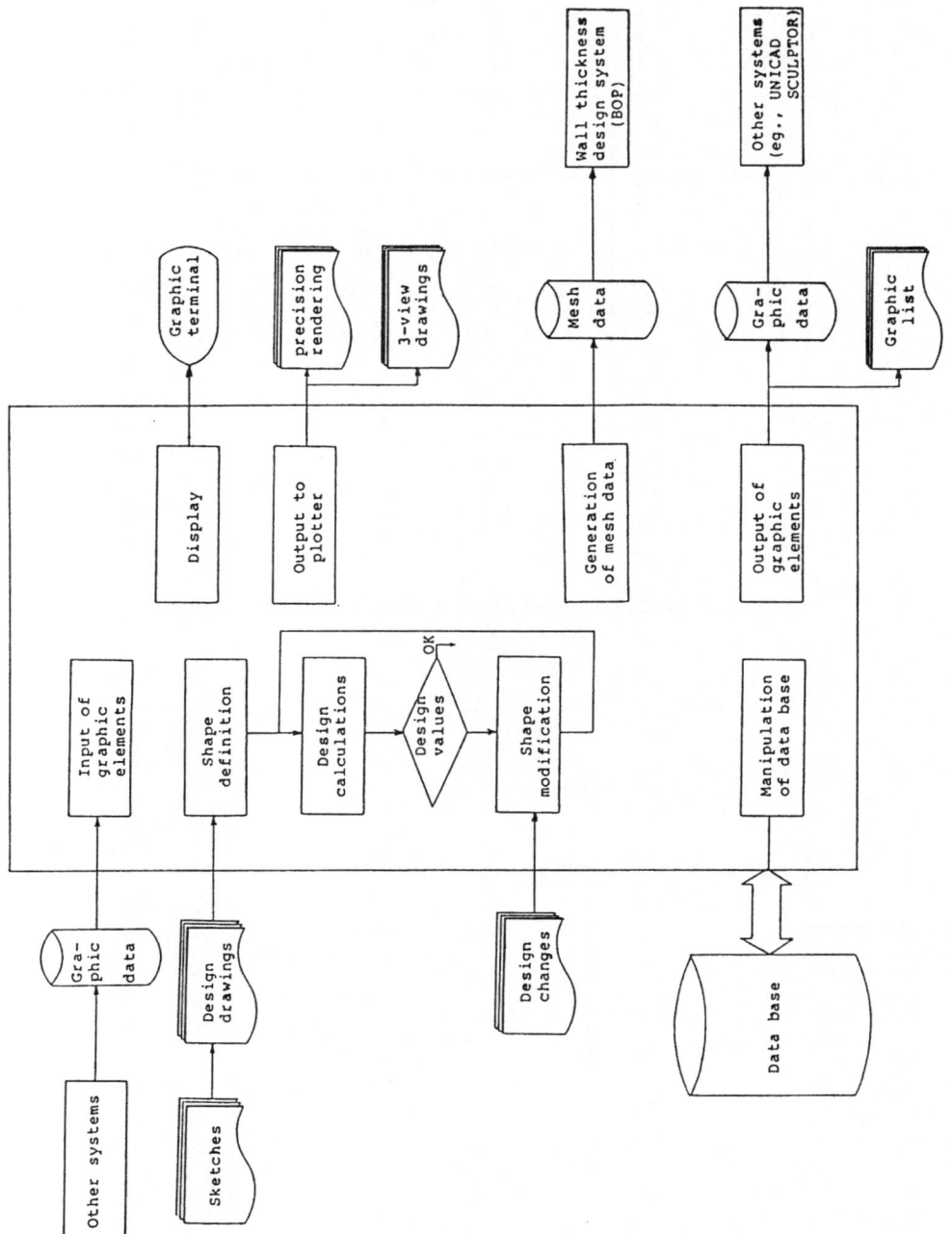

Fig.3 BDAS System

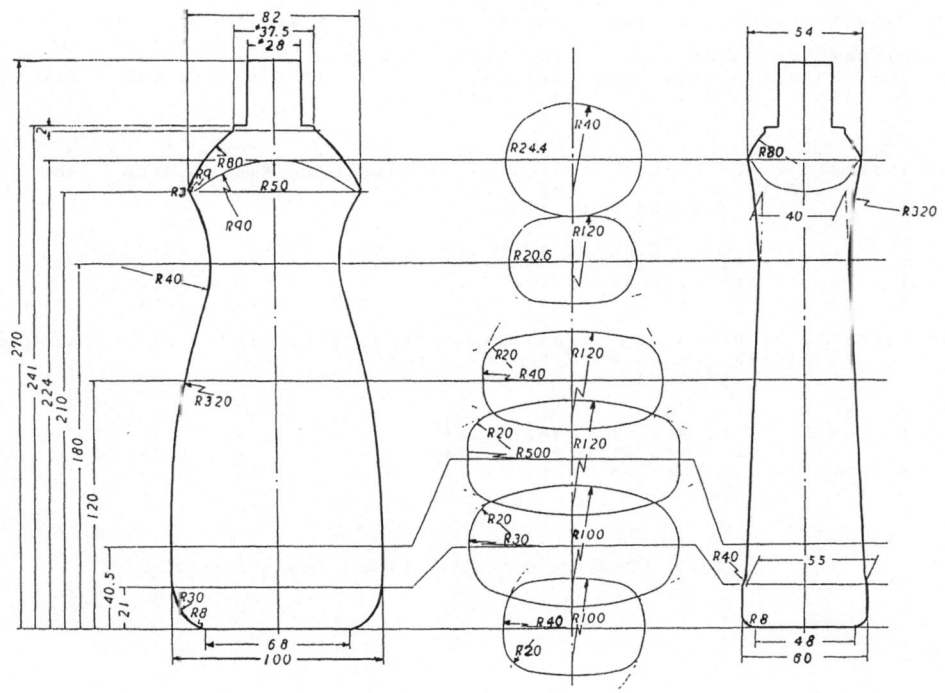

Fig. 4 Design Drawings

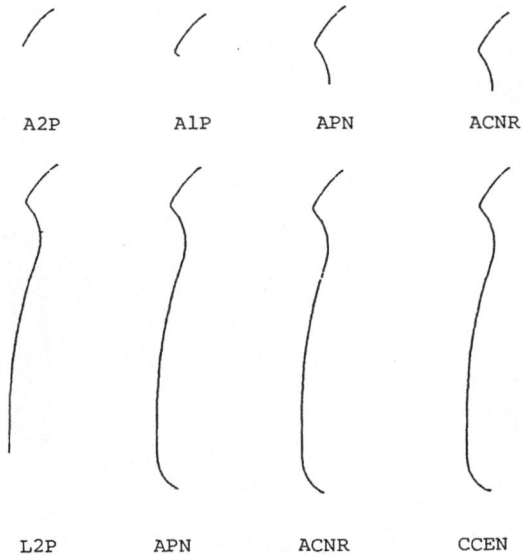

Fig. 5 Example of Definition of Connected Lines and Output of the Result

```
*** FIGUER NAME = T003 ***    GENERATED AT 01/26/84   07: 26: 12

    FIGURE TYPE = CONNECTED LINE (410)
        PARENTS = S004 S003 S002 T023 T021 T020 T019 T018 T017 T016 T015
                  T014 T013 T012 P001 BOTL

        SONS = NONE

** INTERNAL FIGURE NAME = T003-1 ** ATTRIBUTE ** FIGURE TYPE = ARC(329)
        CENTER(X, Y, Z) = ( .00, 31.42, 176.69)
                RADIOUS = 20.00(mm)

    N    X      Y        Z        I       J       K      IN      OUT
    1   .00   -18.75   239.00    .000   -.774   -.627   17.84   17.84
    2   .00   -31.28   226.38    .000   -.621   -.784   17.84   17.84
    3   .00   -40.70   211.30    .000   -.433   -.902   17.84   17.84

** INTERNAL FIGURE NAME = T003-2 ** ATTRIBUTE ** FIGURE TYPE = ARC(329)
        CENTER(X, Y, Z) = ( .00, -38.42, 210.00)
                RADIOUS = 3.00(mm)

    N    X      Y        Z        I       J       K      IN      OUT
    1   .00   -40.70   211.30    .000   -.423   -.902   1.78    1.78
    2   .00   -40.97   209.57    .000    .142   -.990   1.78    1.78
    3   .00   -40.23   207.99    .000    .638   -.744   1.78    1.78
```

Fig. 6 Checking Connected Line Numerical Data

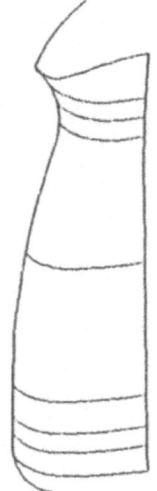

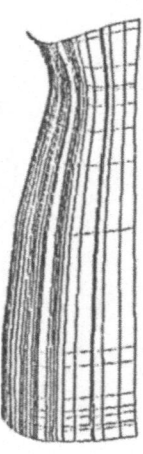

Fig. 7 Basic Surface Input Lines

Fig. 8 Basic Surface Display

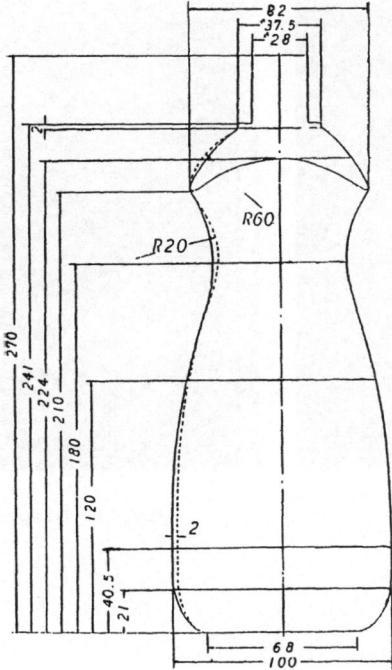

Fig. 9 Shape Modification

```
*** BOTTLE INFORMATION ***

    BOTTLE NAME                B001
    DIVIDED                      15

    SPACE UNDER BOTTOM         2.00  (    ml)
    WEIGHT OF PLASTIC         25.00  (     g)
    DENSITY OF PLASTIC         .955  ( g/cm3)

    THICKNESS OF TOP PART      1.80  (    mm)
    THICKNESS ON SHOULDER      1.20  (    mm)
    THICKNESS OF BOTTOM        1.50  (    mm)

    THICKNESS OF BODY           .30  (    mm)
    FULL CAPACITY            828.91  (    ml)
    HEIGT OF FILLING VOLUME  231.75  (    mm)
    FILLING VOLUME           800.00  (    ml)
    AREA OF SURFACE          592.21  (   cm2)
```

Fig. 10 Checking Design Values

Fig. 11 Display Example 1

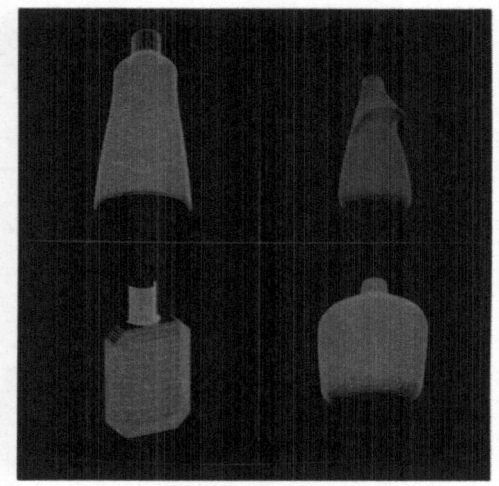

Fig. 12 Display Example 2

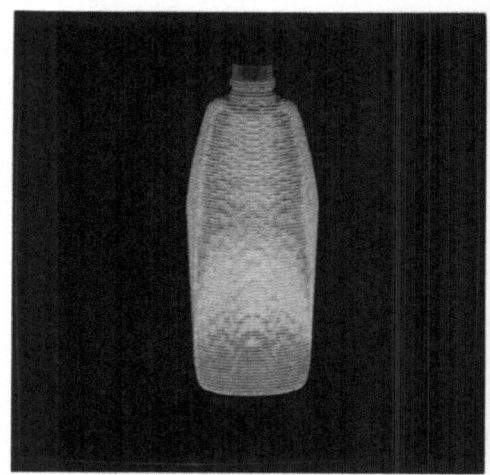

Fig. 13 Display Example 3

Fig. 14 Display Example 4

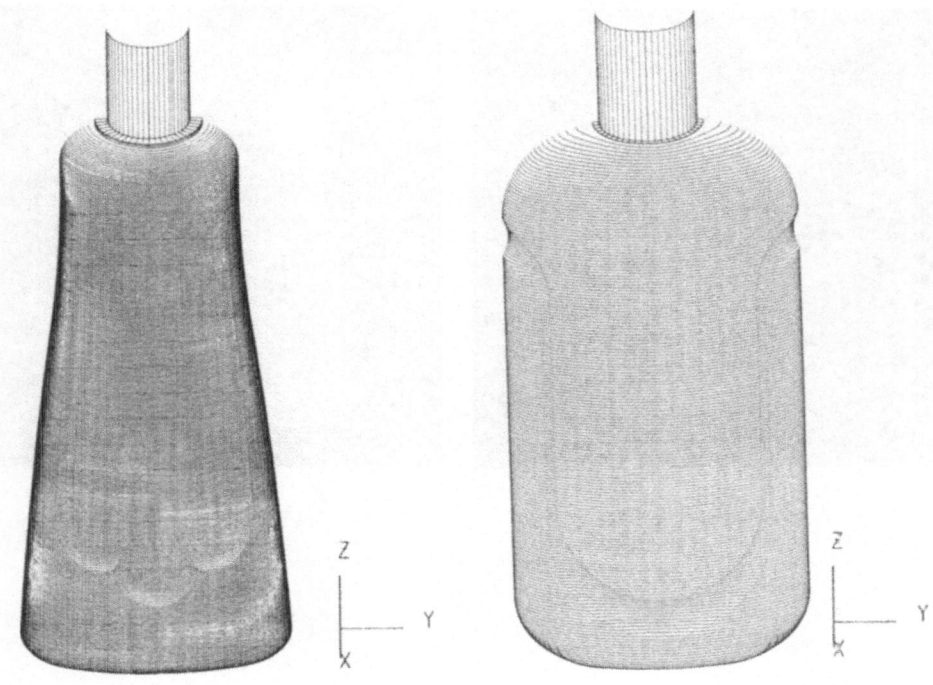

Fig. 15 Plotter Output 1   Fig. 16 Plotter Output 2

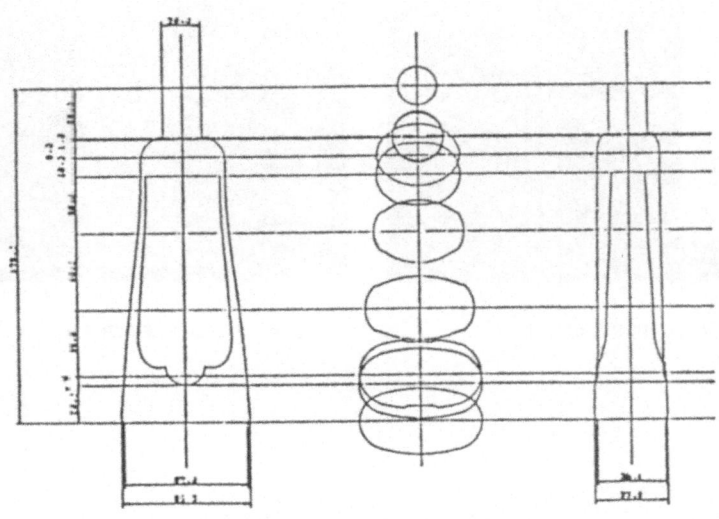

Fig. 17 Plotter Output 3

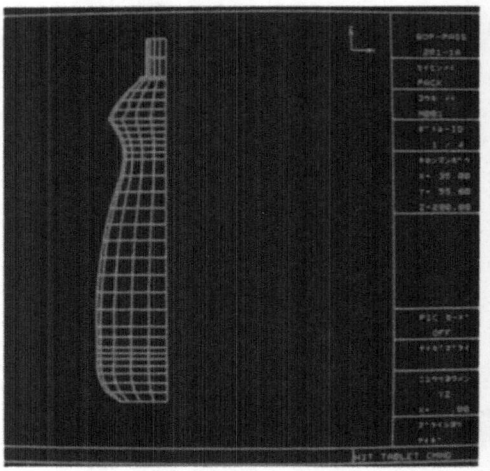

Fig. 18 Mesh Data   Fig. 19 BOP Output 1

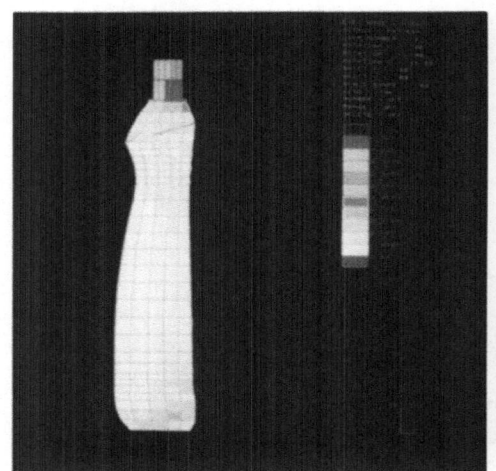 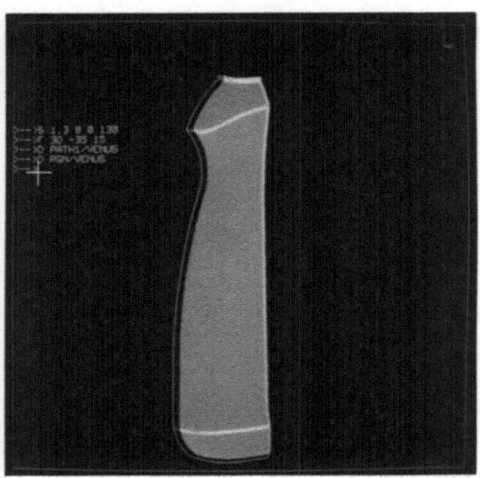

Fig. 20 BOP Output 2   Fig. 21 SCULPTOR Cutter Path

Interactive VLSI Chip Floor Design Using Color Graphics

Kazuhiro Ueda, Hitoshi Kitazawa and **Ikuo Harada**
Atsugi Electrical Communication Laboratory
Nippon Telegraph and Telephone Public Corporation
Ono, Atsugi-shi, Kanagawa 243-01, Japan

ABSTRACT

In a hierarchical VLSI design, the block-level layout design is called 'chip floor plan'. This paper presents a semi-automatic VLSI chip floor plan program CHAMP, which utilizes a color graphic terminal to the fullest. It has an automatic initial placement and semi-automatic block packing procedures. In the chip floor plan problem, because of the variety of block sizes and shapes, it is very difficult to minimize the chip area by only an automatic process using a computer. Consequently, in most cases, the optimum solution is not obtained without the help of a human designer. To facilitate the manual optimization process, CHAMP is provided with a set of interactive commands using a color graphic terminal. In this paper, chip floor plan program CHAMP is described, in which its interactive facilities are emphasized, and the application results are discussed.

INTRODUCTION

As VLSI chips contain more than tens of thousands of gates, it becomes necessary to take a hierarchical approach to their design. In such a hierarchical approach, it is essential to attain a high-quality block-level layout, i.e., chip floor plan at the first stage in the chip layout design. At present, in most hierarchical layout systems, the chip floor plan design is performed manually. Several algorithms for automatic floor plan have been reported (1-5), however, they do not seem to be practical. In each of these methods, it is either difficult to handle various types of blocks at the same time, or to apply them to interactive design environment. This paper presents a new semi-automatic floor plan algorithm and its program.

In the chip floor plan placement problem, a placement unit is a block which can have various sizes and shapes. This placement irregularity is one of the most important factors to be considered in the chip floor plan placement problem. Because of that irregularity, a manual process is indispensable and, as a result, a color graphic terminal plays an important role in the floor plan problem. The present chip floor plan program CHAMP has some automatic facilities for the initial placement and the following block packing process. It also has a set of powerful interactive commands making full use of functions of a color graphic terminal.

CHIP FLOOR PLAN OVERVIEW

The VLSI chip consists of blocks, and each block consists of several hundreds or thousands of cells or several subblocks. Further, the cell performs a basic function, such as NAND, NOR, or Flip-flops. From the layout point of view, blocks can be classified into two categories: fixed-shaped blocks, such as RAMs or ROMs, and variable-shaped blocks composed of standard cells.

The system's design flow is as follows. The LSI network data are described by HSL (Hierarchical Specification Language) (6). The network data is processed by HIDEMAP system (6) and stored into the logic network database. The block interconnection data and the block area estimation parameters, which are extracted by a part of a hierarchical, standard-cell VLSI layout program ALPHA (7) from the logic network database, are entered into CHAMP. After the floor plan design, the CHAMP output data, which consists of block shapes and locations, are handed over to ALPHA. The CHAMP programs are written in APL and are using its graphic library. Therefore, most of its functions can be performed in an interactive manner, and some of them can be performed by specifying them directly on the graphic display screen.

The chip floor plan objectives are as follow:
(a) To accommodate blocks within a nearly square-shaped chip boundary having as small an area as possible.
(b) To determine the height/width ratio (or the number of cell-rows) for each variable-shaped block, and the location for all blocks.
(c) To estimate the chip area based on parameters associated with blocks.

INITIAL BLOCK PLACEMENT

The chip floor plan processes with CHAMP are divided into two phases. First is the initial placement phase and second is the block packing. There are two alternatives for obtaining an initial placement. One is an automatic initial placement procedure, using the AR method (8). By using the AR method, an initial placement can be obtained, in which strongly-connected blocks are located near each other and in which weakly-connected blocks are located far from each other. If the layout designer wants to modify the initial placement, he or she can rotate the block locations in an arbitrary angle and/or move some blocks by specifying a distance. Figure 1 shows an example of initial placement obtained by the AR method.

Another initial placement method is a manual placement by an interactive graphic function, called MBP (Manual Block Placement). Figure 2 (a) shows an initial MBP state. The main display area is the window surrounded by a dotted line. The dotted line is assumed as a chip boundary. By selecting a command from the menu, the designer can locate each block at the position specified by the cursor, move the specified block to another position and/or delete the selected blocks from the screen.

MBP is useful if the designer has appropriate information for the block locations. Otherwise, the AR method gives a better initial placement. Figure 2 (b) shows a typical example of initial placement result with MBP.

Note that, in this stage in the chip floor plan, each block has a nearly-square shape, except for the fixed-shaped blocks. The variable-shaped blocks vary their shapes so as to match each other in the final stage of the chip floor plan.

BLOCK PACKING

An initial placement usually has some overlaps and/or dead spaces between blocks (See Fig. 3). The block packing is a phase to eliminate such overlaps and dead spaces by moving and/or reshaping blocks and, at the same time, put them into a nearly squared-shaped chip boundary that has as small an area as possible.

Figure 3 also shows a display screen format. The main portion of the screen is the design window that shows the current block locations and shapes. The dotted line represents the chip boundary that is set sufficiently large to enclose all the blocks at the initial state and is shrunk during the block packing phase. The inter-block interconnections are displayed as color lines. Every inter-block interconnection is classified into four colors; Red, Pink, SKy-blue and Navy-blue, according to the number of interconnections. The classification criteria are shown on the right-upper portion of the screen. The right-middle and right-bottom portions are the menu table and its specification areas. Most frequently used functions are displayed in the menu table. One or more of them are performed by being specified with some parameters in the specification area. Other functions are performed by command string input with parameters.

Each block represented in the design window has its own block width, height and number of cell-rows. Block width W and block height H are considered as functions of the number of cell-rows R, the widths of cells included in the block and some other parameters. W and H can be calculated by using empirically-obtained functions. The number of cell-rows R is indicated on the shoulder of each block number.

In the block packing phase, semi-automatic functions, called BLP and BLPGC, are often used. They are used to move and reshape the blocks gradually in order to eliminate the overlaps between blocks and/or between the chip boundary and blocks. The careful repetition of move and reshaping of blocks with chip boundary shrinking gives the designer a final chip floor plan. However, the resultant floor plans are not necessarily satisfactory. Therefore, a set of interactive functions are prepared for the designer to refine the floor plan. Such interactive commands and semi-automatic functions can be used in an intermixed way.

CHIP AREA ESTIMATION

As mentioned above, each block has its own width W and height H that can be calculated based on empirically-obtained equations. Adding to such estimations, CHAMP also estimates the channel areas occupied by inter-block interconnections.

In the present layout system, the cellrows through lateraly adjacent
blocks must have common channels, i.e., the height of the heighest
cell-row constrains the height of cell-rows in the laterally adjacent
blocks. Under such conditions, the chip area is estimated. Figure 4
shows an example of the chip area estimation result. Spaces between
blocks in Fig. 4 (a) represent unused areas caused by making cell-rows
have common channels through several blocks or dead areas caused by
mismatching of block shapes. Figure 4 (b) shows another representation of
the block layout for the chip area estimation. The most congested portion
of the cell-rows is indicated by the hatched region in Fig. 4 (b).
Observing this screen, the designer can see where the most congested
portion is and where unused areas exist, etc.

INTERACTIVE COMMANDS

A variety of block and chip boundary move/reshaping commands are provided
for the layout designer. These kinds of functions are used most frequently in the block packing process.

Using these commands, blocks may be moved by a given distance, moved by
referencing another block, changed their shapes, etc. The chip boundary
also may be moved by a given distance. Some typical commands are as
follow:
    FIT :   Move selected block(s) to be attached to the specified
        edge (or its extension) of another specified block so that
        the related blocks come outside each other.
        ex) In Fig. 5, block 15 and 16 are FITed to the upper-side of
        block 12.
    FITALL : Pack all the blocks to the leftbottom corner of the
        chip boundary without any overlap, keeping the current
        relative locations. (This command is useful at the end of the
        block packing phase.)
        ex) See Fig. 6.
    BMOVEGC : Move a selected block to its gravitational center
        (a point where the sum of force vectors determined by the
        connectivity to the other blocks becomes zero).
    TYC :   Change the number of cell rows of selected block(s)
        by given numbers. According to the change, their shapes are
        modified.
    WAKU :   Shrink or expand the chip boundary by a given distance.

Local database commands allow the designer to store and refer to intermediate forms during the chip floor plan process. Some other commands are
prepared for indicating parameters of the current status or connection
data. The other commands are for parameter setting, displaying mode
setting, etc. The list of typical commands is summarized in Table 1.

Figure 7 shows an example of a chip floor plan for a 16-bit CPU circuit
obtained by CHAMP.

CONCLUSIONS

Chip floor plan program, CHAMP, which makes use of color graphics to the fullest extent, has been described. From application to practical VLSI circuits, it is known that CHAMP can handle various kinds of blocks by interactive commands with ease, and its chip area estimation function gives the designer some information for a better floor plan. It is also known that the color graphics are very useful in the chip floor plan interactive design phase.

Further improvement in the system is expected, such as power line manipulation and floor plan modification by feedback from the following layout results, especially in the case where 'super blocks' (a block consiting of several blocks) must be handled.

ACKNOWLEDGEMENT

The authors would like to express their appreciation to Dr. M. Watanabe, Dr. H. Mukai and Dr. T. Sudo for their continuous encouragement and valuable suggestions. They also wish to thank K. Takeda for his effort in preparing parts of the program, and to K. Tansho for his valuable comments and discussions through the intensive program usage.

REFERENCES

(1) C. S. Horng and M. Lie, "An automation/interactive layout planning system for arbitrarily-sized rectangular building blocks," Proc. 18th Design Automation Conference, pp. 293-300, June 1981.
(2) R. H.J.M. Otten, "Automatic floorplan design," Proc. 19th Design Automation Conference, pp. 261-267, June 1982.
(3) W. R. Heller, G. Sorkin and K. Maling, "The planar package planner for system designer," Proc. 19th Design Automation Conference, pp.253-260, June 1982.
(4) K. Maling, S. H. Mueller and W. R. Heller, "On finding most optimal rectangular package plans," Proc. 19th design automation Conference, pp. 663-670, June 1982.
(5) A. Leblond, "CAF: A computer-assisted floorplanning tool," Proc. 20th Design Automation Conference, pp. 747-753, June 1983.
(6) T. Sudo, T. Ohtsuki and S. Goto,"CAD systems for VLSI in Japan," Proc. of IEEE, Vol. 71, No. 1, pp. 129-143 (January 1983).
(7) T. Adachi, H. Kitazawa, M. Nagatani and T. Sudo,"Hierarchical top down layout design method for VLSI chip," Proc. of 19th Design Automation Conference, pp. 785-791 (June 1982).
(8) K. Ueda,"Placement algorithm for logic modules," Electron. Lett., 10, 10, pp. 206-208 (1974).
(9) K. Ueda and H. Kitazawa,"Algorithm for VLSI chip floor plan," Electron. Lett., 19, 3, pp. 77-78 (1983).
(10) H. Kitazawa and K. Ueda, "Chip area estimation method for VLSI chip floor plan," Electron. Lett., 20, 3, pp. 137-139 (1984).

Fig. 1   Initial placement example by AR method.

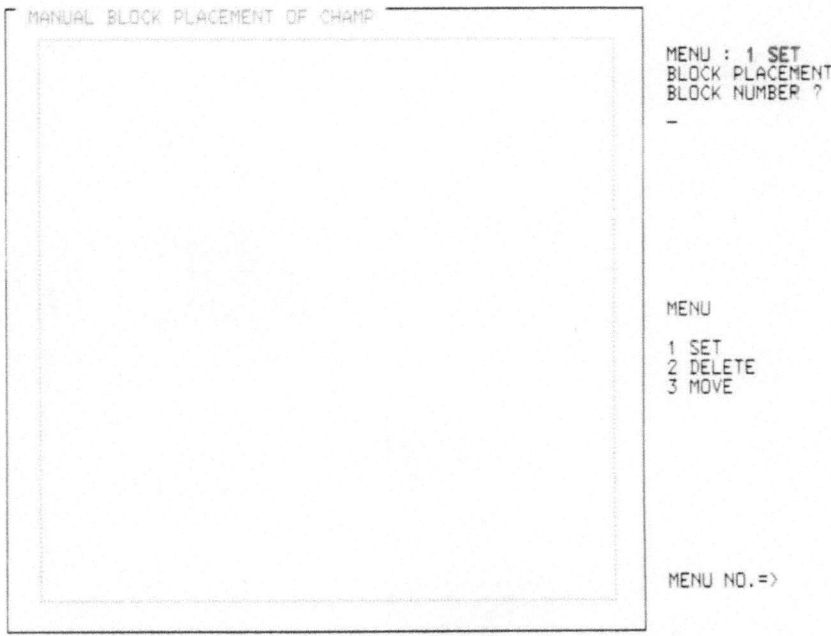

(a) Initial state.

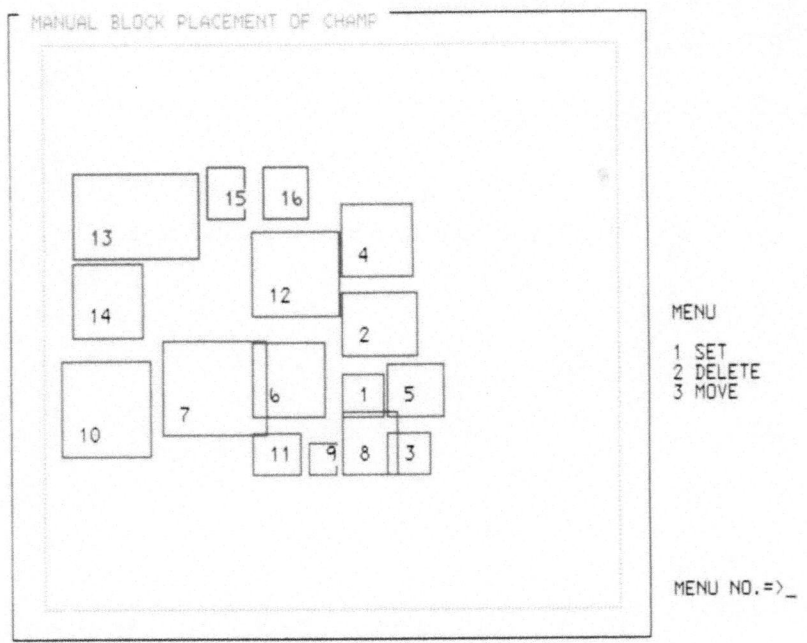

(b) MBP result.

Fig. 2 Manual block placement MBP.

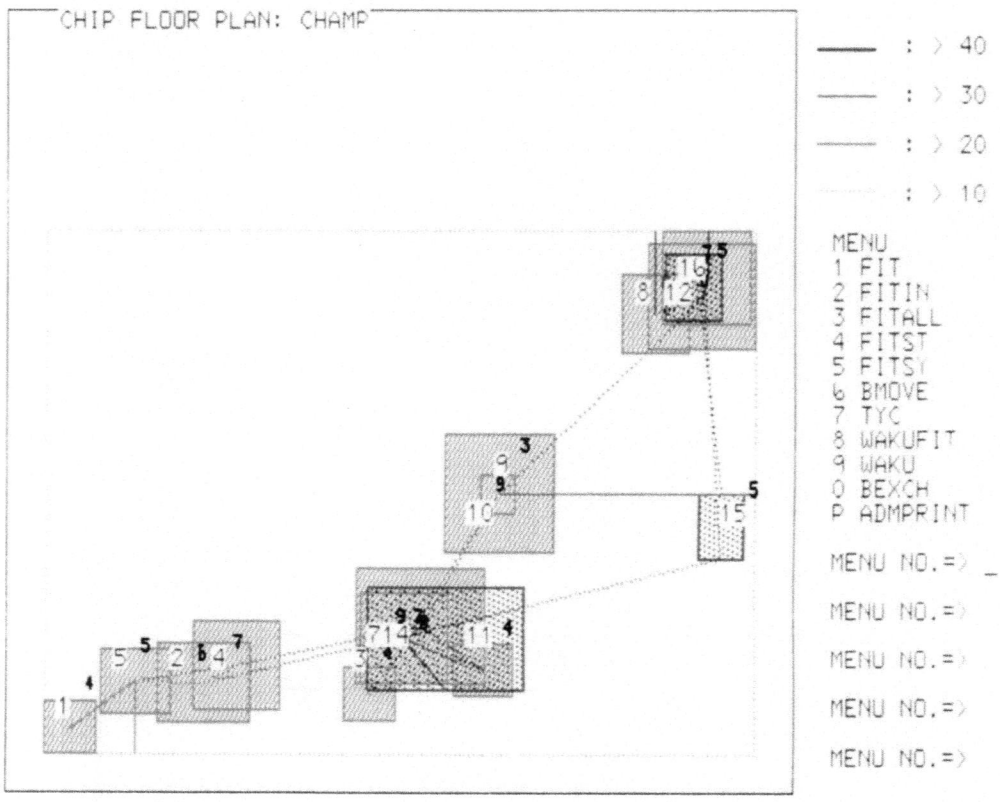

Fig. 3 Display screen format for block packing.

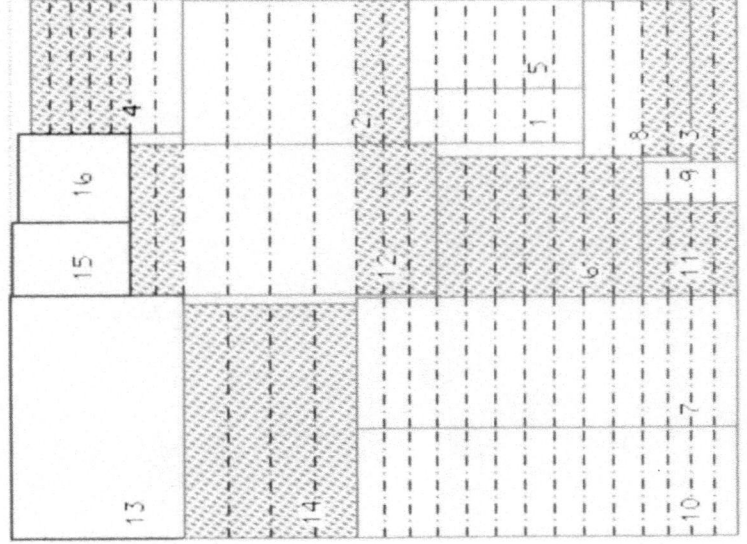

(b) Cell-row representation.

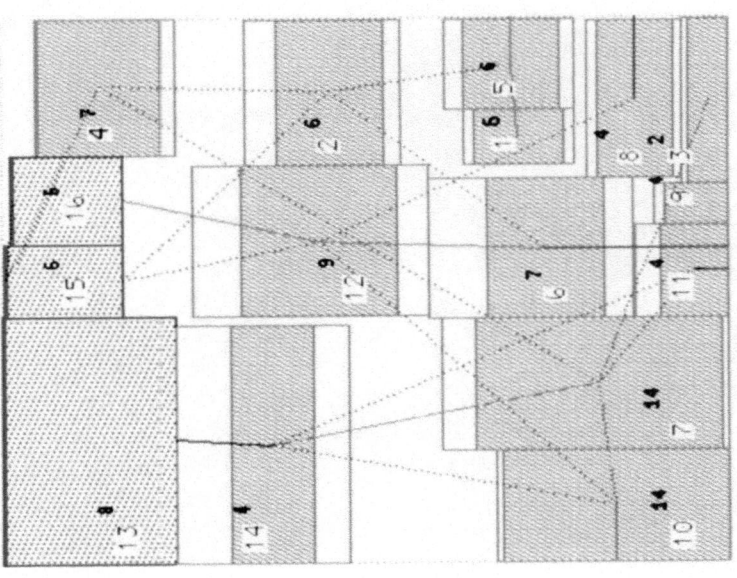

(a) Intra- and inter-block representation.

Fig. 4 Chip area estimation.

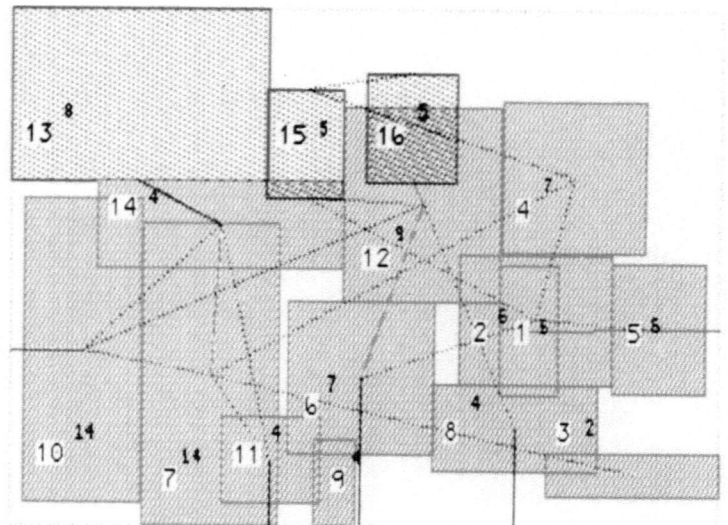

(a) Before FIT.

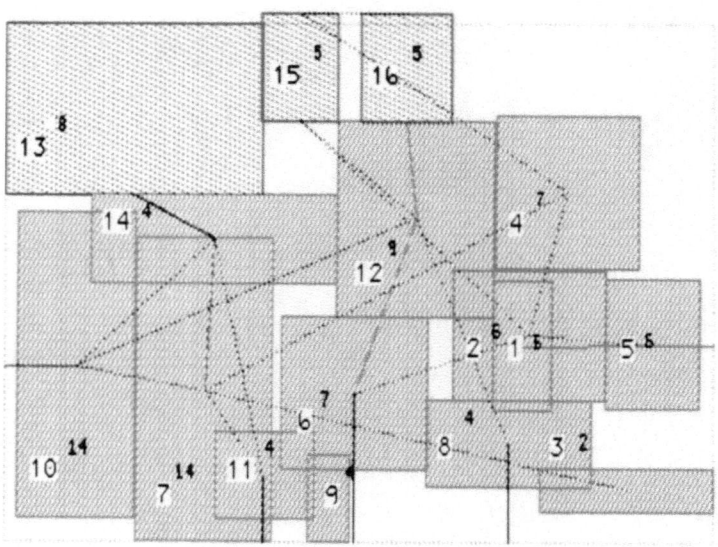

(b) After FIT.

Fig. 5   Move block to another block : FIT.

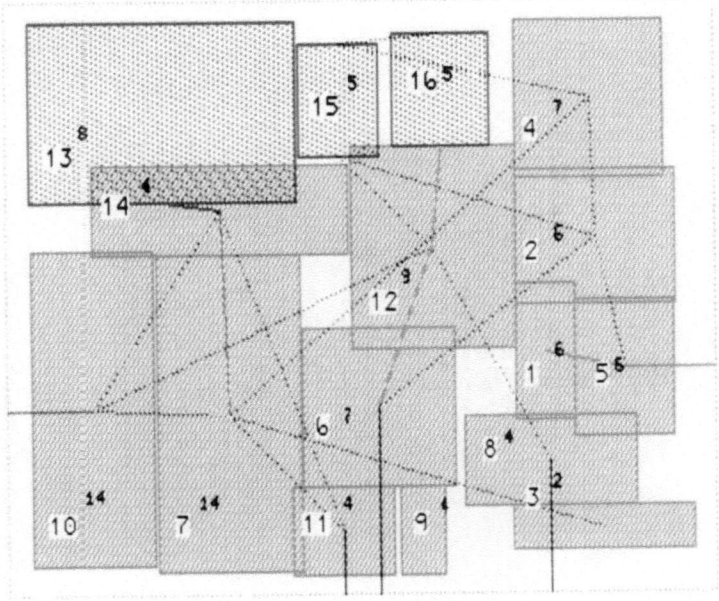

(a) Before FITALL.

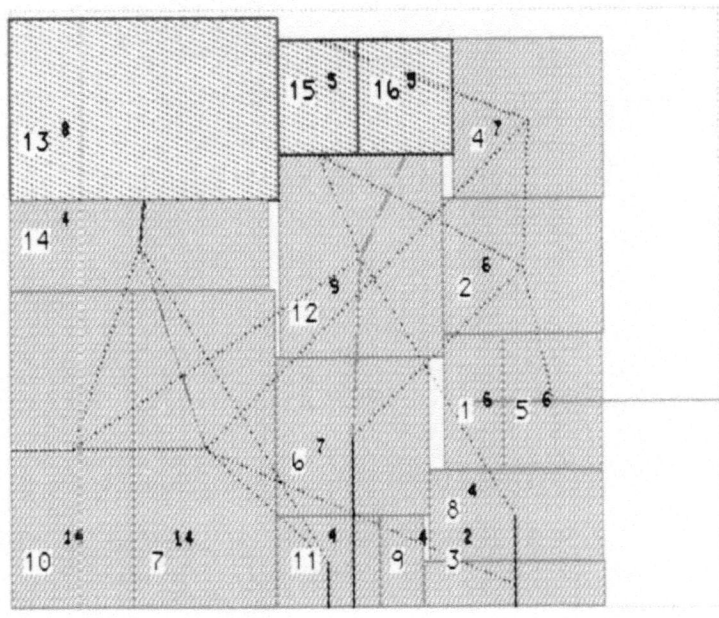

(b) After FITALL.

Fig. 6   Pack all blocks in the left-bottom corner : FITALL.

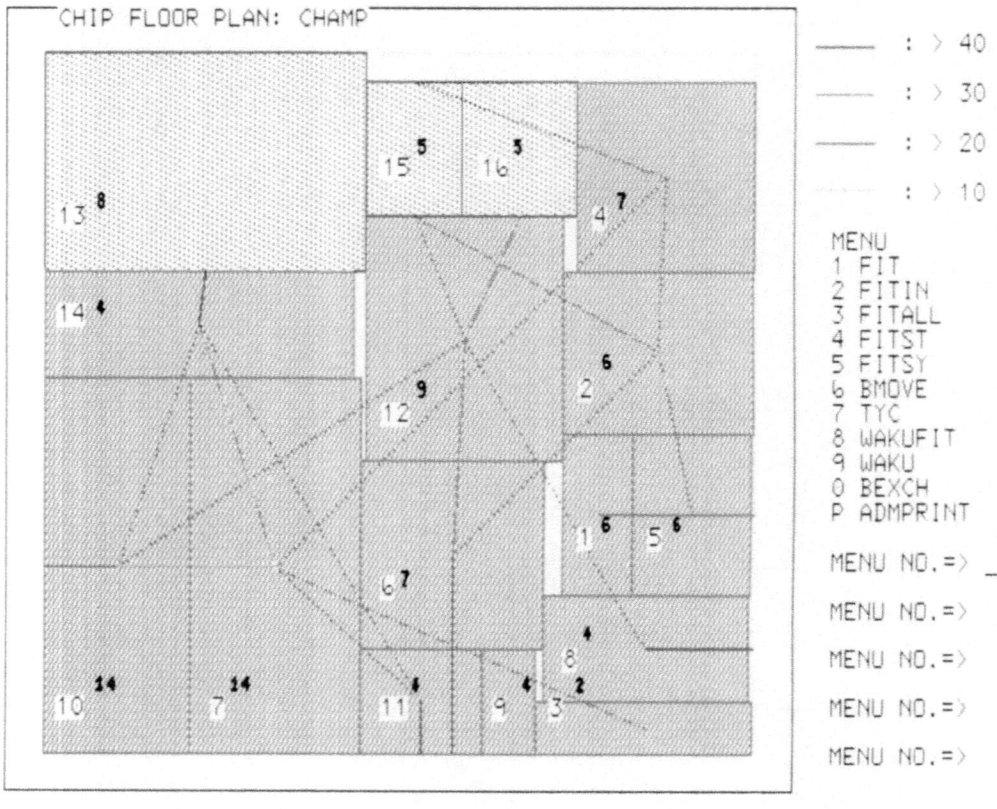

Fig. 7 An example of the chip floor plan by CHAMP.

Table 1. MAJOR INTERACTIVE COMMANDS

ITEM	COMMAND	FUNCTION
Block move /reshape	BLP, BLPGC	move and/or reshape blocks automatically
	BMOVE	move block(s) by given distance
	BMOVEGC	move block(s) to gravitational center
	BEXCH	exchange a pair of blocks
	FIT	move block(s) to outside of another block
	FITIN	move block(s) to inside of another block
	FITST	align blocks vertically in specified order
	FITSY	align blocks horizontally in specified order
	FITALL	pack all blocks into the left-bottom corner
	FITBH	adapt block height to distance between two other blocks
	TYC	change number of cell-rows
Inter-connection Display	COLCON	set color-connectivity correspondence
	BUSSET	set bus name-block numbers correspondence
	RECON	make interconnection pattern be shortest spanning trees
Chip Boundary Move	WAKU	shrink or extent chip boundary
	WAKUFIT	fit chip boundary to enclose all blocks
Database Management	DBINIT	initialize database
	DBWRITE	write block placement and shape data into database
	DBREADC	read out comments on stored data
	DBREAD	read out stored data
Data References	BCON	display inter-block connectivity
	BDATA	display block placement, shape and area data
	CHIPSIZE	display chip size and area
	CHIPR	display chip area efficiency
	INLIST	display summary of input data
	PARAM	display status of parameters

On Fifth Generation Systems and Their Implications for Computer Aided Design

David B. Arnold
School of Computing Studies and Accountancy
University of East Anglia
Norwich, NR4 7TJ, UK

ABSTRACT

While much discussion is currently taking place on the importance of the "fifth generation" and Intelligent Knowledge Based Systems (IKBS) to the future of computing, it seems difficult for CAD users to see how what might happen relates to current CAD systems. This paper suggests a relationship in terms of models of "the design process", by categorising current CAD practice and discussing the potential role of IKBS in relation to this practice. The probable differences in the "feel" of the Man/-Machine interface of 5th generation systems is predicted and the paper concludes by considering whether these systems will affect the nature of the designs produced.

CAD Systems and their Relation to the "Design Process"

"A CAD system is characterised by the basis on which the work is allocated between the designer and the computer" [12].

Design is commonly accepted as an iterative process, in which the designer produces a design proposal, analyses it according to certain criteria, and then produces a different proposal based on the results of the analyses, until the criteria are satisfied. Mitchell [14,15] for example, isolates these processes as "solution generation" and "solution evaluation", while March [13] proposes a loop containing three types of thought process - production, deduction and induction (the PDI model of design - figure 1). He considers that production and induction are both "intuitive" processes, while deduction is an "analytic" process, and however one defines the design process, these two methods of information processing appear to be involved. Krause and Vassilakopoulos [11] for instance, state that the "three ways of human information processing are: intuitive, discursive and algorithmic". Discursive information processing may be considered as a combination of the other two types when more than one processor is involved, and other descriptions exist for these remaining two. George [10], for example, uses "imagination and reasoning", while de Bono [7] prefers "lateral and vertical thinking".

Whatever labels we attach to these processes, one involves the execution of a logical sequence of steps to reach a conclusion (analytic), whilst the other involves taking jumps which may, or may not (according to your viewpoint), be based on a logical train of thought, which follows subconscious rules and is therefore unspecified.

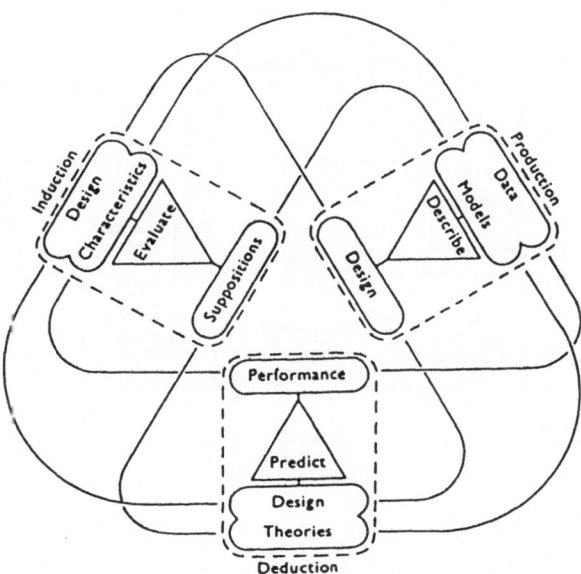

The PDI (production/deduction/induction)-model of the rational design process described in the text. The diagram suggests a cyclic, iterative procedure PDIPDIPD... and so on, with constant refinements and redefinitions being made of characteristics, design and suppositions as the composition evolves. In fact the model is envisaged as representing a critical, learning process in that statements inferred at later stages may be used to modify those used in earlier stages and thus to stimulate other paths of exploration. For this reason no arrows are shown along these paths, although the general direction of argument is clockwise.

Figure 1   The PDI Model of Design (After March [13])

To provide a context for later discussion, I am considering CAD systems in relation to a simplistic design loop (figure 2) of solution generation and evaluation, in which part of the generative process involves the analytical formation of a design proposal from an intuitive proposition, and part of the evaluation process is an intuitive (aesthetic) assessment of the analysed proposal. This is intended to show that both generation and evaluation involve both types of mental process, rather than a simplistic association of analysis with evaluation and intuition with generation.

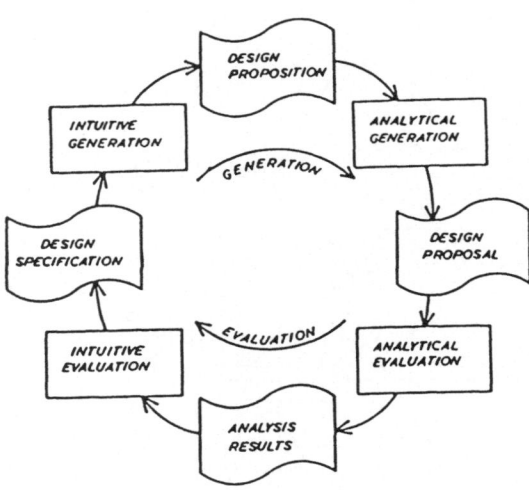

Figure 2   A Simplistic Design Loop

A classification of CAD systems can therefore be made by considering how much of each process is modelled by the computer and which processes remain with the man. Whatever the basic division, it is certain that part of the analytic process will be performed by the machine and part of the intuitive process by the man.

An illustration of one iteration around the design loop might be as follows. An architect is briefed to design a housing estate with a particular mix of dwellings to be built on a specified site. The details of this brief form the design specification. The architect might choose to investigate the possibility of meeting his brief using a particular type of dwelling layout (e.g. "streets"). This would be a very outline design proposition. Given the proposition, the next stage would be to see how streets might fit this site and would probably involve a sketch design. To produce the sketch design a number of rules would be used. For example, generalised rules as to minimum building separation for privacy, minimum road widths, etc. would be used in generating approximate positions for the buildings. Having produced a first approximation the design would be subjected to more detailed analyses, both for the measures used in generation and for other criteria. Parking space and its distribution, dwelling mix layout, services routing,etc. might be analysed to see whether one could be found which showed critical inadequacies in the design, or, perhaps more likely with an experienced designer, where the performance could be improved by amending the design. Additionally the designer would be assessing whether the end result would be something worth building, or whether a completely different approach might be better. The results of this iteration around the design loop, plus the original specification, then become the starting point for the next iteration and the process restarts. Clearly the architect is also contributing knowledge and experience gained over the development of past designs, as part of the basis for the current project. This corresponds to the "habitual notions" described in March's PDI model.

The great majority of current CAD systems involve the use of the computer principally in assisting the analytic evaluation phase of the design loop. The assistance may take the form of tools to human evaluation (e.g. visualisation in 3D, filing systems for drawings) or specific analyses performed by the machine (e.g. finite element calculations), but in both cases the nature of the design has been determined by the human. Notice that however much analysis is performed by the machine, the human will always perform a further evaluation of the acceptability of the analysis results, as well as more intuitive assessment against such subjective criteria as taste and style.

In many cases even in these systems, some detail of the design generation may be left to the machine. An obvious example would be the assistance given by many drafting systems in allowing the user to specify the method of construction of a drawing rather than every line in its minutest detail. In this case although the machine is being used to generate some design information, it is only following instructions which in themselves still completely specify the intended drawing. A more positive contribution is made in some other systems. For example, a building might be described in 3D, but placed on an essentially flat site, with the system providing height information from terrain models. In this case the system is inventing design data which has not been completely specified by the human user, since the height selected for a building might be constrained by many design goals such as view, cut and fill minimisation, privacy, daylight etc. Thus although the level of influence in the overall design may be slight, the automated system is nevertheless beginning to take design decisions based on some algorithmic procedure.

The height finally selected is based on calculations which "optimise" the building's position with respect to the particular design criteria which have been quantified by the system's programmers. These rules might have been selected for simplicity (e.g. terrain model height at the first vertex of the house's plan) or using more sophisticated measures (e.g. cut and fill requirements). However, whatever the criteria chosen, the user's appreciation of the system's response may well be identical - the selected height will probably be accepted without questioning the underlying assumptions built into the procedure which chose that height.

This generation of detailed design information based on design rules falls in the upper right hand quadrant of my design loop, and this is where the principal influence of IKBS will be - in the analytic generation of design proposals from design propositions (e.g. see [17]). In fact people have been experimenting with systems which address this portion of the design loop for quite a number of years. A classic example in architecture is the work by Yessios [20] in the early 70s, in the use of shape grammars [15] to describe prototypical housing layouts (in plan) and to transform these prototypes to fit the shape of any particular site (figure 3). This is clearly the analytic generation, based on the architect's decision to use streets (in terms of my previous example), as opposed to courts or tower blocks.

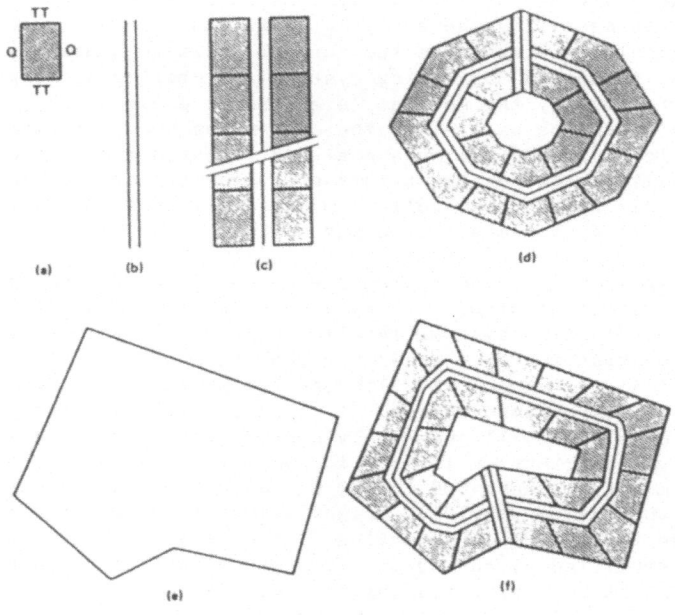

Figure 3   An example of Yessios' SIPLAN System (After Mitchell [15])
(a-c) Steps in defining Prototype (d) Prototype layout
(e) Actual Site Boundary   (f) Prototype Layout Matched to Site

This approach to the problem of automating design generation is attempting to rationalise the designer's actions into computable procedures, based on known facts, as in, for instance, the SPA system (Space Planner for Architects [18]) used for designing bathroom layouts. In this approach, as with real designer's, some of the evaluation phase is embedded in the generative phase (c.f. March's "habitual notions" [13]). Thus the system does not investigate any layouts which are based on a particular decision, because it embodies an expectation that none of the layouts generated this way will achieve the design criteria. It is obviously essential if this type of assistance is to work that man and machine share the same model of the abstract concepts defined in high level descriptions of design propositions. Since individual designers rarely share precisely the same definitions an element of machine training is bound to be required.

Systems of this type have been intended primarily to provide a stimulus
to the designer by proposing outline sketch designs which could then be
refined by more conventional techniques. In some cases they have also
been used to act as pump-priming to the intuitive generation (upper
left hand quadrant) by providing sketch layouts which are not completely
rule based, but also involve a certain degree of randomness in an attempt
to simulate intuition.

Typically in this approach a random number generator is used to "guide"
the generation and the randomly generated composition is checked against
some basic criteria. As a very early example of this, the BAID-1 system
[4,5] evaluated randomly generated housing layouts against criteria of
sunlight, daylight and privacy before presenting the results to the
architect for further design development and analysis.

To summarise current CAD systems in terms of the design loop, almost all
involve the analytic evaluation of design proposals. Most will also
involve some rule based assistance to the generation of design data,
or of data describing the design in a format suitable for specialised
analysis programs (e.g. preprocessors for finite element analysis).
There have been some attempts at computer assistance earlier in the design
loop and I anticipate that the main thrust of fifth generation developments will address this part of the design process.

The "Feel" of Fifth Generation Man/Machine Interfaces

Having considered where the assistance of IKBS will be most noticed in
CAD systems, I want to consider how this assistance may be perceived by
the designer using such systems.

Much emphasis has been placed on the invention and development of new
interactive tools in conjunction with the next generation of computing
systems. Particularly noticeable on the input side is voice recognition,
which is often presented as the answer to all prayers, but can in fact
only ever be a small part of the input to CAD systems and therefore only
a small part of its feel. Design is concerned with shapes and natural
language, whether spoken or written, has never been an adequate tool for
shape description. No one would dispute the usefulness of being able
to have verbal commands interpreted, but for CAD work this will never
act as more than comment on other forms of description. The main impact
of voice input will be in revamping the feel of existing input tools by
allowing verbal selection of menu options, etc. In addition, new and
more natural input tools for other types of communication will undoubtedly
be developed, but, if the new tools were merely used to convey the same
dialogue and information, this would not radically affect the feel of the
system. The major changes will occur through changing the level of the
dialogue.

Consider the amount and type of information required to describe the
state of the project at each stage around the design loop. At the design
specification stage we have a relatively brief specification of the
technical requirements, plus, after the first iteration, feedback from the
analysis phase of the previous iteration. This feedback will be condensed abstraction of the more important analysis results. The amount

of information in the design is then expanded during the generative phase
to provide, by the time the design proposal has been formulated, sufficient detail for analysis. This description then provides the inputs
to the analyses, which add additional information on the design's
performance, with respect to particular measures. Thus the amount of
information expands around the loop reaching a maximum with the
production of detailed analysis results. These are then interpreted
and condensed by the designer to produce a specification for the next
iteration. From this consideration it should be apparent that the
position of the Man/Machine interface within the design loop radically
affects the amount and type of information to be conveyed (figure 4).

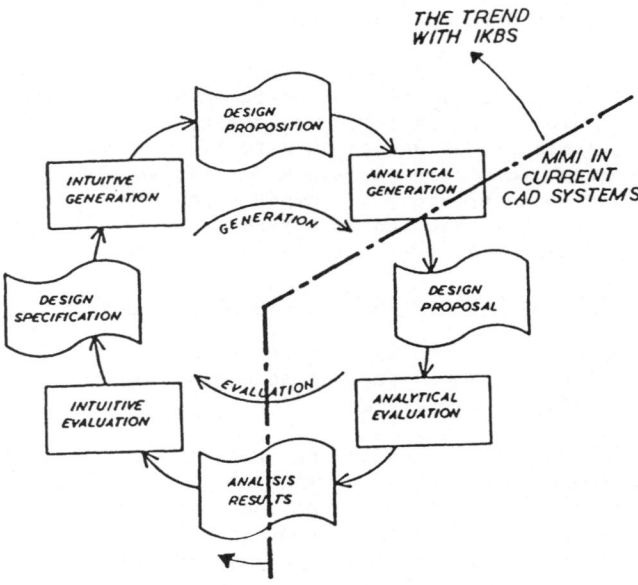

Figure 4 The Man/Machine Interface in CAD Systems

On the input side we can see that if the CAD system is only performing
analytic evaluation then the detail of the design proposal must be
conveyed exactly, and in detail, to the analysis programme. On non-trivial designs this is bound to involve long interactive sessions and
lengthy data checking before the design can be considered as correctly
defined for analysis. This is the situation in many current CAD systems.

As the input side of the Man/Machine Interface is pushed earlier into
the design loop then the volume of data to be described will be radically
reduced and its level of abstraction increased. One consequence of
this is an increasing reliance on the rule based generation system to
interpret design requirements as opposed to the passive acceptance of
design descriptions. The influence of this on the eventual products is
considered later. Experiments with interpretation procedures for some

input processes have been taking place for a number of years (see [1],[9]).

The reliance on an automated generator, working from condensed statements of a problem to design details, has a number of consequences for the design of the Man/Machine interface. In particular care must be taken to achieve a balance between too much interpretation of the designer's requests and too little. No interpretation is the norm for most current systems, with much associated frustration for the person inputting the design description, but too much interpretation could be just as distressing. For example, an architect confronted by a green field site might wish to consider in outline how streets might fit. If the system responds with "the drains to No.47 are too expensive to route", then the designer is left without much guidance as to how and why the original proposition failed and what assumptions and alternatives lead the system to consider No.47's drains a problem.

Designers would appear to work in parallel with several alternatives, but with limited lookahead. An automated system might attempt to match this approach, rather than pursue each avenue to its logical conclusion before exploring the next at all. A suitable response must therefore be one which balances the designer's expectation of a suitable response, even if in the end the drains to No.47 are a problem. Without this balance the system can never feel "natural".

A properly balanced system would include some assistance for the output side of the interface. This will hopefully take the form of evaluation of analysis results in order that the volume of results thrown back at the designer was reduced to include only the most significant trends. Obviously this does not affect the need to allow the designer to interrogate the details of the analysis results if required, but the objective should be to avoid swamping the user with too much detail in the same way as the objective for input dialogues should be the removal of the need for exhaustive systematic coding of all the design details. Obviously this places a considerable burden of responsibility on the designer of the part of the system which extracts the "significant" trends in the analysis results.

A second difficulty in the use of automated systems is comparable to the introduction of pocket calculators in many schools and the subsequent fall in the level of competence in mental arithmetic. As the level of complexity of rule based generation systems grows, then the number of pre-programmed "habitual notions" involved in the use of such a system may well be forgotten. As Willey [19] points out "In the computer-aided design of housing layouts Auger, Willey and Yessios have made general assumptions about the nature of the final built form. Decisions have been made affecting the way in which roads will relate to dwellings, the types of dwellings and the kinds of densities which will be used". For instance, some knowledge of maximum allowed distortion of particular elements must be assumed or given as data (e.g. minimum road widths, maximum and minimum plot-size, plot proportions etc.). Thus, if the system has defined typical road widths of say 6 metres, the architect may in time forget this assumption and cease to investigate road width as a variable of the system.

A third problem which might arise with IKBS applied to design is that
the CAD system may well begin to impose a style on the individual
designer using the system. This is really only a problem in those
design situations where aesthetics are of appreciable importance. For
example, the choice of which mechanical component, out of many which
perform the same job at equivalent cost, may be unimportant, and hence
a directed style in designing such components may not affect the quality
of the product. However in fields such as car design or architecture
style is a major factor influencing the success or otherwise of the
product. Even then the imposition of an overall style may be seen as
desirable. A "house" style, identifying products from a particular manufacturer, may well be preferable to many uncoordinated individual styles
and might be achievable by constraining individual product designers
using systems based on common rules. However, before considering the
implications of imposed style it is necessary to see how and why it
could occur and I will therefore consider next the origins of style
and the ways in which fifth generation CAD systems may impose, perhaps
unwittingly, a style on the individual designer.

The Imposition of Style

"Design problems do not have unique optimal solutions, hence we may
choose any one of many satisfactory solutions" (Simon, [16]).

It is this degree of freedom and the designer's characteristic method
of selection from the available satisfactory solutions which give rise
to style. Simon goes on to say that "the order in which possibilities
are considered may have a major influence on which solution is
discovered. Hence autonomous characteristics of the generator that
determine the order of search are an important aspect of style".

Mitchell [14,15] in considering style, used a set U to represent all
possible artifacts and a subset G of U to represent all those artifacts
which meet the design criteria (i.e. the goals, or set of acceptable
solutions). Style according to the above definition would be defined
as a tendency to select solutions from only one part of the goal set G
(figure 5(a)), but how could this arise with computer aided generators?
In the previous sections we have considered two mechanisms which allowed
the system to assist the designer in formulating a design proposal. The
first involved defining rules which simulate the procedures used by the
designer in fleshing out the details of a design proposal. Thus a system
for automating the layout of bathroom fittings might consider a particular
placement of the bath as optimal and attempt to place the other fittings
around this. The decision to attempt to find solutions involving this
particular position for the bath first clearly affects the order in
which members of the solution set G are found. Hence "different solution-
generating procedures may tend to generate characteristically different
subsets of G ..... So, in principle, we may expect that an automated
design system might display ..... a characteristic style"[14].

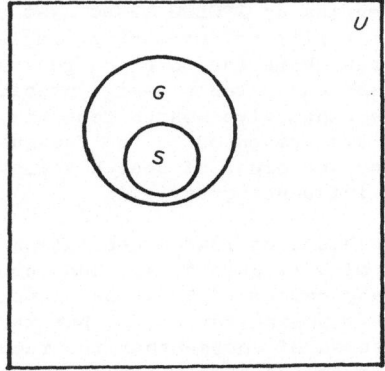

S IS A STYLISTIC SUB-SET OF G

Figure 5(a)   Set Demonstration of Style

Since this type of solution generator has a style of its own, even if the solution is passed to a designer for analysis and modification, the designer is still constrained to a starting point which is from the same stylistic subset of possible solutions. Even if he completely rejects the solution and reformulates the whole problem, the solution generator is still going to suggest a new scheme from the same characteristic subset. Bazjanac [6], for instance, reports that in tests on the Building Optimisation Program "it was conclusively proved that BOP in fact limited the solution space to only one morphological type and discouraged exploration of any innovative ideas". This type of restrictiveness is symbolised by set R1 in figure 5(b).

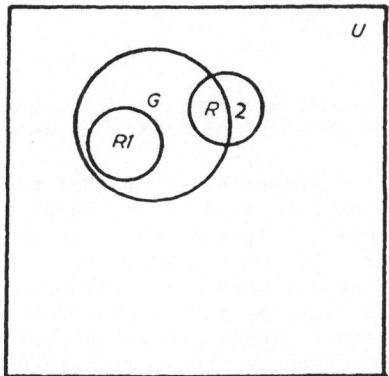

R1 & 2 ARE RULE BASED SUBSETS OF U

Figure 5(b)   Rule Based Imposition of Style

One of the perceived strengths of PROLOG based systems (e.g. [17]) is that the solution generator will not present a single answer, but a list of alternatives. Even where the solution generator is capable of finding all valid solutions and given a design problem where the size of the solution set makes exhaustive search feasible, the order in which possible solutions are presented to the designer will affect the final choice, and assuming the order of search follows a pattern, then the system will still be influencing style.

In contrast, the approach based on random generation produces a simplistic solution from a subset S of U (figure 5(c)), and, provided that S includes all members of G, since any member of S may be chosen with equal probability, the generator is not imposing any style, but may be providing a useful stimulus. (It is assumed of course that the random number generator is not constrained to produce the same sequence every time it is invoked!)

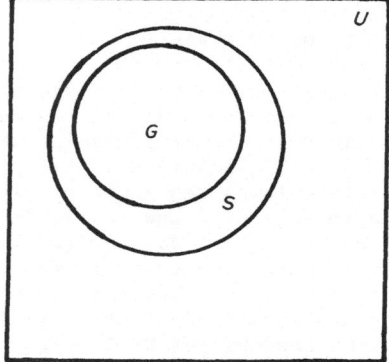

Figure 5(c) Provided S includes all members of G, and members of S are produced with equal probability, no style is imposed.

In defining their reasons for proposing the BAID-1 system, Auger et al [4] said "designers frequently prepare layouts for hundreds or even thousands of nearly identical dwellings. This can result in repetitive and often uninteresting schemes which .... compare badly in aesthetics and social standing with other longer established developments". In such circumstances a randomly generated initial layout provides a local variation in the stimulus to the designer, where otherwise the site might appear as an infinite and boring continuum. Interestingly enough Dijkstra [8] has warned of the dangers and difficulties of using repetitive techniques in large design problems, but in that case the activity concerned was the design of programs.

In cases where random "designs" are being produced, style is generated by the designer's choice and modification of parts of the randomly generated proposition or by the imagination of the viewer. As de Bono points out "If you offer a random arrangement of lines to a group of people they will soon start to pick out significant patterns. They will be convinced that the patterns have been put there deliberately or that the random arrangements are not random at all, but actually constructed out of special patterns" [7].

In Conclusion

This paper has attempted to show where, how and why the advent of IKBS and fifth generation computing systems will affect the designer's role in using CAD systems. By showing the limited impact of most current CAD systems on the design process, the new areas of influence were highlighted and their significance to the design loop demonstrated. A number of points arose:-

1. The volume of data communicated, both input and output, should decrease in keeping with the system's ability to interpret and infer.

2. Novel input tools affect the ease of communicating a piece of information. IKBS, in affecting the volume and type of dialogue, will have a more dramatic effect on the "feel" of the system.

3. The designers of knowledge based systems, which infer from high level specification and designer's instructions, will have to strike a delicate balance between too little and too much inference drawn from each command. This balance will be greatly affected by the nature of the design problem itself, whether it be largely unconstrained or offer few alternative solutions.

4. It is important that designer and machine share common definitions of "habitual notions" as to the meaning of abstract design descriptions. This will involve tailoring the CAD systems for individual designers and/or re-education of those designers to slightly different terms.

5. There is a definite risk of constraining the designer into not exploring the full range of options available.

6. IKBS will almost certainly affect the style of the artifacts designed. Whether this is important or not depends on the nature of the products being designed and on the importance attached to individual style.

References

[1] Aldefeld, B. On automating recognition of 3D structures from 2D representations, in Computer Aided Design, Vol.15(2)(March 1983) pp.59-64.

[2] Arnold, D.B. A Computer Model of Housing Layout, PhD Thesis, School of Architecture, University of Cambridge, England (1978).

[3] Arnold, D.B. Some Relationships Between Design, Style and Automation, CGP Memo 79/10, Computational Geometry Project, School of Computing Studies and Accountancy, Univ. of East Anglia, Norwich, England (Oct. 1979).

[4] Auger, B., Butlin, G. and Hubbold, R.J. A High Density Housing Layout Program, Computer Graphics Workshop Report No.2, Univ. of Leicester, Engineering Department Report No.71 (1971).

[5] Auger, B. The Architect and the Computer, London, Pall Mall Press (1972).

[6] Bazjanac, V. The Promises and Disappointments of Computer Aided Design, in (Reflections on) Computer Aids to Design and Architecture (Ed. N.Negroponte) Petrocelli/Charter, New York (1975).

[7] de Bono, E. Lateral Thinking - A Textbook in Creativity, Ward Lock Educational, London (1970).

[8] Dijkstra, E.M. Notes on Structured Programming, in O.-J.Dahl, E.M. Dijkstra and C.A. Hoare - Structured Programming, Academic Press, London (1972).

[9] Earl, D.J. From Sketch to Solid: Pictorially Aided Techniques for Converting Collections of Lines into Planar Faced Objects, PhD Thesis, Computational Geometry Project, Univ of East Anglia, Norwich (1983).

[10] George, F.H. Models of Thinking, Advances in Psychology Series No.1 (Series Editor J. Cohen), George Allen and Unwin, London (1970).

[11] Krause, F.-C. and Vassilakopoulos, V. A Way to Computer Supported Systems for Integrated Design and Production Process Planning, in CAD Systems, IFIP Working Conference (Ed. J.J. Allen), North Holland Publishing Co., Amsterdam (1977).

[12] Latombe, J.C. Artificial Intelligence in Computer Aided Design: The TROPIC System, in CAD Systems, IFIP Working Conference (Ed. J.J. Allen), North Holland Publishing Co., Amsterdam (1977).

[13] March, L. Introduction - The Logic of Design and the Question of Value, in The Architecture of Form (Ed. L. March), Cambridge Urban and Architectural Series No.4, Cambridge University Press (1976).

[14] Mitchell, W.J. The Theoretical Foundations of Computer Aided Architectural Design, Environment and Planning B., Vol.2(2)(1975).

[15] Mitchell, W.J. Computer Aided Architectural Design, Petrocelli/-Charter, New York (1977).

[16] Simon, H.A.   Style in Design, in <u>Spatial Synthesis in Computer Aided Building Design</u>, (Ed. C.M. Eastman), Applied Science Publishers Ltd., London (1975).

[17] Swinson, P.S.G., Pereira, F.C.N. and Biji, A.   A Fact Dependency System for the Logic Programmer, <u>Computer Aided Design</u> Vol.15(4) (July 1983) pp.235 243.

[18] Toller, D.R. and Willey, D.S.   Framed Bathrooms, Bargains and Architectural Designing, <u>Computer Aided Design</u>, Vol.15(1) (Jan 1983) pp.7-13.

[19] Willey, D.S.   Approaches to Computer Aided Architectural Sketch Design, <u>Computer Aided Design</u>, Vol.8(3) (July 1976).

[20] Yessios, C.I.   Formal Languages for Site Planning, in <u>Spatial Synthesis in Computer Aided Building Design</u>, (Ed. C.M. Eastman), Applied Science Publishers Ltd., London (1975).

Chapter 7
Graphic Displays and Peripherals

New Trends in Graphic Display System Architecture

Ender M. Kaya
Ramtek Corporation
2211 Lawson Lane
Santa Clara, CA 95050, USA

ABSTRACT

This paper discusses a 4th generation graphics computing and display system. It defines the following as components of 4th generation graphics architecture: a combination of pipelined parallel co-processors, custom VLSIs for vector drawing, bit slice and mathematics chips for geometry processing, a 32-bit VMEbus structure, and a new display list data structure. The paper shows how these components and modular architecture add high performance-to-cost effectiveness of raster-scan graphics display systems.

INTRODUCTION

Computer graphics has passed through several important stages of evolution, encompassing monochrome stroke writers through color raster-scan display generators. The industry began to visibly mature several years ago when raster graphics systems, based on standard graphics controller chips and other off-the-shelf technology, appeared. These developments have brought the price of color displays down, but at the cost of performance.

For that and other reasons (one being that software developers have remained device-independent, often leaving display features underutilized), graphics applications have remained predominately oriented to a host computer. One consequence is that basic recurring graphics processing operations take significant time to complete.

THE 4TH GENERATION GRAPHICS COMPUTING SYSTEM

To improve the integrated performance of graphics systems for CAD/CAM, command and control, CAE, and simulation requires substantial increases in performance and functions.[1,2] The Ramtek New Model 2020 provides a concrete approach to meeting these requirements.

The Ramtek New Model 2020 features a combination of pipelined parallel co-processors, custom VLSIs for vector drawing, bit slice and mathematics chips for geometry processing, a 32-bit VMEbus structure, and a new display list data structure. These are combined in a series of modular high-performance raster-scan graphics display systems. Pixel access speeds reach 74 ns -- the equivalent of 337,000 vector-cm/s. That is 35 times faster than previous raster graphics systems, and meets the needs of most CAD/CAM graphics design applications.

A geometry co-processor handles fast two- and three-dimensional modeling transformation, translation, rotation, scaling, windowing, and orthographic and perspective projections. The large virtual coordinate space ($\pm 2^{15}$ for integers or $\pm 1.7 \times 10^{38}$ for floating-point numbers) is especially important when complex VLSI designs need to be stored and manipulated locally. And since a great many vectors tend to be horizontal in electronic CAD applications, the system's 60 Hz noninterlaced refresh eliminates flicker and eye strain.

Depending on the model, a system may have up to five co-processors to handle the graphics geometry, the display list, peripheral devices, and communications with the host computer. With the addition of these modules, the system becomes an ultra high performance 3-D graphics computer that can manipulate complex data structures and display them on a CRT at speeds approaching screen refresh rates.

The system's modular bus structure and expandable architecture is achieved with the VMEbus. This bus, which uses two 96-pin connectors and has a data transfer rate of 20M bytes/s, is organized for 16- or 32-bit operation. The system uses this structure to support the multiple co-processors. And instead of relying on a permanent master, the bus includes arbitration logic, which gives each processor access at any time. Shared memory for message transfers and interrupt-driven signal registers for control provide interprocessor communication.

All configurations include refresh memory, a video processor,[3] a CRT screen, and a micro floppy-disk drive that loads the machine's internal instructions (Fig. 1a). The refresh memory, addressed on a separate memory bus, is dual-ported to allow simultaneous access by the video processor(s) and the drawing processor. It is arranged in planes of 1280 by 1024 bits, and comes in 4-bit increments up to 16-bits.

SUB-VIDEO SYSTEM

Up to 12 planes feed an internal color look-up table, thereby permitting 4096 simultaneous colors -- from a palette of over 16 million -- to be displayed. The other four planes can be used as video overlays in applications where text or map outlines must be superimposed onto screen images.

The video processor, which contains a multiplexor and a video look-up table, maps refresh data to the CRT. The table accepts up to 12 bits of pixel data and displays 25 bits of color information (8 bits per color gun and a blink control bit). The multiplexor is programmable, permitting the user to specify which bits of the pixel data in the refresh memory should be used as inputs to the look-up table, and in what order. This capability allows any arbitrary combination of the 12 permissible bit planes of display memory to be used to construct a screen image. It is especially helpful in animation and other double-buffering applications, where one set of memory planes must sometimes be displayed while another is being modified.

SOFT-LOADED INSTRUCTIONS

Because all of the system processors operate out of RAM, rather than under ROM control, they can have instructions downloaded from any MC68000 on the bus or from the floppy disk provided with the system. The 3.5-in. floppy-disk drive adds another advantage as well; the disk with the standard operating software can be replaced with one that contains special diagnostics. And protocol definitions for communication or graphic generation, as well as storage configuration information, can be stored on disk for use in tailoring the system.

The drawing processor is based on the AMD2903 bipolar bit slice processor with a 4K-word control store implemented in RAM. The control store can be reprogrammed to suit specific applications, thus increasing system flexibility.

Special-purpose hardware provides vector generation and assists for polygon fill. It can, for example, generate special vectors where the pixel values vary along the vector. This feature is used for textured vectors, depth cueing and, when used with the fill function, shaded polygons (for modeling of solids).

The drawing processor accepts 2-D picture primitives and translates them into complex screen images composed of vectors, text characters, and polygons. A general-purpose 16-bit parallel interface is included for host communications.

A communications co-processor, based on an MC68000 16-bit microprocessor, provides DMA circuitry for transferring data quickly to and from the host computer. It also provides two 16-bit parallel interfaces capable of transferring 1 million 16-bit words/s. A 16K-byte ROM holds power-up routines and 128K bytes of RAM are available for storing programs. Standard instructions download software from the host and begin display execution. Other I/O interfaces include a 10M-bit/s Ethernet link.

Models are created by adding additional co-processors on the VMEbus. Models available later this year will include one for solid display list processing and one for three-dimensional solids processing (Fig. 1b). The display list processor, based on an MC68000 16-bit microprocessor, builds and maintains hierarchical display list structures. A display list contains the data to be displayed in terms of objects, which are created by Move, Draw, Line, Fill Area, and other such commands. Complete pictures and subpictures (picture components) are composed from these objects and scaling and rotation commands.

The display list processor also has a 16K-byte bootstrap ROM and 256K bytes of RAM for program storage. Four RS-232-C serial ports provide connection to a local terminal for debugging, and to peripherals. A 500 ns timer is also included. The display list memory consists of 768K bytes of RAM on board, with an additional 3.75M bytes available through the VMEbus.

The geometry processor serves applications that require 3-D representations and floating-point accuracy. This 64-bit processor is organized from AMD2903 bit slices. It has a special VLSI floating-point circuit to increase speed, and operates on graphics data conforming to the IEEE specifications for 3-D information for coordinates, transformations, clipping, and perspective.

Graphics information, represented as display lists, describes objects in terms of Cartesian coordinates. An object may consist of a series of high-level forms, such as the end points of a line or the start, end, and center points of arcs or circles. Transformation from high-level information into actual bit patterns in the display memory normally requires significant mathematical manipulation, such as matrix multiplication.

The geometry processor's major task is to transform the user's coordinate space to the two's complement 16-bit integers of the drawing processor's coordinate space. It executes its own instructions for vectors and generates the equivalent drawing processor instructions. Working with the VLSI floating point circuit, it can generate more than 200,000 transformed vectors/s. Systems not configured with the geometry processor depend on the MC68000 display-list-processor module to do 3-D calculations. The graphic processor, when available, will act as a 3-D accelerator.

The last of the co-processor modules, the peripheral processor, accommodates such devices as joysticks, data tablets, cursor mice, trackballs, data terminals, and modems through four RS-232-C serial ports. It also serves as a fast interface with the graphic system's video look-up table.

The display list data structure, the geometry processor, and the pipelined communications system provide the keys to the excellent performance of the graphics system series.

The communications network establishes a message route among processors. Any individual processor can operate independently on a portion of the display task. And each processor can generate additional work for the next processor while the latter performs work it has already received. By having the processors work together in this way, system throughput is much greater than with single-processor designs.

DISPLAY LIST STRUCTURE

The data in the display lists is organized into hierarchical trees (Fig. 2a). Each node in a tree is called a subpicture and can have any number of subpictures -- children -- subordinate to it. And each subpicture can have default attributes, a transformation, and graphical data associated with it.

There are three types of nodes: normal subpictures, subtree root subpictures, and subtree invocation subpictures. Each has a control block containing display information. Subpictures are referred to by name, data type, and software switch setting with a number of attributes determining color, viewport, and type of transformation. Trees are maintained by pointers linking each subpicture with its parent, its children, and its siblings.

Trees may be "grafted" onto other existing tree structures to create separate display elements without duplicating the data in the primary tree. This is done by creating a special invocation subpicture that contains no graphical data but instead points to a root of the tree to be grafted.

In the data structure shown in Fig. 2b, nodes B and C are both subtree invocation subpictures whose subtree field points to subpicture X. Colors and patterns can be specified with the various data types -- vectors, stroked text, polygon edges, and polygon interiors -- that are associated with each subpicture. If a color or pattern value is not specified in a subpicture, the default values become those of the parent node.

The data for a subpicture is maintained as an extensible buffer, a group of fixed-length buffer segments that are linked by pointers. This scheme accommodates large amounts of data but does not waste space when only a small amount of data is present.

The hierarchical tree structure is defined using a block-structured approach, traversing the structure in a left-to-right, top-to-bottom manner. The tree shown in Fig. 2a would have its image generated by processing the subpictures in the order A, B, E, F, C, D (Fig. 3).

The displayed image of any subpicture is a combination of the subpicture data and the cumulative effects of attributes inherited from the subpictures above it in the data structure. Each time a subpicture is processed, its transformation matrix is concatenated with the composite matrix of its parent. The composite matrix of a subpicture is used to transform all data associated with it during image generation.

Similarly, the viewport specified with a subpicture will be "boxed" within the composite viewport calculated for the subpicture directly above it in the data structure. This boxing operation consists of calculating the intersection of the parent's composite viewport with the subpicture's viewport. The resulting viewport then becomes the composite viewport for the subpicture.

INTERPROCESSOR COMMUNICATIONS

Interprocessor communications is implemented with shared memory and signal registers. Each processor has a data buffer and two signal registers -- one for request and one for acknowledgments (Fig. 4) -- accessible to all the other processors over the system VMEbus. The buffer is used to build messages for other processors, which then perform memory reads to it.

Writing into either of the two signal registers will cause the receiving processor to be interrupted. One or more processors write into the request register to indicate that they have a message for it.

One processor writes into another's acknowledge register to signal
that action has been completed on the last message sent by the latter.
One bit is assigned to each processor to indicate which one has sent a
message or an acknowledgment. Thus each processor can keep track of
the message flow, making possible true parallel sharing of tasks.

One processor communicates with another by building a message in its
data buffer; setting the bit corresponding to it in the request
register of the processor the message is intended for; and either
waiting for the interrupt indicating that the message was acted upon
and acknowledged or continuing processing until the interrupt arrives.

The buffers are formatted as shown. A block of four 32-bit words is
allocated for each processor in the system. This block can hold short
messages or pointers to an extensible buffer containing longer pieces
of information. Messages are always instructions for the receiving
processor, and successful execution of the instruction is always
followed by an acknowledgment to the sending processor.

In the state depicted in Fig. 4, the display list processor has just
requested that the graphics processor store a matrix at the address
defined by aaaa. The geometry processor will be interrupted, read its
request register, and realize that it has a request from the display
list processor. The message is then read and executed and an
acknowledgment is sent. The request bit is then cleared, ending the
communication, which is a pipelined sequence.

The pipeline flows from display list processor to geometry processor,
and then to drawing processor. The display list processor initiates
the generation of all data from the display list memory. Its task in
the image creation process is to traverse the hierarchical tree data
structure and identify which data and attributes within the structure
should be sent to the other processors in the pipeline. Once it has
identified data or attributes, it will build instructions to transfer
the information to the next stage in the pipe. These commands are
placed in an extensible buffer that will be read by processors further
down the line.

Once a message has been sent to the next processor, the sending
processor may construct a new message in another extensible buffer.
In that way, one processor can continue to fill the pipeline without
waiting for the execution of a previous instruction.

DISCUSSION

All of the figures stated here are achieved in the 2020 4th generation
graphic system. This system provides not only the best performance of
all graphics systems on the market today, it also offers a unique
concept in model compatibility. The 2020 series allows the graphics
user to select the level of performance that best fits the application
and budget -- and without sacrificing needed functionality. The 2020
provides a truly outstanding level of performance.

CONCLUSION

Ramtek has done much to improve the integrated performance of graphics systems. We have increased drawing speed by an order of magnitude, and have developed a parallel system architecture that permits more graphics operations to be shifted from the host computer to the local display unit.

REFERENCES

1. Tsuneo Ikedo, "High-Speed Techniques for the 3-D Color Graphic Terminal," to appear in IEEE Computer Graphics and Applications, 1984.

2. Akira Fujimoto, C.G. Perrott, and Kansei Iwata, "3-D Color-Shaded Graphics Display with Depth Buffer and Pipeline Processor," to appear in IEEE Computer Graphics and Applications, 1984.

3. Mary C. Whitton, "Memory Design for Raster Graphic Displays," IEEE Computer Graphics and Applications, pp. 48 to 65, Vol. 4, No. 3, 1984.

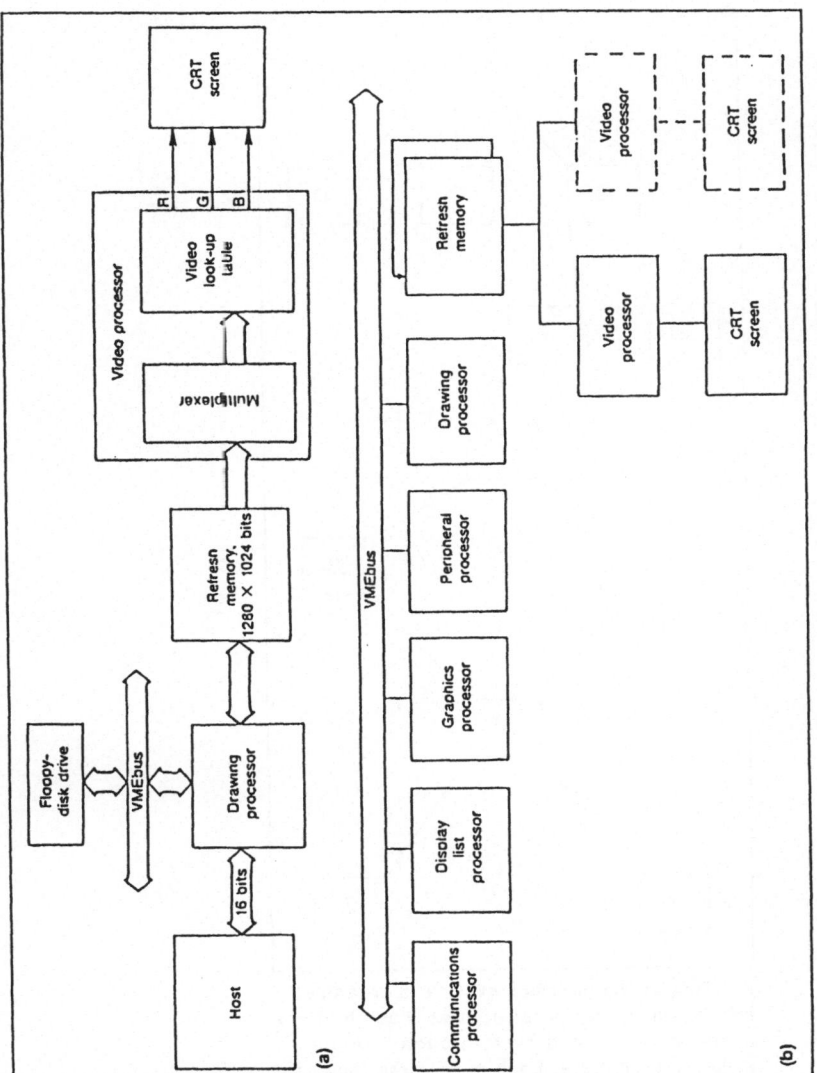

1. The basic configuration of the raster-scan graphics system (a) provides a straightforward frame buffer for control by a host computer. The integral floppy disk drive is used to load configuration attributes that allow correct communication with the host. (A second video processor and CRT screen are optional.) The VMEbus allows the system to be extended by adding one or more coprocessors. When fully configured (b), the system becomes a high-performance stand-alone graphics system capable of accomplishing a plethora of tasks and communicating with a host system.

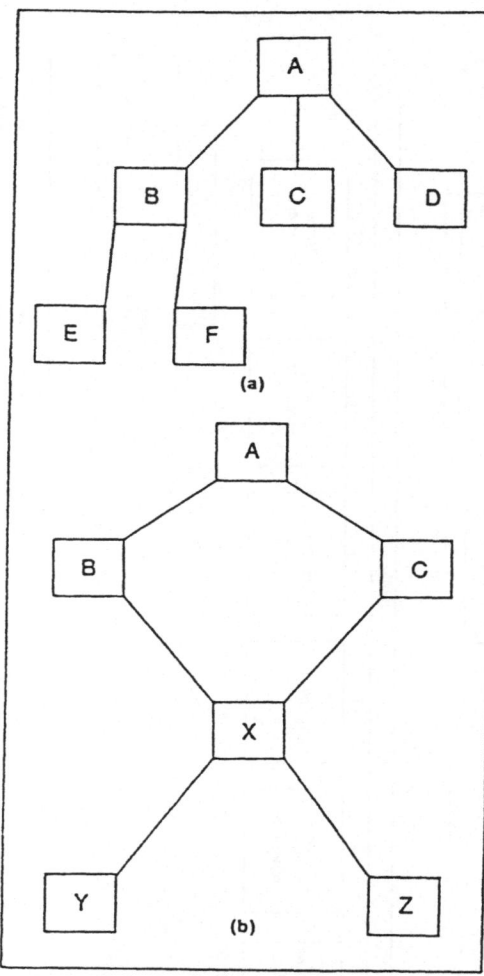

2. Data in the graphics system is organized into hierarchical tree structures. Each node in a tree, here denoted by A through F (a), is called a subpicture. Each subpicture (such as B) can have subordinates, or chldren (E and F). Additionally, subpictures can have specific attributes describing transformation and the graphical data associated with it. Also, subpictures can share children (b). For example, nodes B and C are both subtree invocation subpictures whose subtree field points to, or shares, subpicture X.

```
       SUBPICTURE_CREATE 0 A          /* Begin A with default segment size*/
         SUBPICTURE_CREATE 0 B        /* . Begin B */
           SUBPICTURE_CREATE 0 E      /* .. Begin E*/
           SUBPICTURE_END E           /* .. End E */
           SUBPICTURE_CREATE 14 F     /* .. Begin F with segment size 14*/
           SUBPICTURE_END F           /* .. End F */
         SUBPICTURE_END B             /* . End B */
         SUBPICTURE_CREATE C          /* . Begin C */
         SUBPICTURE_END C             /* . End C */
         SUBPICTURE_CREATE D          /* . Begin D */
         SUBPICTURE_END D             /* . End D */
       SUBPICTURE_END A               /* End A */                    (a)


       SUBPICTURE_CREATE 0 A          /* Begin A */
         SUBPICTURE_CREATE 0 B        /* . Begin B */
         SUBPICTURE_END B             /* . End B */
         SUBPICTURE_CREATE C          /* . Begin C */
           SUBPICTURE_CONTINUE B      /* . Continue B */
             SUBPICTURE_CREATE 0 E    /* .. Begin E */
             SUBPICTURE_END E         /* .. End E */
             SUBPICTURE_CREATE 14 F   /* .. Begin F with segment size 14*/
             SUBPICTURE_END F         /* .. End F */
             SUBPICTURE_CONTINUE A    /* Continue A (active twice)*/
               SUBPICTURE_CREATE D    /* . Begin D */
               SUBPICTURE_END D       /* . End D */
             SUBPICTURE_END A         /* End A */
           SUBPICTURE_END B           /* . End B*/
         SUBPICTURE_END C             /* . End C*/
       SUBPICTURE_END A               /* End A */                    (b)
```

3. The data structure in Fig. 2a could be constructed by executing the first set of instructions (a). However, many different specifications are possible, and the second set of instructions (b) will create a similar structure. The dots in the comments indicate the level within the tree structure being defined, and the indentation reflects the stacking level of active subpictures. Although the second approach may seem cumbersome, it has the flexibility of allowing user modules to generate tree structures without knowing the attributes of other trees in the overall system.

4. Each processor has two signal registers with tag bits to indicate which of the other processors has requested or acknowledged an action. A data buffer of four 32-bit words also is associated with each processor. Here, the display list processor (a) has sent a request to the graphics processor (b) to store the matrix located at address "aaa." If the instruction message is greater than four 32-bit words, an extensible buffer pointer is placed in the data buffer. The pointer thereby links the data buffer to a block of memory containing the message.

Morphological Binary Image Processing with a Local Neighborhood Pipeline Processor

William K. Pratt and **Ihtisham Kabir**
Vicom Systems, Inc.
2025 Junction Avenue
San Jose, CA 95134, USA

ABSTRACT

This paper presents a flexible pipeline image processor architecture for performing morphological image processing at digital video rates. Algorithms for additive, subtractive and hierarchical morphological operators is also presented.

1. Introduction

Morphological image processing is a type of processing in which the spatial form or structure of objects within an image is modified for purposes of image enhancement or image analysis. Dilation, erosion and skeletonization are three fundamental morphological operations. With dilation, an object grows uniformly in spatial extent, while with erosion an object shrinks uniformly. Skeletonization results in a stick figure representation of an object. Figure 1 provides examples of dilation, erosion and skeletonization of a binary object.

The basic concepts of morphological image processing began with the research of Matherton on topology [1]. Serra [2], at the School of Mines in France, applied morphological techniques to the analysis of microscopic rock samples, and in the process, developed much of the foundation of the subject. Sternberg [3-5], at the Environmental Research Institute of Michigan, used morphological methods for a variety of industrial vision applications. This research work led toward the development of the Cytocomputer for rapid morphological image processing [6]. References [7-13] discuss algorithms and applications of morphological image processing.

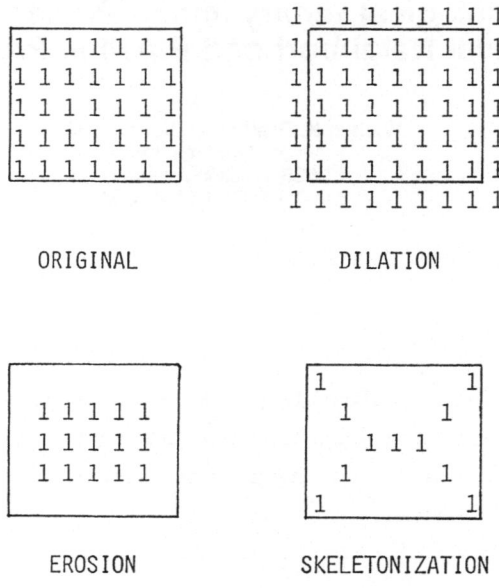

FIGURE 1. EXAMPLES OF DILATION, EROSION AND SKELETONIZATION OF A RECTANGULAR OBJECT.

This paper presents a pipeline processor architecture for morphological image processing of binary-valued images in which a complex morphological operation is decimated into a sequence of point, ensemble and local neighborhood spatial functions. This local neighborhood approach has been previously applied to convolution [14] and other conventional methods of image processing [15].

2. Morphological Definitions

Morphological image processing operations apply to both binary and grey scale images. However, the discussion in this paper is limited to binary images.

The local neighborhood relationship between a binary-valued pixel $F(j,k) = X$ at row, column location (j,k) and its eight nearest neighbors is as follows

$$\begin{array}{ccc} X_3 & X_2 & X_1 \\ X_4 & X & X_0 \\ X_5 & X_6 & X_7 \end{array}$$

Pixel $F(j,k)$ is said to be 4-connected to a neighbor if it is a logical one and if its East, North, West or South (X_0, X_2, X_4, X_6) neighbor is a logical one. Pixel $F(j,k)$ is said to be 8-connected if it is a logical one and if one of its eight neighbors is a logical one. Pixels in a binary object (logical 1) are usually considered to be 8-connected, while the background pixels (logical 0) are considered 4-connected. This eliminates ambiguity in the definition of the interior and exterior of ring-shaped objects [16]. Figure 2 contains definitions of the center pixel of several 3 x 3 pixel patterns.

3. Pipeline Image Processor

The basic architecture of a pipeline image processor is shown in Figure 3. In operation, data moves from image memory through a Point Processor, Ensemble Processor or a Spatial Processor and back to image memory at digital video rates to complete a single pass of a multi-stage algorithm. The Point Processor performs a linear or nonlinear mapping between input and output pixels. It is implemented as a 16-bit input, 16-bit output look-up table (LUT). The Ensemble Processor performs pixel-by-pixel addition, subtraction, and multiplication of grey level images and logical combination (AND, OR, NOT, XOR, etc.) of binary images. The Spatial Processor performs linear convolution or nonlinear spatial combination of pixels of an input image over a 3 x 3 pixel neighborhood to produce a single output pixel. The pipeline image processor of Figure 3 can be used to execute conventional image processing algorithms for image enhancement, edge detection and other forms of pre-processing prior to image analysis. The pipeline image processor can also be programmed to perform morphological image processing for binary and grey level images.

```
0 0 0            0 0 0            0 0 0
0 Y X            0 Y X            0 Y 0
0 X 0            0 0 X            0 0 0
4-CONNECTED      8-CONNECTED      ISOLATED


0 0 0            X 0 0            X X X
0 Y 0            X Y X            0 Y 0
0 0 X            X 0 X            X X X
   SPUR            BRIDGE         H-CONNECTED


0 0 0            0 X X            0 X X
0 Y X            X Y X            0 Y X
0 X X            X X X            0 X X
  CORNER          INTERIOR         EXTERIOR
```

FIGURE 2. BINARY MORPHOLOGICAL DEFINITIONS

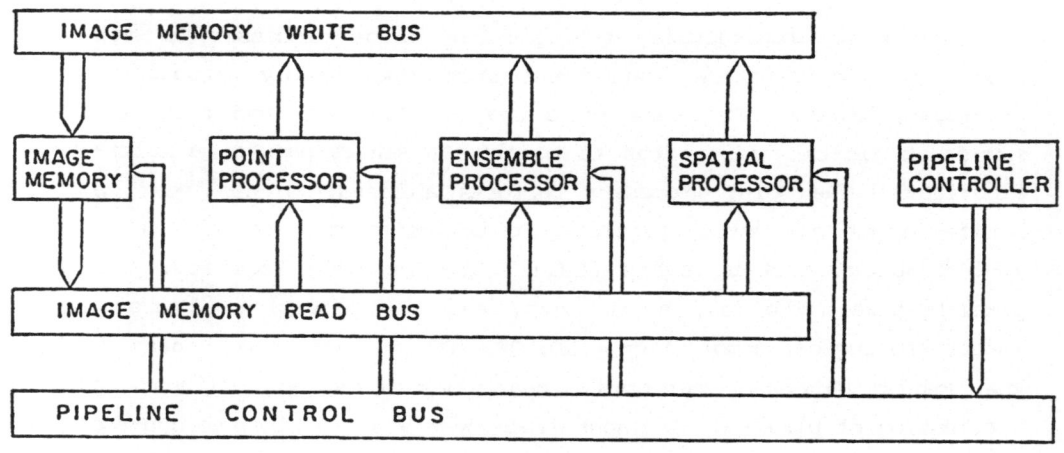

FIGURE 3. PIPELINE IMAGE PROCESSOR

Figure 4 shows the structure of a binary morphic processor that can be effectively created by sequentially combining the Spatial Processor and the Point Processor. Three adjacent rows of an image are scanned into the tapped delay line circuits of the Spatial Processor to gain parallel access to the nine pixels in the 3 x 3 window. The Spatial Processor acts as a "pixel stacker." The LUT of the Point Processor then performs the logical combination of the center pixel and its eight neighbors to execute a morphological operation. Figure 5 describes the logic flow for unconditional neighborhood operations.

4. Additive Operators

The additive operators cause the center pixel of a 3 x 3 pixel window to be converted from a logical 0 state (white) to a logical 1 state (black) if the neighboring pixels meet certain pre-determined conditions. The basic additive operators are defined below.

INTERIOR FILL. Creates a black pixel if 4-connected neighbor pixels are all black.

```
        D 1 D         D 1 D
        1 0 1         1 1 1
        D 1 D         D 1 D
        input         output
```

where D denotes a "don't care" state. There are 16 qualifying patterns.

BRIDGE. Creates black pixel if creation results in connectivity of previously unconnected neighboring black pixels.

```
        1 0 0         1 0 0
        1 0 1         1 1 1
        0 0 1         0 0 1
        input         output
```

There are 120 qualifying patterns.

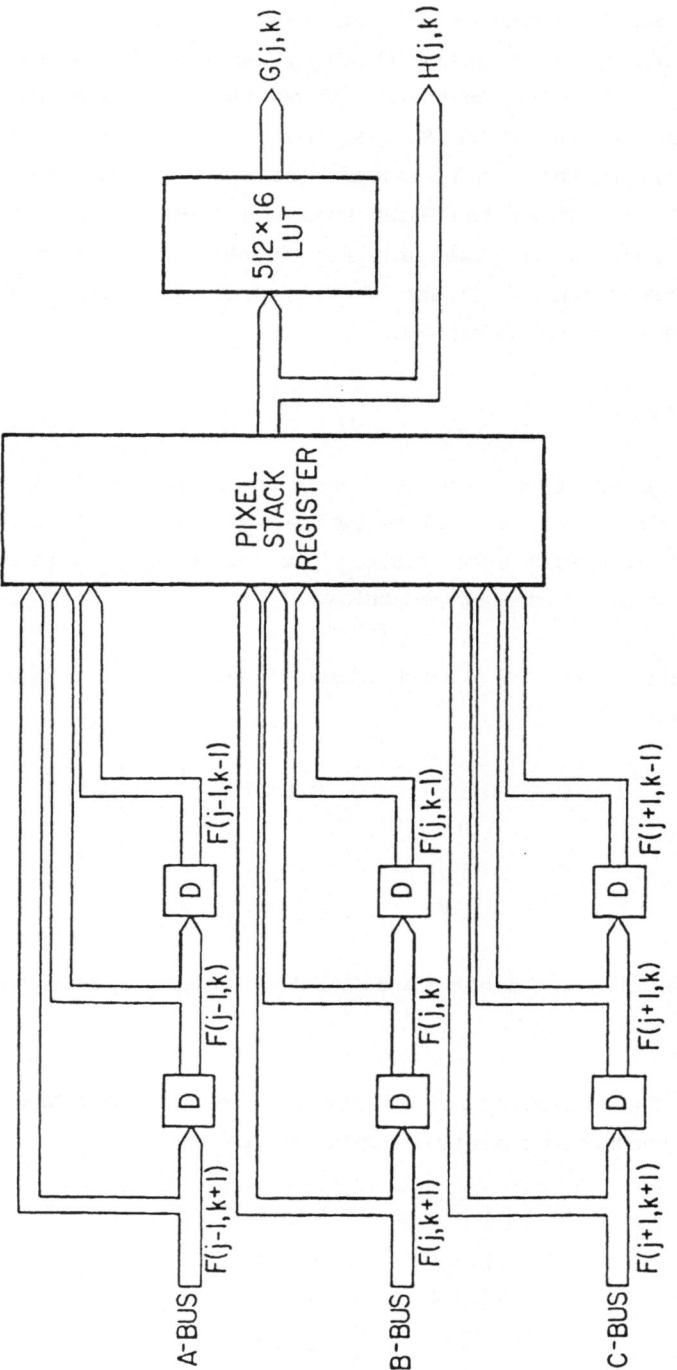

FIGURE 4. BINARY MORPHIC PROCESSOR

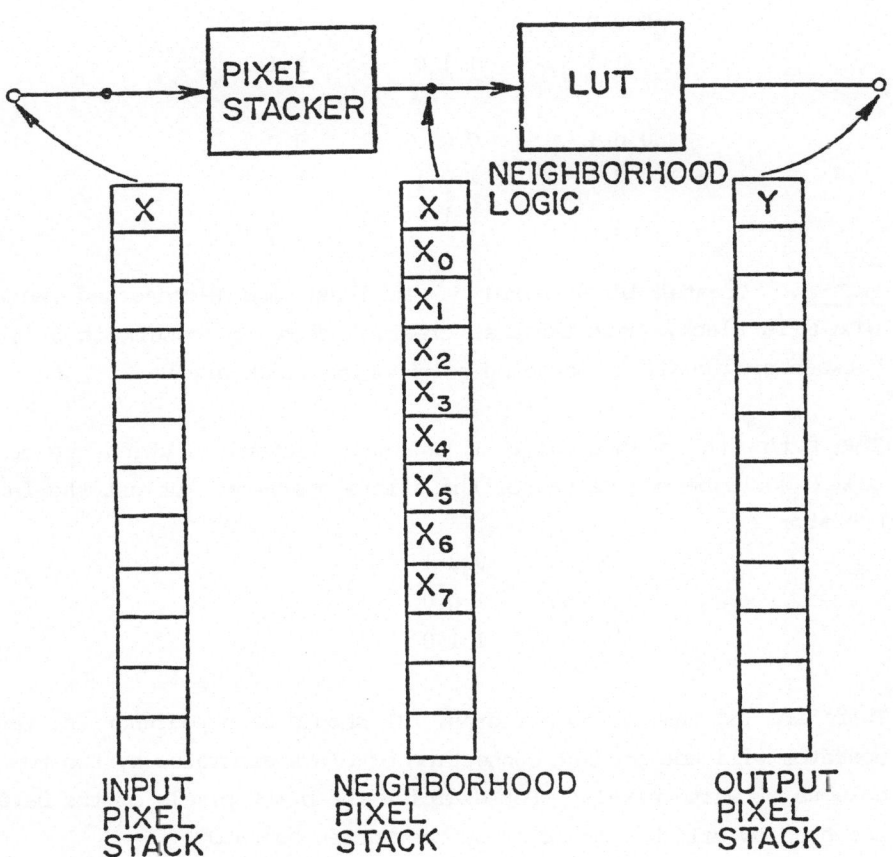

FIGURE 5. UNCONDITIONAL NEIGHBORHOOD OPERATIONS

DILATE. Creates black pixel if at least one 8-connected neighbor pixel is black.

In the following examples, the center pixel is set black. There are 255 qualifying patterns.

```
0 0 0      0 0 0      0 0 0
0 0 0      0 0 0      0 0 0
0 0 1      0 1 0      1 1 0

0 0 0      0 0 0      0 0 0
0 0 0      1 0 0      1 0 0
1 1 1      1 1 0      1 1 1

0 0 1      0 0 0      0 0 1
0 0 1      1 0 1      1 0 1
1 1 1      1 1 1      1 1 1
```

FATTEN. Creates black pixel if at least one 8-connected neighbor pixel is black, provided that creation does not result in a bridge between previously unconnected neighboring black pixels.

The following is an example of an input pattern in which the center pixel would be set black for the dilate operator, but not the fatten operator.

```
0 0 1
1 0 0
1 1 0
```

There are 135 qualifying patterns. It should be noted that the fatten operator will not prevent connection of blobs separated by two rows or columns of white pixels. For example, the black pixels of the data shown below will be connected by the fatten operator.

```
0 0 0 0 0 0 0 0
0 1 1 0 0 1 1 0
0 1 1 0 0 1 1 0
0 0 0 0 0 0 0 0
```

The bridge, dilate and fatten operators can be applied recursively. With the dilate and fatten operators, objects will grow by a ring of exterior pixels upon each pass.

Figure 6 contains a test image used to show the results of the binary morphological operators. Results of the dilate operation are shown in Figure 7. In each example, the original pixels are colored red and the modified pixels are colored yellow-green. Figure 8 contains a blowup of the blob for dilation and fattening. All other objects in the test image are treated the same for dilation and fattening.

5. Subtractive Operators

The subtractive operators cause the center pixel of a 3 x 3 pixel window to be converted from black to white if its neighboring pixels meet pre-determined conditions. The basic subtractive operators are defined below.

ISOLATED PIXEL REMOVE. Erases black pixel with eight white neighbors.

```
0 0 0        0 0 0
0 1 0        0 0 0
0 0 0        0 0 0
input        output
```

SPUR REMOVE. Erases black pixel with a single 8-connected neighbor.

```
0 0 0        0 0 0
0 1 0        0 0 0
1 0 0        1 0 0
input        output
```

There are four qualifying patterns.

FIGURE 6. TEST IMAGE

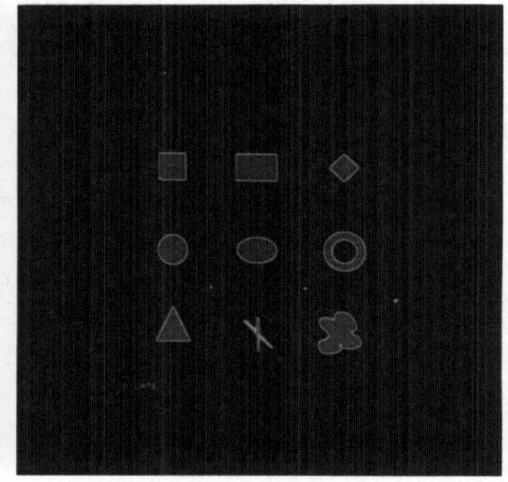

FIGURE 7. DILATION EXAMPLE

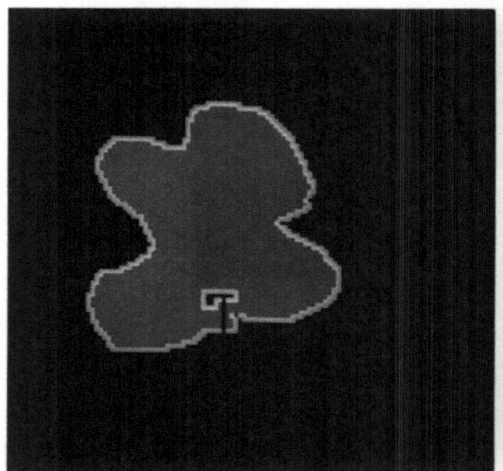

DILATE

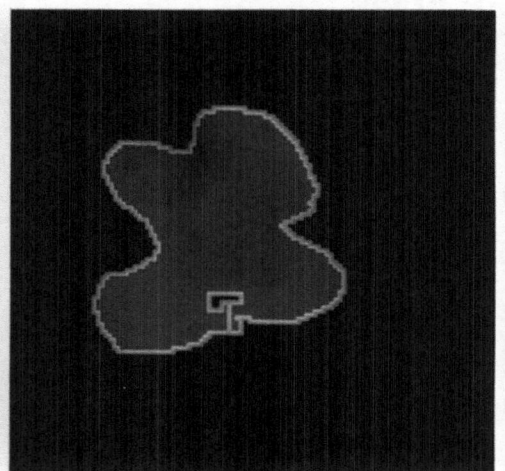

FATTEN

FIGURE 8. EXAMPLES OF DILATION AND FATTENING

INTERIOR PIXEL REMOVE. Erases black pixel if all 4-connected pixels are black.

```
D 1 D         D 1 D
1 1 1         1 0 1
D 1 D         D 1 D
input         output
```

There are 16 qualifying patterns.

BREAK. Erases black pixel which is 8-connected.

```
1 1 1         1 1 1
0 1 0         0 0 0
1 1 1         1 1 1
input         output
```

There are two qualifying patterns.

ERODE. Erases black pixels meeting erosion conditions.

Table 1 lists the erosion patterns. Figure 9 is an example of single pass erosion. Recursive application of the erosion operator will eventually erase all black pixels.

SHRINK. Erases black pixels meeting erosion conditions, provided that erasure does not break connectivity nor completely erase an object.

The shrink erase patterns are identical to the erosion erase patterns of Table 1. The shrink algorithm is executed in two phases per pass to prevent total erasure of an object and to prevent connectivity breakup. Figure 10 contains a flow chart of the conditional erase operation for each stage. In the first phase of the algorithm, the A patterns of Table 1 are entered in the conditional erasure LUT. The center pixel of those patterns meeting the shrink criteria are labelled for conditional erasure. Next, the erasure states and pixel

TABLE 1
ERODE PATTERNS

```
0 0 0     0 0 0     0 0 1     1 0 0
0 1 0     0 1 0     0 1 0     0 1 0
0 0 1     1 0 0     0 0 0     0 0 0
 A,B       A,B       A,B       A,B

0 0 0     0 0 0     0 0 0     0 1 0
0 1 0     0 1 1     1 1 0     0 1 0
0 1 0     0 0 0     0 0 0     0 0 0
 A,B       A,B       A,B       A,B

0 0 0   0 0 0   0 0 0   0 0 1   0 1 1   1 0 0   1 1 0   0 0 0
0 1 0   0 1 0   1 1 0   0 1 1   0 1 0   1 1 0   0 1 0   0 1 1
1 1 0   0 1 1   1 0 0   0 0 0   0 0 0   0 0 0   0 0 0   0 0 1
 A,B     A,B     A,B     A,B     A,B     A,B     A,B     A,B

0 0 0     0 0 1     1 0 0     1 1 1
0 1 0     0 1 1     1 1 0     0 1 0
1 1 1     0 0 1     1 0 0     0 0 0
 A,B       A,B       A,B       A,B

0 0 0     0 1 1     0 0 0     1 1 0
1 1 0     0 1 1     0 1 1     1 1 0
1 1 0     0 0 0     0 1 1     0 0 0
 A,B       A,B        A         B

0 0 0   0 1 1   1 0 0   1 1 1   0 0 0   0 0 1   1 1 0   1 1 1
1 1 0   0 1 1   1 1 0   0 1 1   0 1 1   0 1 1   1 1 0   1 1 0
1 1 1   0 0 1   1 1 0   0 0 0   1 1 1   0 1 1   1 0 0   0 0 0
 A,B     A,B     A,B     A,B     A,B     A,B     A,B     A,B

1 0 0     1 1 1     0 0 1     1 1 1
1 1 0     0 1 1     0 1 1     1 1 0
1 1 1     0 0 1     1 1 1     1 0 0
 A,B       A,B       A,B       A,B

0 0 0     0 1 1     1 1 0     1 1 1
1 1 1     0 1 1     1 1 0     1 1 1
1 1 1     0 1 1     1 1 0     0 0 0
  A         A         B         B

0 0 1   0 1 1   1 0 0   1 1 0   1 1 1   1 1 1   1 1 1   1 1 1
1 1 1   0 1 1   1 1 1   1 1 0   1 1 0   1 1 1   1 1 1   0 1 1
1 1 1   1 1 1   1 1 1   1 1 1   1 1 0   0 0 1   1 0 0   0 1 1
  A       A       A       A       B       B       B       B
```

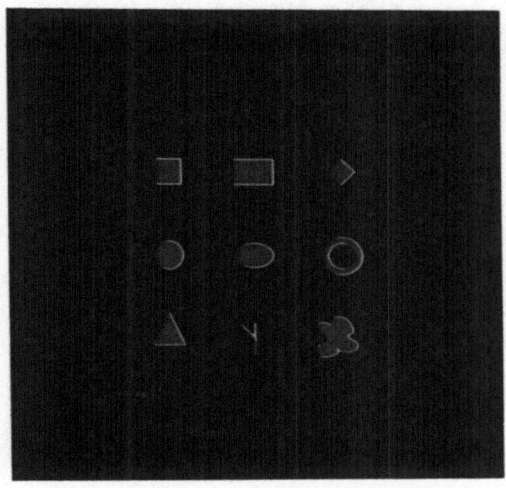

FIGURE 9. EXAMPLE OF EROSION

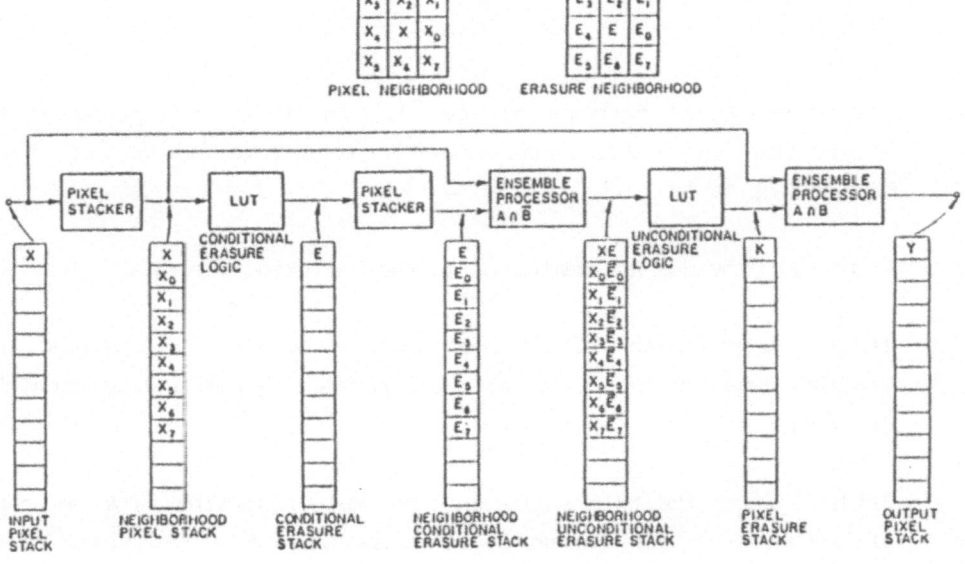

FIGURE 10. CONDITIONAL ERASURE OPERATIONS

states in the 3 x 3 window are examined to determine if a conditional erasure is to be made unconditional or to be rejected. The unconditional erasure logic is

$$G(j,k) = [F(j,k)] \cap [P(E, X_0\bar{E}_0, X_1\bar{E}_1, \ldots, X_7\bar{E}_7)]$$

where P(.) denotes an unconditional erasure pattern of its arguments and E_i represents a conditional erasure of the i-th neighbor of F(j,k). As an example, the pattern of the center E and neighbor $X_i\bar{E}_i$ terms

```
0 0 0
0 1 0
1 1 0
```

causes F(j,k) to be erased, while the pattern

```
0 0 0
0 1 0
1 0 1
```

prevents F(j,k) from being erased. In the second phase of the algorithm, the conditional erase logic LUT is filled with the B patterns of Table 1.

Figure 11 provides an example of in the shrinking process.

<u>THIN</u>. Erases black pixels meeting thin conditions, provided that erasure does not break connectivity nor shorten minimally connected strokes.

Table 2 lists the thin patterns. The thin algorithm is a two phase algorithm, with its second phase consisting of unconditional erase logic identical to that of the shrink algorithm.

Figure 12 contains an example of thinning of the test image. A result of the application of thinning to an edge map is shown in Figure 13.

TABLE 2

THIN PATTERNS

```
0 0 0     0 0 1     1 0 0     1 1 1
0 1 0     0 1 1     1 1 0     0 1 0
1 1 1     0 0 1     1 0 0     0 0 0
 A,B       A,B       A,B       A,B

0 0 0     0 1 1     0 0 0     1 1 0
1 1 0     0 1 1     0 1 1     1 1 0
1 1 0     0 0 0     0 1 1     0 0 0
 A,B       A,B        A         B

0 0 0   0 0 0   0 0 1   0 1 1   1 0 0   1 1 0   1 1 1   1 1 1
0 1 1   1 1 0   0 1 1   0 1 1   1 1 0   1 1 0   0 1 1   1 1 0
1 1 1   1 1 1   0 1 1   0 0 1   1 1 0   1 0 0   0 0 0   0 0 0
 A,B     A,B     A,B     A,B     A,B     A,B     A,B     A,B

0 0 1     1 0 0     1 1 1     1 1 1
0 1 1     1 1 0     0 1 1     1 1 0
1 1 1     1 1 1     0 0 1     1 0 0
 A,B       A,B       A,B       A,B

0 0 0     0 1 1     1 1 0     1 1 1
1 1 1     0 1 1     1 1 0     1 1 1
1 1 1     0 1 1     1 1 0     0 0 0
  A         A         B         B

0 0 1   0 1 1   1 0 0   1 1 1   1 1 0   1 1 1   1 1 1   1 1 1
1 1 1   0 1 1   1 1 1   0 1 1   1 1 0   1 1 0   1 1 1   1 1 1
1 1 1   1 1 1   1 1 1   0 1 1   1 1 1   1 1 0   0 0 1   1 0 0
  A       A       A       A       B       B       B       B
```

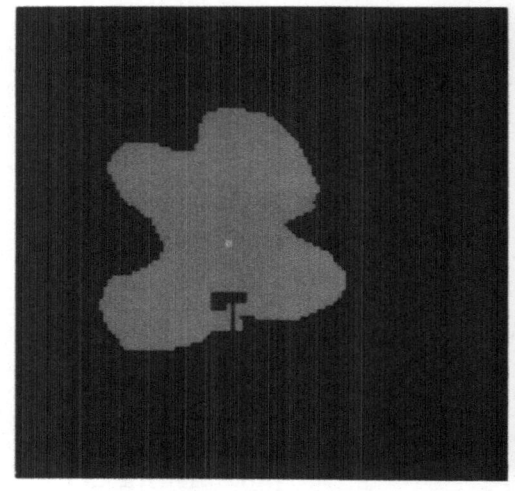

FIGURE 11. EXAMPLE OF SHRINKING

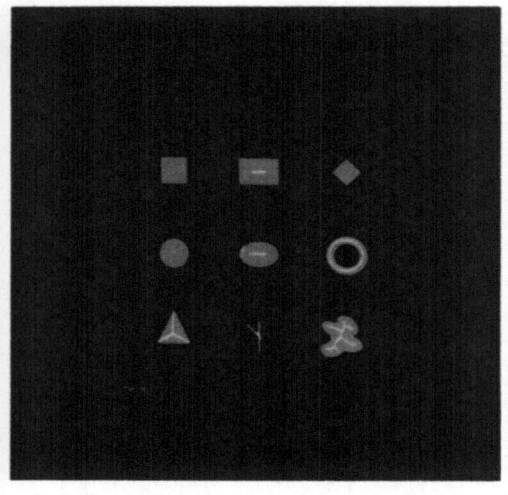

FIGURE 12. EXAMPLE OF THINNING

SOBEL EDGE MAP

THINNED SOBEL EDGE MAP

FIGURE 13. THINNING APPLIED TO AN EDGE MAP

SKELETONIZE. Creates medial axis transform of objects.

The medial axis transform [17] of a binary object consists of the locus of pixels that are equi-distant from the nearest boundary of the object.

Table 3 lists the skeletonize patterns.

Figure 14 contains an example of the skeletonization process.

6. Hierarchical Operators

The primitive additive and subtractive morphological operators are often combined sequentially to perform enhancement or analysis tasks. For example, erosion can be performed a pre-determined number of times followed by shrinking. The erosion operation will eliminate small size blobs, and the subsequent shrink operation will reduce the resultant blobs to single pixels, which can then be counted to determine the number of blobs in an image of minimal size. The two most widely employed hierarchical operators are the open and close operators.

OPEN. Performs erode then dilate operations successively.

The open algorithm executes n passes of erosion followed by n passes of dilation. Rectangularly shaped objects remain invariant to the open process, if they are not completely eroded. Other objects are modified by the open process.

Figure 15 presents the results of the single pass open operator on the test image. The open operator is useful for detecting thin strokes in an image. For example, note the elimination of the double width stroke of the sloping cross object. As a practical application example, Figure 16a shows an original thick film electronic circuit and Figure 16b is the result of single pass erosion. Note the loss of connectivity of the narrow trace. Figure 16c contains the final result of the open process. The breakup of the narrow trace is clearly visible.

TABLE 3
SKELETONIZE PATTERNS

```
0 0 0    0 0 0    0 0 1    0 1 1    1 0 0    1 1 0    1 1 1    1 1 1
0 1 1    1 1 0    0 1 1    0 1 1    1 1 0    1 1 0    0 1 1    1 1 0
1 1 1    1 1 1    0 1 1    0 0 1    1 1 0    1 0 0    0 0 0    0 0 0


0 0 1    1 0 0    1 1 1    1 1 1
0 1 1    1 1 0    0 1 1    1 1 0
1 1 1    1 1 1    0 0 1    1 0 0


0 0 0    0 1 1    1 1 0    1 1 1
1 1 1    0 1 1    1 1 0    1 1 1
1 1 1    0 1 1    1 1 0    0 0 0


0 0 1    0 1 1    1 0 0    1 1 0    1 1 1    1 1 1    1 1 1    1 1 1
1 1 1    0 1 1    1 1 1    1 1 0    0 1 1    1 1 1    1 1 1    1 1 0
1 1 1    1 1 1    1 1 1    1 1 1    0 1 1    0 0 1    1 0 0    1 1 0
```

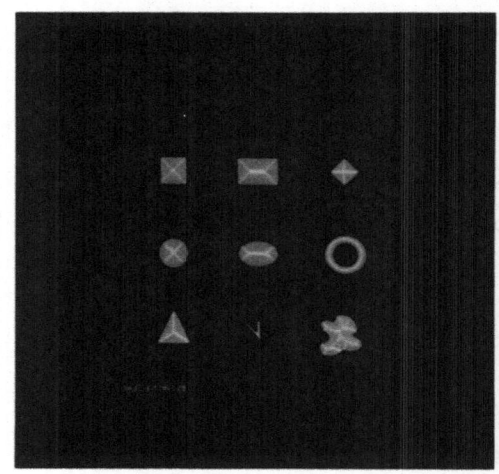

FIGURE 14.
EXAMPLE OF SKELETONIZATION

FIGURE 15.
EXAMPLE OF OPEN OPERATION

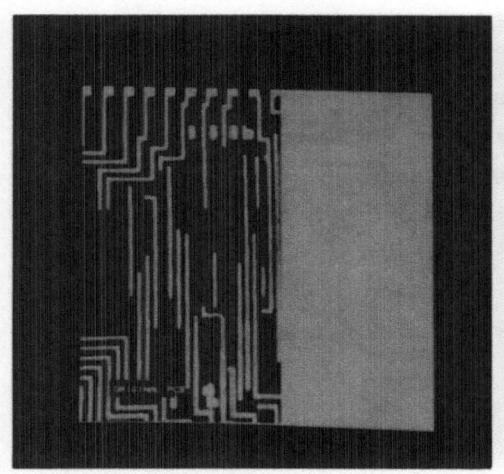 ORIGINAL

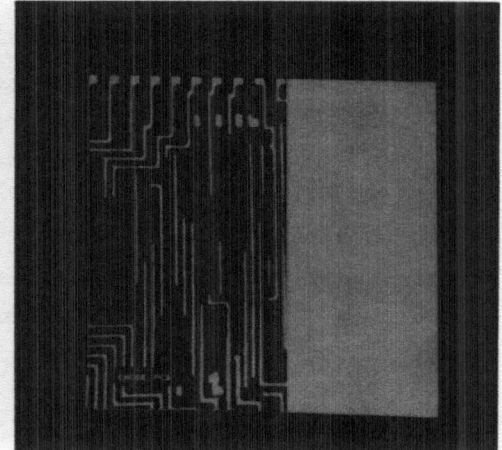 EROSION

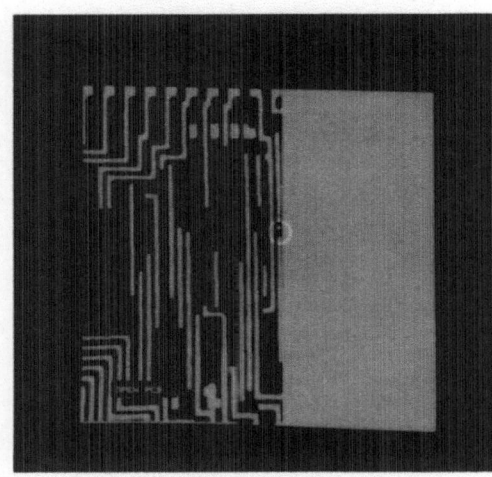 OPEN

FIGURE 16. OPEN OPERATION APPLIED TO THICK FILM CIRCUIT IMAGE

CLOSE. Performs dilate then erode operations successively.

The close algorithm executes n passes of dilation followed by n passes of erosion. As with the open operator, rectangularly shaped objects remain invariant, but other shapes are affected.

Figure 17 presents the results of the single pass close operator on the test image. Figure 18 shows the effect of the close process on a thick film circuit. In this example, two closely-spaced traces are fused together.

7. **Summary**

This paper has presented a flexible pipeline image processor architecture for performing morphological image processing at digital video rates. Algorithms for additive, subtractive and hierarchical morphological operators have also been presented.

8. **Acknowledgement**

The authors wish to express their gratitude to Dr. Ted J. Cooper of Vicom Systems, Inc. for helpful technical discussions during the algorithm development.

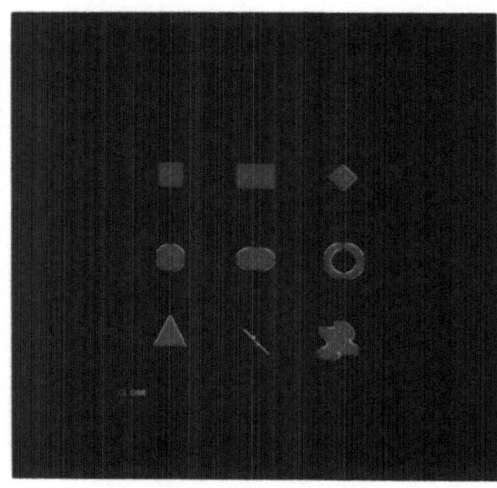

FIGURE 17.
EXAMPLE OF CLOSE OPERATION

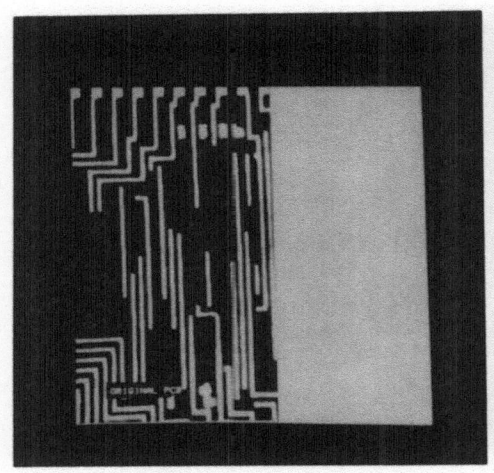
ORIGINAL

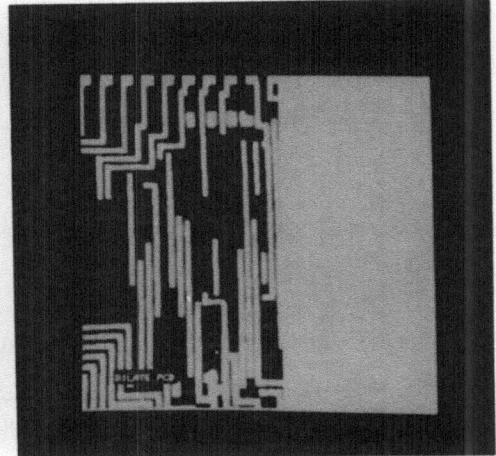
DILATION

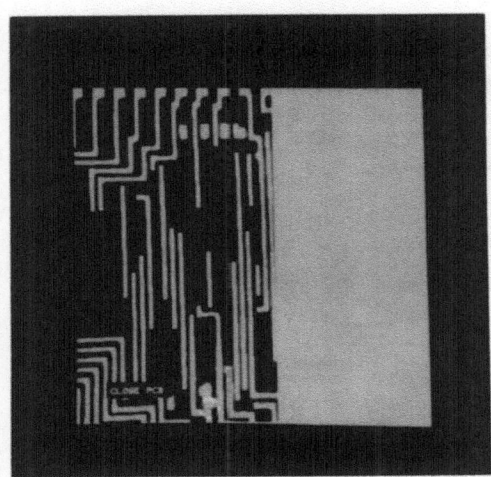
CLOSE

FIGURE 18. CLOSE OPERATION APPLIED TO THICK FILM CIRCUIT IMAGE

REFERENCES

1. G. Matherton, <u>Random Sets and Integral Geometry</u>, New York, Wiley, 1975.

2. J. Serra, <u>Image Analysis and Mathematical Morphology</u>, Academic Press, London, 1982.

3. S.R. Sternberg, "Language and Architecture for Parallel Image Processing", <u>Proceedings of the Conference on Pattern Recognition in Practice</u>, Amsterdam, The Netherlands, May 1980.

4. S.R. Sternberg, "Architectures for Neighborhood Processing", <u>IEEE Pattern Recognition and Image Processing Conference</u>, August 1981.

5. S.R. Sternberg, "Parallel Architectures for Image Processing", <u>Proceedings of 3rd International IEEE Compsac</u>, Chicago, 1981.

6. S.R. Sternberg, "Automatic Image Processor", <u>U.S. Patent 4,167,728</u>.

7. A. Rosenfeld, "A Characterization of Parallel Thinning Algorithms", <u>Information and Control</u>, Vol. 29, 1975, pp. 286-291.

8. T. Pavlidis, "A Thinning Algorithm of Discrete Binary Images," <u>Computer Graphics and Image Processing</u>, Vol. 13, 1980, pp. 142-157.

9. C. Arcelli and G. Sanniti Di Baja, "On the Sequential Approach to Medial Line Thinning Transformation", <u>IEEE Transactions on Systems, Man and Cybernetics</u>, Vol. SMC-8, No. 2, 1978, pp. 139-144.

10. T.N. Mudge, W.B. Teel and R.M. Lougheed, "Cellular Image Processing Techniques for Checking VLSI Circuit Layouts", <u>Conference on Information Sciences and Systems</u>, 1981.

11. S.R. Sternberg, "Cellular Computers and Biomedical Image Processing", Proceedings of the U.S. - France Seminar on Biomedical Image Processing, Grenoble, France, May 1980.

12. D.L. McCubbrey, "Real-Time Bin Picking Using Cellular Neighborhood Operations", Applied Machine Vision Conference, April 1982.

13. D.J. Svetkoff, J.B. Candlish and P.W. VanAtta, "High Resolution Imaging For Automatic Inspection of Multi-Layer Thick Film Circuits", Applied Machine Vision Conference, 1983.

14. J.F. Abramatic and O.D. Faugeras, "Sequential Convolution Techniques for Image Filtering", IEEE Transactions on Acoustics, Speech, and Signal Processing, Vol. ASSP-30, pp. 1-10, Feb. 1982.

15. T.J. Cooper and W.K. Pratt, "System Architecture Speeds Multitasking Image Processing", Computer Design, July 1983.

16. W.K. Pratt, Digital Image Processing, Wiley Interscience, New York, 1978.

17. J.C. Matt-Smith, "Medial Axis Transforms", Picture Processing and Psychopictorics, B.S. Lipkin and A. Rosenfeld, Eds., Academic Press, New York, 1970.

Continuous Color Presentation Using a Low-Cost Ink Jet Printer

Sachio Kubo
Department of Geography
The University of Tokyo
3-1, Hongo 7-chome, Bunkyo-ku
Tokyo 113, Japan

Summary
This paper discusses continuous color hardcopies using a low cost color ink jet printer. On the basis of simple fomulae to transform luminous primaries to printing primaries, several dot patterns making gray scales for each color ink are tested. As a conclusion, the rotated regular pattern gives the best visibility when the resolution of the original image is high enough, but random point patterns give more natural images when the original resolution is low. Using the segmented pattern method, the dot matrix size for a pixel can be reduced to 2 by 2 without destroying the expression.

Introduction
Continuous color hardcopies, which are defined here as hardcopies with more than 512 (8 gray scale levels to each primaries) colors, became neccesary with recent development of computer graphics. One of the motivations is the generalization of multi-color graphic terminals, which can present near-natural colors. Furthermore, some applications of color image analysis such as remote sensing, landscape analysis, bio-medical analysis, video image processing have become more popular. Even in the field of computer arts, artists are no longer satisfied with a color CRT imagery which can be presented to public only on the machine or by taking photographs.

Optical methods
Optical methods have been the most popular way to make continuous color hard copies. The simplest and cheapest way to make hardcopies is to take photographs of the color CRT with cameras, either conventional or instant ones. These methods necessarily have distortions, for any color CRT now available has a curved surface which generally causes distortions, adding to those coming from camera lenses.

Systems with less distortion are needed for industry and laboratory uses. Optical color hardcopy systems usually use high resolution monochromatic CRT or beam generators (e.g. lasers) with red, green and blue filters, and photographic media such as color photographic papers or films. One of the advantages of optical color hardcopy systems is that most technologies are based on popular COM (Computer Output on Microfilm) systems, so that only minor technological developments are needed. According to the nature of photographic media, it is easy to achieve high resolutions.

On the other hand, several disadvantage arise: One is the high initial cost of those precision systems. Most of the recorders cost more than 10,000 U.S. dollars and are too expensive for personal usage. A further problems are the running costs. The cost of color films is relatively low, but paper printing pushes up the running costs (e.g. a 8 in. by 10 in. print usually costs more than 8 U.S. dollars). Thus less expensive color hardcopy systems are required, which nevertheless provide less distortion.

Non-optical hardcopy
The other method for making a color hardcopy is to use color printers. Color printers have been expensive devices whether they are non-impact (e.g. ink jet, thermal, thermal transparency) or dot impact ones. But the recent appearence of low-cost color printers (i.e. less than 1100 U.S. dollars) on the market enabled the development of personal continuous color printing systems. An experimental system used in our laboratory is composed of a video camera with RGB independent tubes, a remote controller for the video camera, a color graphic display of 256 by 240 resolution with 12 bit planes (Nexus 5500), a micro-computer with 8086 CPU (Sord M343), and a color ink jet printer (SHARP IO-700) (Fig.1 and 2). Video images from a camera are converted to digital RGB signals by an interface attached to the Nexus 5500, which can convert a single frame within 400 milliseconds.

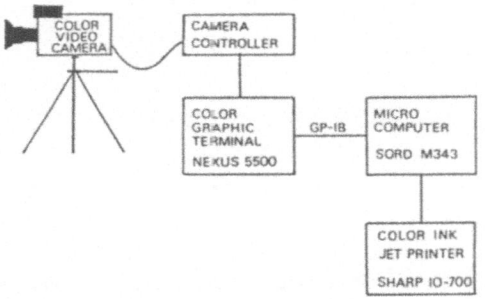

Fig. 1. The experimental system used in this study. The system is controlled by a SORD M343 micro computer. A Sharp IO-700 color ink-jet printer is used as the output device. Images are taken by a video camera, then digitized by a Nexus color graphic terminal.

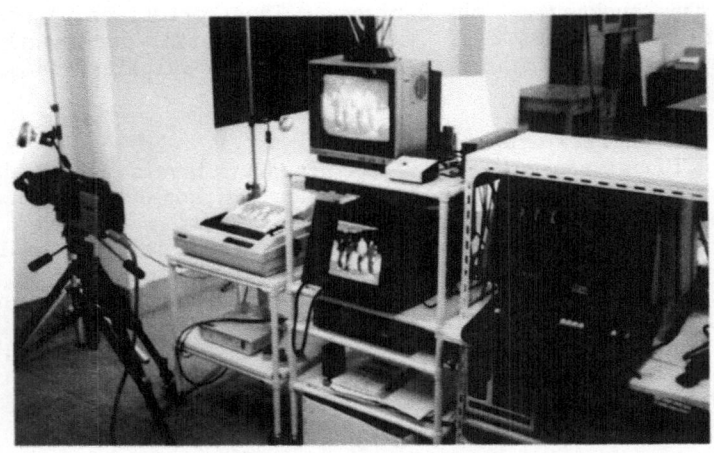

Fig. 2. The system in work.

Color signal transformation

It is well known that the colors on CRT are produced by additive mixture of luminous primaries, red, green and blue, which are usually labeled as R, G and B, and that each pixel has an intensity level for each of these three. In the optical recording, no transformation of those color signals is needed. However, in printing, colors are produced by subtractive mixture of printing primaries, magenda, cyan and yellow. Thus a transformation of color signals is required.

The basic formulas of the transformation are;

$$\begin{aligned} M &= t - G \\ C &= t - R \\ Y &= t - B \end{aligned} \quad \dots \dots 1)$$

where C, M and Y are the densities of cyan, magenda and yellow ink respectively, and t is the maximum intensity of R, G and B. Most colors are reproduced by this formula except black and gray, as an equal mixture of the three printing primaries produces brownish colors rather than black or gray. Thus black ink is usually added to these three primaries.

In this case, the formulas above are changed to;

$$\begin{aligned} M' &= M - \min(M,C,Y) = \max(R,G,B) - G \\ C' &= C - \min(M,C,Y) = \max(R,G,B) - R \\ Y' &= Y - \min(M,C,Y) = \max(R,G,B) - B \\ B1 &= \min(M,C,Y) = t - \max(R,G,B) \end{aligned} \quad \dots \dots 2)$$

where B1 is the density for black ink.

The actual printing colors are affected by the ink colors and physical characteristics of the paper, especially the surface reflection rate. In the case of ink jet printers, special paper with small holes on the surface is used to secure absorption of ink mist, which causes lower reflection rate coming from the roughness of the surface. Thus correction parameters have to be added to the formulas 2). Though the correction parameters form non-linear functions, they can be regarded as simple multipliers in operational uses.

Dot patterns for density expression

Multi-color CRT can present 8 to 4096 intensity levels for each luminous primary, most color printers either impact or non-impact, however, can present three to eight colors on one single dot. In order to obtain continuous colors, a pixel is composed of an agglomeration of smaller dots. The densities for each printing primaries are determined by the number of colored dots in the agglomeration. If a pixel is composed of 3 by 3 dots, 10 density levels for each primary are available, yielding 1000 colors in total. If a pixel is enlarged to 4 by 4 dots, 17 density levels for each primary give 4913 colors. This pixel size has the ability to produce hardcopies of natural color CRT with 12 bit planes (4 bits for each luminous primaries).

Making the dot agglomeration larger increases the available density levels, but of cource the pixel size also becomes larger. In order to make hardcopy of CRT with 18 bit planes, an 8 by 8 dot size is necessary.

Regular dot patterns

Several types of dot patterns can be considered. The simplest and most popular patterns are the fixed regular patterns (Fig. 3). This method uses the same patterns for all printing primaries. Although this method has been common, there are several disadvantages. As all the primaries tend to be placed on the same dot, the portion of white (not painted) generally increases. This causes a faint of color more than intended (see Fig. 4-a,b,c). Furthermore, when a black dot is placed on a dot with a different color, this dot will be black only. Thus, the color is changed compared to the correct color mixture (Fig. 4-d,e).

Fig. 3. A sample of the fixed regular patterns.

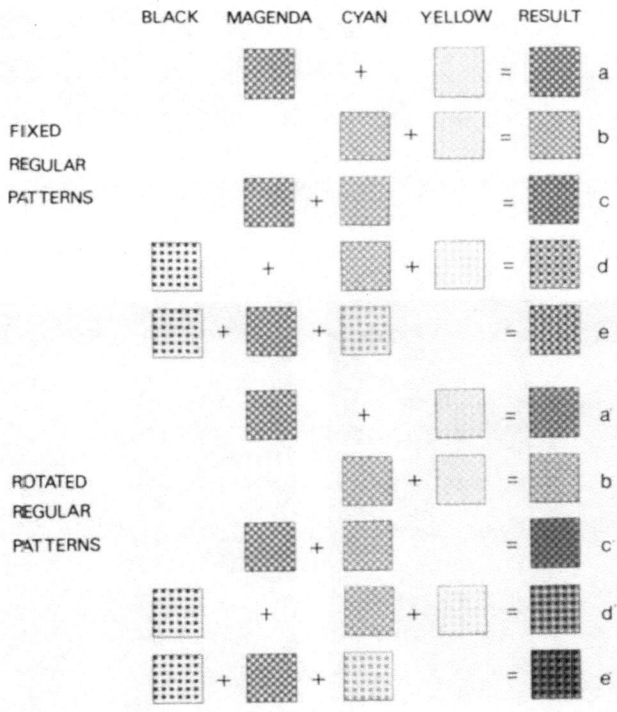

Fig. 4. A test chart to explain the differences between the fixed regular patterns and the rotated regular patterns. By the fixed regular pattern method (a-e), most dots are placed on the same points, but by the rotated regular pattern method (a'-e'), most dots are placed on the different points. Thus obvious differences are seen between the corresponding colors.

To solve this probem, a rotated regular dot pattern method is effective. Dot patterns are rotated by 90° for each primaries as well as for black (Fig. 5). Differences in color presentation between the fixed pattern method and the rotated method are quite apparent (Fig.4 a-a' to e-e'). By this rotated method, problems are reduced to a certain extent. A color chart printed by this method is shown as Fig. 6-a. In operational usage, especially in reproducing natural imagery like photographs, this problem almost doesn't matter compared to color chart tests. Comparing the two samples (Fig. 7-b,c), it is difficult to find defferences. However, in general, the rotated patterns are recommended.

In both fixed and rotated regular pattern methods, interferences (moires) may appear for certain combination ofs dot patterns. Interferences cause coherent noises which destroy the visibility of the printed pictures.

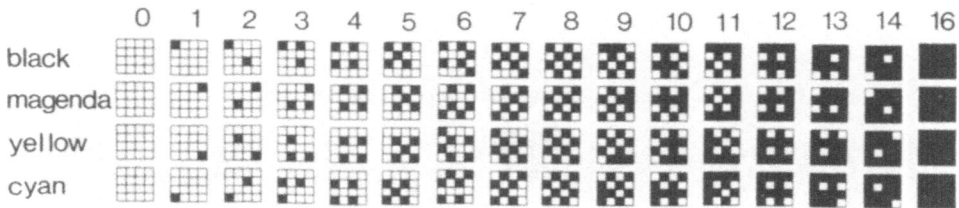

Fig. 5. A sample of the rotated regular patterns.

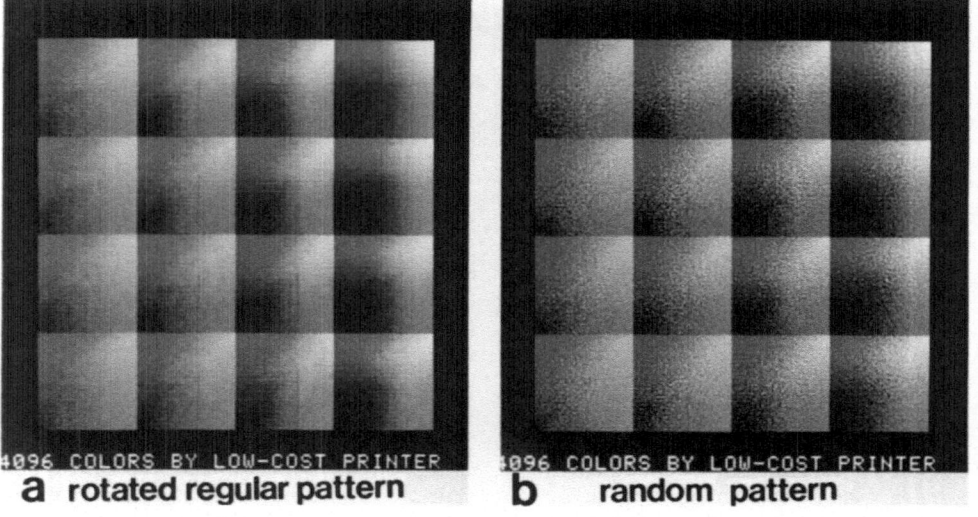

Fig. 6. Color charts made by the rotated regular pattern method (left) and the random pattern method (right).

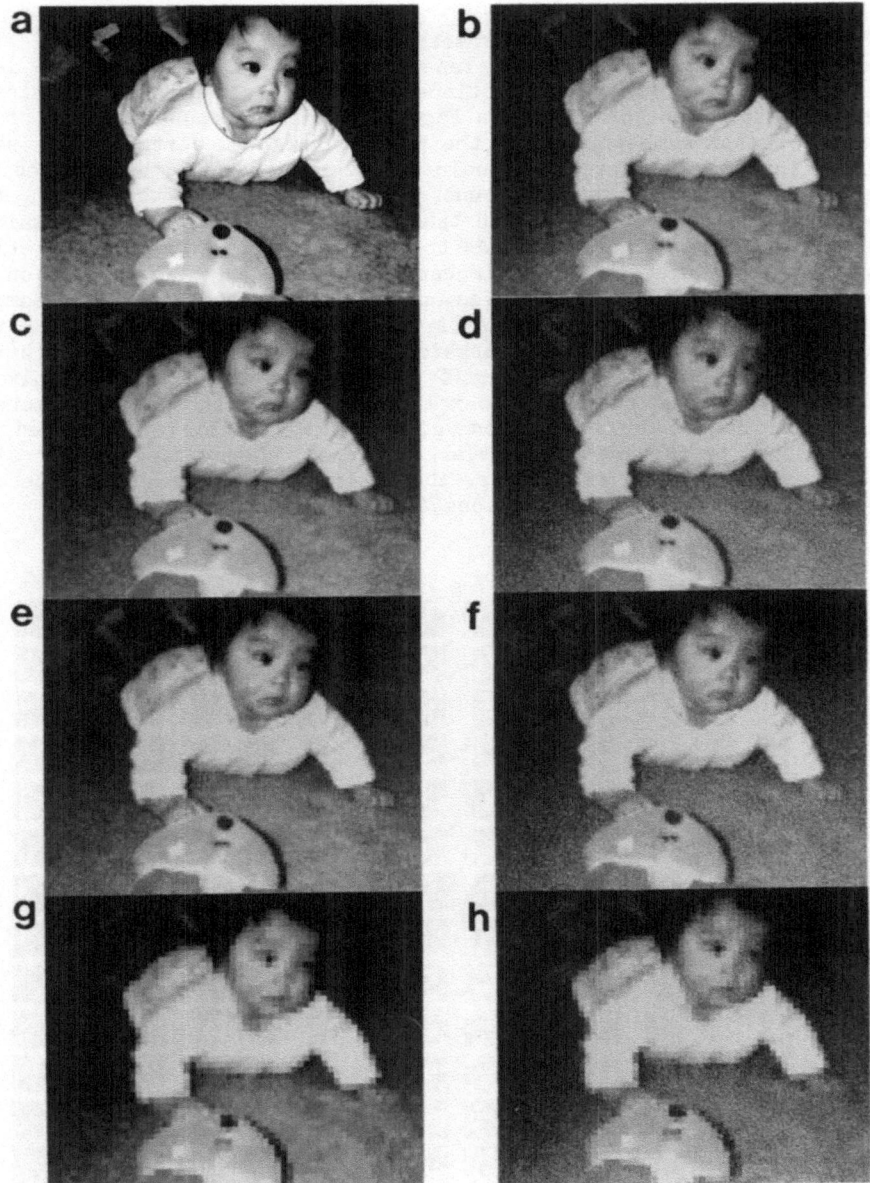

Fig. 7. The original photo and the printed samples by the color ink-jet printing system. (7-a) the original photo, (7-b) by the fixed regular pattern method, (7-c) by the rotated regular pattern method, (7-d) by the random pattern method, (7-e) by the rotated regular pattern method on reduced resolution (1/2) image, (7-f) by the random pattern method on reduced resolution (1/2) image, (7-g) by the rotated regular pattern method on reduced resolution (1/4) image, (7-h) by the random pattern method on reduced resolution (1/4) image.

Random dot patterns
The random point method is another method to define dot patterns. The place of the dots is determined by random numbers so that there are less possiblities to cause the above mentioned difficulties. Random patterns used in this experiment are shown in Fig. 8. In order to reduce the time to generate random numbers, one of the preset 16 random patterns for each density is randomly selected. A color chart produced by this method is shown as Fig. 6-b and a picture is shown as Fig. 7-d. In this case, the edges of figures become blurred and the picture gives a hazy impression. This "hazy" characteristic is related to the size of the dot agglomeration and the original resolution of the imagery. When the dot aggromelation is 8 by 8 or larger, this method gives quite good presentations. Sample photos (Fig. 7-c to h) show changes of the presentation according to the enlargement of the dot agglomeration size and the reduction of resolution of the original imagery. In case of Fig. 7-g and h, four original pixels are merged to one pixel resulting 16 x 16 random dot patterns. A picture printed by the random pattern method gives better visibility compared to picture produced by the rotated regular patterns. However, when the size of the dot agglomeration is smaller, the quality of the print-out become worse but somewhat artistic impressions (Fig. 9-a,b).

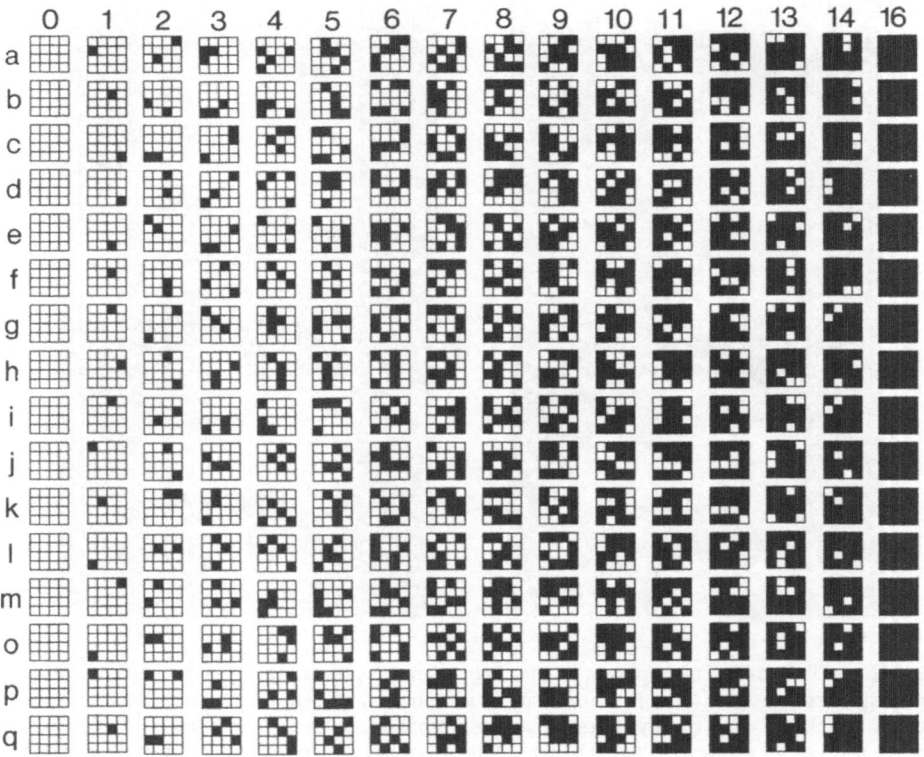

Fig. 8. The random patterns used in this article. In order to save time to generate random numbers, the random patterns are preset. One of the 16 preset patterns for each density is randomly selected.

Fig. 9. A comparison of the print-out by the "patchworked" 2 x 2 rotated regular pattern method and the one by the random pattern method.

Dot size and ability of color presentation

Expensive high quality ink-jet printers such as Applicon or Sanyo have high resolutions, that is 10 to 12 dots per millimeter. If a 4 by 4 dot agglomeration has a size of 0.33 or 0.4 millimeter, 512 pixels in line come to 171 or 205 millimeters respectively which is nearly the same size as the images on 12 or 14 inch CRT screens. From this point of view, the reproduction of about 4000 colors provides almost no resolution problems for high-quality printers.

In case of low-cost personal color printers, regardless of printer types (dot-impact, thermal, thermo-transparency, ink-jet), the resolution is 3 to 5 dots per millimeter. In this case, a pixel composed of 4 by 4 dots makes almost 1 mm square. A hardcopy of 512 x 512 pixels sizes 50 x 50 cms, which may be regarded as too large. Moreover, those low-cost printers usually limit the dot numbers in horizontal direction to about 800 to 1600. Thus by a 4 by 4 dot agglomeration, presentation of 200 to 400 pixels are a technical limit unless the users want to use the "scissors and paste" techniques. To overcome these problems, more techniques are required.

Making continuous colors with smaller dot patterns

The patchwork method can solve the problem. When the required dot size for a print is different from the prepared dot pattern size, a subsegment is picked up from the corresponding location of the original dot pattern, and is patched to the painting pattern. Figure 10 shows usage of this method for a 2 x 2 dot size.

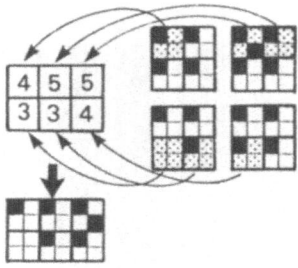

Fig. 10. The patchwork method to reproduce reduced or enlarged pattern size. The corresponding segments of dot pattern are cut from the original pattern and are patched to the printing dot patterns.

Fig. 11. Samples of prints by the "patchwork" method. (11-a) by the rotated regular pattern method using 4 x 4 dot patterns, (11-b) a pixel is represented by 2 x 2 dots using the patchwork method, (11-c) a pixel is represented by a single dot. (11-d) enlargement of (11-b), (11-e) enlargement of (11-c).

An sample shown in Fig. 11-b is produced by this method using a 2 x 2 dot attribution for one pixel. There are only little significant differences compared to the prints using the 4 x 4 dot rotated regular patterns (Fig. 11-a). In a further reduction, 1 x 1 dot attribution to a pixel, although the details of the image are lost, most colors are reproduced (Fig. 11-c). Enlarged photos (Fig. 11-d,e) show the details of patchworked dot patterns. This patchwork method can be used not only for a reduction of the printed picture size, but is also effective for enlargement. The same dot patterns are used regardless of the numbers of attributed dot to a pixel.

Conclusion
With certain techniques, rotated regular patterns and the patchwork dot pattern merging, low-cost personal ink-jet printers can be used as a continuous color hardcopy device. The price of the system is much cheaper than the present professional hardcopy devices, so the efficiency is very high compared to the cost.

Bibliography
Optical Society of America, Committee on Colorimetry. **The Science of Color.** Washington. D. C., 1963.
Kubo, S. **ALIS Graphics Program Manual (The First Edition),** The University of Tokyo Computer Center, 1978.
Jern, M. **The Color Plotting System.** Harvard Library of Computer Graphics Vol.2, pp.131-135, 1979.
Pope, A. **The Form of the Color Solid.** Harvard Library of Computer Graphics, Vol.6, pp.115-133, 1980.
Orr, J. N. **Matching User Requirements with Hardware Capabilities:** Graphic **Hard-copy Output Devices.** Harvard Library of Computer Graphics, Vol.9, pp.68-73, 1980.
Gruber, L. S. and Barney, H. **Color Computer Graphics and Imaging with Polaloid 8 x 10 PolacolorLand Film and the Dunn 631 Color Camera.** Harvard Library of Computer Graphics, Vol.9, pp.47-54, 1980.
Kobayashi, M. et al. **MultiColor and Multitone Ink Jet Printing Method.** EMC81-15, The Institute of Electronics and Communication Engineers of Japan, 1981.
Nishimura, T. et al. **Color Processing Method in Color Ink Jet Printer.** EMC 82-2, The Institute of Electronics and Communication Engineers of Japan, 1982.
Kubo. S. **ALIS Graphics Program Manual (The Second Edition),** The University of Tokyo Computer Center, 1983.
Nishimura, T et al. **Ink Jet Printing of Color Image by TV Camera Input.** IE83-6, The Institute of Electronics and Communication Engineers of Japan, 1983.

Mechanically Feedbacked Touch Sensor for Electronic Painting by Skilled People

Shigeru Kimura
Information Processing Center
Kyushu Institute of Design
9-1, Shiobaru 4-chome, Minami-ku
Fukuoka 815, Japan

ABSTRACT

Mechanically Feedbacked Touch Sensor (MFTS) is introduced by the author for manual analog input to Electronic Painting (EP) by skilled people, e.g. visual artists, animators and so on. The main reason to introduce MFTS is to give EP parallelism of manipulations to those of conventional paintings. Parallelism will make EP systems acceptable by skilled people. They will be able to use EP systems with little training, and yield better works by utilizing their acquired skill. MFTS consists of a pressure/displacement sensor and related electronic circuits. Users can adjust analog input values by sensing the feedback of the input values to their fingertips by the spring of MFTS. MFTS can be used in home or office computings.

1. Introduction

Man-machine interface has been improved during this decade so that we can choose among many alternatives. Among them, we will find speech input/output, pointing devices and so on. Nevertheless, we cannot find any appropriate devices for manual analog input other than control dial. Although most of computer users at terminals or workstations want to input text data or point coordinates, there are some users who want to input analog values with their hands or fingers.

A visual artist, for example, may want to change the width of drawing line continuously in electronic painting. He may want to control the size or density of a shot of air brush. Or he may want to create a new color on the electronic palette by the mixture of two or more different colors. He may, of course, use alphanumeric keyboard to designate the values. But the use of keyboard will turn his attention from CRT screen to keyboard, and interrupt the natural flow of creative thought.

I introduce Mechanically Feedbacked Touch Sensor (MFTS) for manual analog input. MFTS consists of a pressure/displacement sensor and related electronic circuits. MFTS sends A/D converted digits to the CPU. Mechanical feedback is realized by a spring connected to the push button of MFTS. MFTS is advantageous over control dial, because user can know the analog input value at that moment by sensing feedbacked input value to his fingertip and concentrate his attention on the screen. I will show MFTS mounted on a pointing device will give powerful input facilities to electronic painting systems.

2. Input Devices for Direct Manipulation

Ben Shneiderman introduced the term "direct manipulation" to designate some type of conversational systems. Direct manipulation is a real-time manipulation of textual and/or graphic objects on the CRT screen with no or few keyin commands. Examples of direct manipulation are screen editors, CAD/CAM, CAI/CMI, video games and electronic painting systems. Direct manipulation seems the best man-machine interface so far, because of little training needed, high quality achievements and, above all, users' favor.

We can use various input devices for direct manipulation. Among them are alphanumeric keyboards, programmable function keys, function switches, control dials and several kinds of pointing devices. Although alphanumeric keyboard is preferable for text input, it seems pointing devices acquired the best favor of users as input device for direct manipulation. The most advantageous point of pointing devices over other input devices is that user can concentrate his attention on the screen and most of the manipulations can be done with one device.

There are two different uses of pointing devices. One is graphic use, and the other is logical or selective use. In the graphic use, devices are used to input graphic objects as dots or lines. In this case, high resolusion, smooth movement and similarity of manual operations to those of pens, pencils or brushes are needed. In the logical use, on the other hand, devices are used to select one object among a list of menu entries or icons. In this case, easy care, small size and inexpensiveness are needed.

We have two methods to input point coordinates. One is relative or dynamic method, and the other is absolute or static method. In the relative method, pointing devices are used to input the quantity of cursor movement from the present cursor position. Cursor keys, track ball and mouse use this method. In the absolute method, pointing devices are used to directly input point coordinates. Joystick and tablet digitizer use this method.

Mouse has the best characteristics of logical and relative input device, and acquired favor of large amount of users. It is used as a standard input device of laboratory or office workstations or even low-cost personal computers. Tablet has the best characteristics of graphic and absolute input device. It is used in the systems in which graphic input is very important. CAD/CAM systems and electronic painting systems are examples of these.

Disadvantage of these pointing devices other than difficulties in text input is that any input other than graphic ones must be menu selection or command keyin. This results in increase in the number of menu entries and keyin commands. Large and complicated system will have many menu entries and keyin commands, and this results in increase in user training time.

3. Mechanically Feedbacked Touch Sensor

MFTS is a touch sensor which converts pressure upon the push button to output voltage. Output voltage is converted to digital value and sent to the CPU. Sensor may be displacement sensor, because displacement is converted to pressure by the spring connected to the push button of MFTS. I think the best displacement sensor is Linear Variable Differential Transformer (LVDT) and the best pressure sensor is Piezoelectric element, because they have very simple structures.

LVDT consists of a bobbin with three coils on it and a movable iron core at the center. Figure 1 shows the structure of LVDT and Figure 2 shows the circuit diagram. The primary coil E is for the power supply and secondary coils E_1 and E_2 are for the output. E_1 and E_2 are differentially connected, or have opposite polarities.

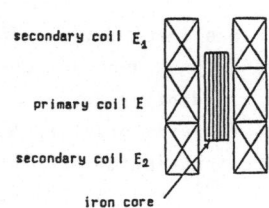

Figure 1 Structure of LVDT

If the movable core stays at the home position, there is no output voltage between the output terminals. If, on the other hand, the core is displaced to either direction, say downwards, the magnetic flux crossing E_1 or E_2 will decrease or increase, respectively, which causes output voltage at the output terminals. Figure 3 shows that the rectified output voltage is proportional to the amount of displacement of the core.

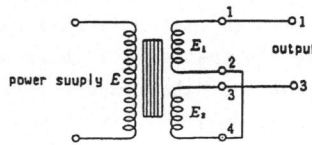

Figure 2 Circuit Diagram of LVDT

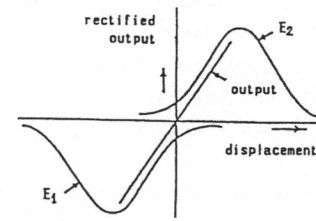

In order to efficiently utilize the linear domain shown in Figure 3 and to get a large stroke of the push button, the mechanical home position should not be at the same position as the electric home position. Mechanical home position is shown in Figure 4.

Figure 3 Input/Output Function

The electronic circuits of MFTS are LVDT interface, A/D converter, and a control processor. LVDT interface circuit provides LVDT with AC power supply, rectifies AC output to DC and so on. The functions of A/D converter and control processor will be discussed later.

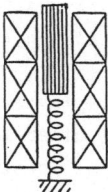

Figure 4 Mechanical Home Position

MFTS has two operating modes. One is stream mode and the other is one shot mode. In the stream mode, MFTS will send the CPU a stream of output digits, values of which are proportional to input pressure values. In the one shot mode, on the other hand, the control processor will not send any digits to the CPU until the end of the input shot. Because input pressure causes positive output, a shot begins with the first non-zero input and ends with zero input. After the end of the shot, control processor will send the CPU several digits which are gotten by calculation from the sequence of input digits. Thus we can designate several different values with a single shot. Details of one shot mode will be discussed later.

4. MFTS in Electronic Painting

We have many stories that tell about new technology impacting on fine arts, music or other kinds of art. I think that Electronic Painting (EP) is one of the most exciting achievements in computer applications. EP systems will provide artists with powerful new tools.

I think, however, we have many problems to overcome in EP systems. Among them are the costs of the systems, appropriate hardcopy devices and so on. The most important, but difficult problem is the trade-off between accessibility and trainability. Systems should easily be accessed by artists with no or little training. But systems should be sophisticated enough that their acquired skill and continuous use of the systems can yield much better works.

If users are young or even newcome, the problem may not be so important. They may easily be accustomed to EP system, and yield good works after a few months of training. If, on the other hand, users are skilled in painting by conventional methods, the problem is vital. Skilled people have their own style of working, want to believe their acquired skill will yield better works, and their rather high labor costs will not permit long period of training.

If a new technology is supported by only young people, its impact on the public will not be so great. But if it is supported by some portion of older people, its impact will be very important. If EP is supported by skilled artists, it will be used not only by animators or commercial artists but by traditional fine artists.

Solution to the problem of the trade-off between accessibility and trainability must be the parallelism of manual operations between conventional method and EP. If users can find counterparts to their conventional methods in EP system they will easily be accustomed to the system. The main purpose to introduce MFTS is to give this parallelism to EP systems.

As an example, let me discuss a line drawing with a brush. Painter will select a brush with appropriate size, shape and stiffness. He will continuously change the pressing force and moving speed in order to control width or other features of the line. In EP systems available so far, user cannot continuously change the line width. Instead, he will draw a thick line with a brush. Then he will select another brush to erase some portion of the drawn line to make it thinner. Or he will select another brush to make it thicker. Thus, the number of brushes to be selected increases. This increases the number of menu entries or keyin commands.

If he uses MFTS mounted on the stylus of a tablet, he can continuously change the width of a line after selecting a brush. Thus, the number of brushes to be selected will drastically decrease. Painter can draw a line in such a way as conventional one.

Let me discuss, as another example, a shot of air brush. Painter will control the pressure or duration of the shot to control the size and density of the shot. In EP systems, he must designate the size, density and density distribution pattern with menu selections or keyin commands. If he uses MFTS in the one shot mode, he can input those values with a shot of MFTS, and can simultaneously designate the place of the shot by the stylus. In other words, an air brush shot can be done with a single shot of MFTS.

These two examples show the parallelism of manipulations between the conventional paintings and EP system with MFTS. And this means that skilled people can utilize their acquired skill to yield better works by EP system.

Advantage of MFTS over control dial was discussed before. Now I will compare MFTS to pointing devices. Absolute pointing devices may virtually be manual analog input devices. Indeed, some kind of joysticks have similar functions to those of MFTS. I refer to "return to neutral" joystick which returns to neutral position when there is no pressing force.

But pointing devices including this kind of joysticks are not suitable for simultaneous input of both point coordinates and analog values, because simultaneous manipulation of two such devices is difficult. MFTS can be small enough to be mounted on pointing devices. And simultaneous manipulation will be easier. I think MFTS on the stylus of a tablet is best suited to EP systems because of high resolution and smooth movement.

I think there are two advantages of MFTS due to mechanical feedback over devices without feedback. One is fine adjustment capability, and the other is psychological or physiological effects. We can sense with our fingertips the counterbalance of the spring of MFTS to input pressure. And we can precisely adjust input pressure by sensing the counterbalance as well as by watching the programmed feedback on the screen.

Psychological or physiological effects are that appropriate stroke of push button and appropriate counterbalance of the spring will give some kind of pleasure to users, and stimuli to fingertips are thought to be especially good for creative thought. Parallelism to conventional paintings and this kind of psycological or physiological effects will acquire better favor of users.

5. MFTS in detail

Figure 5 shows the block diagram of MFTS using LVDT. LVDT interface circuit sends DC analog values to A/D converter. Input to A/D converter should be biased so that valid input may yield positive output value and zero input must stably yield zero output. The input/output function of A/D Converter is shown in Figure 6.

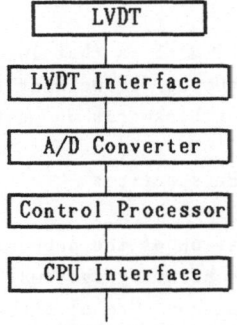

Figure 5 Block Diagram of MFTS

As mentioned before, MFTS has two operating modes. They are stream mode and one shot mode. Control processor sets the mode bit in order to identify the mode.

In the stream mode, control processor sends output digits to CPU. Digits of 8 bits each and a rate of input/output stream of less than 100 digits per second will satisfy most of application requirements.

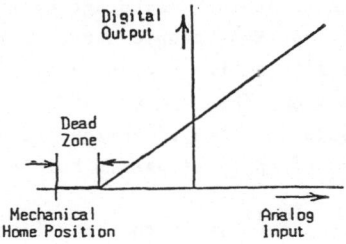

Figure 6 Function of A/D Converter

In the one shot mode, control processor will not send any digits until the end of a shot. Figure 7 shows a shot in one shot mode. Control processor processes input digits and sends output digits to CPU. Among the output digits, we will find the following values:

(1) Peak Value   Vp
(2) Integrated Value   Vi
(3) Duration   D
(4) Peak Position   P
(5) Sharpness   S

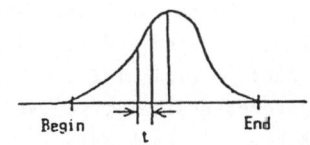

Figure 7 Shot in One Shot Mode

Peak value is the maximum value of the input digits. Integrated value is the sum of all the input digits. And duration is the number of input digits. All of them can easily be gotten by simple calculations. Vi must be of double length. Peak position should be normalized so that the center of the shot is 128 and the beginning or the end is 0 or 255, respectively, when a digit is 8 bits. Sharpness is defined in some way or another. These two values can also be gotten by simple calculations.

Note that any of the output values is independent of the others. We can, for example, give a high peak value with low integrated value, or vice versa. Thus, we can simultaneously input several different values in a sophisticated but intuitive manner.

Drawback of MFTS is that input pressure is unidirectional and yield only zero or positive output. If we want to use MFTS to control bidirectional movement, e.g. forwards or backwards, we must use a pair of MFTSs.

6. Future Perspectives

The motivation of the proposal of MFTS is the need for good input devices for electronic painting systems. I think, however, this device has a very large area of applications. One of them is amusement use like video games. Sophisticated tactics can be applied to the video games by the use of MFTS.

I think another advantage of MFTS is that this device is suited for decisions in outline. Many people cannot make rigid decision or selection at workstations, especially at the beginning of a work. They will want to go on working without rigid decision. They can use MFTS in order to input ambiguous values. They can fix the ambiguous value afterwards. Due to this advantage, MFTS will have a very large area of applications in home or office computings.

We are now fixing the specifications of MFTS, testing elements of hardware, and making simulations of electronic paintings on a general-purpose computer. I hope that mass production will reduce the manufacturing costs of MFTS to less than 100 dollars a device.

ACKNOWLEDGEMENTS

Mr. Aihara told me about LVDT and is taking part in designing the prototypes. Mr. Asakura selected and tested appropriate ICs, drew detailed block diagrams and is taking part in designing the hardware and software of prototypes. Mr. Ogasawara has sponsored designing and manufacturing of prototypes. I will give graet thanks to Mr. Kobayashi who kindly introduced these persons of ability to me and coordinated the discussions.

REFERENCES

1. Gerland Stern, "SoftCel - An Application of Raster Scan Graphics to Conventional Cel Animation." Computer Graphics, vol. 13, no. 2, pp. 284-288, Aug. 1979
2. Ben Shneiderman, "Direct Manipulation: A Step Beyond Programming Languages," Computer, vol. 16, no. 8, pp. 57-69, Aug. 1983
3. Robert A. Moog, "The Human Finger - A Versatile Electronic Musical Instrument Component," Journal of The Audio Engineering Society, vol. 26, no. 12, pp. 958-960, Dec. 1978

Chapter 8
Graphics Standardization

GKS, a Standard for Software OEMs

Clinton N. Waggoner
Nova Graphics International Corporation
1015 Bee Cave Woods
Austin, TX 78746, USA

1.0 INTRODUCTION

The information age is upon us. The information industry, equivalent in importance to steel, railroads, oil, automobiles, and electronics is still in its infancy. The rapid decrease in cost and increase in performance of computers is making it possible. However, now the challenge is for software developers to design software applications packages which utilize all the available information in an effective manner. The key is for the software to be able to present information to and interact with humans in a wide variety of capacities. Graphics is an effective approach to handling the human interface. Thus graphics software will become a major market within the information industry. In order to serve this market in an effective and responsible manner, systems and software OEMs must utilize standards. This article summarizes the current status of graphics standards and discusses their use by software OEMs.

1.1 BACKGROUND

De facto standards in computer graphics have been common for a long time. For example a pseudo standard for interfacing to pen plotters has been the basis of many graphics software packages. Similar pseudo standards for storage tube based graphics devices exist. However, these pseudo standards have two basic shortcomings which prevent them from being appropriate today. First of all they are generally based on an output only model. The ability to interact with graphical information and use graphical input techniques is now very important. Second, the pseudo standards do not have the workstation model. Increasingly graphics devices in addition to having a display surface also contain one or more input devices and an intelligent processor.

In the early to mid 1970s national study groups were formed to address more comprehensive graphics standards. In 1977 the Graphics Standards Planning Committee (GSPC) of ACM (SIGGRAPH published the CORE system.[1] In the same time frame the German Standardization Institute, DIN, produced the Graphical Kernel System (GKS). Several excellent articles give a detailed history of the development of the GSPC CORE and GKS.[2,3] However, the result is that GKS has become a draft international standard and should become an ANSI standard in late 1984 after undergoing a four month public review period which is now in process.

1.2 GKS AND CORE

Those who follow technical developments in the graphics standards arena are aware of the controversy between supporters of GKS and CORE. At this point there does not appear to be any question that GKS will become an international standard. There is still consideration being given by the ACM to support CORE as an ACM standard. For the most part the two standards are similar. Some of the details are specified differently but the same result can be achieved by the applications programmer.

At this point the major differences are:

1) GKS is 2D and CORE is 3D
2) GKS has standard language bindings, CORE does not
3) GKS has bundled attributes concept
4) GKS is accepted internationally

GKS is presently a 2D standard whereas the CORE "standard" is 3D. However, work is in progress within ANSI and ISO to extend GKS to 3D. A serious flaw of CORE is that it became a pseudo standard without standardized language bindings being developed. Thus the applications programmer is faced with different interfaces to each "CORE" implementation. On the other hand standard GKS language bindings are already developed or are in the process of being defined for major programming languages. GKS has the ability to handle bundled attributes and individual attributes whereas "CORE" only specifies individual attributes. However, the most important factor supporting GKS is that it has become accepted on an international basis. Many hours of work have been committed to developing the GKS model. In particular the workstation model has been developed far more than "CORE". It is unlikely that the "CORE" model could ever gain international acceptance.

Given the international acceptance of GKS it appears that GKS will become the tool to be used by software OEMs to develop graphics-based software application packages. By using GKS, developers can offer a product which has the greatest potential for gaining a world-wide market appeal.

1.3 RELATIONSHIP OF GRAPHICS STANDARDS

It is easy to become quickly confused by a wide variety of acronyms having to do with graphics standards. How do all of these standards relate to one another? The key to understanding the relationship between the various standards is to realize that each standard is addressing a different interface. For example, GKS is the definition of an interface at the applications level between the applications program and graphics. A virtual grahics model is defined by GKS and the applications programmer writes his applications program around this model. Figure 1 shows a complete graphics environment and illustrates the major interface points.

A standard exists (at least in draft form) for each of the interface points. The major standards which one hears about are:

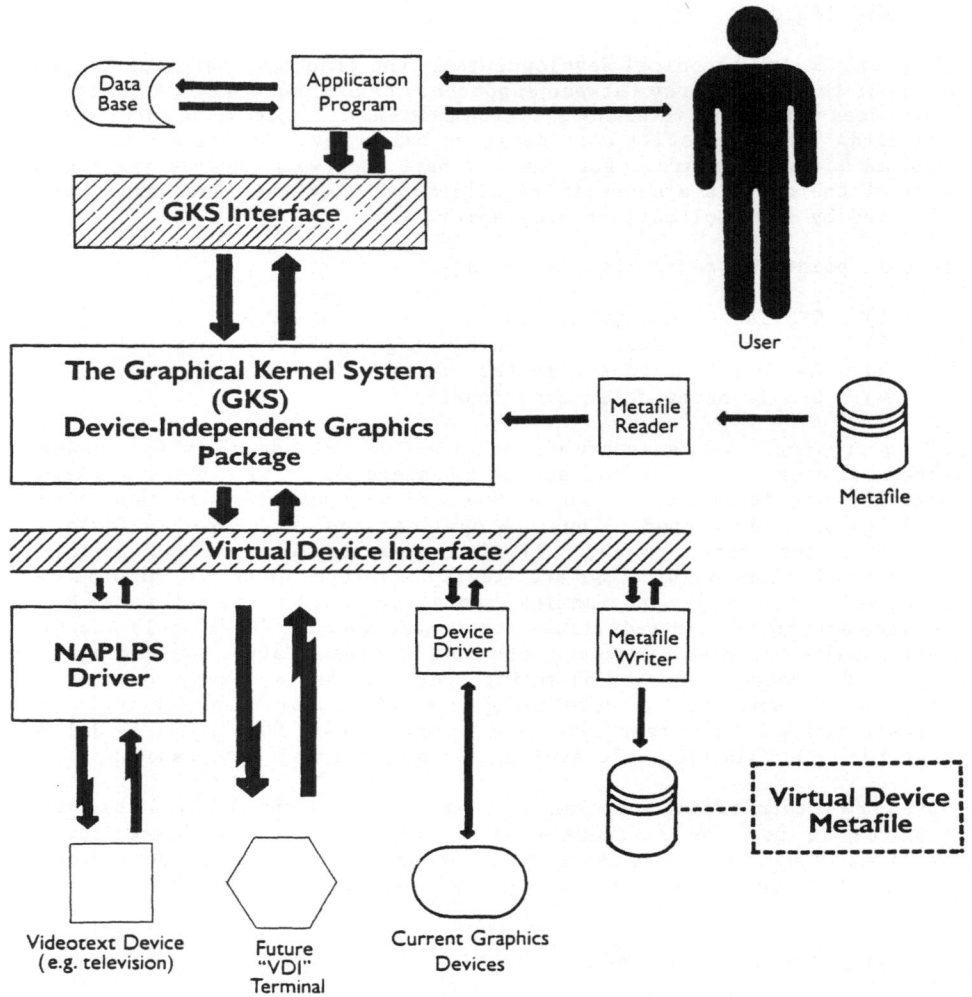

FIGURE 1

GRAPHICS ENVIRONMENT

GKS -   The definition of an interface between an applications program and a graphics model.

VDI -   The definition of device independent interface to device dependent graphics equipment and services.

VDM -   The definition of a mechanism for storing or transmitting graphical images.

NAPLPS - The definition of a standard method for encoding visual information including both text and graphics. This encoded information can then be used to drive videotext devices for a wide variety of applications.

2.0 FUNCTIONALITY OF GKS

Let us now examine the functionality which GKS provides for the software developer. Just to duplicate this functionality for a single graphics device would be a significant undertaking.

GKS provides the following major areas of functionality:

- 2D output primitives (3D specification in progress)
- multiple workstations
- individually controlled and bundled attributes
- workstation dependent and workstation independent segments
- multiple normalization transformation
- workstation transformation
- six input classes
- three input modes
- extensive inquiry

2.1 OUTPUT PRIMITIVES

GKS provides six basic output primitives: polyline, polymarker, fill area, text, fill array, and generalize drawing primitives. Table 1 illustrates each of the output primitives.

For polyline the user can control the line style, line width and color. Polymarker attributes include marker type, marker size, and marker color. Fill area provides the ability to fill a polygon of complex shape. The example in Table I is a single polygon. Notice how it has the effect of producing an eye for the aardvark. The polygon actually crosses back over itself and the definition of inside/outside for GKS polygon results in the eye area being considered outside. Polygons can have four fill styles (hollow, solid, pattern, hatch). Additionally, the user can specify color, hatch style, pattern size, pattern reference point, and pattern style.

GKS provides extensive text facilities. Three character precisions are supported. String precision is specified to take advantage of hardware character generators. Character precision similarly is intended to take

TABLE I

GKS OUTPUT PRIMITIVES

POLYLINE: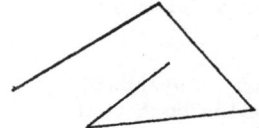

POLYMARKER:
+   +   +   +
    +   +   +

FILL AREA:

TEXT: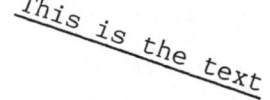

CELL ARRAY:

GENERALIZED DRAWING PRIMITIVE: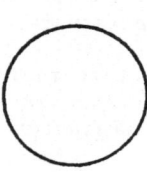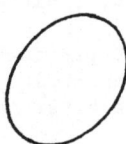

advantage of hardware character generators but on a character by character basis. Stroke precision supports the full range of text attributes: expansion factor, spacing, color, height, orientation, path, and alignment.

Cell array provides a means of specifying an array of colors and is useful in image processing. Generalized drawing primitives are provided to allow primitives to draw common geometric shapes to be specified in a well-defined, implementation-dependent way. Where possible advantage will be taken of hardware capabilities such as circle generators.

2.2 WORKSTATIONS

One of the major strengths of GKS is the formalization of the concept of a workstation. Many graphics devices already provide all or most of the facilities defined to be a GKS workstation. Figure 2 is an illustration of a distributed approach to implementation of GKS. Notice the multiple workstations. A distributed implementation of GKS allows processing to be off loaded to graphics workstations with local intelligence. GKS supports the following types of workstations:

    Output - output only (plotter)
    Input - input only (digitizer)
    Outin - output and input (CRT)
    WISS - Workstation Independent Segment Storage
    MO - metafile output
    MI - metafile input

2.3 ATTRIBUTES

GKS provides for specification of primitive attributes in three ways: bundled, individual and mixed. The concept of a bundle is that of a logical pen. For example a polyline bundle might be a dashed line of nominal thickness and of color red. Once a bundle is defined then it is only necessary to refer to it by its bundle identification. GKS implementations provide pre-defined bundles for each output primitive or the user may provide his own.

2.4 SEGMENTS

Segments provide the ability to group a set of primitives. That set of primitives is given a segment name and can be manipulated as a single entity. Segments can be transformed, made visible or invisible, and highlighted. A typical example is to define a single segment to represent part of a picture and then replicate it. For example a single wheel of a car could be defined and then transformed and copied to create three additional wheels. Segments are stored on those workstations that are active when the segment is created. This is known as workstation dependent segment storage (WDSS). In addition GKS provides a workstation independent segment storage (WISS). Segments can be copied from workstation independent segment storage to any workstation.

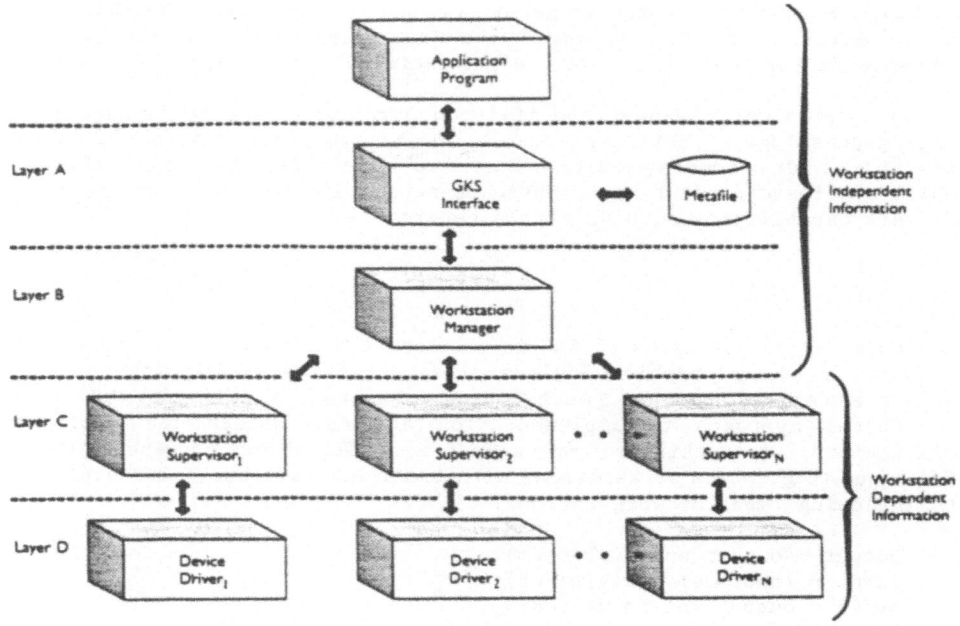

FIGURE 2

NOVA*GKS SYSTEM ARCHITECTURE

2.5 COORDINATES AND TRANSFORMATIONS

Figure 3 illustrates the coordinate systems and transformations available in GKS. World coordinates are provided for the user to define his graphics. World coordinates are then transformed to normalized device coordinates (NDC). The transformation from world coordinates to normalized device coordinates is called the normalization transformation. There may be multiple normalization transformations so that a picture can be composed in NDC space from different sections of world space or even different world spaces. An additional transformation called the workstation transformation allows any portion of the picture in NDC space to be selected and positioned on each device. Separate workstation transformations may exist for each workstation. Thus different workstations may display different aspects of a picture.

2.6 INPUT

GKS provides a formal model for input. There are six logical input classes:

    locator   choice
    valuator   string
    stroke   pick

These logical input devices allow for handling interactive processing. Locator provides a mechanism for the user to point to a position on the screen and cause the coordinates of that position to be returned in world coordinates. A light pen, joystick or mouse are typical physical realizations of a locator. Valuator returns a real number. A dial is a physical example of a valuator. Stroke provides a sequence of points in world coordinates. A digitizer is a common physical realization of a stroke device. Choice provides a non-negative integer which represents a selection from the available choices. It is commonly used for menu processing. String provides the capability to input a character string, typically from a keyboard. Pick is used in conjunction with segments to allow the user to identify a segment by pointing to it with a device such as a light pen. Pick returns the identity of the "picked" segment.

Each input device can be independently operated in three different modes:

    request
    sample
    event

Request mode causes the program to pause and wait until an input device is triggered. Sample mode provides the current "measure" of an input device. For example, sample valuator will return the current value of the valuator input device without any operator intervention. Event input provides for asynchronous input. An input device can be placed in event mode and the program can go on and do other things. When the input device is triggered an interrupt occurs and the measure of the input device is placed in an event queue.

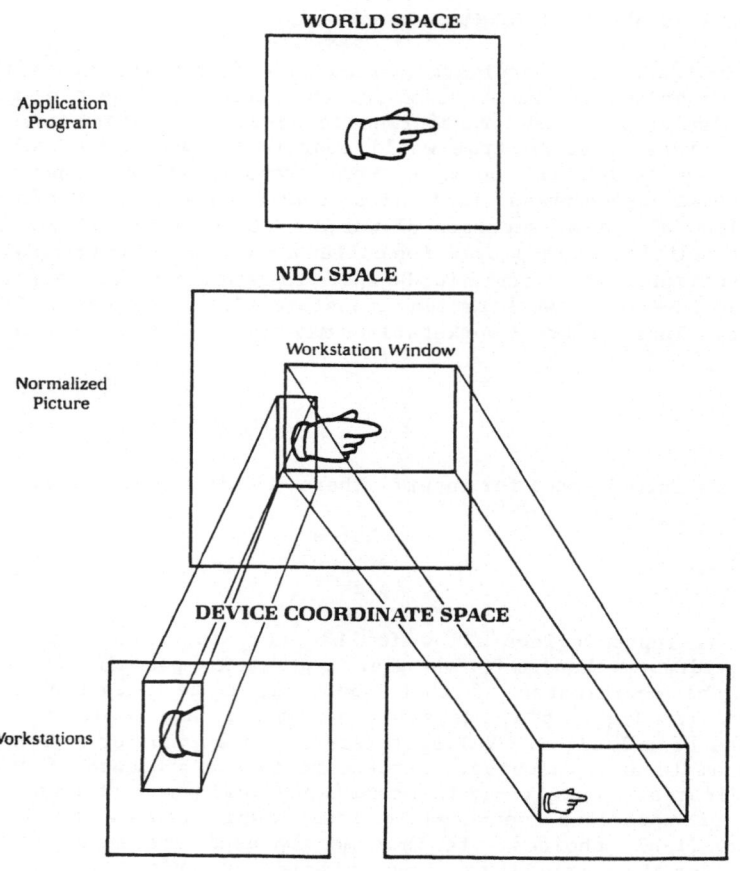

FIGURE 3

WINDOWS AND VIEWPORTS

2.7 INQUIRY FUNCTIONS

In order to assist the applications programmer in writing device independent applications programs, GKS provides an extensive set of inquiry functions. These functions allow the application program to inquire about the characteristics of the GKS implementation and each supported workstation. The application program can then make intelligent choices based upon the available facilities. For example, if color is not available, the program may utilize different line styles to discriminate between two objects.

2.8 GKS LEVELS

GKS defines various levels of implementation. The functionality supported at each level is strictly defined. Table II describes the various levels. One axis defines levels of input functionality and the other defines levels of output functionality. The careful definition of levels allows OEMs to choose a level consistent with their needs. Thus OEMs requiring minimal functionality are not burdened with the resource requirements of higher levels but still retain device independence and upwards compatibility.

3.0 GKS FOR OEM APPLICATIONS

A potentially very large market exists for graphics-based software applications packages. However, to be viable in this market the applications software or systems developer must address the issues of portability and device independence. The inability of software developers to achieve productivity gains which match the price/performance gains achieved in hardware is causing a change in the software business.

Software must be written so that it has the longest possible life cycle and the widest possible market appeal. Software designers will have to concentrate their resources on the applications area they are addressing rather than spending resources writing low level software which can be purchased separately. This is especially true in graphics applications because of the wide variety of available graphics devices and the rapid changes in technology. GKS provides for the graphics application programmer what FORTRAN provides to the scientific programmer.

Let us now examine some of the specific approaches available to developers of graphics-based application software and discuss the advantages of utilizing GKS.

3.1 APPROACHES TO GRAPHICS SOFTWARE

As a simple example to use for discussing the approaches to graphics software development let us consider just the ability to draw lines. We will examine three possible approaches and discuss the ramifications of each approach.

TABLE II

GKS LEVELS

	The Graphical Kernel System GKS Levels		
Output Level \ Input Level	a	b	c
m	No input, minimal control, only individually set attributes, subset of output functions.	Request input, mode setting and initialize devices, no PICK input.	SAMPLE and EVENT input, no PICK.
0	No graphic input, minimal control, predefined bundles only.	REQUEST input, mode setting, and initialize input device.	SAMPLE and EVENT input.
1	Full output including full bundle concept, graphic segment support and metafile storage.	All of 0b above, plus REQUEST PICK mode, setting and initialize for PICK.	SAMPLE and EVENT input for PICK.
2	All of 1a above, plus workstation independent segment storage.	All of 1b above.	All of 1c above.

3.1.1 Direct Interface

This approach requires the developer to write a driver for each device. If different line styles are needed then the developer must also write software to provide different linestyles. The advantage of the direct interface is that the software developer can customize the driver for maximum efficiency. The major disadvantage is that his software can only support a single device or a small number of devices without large amounts of work. Additionally, the programmer must learn to talk to the device at the bit level, thus reducing his productivity.

3.1.2 Pseudo Standards Interface

The use of pseudo standards or vendor supplied device drivers removes the need to talk to a graphics device at the bit level. However, the developer is still limited to a small number of devices. Additionally, he must provide the functionality to produce different linestyles. Again work must be done that is not related to the application at hand and there is little or no portability.

3.1.3 GKS Interface

A developer using GKS would utilize the polyline output primitive discussed earlier. His application would be portable to all devices supported by the GKS package. Additionally, the developer is free to concentrate on his applications software and need not concern himself with the details of each graphics device. The buyer of his software package could then be assured that if different graphics equipment were purchased then the software would not become obsolete. Thus the marketability of the software product is enhanced. The example of simple line drawings doesn't tell the whole story. Consider text, polygon fill, different coordinate systems, etc. The work involved to write software to handle these capabilities is non-trivial. To become cost effective software developers must take advantage of existing software.

3.2 CASE HISTORY

The author of this article was one of the designers of a complex interactive contour mapping system. This mapping package was based upon a "CORE"-based system. It is estimated that approximately three man years of programming effort was saved by utilizing a graphics package. In addition the package was immediately available on a wide variety of graphics devices. Thus the product was to market quicker and had a broader market base. GKS would have been even more suitable for the package because of its concept of levels. It would have been possible to choose a level of implementation which matched the functional needs of the application.

3.3 SUMMARY OF GKS ADVANTAGES FOR THE OEM

The significant advantages available to developers of graphics-based application software are:

- graphics device-independence and thus a wider market,
- extended software life,
- programmer portability,
- increased programmer productivity,
- good graphics functionality immediately available,
- resources can be concentrated on the application,
- lower maintenance costs, and
- ability to construct prototypes quickly.

REFERENCES

[1] "Status Report of the Graphics Standards Planning Committee of ACM/SIGGRAPH," Computer Graphics, Vol. II, No. 3, Fall 1977.

[2] "GKS - The First Graphics Standard," Peter R. Bono, Jose L. Encarnacao, F. Robert A. Hopgood, Paul J. W. ten Hagen, July 1982 IEEE CG&A.

[3] "Graphics Standards Evolve to Serve Users and Vendors," Dave Straayer, Computer Technology Review, Winter, 1982.

A Standards Solution to Your Graphics Problems

Mark G. Rawlins
Graphic Software Systems, Incorporated
25117 S.W. Parkway
Wilsonville, OR 97070, USA

Imagine the following scenario. Your department has had a new desktop computer for several weeks now, and you have mastered the word processing software so that you are able to generate a perfect letter in less time and with less effort than it used to take to type it. Having revised an important proposal that absolutely has to get to the airport counter by 6:00 p.m., you feel that it just doesn't create the impact you want it to. What your proposal needs is graphics! But how do you add illustrations at 3:00 p.m. on Friday afternoon.

If only you could do the kind of graphics the financial people did with the mainframe computer for the last quarterly report! Wait. Didn't you hear that the same program is now available to your desktop computer? A half hour with the self-instructing program and you have the charts you wanted on the screen. Now all you have to do is make hard copies of them. But after sending it to the attached dot matrix printer, you realize they are still not good enough. If only they were in color!

From the curious crowd gathered at your desk, out steps a volunteer who promises to help you. Returning shortly with a small multipen plotter, he unplugs your printer and plugs in the plotter, makes a few selections from a special menu and voila', the plotter begins drawing your chart--this time in color!

Not until the proposal is on its way do you have a chance to relax and reflect on how effectively you were able to use computer graphics to solve your problem--thanks to the impact of standards. But it hasn't always been that easy.

Plotting Our Way Through Standards

The cost of hardware has traditionally been blamed for inhibiting the growth of computer graphics. In fact, the lack of universal standards has dulled the impact of the dramatic reduction in component costs in the past decade. The advent of these important standards brings benefits to users on several levels.

In early days of computer graphics, users were obliged to write their own software to make a system work. Without a standard interface to graphics functions, adding on a new device to the system meant developing new software so the parts could talk to each other. Due to the cost of software development, "defacto" standards naturally emerged with the dominance of successful graphics products such as Calcomp plotters and Tektronix graphics terminals. When these companies added software support (Tektronix PLOT-10, for example), their implementation of graphics utilities became the common graphics language for applications. As the industry grew, that wasn't enough.

Current Standards Efforts

Present efforts in standardization are the result of over a decade of work done by European and American organizations. They apply to two main interface levels: the programmer interface and the device interface. The programmer interface refers to the conceptual model as well as the syntax a programmer uses when incorporating graphics functions into an application program. The device interface refers to the protocol between the device-independent and the device-dependent functions. The programmer level interface standardizes the referencing and functions of a graphics subroutine library; the device interface defines a device driver protocol that is consistent for all graphics devices.

The Graphical Kernel System

The Graphical Kernel System (GKS) is the proposed standard at the programmer level. GKS originated in Europe but has felt the influence of many national organizations, including ANSI in the United States, and is now in the process of being adopted as an American National Standard. GKS achieves source code portability. It allows graphics applications programs to be transported between different computer installations by providing a consistent interface in high level languages such as FORTRAN. This also ensures that graphics programmers--a scarce commodity today--will be able to work on different hardware without going through a costly learning curve. GKS provides a common graphics model and syntax to the programmer by standardizing the way graphics functions are accessed, and by providing graphics output on a virtual device surface.

The basic drawing primitives in GKS are the polyline, the polymarker and text primitives. The polyline primitive draws vectors (straight lines) between a sequence of points specified as an array. The polymarker primitive is similar to the polyline except it draws a marker symbol at each specified point rather than a vector. And the text primitive displays text strings at any position with any orientation.

GKS also supports raster devices with fill and cell array primitives. The fill operation "paints" the interior of a closed polyline (a polygon) with a specified color or pattern such as a cross hatch. The cell array primitive defines a two-dimensional array of pixels of different colors. The cell may then be replicated over an area by specifying the desired boundaries. These operations are used in imaging applications such as video frame displays, cartography and other scientific areas.

Besides providing device independence for standard functions, GKS also supports non-standard operations through a Generalized Drawing Primitive, a well-defined escape mechanism allowing access to the unique graphics capabilities of a particular device. This is necessary because some graphics devices have special features such as the ability to draw arcs, circles and bars. GKS allows an application program to access these capabilities by passing a function number and the required parameters to the driver.

Each output primitive has attributes that alter its appearance. For example, the polyline primitive has linetype (solid, dashed, etc.), width and color attributes. Polymarkers have attributes of type (. + * o x), size and color. Text primitives have attributes of size, color and orientation. In addition, multiple fonts can be accessed if they are available in the graphics device.

GKS also defines color indices by associating a desired color specified in RGB (red, green and blue) intensities with a color index number; the color values of primitives are then given as the appropriate index.

GKS supports the concept of multiple workstations. This enables several workstations (defined as a single display surface and one or more input devices) to operate in a single, interactive graphics session that might include, for example, a raster display, a plotter and a storage tube. GKS provides the logical interface through which the application program controls physical devices by redirecting graphics I/O at any time.

GKS maps the coordinate space of the application (called the world coordinate space) to device coordinates through two sets of transformations--Normalization and Workstation transformations.

First, GKS transforms world coordinates into a Normalized Device Coordinate (NDC) Space by setting a world window. NDC Space is actually an abstract viewing surface, or an intermediate space between applications and devices. Then it transforms the NDC Space into the Device Coordinates (DC) of the workstation. In the case of multiple workstations, each may have a distinct view of the application by setting a workstation window. The last transformation lets the workstation set a viewport that can be used for scaling and translating the original picture.

A full set of input operations allows an application program to receive input from a broad range of interactive input devices. The input operations are grouped into five classes: CHOICE, LOCATOR, PICK, STRING and VALUATOR. A vital capability, this allows GKS to support the optimum input device for a particular working environment. The result is improved interactivity through which the full potential of the graphics man-machine interface can be realized. The REQUEST LOCATOR function returns a position in world coordinates while the REQUEST VALUATOR function indicates the current value of a continuous valuator device such as a potentiometer. The REQUEST CHOICE function returns an integer that represents one of a set of choices. The PICK function returns the graphics segment number that corresponds to the objects being selected witn graphics input. Finally, the REQUEST STRING function reads character input from a keyboard device. The way these logical function are implemented (joystick, mouse, function keys, etc.) is workstation dependent.

To aid the programmer, GKS also provides an Inquire capability that allows the application program to determine the current operating state, primitive attributes, viewing operations and transformation, as well as device capabilities.

Two emerging standards are addressing the hardware driver interface level. One, the North American Presentation Level Protocol Syntax (NAPLPS), is based on the concept of videotex. Developed in Europe and modified by the Canadians, this idea was adopted by AT&T as a standard for transmitting text and graphics over tele-communications lines. NAPLPS is aimed primarily at providing a way to connect television sets and other very low cost raster devices to telephone lines so consumers can access public commericial data bases. It provides only "one-way at a time" communication, precluding interactive graphics applications. Its value lies in powerful data compaction that allows complicated graphics to be quickly transmitted over low cost communications lines. Although NAPLPS is important because of the number of devices that could potentially use this standard, it is not an optimal interface for general computer graphics applications. It probably will sit beside another, more general device interface called the Virtual Device Interface (VDI).

The Virtual Device Interface

VDI is being developed by the ANSI X3H33 Technical Committee as a standard interface between device-independent software and graphics devices. VDI makes all devices appear as "identical" graphics devices by defining a standard input/output protocol. This isolates the unique characteristics of the physical graphics device in the device driver software module.

For the graphics equipment manufacturer, the adoption of this standard means that a VDI driver for a particular graphics device need be written only once. All graphics applications that conform to VDI will then be able to utilize the standard device drive. Long range benefits will be more evident as equipment and semiconductor manufacturers begin to implement more of the software driver functionality in hardware--in effect moving the VDI interface down into the graphics device itself. This approach offers many benefits to the industry: less design effort expended "reinventing wheels," numerous second-sources, higher reliability with a proven design, reduced costs, and larger markets.

By now the importance of standards should be clear, but all of this activity is little more than an academic exercise if the standards are not implemented on several operating systems--no mean task considering architectural differences among operating systems. Several major hardware and software vendors have already declared support of the proposed VDI standard. Graphic Software Systems has implemented the standard on multiple operating systems and it is available for graphics application and system tools. An application developer utility set, GSS-TOOLKIT, contains a GKS implementation called the Kernel System, a linkable run-time graphics utility library. This system multiplies programmer productivity while providing program portability through the VDI interface. Applications using Kernel System will be source code compatible with mini and mainframe computer systems running GKS procedure libraries.

Built on the basic graphics subsystem are increasingly friendly graphics tools. These include the Plotting System, a data representation plotting utility library; and GSS-CHART, an end user graphing package for scientific and business use.

GSS-TERMINAL is a terminal emulator that makes the vast installed base of minicomputer and mainframe graphic software available to the latest microcomputer workstations. It also emulates popular alphanumeric terminals as well as allows uploading and downloading of data to a host. This capability means more applications can be migrated to microcomputers.

To technical users, adoption of the GKS and VDI standards at the programmer and device interface levels means source code portability for graphics applications programs. Not only will they see a consistent interface to graphics functions at the language level, but compilers and graphics run-time libraries can be generic, with device-dependencies residing in the operating system.

To the hardware OEM this means installing the graphics portion of an operating system only once. Compilers and other utilities that conform to the VDI standard will then be able to access the virtual devices of a system without special adaptation. Higher level functions will be put into the device hardware (or firmware) and, eventually, graphics devices may incorporate a full VDI interface, eliminating the need for device drivers entirely.

And to the end user? Remember the proposal that made it on time!

Sidebar--A GRAPHICS GLOSSARY

ANSI The American National Standards Institute

Attributes Characteristics associated with graphic primitives that affect the appearance of those objects.

Cell Array An output primitive consisting of a rectangular grid of equal size rectangular cells, each having a single color.

Device driver Device-dependent software that generates instructions specifying items to be drawn on a display surface.

GKS Graphical Kernel System

NAPLPS North American Presentation Level Protocol Syntax

NDC Space Normalized Device Coordinate Space, a concept that provides improved device independence for a graphics system by allowing the viewing operations to be carried out without regard for device specifics. NDC coordinates are then converted to specific device coordinates by the device driver.

Primitive The graphical world the programmer describes consists of one or more objects. These are created and modified in world coordinate space by invoking the graphic primitives provided by GKS. These functions describe polylines, polymarkers, text strings, cell arrays, fill areas and generalized drawing primitives. The appearance of these output primitives is affected by the values of primitive attributes.

Raster Graphics device with a display surface composed of a matrix of pixels arranged in rows and columns.

Segment A related set of graphic elements that may be operated on as a whole.

SIGGRAPH Special Interest Group on Computer Graphics

Transformation Mapping of objects from one coordinate space to another.

VDI Virtual Device Interface

Vector A straight line specified by endpoints.

Sidebar--GRAPHICS STANDARDS TIMELINE

1974 The Special Interest Group on Computer Graphics of the Association of Computing Machinery conducted a workshop on machine independence--the beginning of formal work on graphics standardization.

1976 International Workshop of Graphics Standards Methodology held in Seillac, France. The goal--to develop a methodology for accomplishing program portability as well as a functional specification for a core graphics system.

1977 SIGGRAPH Graphics Standards Planning Committee presented draft of Core Standard Proposal which addressed vector graphics.

1979 SIGGRAPH published a revision of the CORE Report that addressed raster functions, metafiles (device-independent plot files) and distributed graphics systems. ANSI committee X3H3 established to continue standards work. International Standards Organization (ISO) began process of adopting Graphical Kernel System as an international standard.

1981 ANSI subcommittee X3H33 began work on a Virtual Device Interface Standard that was formally supported by 15 corporations including software companies, equipment manufacturers and component manufacturers.

1982 GKS adopted by ISO as a Draft International Standard. ANSI began process of adopting it as an American National Standard (formal adoption expected in the fall).

Author Information

Mark Rawlins is the Director of Marketing for Graphic Software Systems, Inc., a software company developing computer graphics tools and applications for OEMs, ISVs and graphics peripheral vendors.

Trademark Information

The names GSS-CHART, GSS-TOOLKIT and GSS-TERMINAL are trademarks of Graphic Software Systems, Inc. The name PLOT-10 is a trademark of Tektronix, Inc.

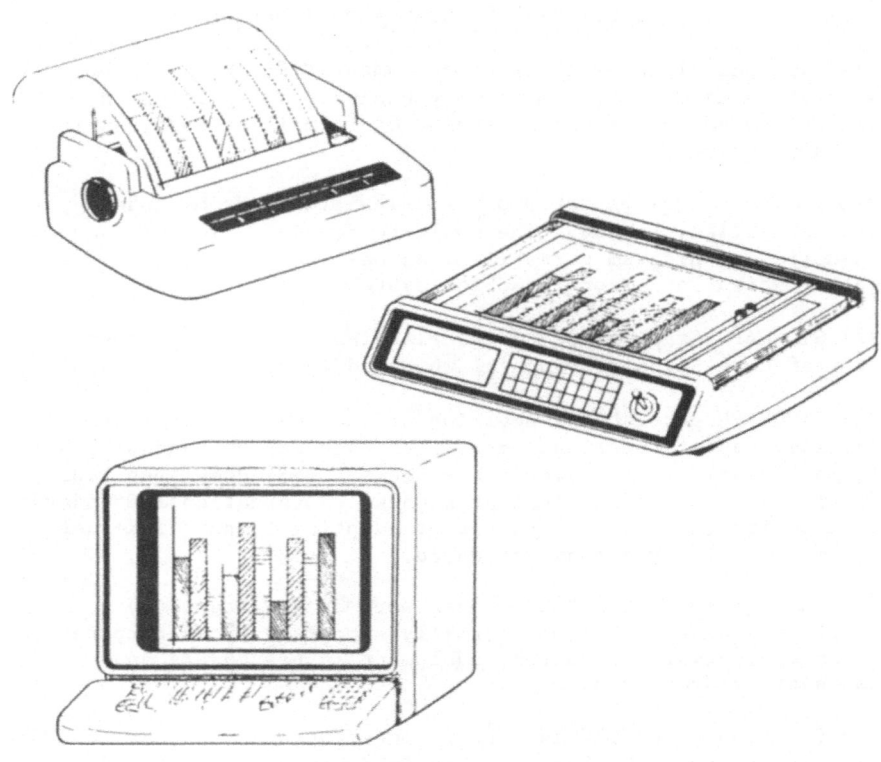

Figure 1 Device-independent Graphics. Standards are evolving
today that make device and host independent graphics a reality.
To the Applications Programmer of Systems Integrator this means
the freedom to design solutions without regard to device or
system specifics. To the End User it means protection for a
software investment and the freedom to upgrade or modify a system
without incurring additional software development costs.

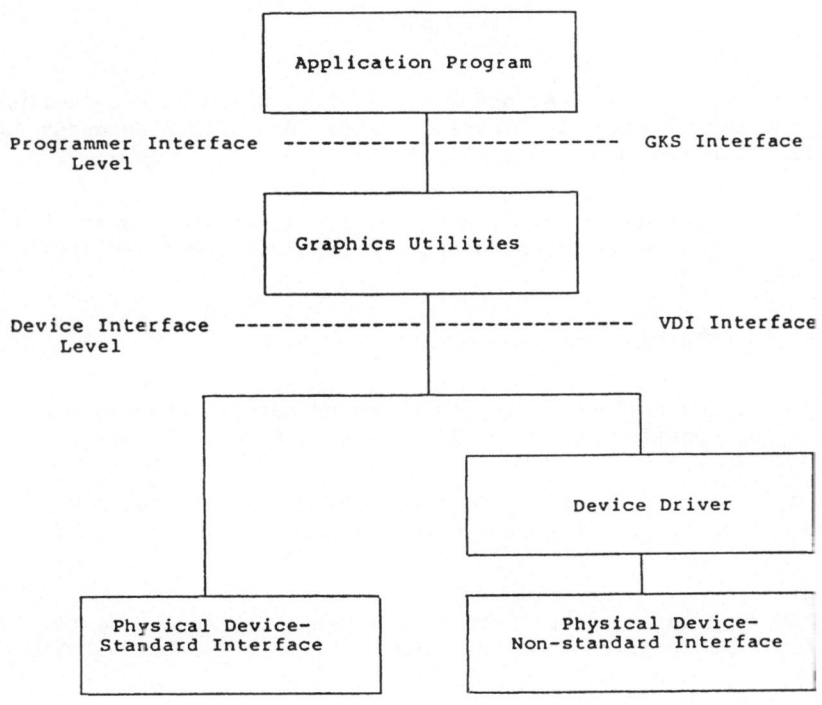

Figure 2 Architecture of Graphics Standards. The two main levels of graphics standards are the programmer and device interface levels. The Graphical Kernel System (GKS) provides the standard interface between the application program and graphics utilities. The Virtual Device Interface (VDI) provides a standard interface between graphics utilities and device drivers.

REFERENCES

Bergeron, R.D., Bono, P.R. and Foley, J.D., 'Graphics Programming Using the Core System' in "Special Issue: Graphics Standards" ACM Computing Surveys 10(4), 389-443 (1978)

Bono, P.R., Encarnacao, J.L., Hopgood, F.R.A. and ten Hagen, P.J.W., 'GKS - The First Graphics Standard' in IEEE Computers and Applications 2(5), 9-23 (1982)

DIN IN 5.9 "FORTRAN interface of GKS 7.2" (1983)

Foley, J.D. and Wallace, V.L., 'The art of natural graphic man-machine conversation' in Proc. IEEE 62(4), 462-471 (1974)

Hopgood, F.R.A., Duce, D.A., Gallop, J.R. and Sutcliffe, D.C., "Introduction to the Graphical Kernel System (GKS)", Academic Press (1983)

"ISO/DIS 7942 Information Processing - Graphical Kernel System (GKS) - Functional Description: GKS Version 7.2", ISO/TC97/SC5/WG2 N163 (1982)

Rosenthal, D.S.H., Michener, J.C., Pfaff, G., Kessener, L.R.A. and Sabin, M.A., 'The Detailed Semantics of Graphics Input Devices' in Computer Graphics 16(3), 33-38 (1982)

ten Hagen, P.J.W., 'The Review of GKS version 7.0, The Finishing Touch' in Computer Graphics Forum 1(4) (December 1982)

GKS SPECIFICATIONS

BACKGROUND

The KERNEL SYSTEM is based on a long history of standards efforts for computer graphics. Psuedo standards have been available in the computer graphics field for some time. Originally, dominant computer graphics hardware manufacturers were able to produce software that became defacto standards. The best examples of early defacto standards are the Calcomp Plotting Routines, and Tektronix PLOT-10. Later, ACM Siggraph (Special Interest Group on Computer Graphics) became involved in the creation of standards for computer graphics. Siggraph felt that it was essential to the growth of computer graphics as a unique discipline to create a standard conceptual model for computer graphics. Siggraph created another pseudo standard called the GSPC 1979 CORE System. This pioneering work led to a consistent vocabulary, and a consistent conceptual model that paved the way for later ANSI and ISO standards efforts. The ANSI and ISO efforts have devoted much study to the technical questions surrounding the creation of a computer graphics system. Uncountable man hours have been spent in the debate and study of alternative methods of doing computer graphics. The results are nearly complete. The ISO and ANSI standards committees have been able to create a uniform conceptual model both in terms of the architectural creation of a computer graphics system (Reference Model), and in the programmers conceptual model for computer graphics.

0.1. REFERENCE MODEL

The Reference Model defines three distinct interfaces that are pertinent to computer graphics. The first interface is between an application program and a graphic utility system. The second is between a graphic utility system and a device. The third is between different graphics computing systems. The relevant standard between an application program and a graphic utility system is the GKS. The relevant standard between the graphic utility system and the device is the VDI. The relevant standard for communications between graphics computing systems is the VDM/PLP. The KERNEL SYSTEM is a graphic utility system and is based on the recently frozen ISO and ANSI GKS standard.

0.2. PRODUCT PURPOSE AND SCOPE

The KERNEL SYSTEM is a subroutine library of 2D graphics primitives with retained segments for programmers and application builders. The KERNEL SYSTEM is compatible with Level Mb of the ANSI Graphical Kernel System (GKS) graphics standard. Features from level 0, 1 and 2 have also been included.

Current documentation regarding the draft GKS standard is entitled "Graphical Kernel System (GKS) - Functional Description," Draft International Standard ISO/DIS7942, Version 7.02, August 9, 1982. This document can be obtained for $28 from the American National Standards Institute Inc., 1430 Broadway, N.Y., NY 10081, (212) 354-3300.

1. PRODUCT DESCRIPTION

This section gives a complete functional description of the KERNEL SYSTEM from GSS. The GKS represents much of the discipline of computer graphics. The discipline of computer graphics is fairly new, but is as rich as any other area of computer science such as Languages or Operating systems. Consequently, the novice in the field will find much of the GKS terminology and concepts new. This will change as GKS is taught in the computer science curriculum.

1.1. OVERVIEW

The KERNEL SYSTEM is a linkable library of functions that is designed to link with Compiled Basic, FORTRAN, and C. As stated in the reference model section, it is intended to be a device independent package which allows more functions and controls to the VDI device level. It is appropriate to provide this type of product as a linkable library, since only those functions used by the application will be selected. The product also supports the large 8086 programming model and the 8087 floating point processor. The following section summarizes the basic features of the product.

1.1.1. TRANSFORMATION FUNCTIONS

The KERNEL SYSTEM supports two transformation paths. Normalization transforms are specified by defining the limits of an area in the world coordinate (WC) system (window) which is to be mapped onto a specified area of the normalized device coordinate (NDC) space (viewport). World coordinates are user specified while the viewport is limited to the NDC space confined to $[0,1]\times[0,1]$. Each normalization transformation defined by the user is identified by a transformation number. The user can have one normalization transformation active at a time. The default normalization transformation is the unity transformation which maps $[0,1]\times[0,1]$ in world coordinates to $[0,1]\times[0,1]$ in normalized device coordinates. In addition to normalization transformations the user of the KERNEL SYSTEM can define workstation transformations. The user can independently select some portion of the NDC space to be displayed somewhere on the workstation display surface. A particular workstation transformation is a mapping from NDC space onto the device coordinates (DC) for that workstation. Normalization transformations will perform mappings that include translations and differential scaling while workstation transformations are uniform mappings of NDC onto DC with translations and equal scaling.

1.1.2. GRAPHICS PRIMITIVES

Graphic primitives supported by the KERNEL SYSTEM include polylines, polymarkers, filled areas (polygons), text, and generalized drawing primitives (GDPs). The user of the KERNEL SYSTEM has control over various attributes of the primitives including line style, marker style, hatch and pattern style, text rotation, alignment and size, and color control for all primitives. Color is referenced by indices with the user having the capability to set the color representation for each index. The number of GDPs available is device dependent and includes such primitives as bars, arcs, pie slices and circles.

1.1.3. INPUT

The KERNEL SYSTEM supports four different types of graphic input devices (locator, choice, string and valuator) and two different modes of input (request and sample). In addition, the KERNEL SYSTEM supports both modes of input for the picking of segments. The user has the ability to inquire upon his current workstation various input capabilites including number of logical input devices and the initial state of the a particular device.

1.1.4. SEGMENTS

In the KERNEL SYSTEM, output primitives may be grouped in segments as well as being created outside segments. Each segment is identified by a unique application specified name. The user of the KERNEL SYSTEM has the ability to open/close (create) a segment, rename a segment, and delete a segment from all active workstations. In addition the user can control various attributes of a segment including visibility (display or not), highlighting, detectability (can pick the segment or not), segment priority (viewing priority in overlapping segments), and segment image transforms (scale, rotation, and translation).

1.2. LANGUAGE BINDINGS

1.2.1. FORTRAN Binding

The following FORTRAN binding is from the final negotiated markups between ANSI and ISO of document ISO NI-5.9/. The meeting was in April 1983.

1.2.1.1. ACCUMULATE TRANSFORMATION MATRIX

SUBROUTINE GACTM (MINP, XO, YO, DX, DY, PHI, FX, FY, SW, MOUT)

REAL MINP (6)	transformation matrix
REAL XO, YO	fixed point
REAL DX, DY	shift vector
REAL PHI	rotation in radians
REAL FX, FY	scale factors
INTEGER SW	coordinate switch
REAL MOUT(6)	transformation matrix

1.2.1.2. ACTIVATE WORKSTATION

SUBROUTINE GACWK (WKID)

INTEGER WKID   workstation identifier

1.2.1.3. ASSOCIATE SEGMENT WITH WORKSTATION

SUBROUTINE GASGWK (WKID, SGNA)

INTEGER WKID	workstation identifier
INTEGER SGNA	segment name

1.2.1.4. CLEAR WORKSTATION

SUBROUTINE GCLRWK (WKID, COFL)

INTEGER WKID	workstation identifier
INTEGER COFL	contrl flag (conditionally, always)

1.2.1.5. CLOSE GKS

SUBROUTINE GCLKS

1.2.1.6. CLOSE SEGMENT

SUBROUTINE GCLSG

1.2.1.7. CLOSE WORKSTATION

SUBROUTINE GCLWK (WKID)

INTEGER WKID   workstation identifier

1.2.1.8. COPY SEGMENT TO WORKSTATION

SUBROUTINE GCSGWK (WKID, SGNA)

INTEGER WKID	workstation identifier
INTEGER SGNA	segment name

1.2.1.9. CREATE SEGMENT

SUBROUTINE GCRSG (SGNA)

INTEGER SGNA   segment name

1.2.1.10. DEACTIVATE WORKSTATION

```
          SUBROUTINE GDAWK (WKID)

          INTEGER WKID              workstation identifier
```

1.2.1.11. DELETE SEGMENT

```
          SUBROUTINE GDSG (SGNA)

          INTEGER SGNA              segment name
```

1.2.1.12. DELETE SEGMENT FROM WORKSTATION

```
          SUBROUTINE GDSGWK (WKID, SGNA)

          INTEGER WKID              workstation identifier
          INTEGER SGNA              segment name
```

1.2.1.13. ERROR HANDLING PROCEDURE

```
          SUBROUTINE GERHND (ERRNR, FCTID, ERRFIL)

          INTEGER ERRNR             error number
          INTEGER FCTID             function identification
          INTEGER ERRFIL            error file (a logical unit number
                                    from a standard fortran OPEN statement)
```

1.2.1.14. ERROR LOGGING PROCEDURE

```
          SUBROUTINE GERLOG (ERRNR, FCTID, ERRFIL)

          INTEGER ERRNR             error number
          INTEGER FCTID             function identification
          INTEGER ERRFIL            error file (a logical unit number
                                    from a standard fortran OPEN statement)
```

1.2.1.15. ESCAPE

```
          SUBROUTINE GESC (FCTID, LDR, DATREC)

          INTEGER FCTID             function identification
          INTEGER LDR               length of data record
          CHARACTER*80 DATREC(LDR)  data record
```

1.2.1.16. EVALUATE TRANSFORMATION MATRIX

```
SUBROUTINE GEVTM (X0, Y0, DX, DY, PHI, FX, FY, SW, MOUT)

REAL X0, Y0               fixed point
REAL DX, DY               shift vector
REAL PHI                  rotation in radians
REAL FX, FY               scale factors
INTEGER SW                coordinate switch
REAL MOUT (6)             transformation matrix
```

1.2.1.17. FILL AREA

```
SUBROUTINE GFA (N, PX, PY)

INTEGER N                 number of points
REAL PX(N)                coordinates of points in WC
REAL PY(N)
```

1.2.1.18. GENERALIZED DRAWING PRIMITIVE

```
SUBROUTINE GGDP (N, PX, PY, PRIMID, LDR, DATREC)

INTEGER N                 number of points
REAL PX(N), PY(N)         coordinates of points in WC
INTEGER PRIMID            GDP identifier
INTEGER LDR               length of data record
CHARACTER*80 DATREC(LDR)  data record
```

1.2.1.19. INITIALIZE CHOICE

```
SUBROUTINE GINCH (WKID, CHDNR, ICHNR, PET, XMIN, XMAX, YMIN,
                  YMAX, LDR, DATREC)

INTEGER WKID                    workstation identifier
INTEGER CHDNR                   choice device number
INTEGER ICHNR                   initial choice number
INTEGER PET                     prompt/echo type
REAL XMIN, XMAX, YMIN, YMAX     echo area in device coordinates
INTEGER LDR                     length of data record
CHARACTER*80 DATREC(LDR)        data record
```

1.2.1.20. INITIALIZE LOCATOR

```
SUBROUTINE GINLC (WKID, LCDNR, TNR, IPX, IPY, PET, XMIN, XMAX,
                  YMIN, YMAX, LDR, DATREC)

INTEGER WKID                    workstation identifier
INTEGER LCDNR                   locator device number
INTEGER TNR                     initial transformation number
REAL IPX, IPY                   initial locator position (WC)
INTEGER PET                     prompt/echo type
REAL XMIN, XMAX, YMIN, YMAX     echo area in device coordinates
INTEGER LDR                     length of data record
CHARACTER*80 DATREC(LDR)        data record
```

1.2.1.21. INITIALIZE PICK

```
SUBROUTINE GINPK (WKID, PKDNR, ISTAT, ISGNA, IPKID, PET, XMIN, XMAX
                  YMIN, YMAX, LDR, DATREC)

INTEGER WKID                    workstation identifier
INTEGER PCDNR                   pick device number
INTEGER ISTAT                   initial status (none,ok,nopick)
INTEGER ISGNA                   initial segment name
INTEGER IPCID                   initial pick identifier
INTEGER PET                     prompt/echo type
REAL XMIN, XMAX, YMIN, YMAX     echo area in device coordinates
INTEGER LDR                     length of data record
CHARACTER*80 DATREC(LDR)        data record
```

1.2.1.22. INITIALIZE STRING

```
SUBROUTINE GINST (WKID, STDNR, ISTR, PET, XMIN, XMAX, YMIN,
                  YMAX, BUFLEN, INIPOS, LDR, DATREC)

INTEGER WKID                    workstation identifier
INTEGER STDNR                   string device number
CHARACTER*(*) ISTR              initial string
INTEGER PET                     prompt/echo type
REAL XMIN, XMAX, YMIN, YMAX     echo area in device coordinates
INTEGER BUFLEN                  length of string
INTEGER INIPOS                  initial cursor position
INTEGER LDR                     length of data record
CHARACTER*80 DATREC(LDR)        data record
```

1.2.1.23. INITIALIZE STRING (FORTRAN 77 subset version)

```
SUBROUTINE GINSTS (WKID, STDNR, LSTR, ISTR, PET, XMIN, XMAX, YMIN,
                   YMAX, BUFLEN, INIPOS, LDR, DATREC)

INTEGER WKID                    workstation identifier
INTEGER STDNR                   string device number
INTEGER LSTR                    length of the initial string
CHARACTER*(*) ISTR              initial string
INTEGER PET                     prompt/echo type
REAL XMIN, XMAX, YMIN, YMAX     echo area in device coordinates
INTEGER BUFLEN                  length of string
INTEGER INIPOS                  initial cursor position
INTEGER LDR                     length of data record
CHARACTER*80 DATREC(LDR)        data record
```

1.2.1.24. INITIALIZE STROKE

```
SUBROUTINE GINSK (WKID, SKDNR, TNR, N, IPX, IPY, PET, XMIN,
                  XMAX, YMIN, YMAX, BUFLEN, INIPOS, LDR, DATREC)

INTEGER WKID                    workstation identifier
INTEGER SKDNR                   stroke device number
INTEGER TNR                     initial norm. tranformation number
INTEGER N                       number of points in initial stroke
REAL IPX(N), IPY(N)             points in initial stroke (WC)
INTEGER PET                     prompt/echo type
REAL XMIN, XMAX, YMIN, YMAX     echo area in device coordinates
INTEGER BUFLEN                  buffer length for stroke
INTEGER INIPOS                  initialize editing position
INTEGER LDR                     length of data record
CHARACTER*80 DATREC(LDR)        data record
```

1.2.1.25. INITIALIZE VALUATOR

```
SUBROUTINE GINVL (WKID, VLDNR, IVAL, PET, XMIN, XMAX YMIN, YMAX,
                  LOVAL, HIVAL, LDR, DATREC)

INTEGER WKID                    workstation identifier
INTEGER VLDNR                   valuator device number
REAL IVAL                       initial value
INTEGER PET                     prompt/echo type
REAL XMIN, XMAX, YMIN, YMAX     echo area in device coordinates
REAL LOVAL, HIVAL               minimal and maximal value
INTEGER LDR                     length of data record
CHARACTER*80 DATREC(LDR)        data record
```

1.2.1.26. INQUIRE CHOICE DEVICE STATE

```
SUBROUTINE GQCHS (WKID, CHDNR, MLDR, ERRIND, MODE, ESW, ICHNR, PET,
                  EAREA, LDR, DATREC)

INTEGER WKID              workstation identifier
INTEGER CHDNR             choice device number
INTEGER MLDR              maximum length of data record
INTEGER ERRIND            error indicator
INTEGER MODE              operating mode
INTEGER ESW               echo switch (no echo, echo)
INTEGER ICHNR             initial choice number
INTEGER PET               prompt/echo type
REAL EAREA(4)             echo area
INTEGER LDR               length of data record
CHARACTER*80 DATREC       data record
```

1.2.1.27. INQUIRE CLIPPING INDICATOR

```
SUBROUTINE GQCLIP (ERRIND, CLIP)

INTEGER ERRIND            error indicator
INTEGER CLIP              clipping indicator (noclip, clip)
```

1.2.1.28. INQUIRE COLOR FACILITIES

```
SUBROUTINE GQCF (WTYPE, ERRIND, NCOLI, COLA, NPCI)

INTEGER WTYPE             workstation type
INTEGER ERRIND            error indicator
INTEGER NCOLI             number of colors
INTEGER COLA              color available (mono, color)
INTEGER NPCI              number of predefined color indices
```

1.2.1.29. INQUIRE COLOR REPRESENTATION

```
SUBROUTINE GQCR (WKID, COLI, TYPE, ERRIND, RED, GREEN, BLUE)

INTEGER WKID              workstation identifier
INTEGER COLI              color index
INTEGER TYPE              type returned values
INTEGER ERRIND            error indicator
REAL RED, GREEN, BLUE     color (red/green/blue intensities)
```

1.2.1.30. INQUIRE CURRENT INDIVIDUAL ATTRIBUTE VALUES

1.2.1.30.1. INQUIRE POLYLINE COLOR INDEX

```
        SUBROUTINE GQPLCI (ERRIND, COLI)

        INTEGER ERRIND              error indicator
        INTEGER COLI                polyline color index
```

1.2.1.30.2. INQUIRE POLYLINE TYPE

```
        SUBROUTINE GQLN (ERRIND, LTYPE)

        INTEGER ERRIND              error indicator
        INTEGER LTYPE               linetype
```

1.2.1.30.3. INQUIRE POLYLINE WIDTH SCALE FACTOR

```
        SUBROUTINE GQLWSC (ERRIND, LWIDTH)

        INTEGER ERRIND              error indicator
        REAL LWIDTH                 linewidth scale factor
```

1.2.1.30.4. INQUIRE POLYMARKER COLOR INDEX

```
        SUBROUTINE GQPMCI (ERRIND, COLI)

        INTEGER ERRIND              error indicator
        INTEGER COLI                polymarker color index
```

1.2.1.30.5. INQUIRE POLYMARKER HEIGHT SCALE FACTOR

```
        SUBROUTINE GQMKSC (ERRIND, MSZSF)

        INTEGER ERRIND              error indicator
        REAL MSZSF                  marker height scale factor
```

1.2.1.30.6. INQUIRE POLYMARKER TYPE

```
        SUBROUTINE GQMK (ERRIND, MTYPE)

        INTEGER ERRIND              error indicator
        INTEGER MTYPE               marker type
```

1.2.1.30.7. INQUIRE TEXT FONT AND PRECISION

```
        SUBROUTINE GQTXFP (ERRIND, FONT, PREC)

        INTEGER ERRIND              error indicator
        INTEGER FONT                text font
        INTEGER PREC                text precision
```

1.2.1.30.8. INQUIRE TEXT COLOR INDEX

    SUBROUTINE GQTXCI (ERRIND, COLI)

    INTEGER ERRIND   error indicator
    INTEGER COLI   text color index

1.2.1.30.9. INQUIRE FILL AREA INTERIOR STYLE

    SUBROUTINE GQFAIS (ERRIND, INTS)

    INTEGER ERRIND   error indicator
    INTEGER INTS   fill area interior style

1.2.1.30.10. INQUIRE FILL AREA STYLE INDEX

    SUBROUTINE GQFASI (ERRIND, STYLI)

    INTEGER ERRIND   error indicator
    INTEGER STYLI   fill area style index

1.2.1.30.11. INQUIRE FILL AREA COLOR INDEX

    SUBROUTINE GQFACI (ERRIND, COLI)

    INTEGER ERRIND   error indicator
    INTEGER COLI   fill area color index

1.2.1.31. INQUIRE CURRENT NORMALIZATION TRANSFORMATION NUMBER

    SUBROUTINE GQCNTN (ERRIND, CTNR)

    INTEGER ERRIND   error indicator
    INTEGER CTNR   current transformation number

1.2.1.32. INQUIRE CURRENT SETTING OF PRIMITIVE ATTRIBUTES

1.2.1.32.1. INQUIRE CHARACTER HEIGHT

    SUBROUTINE GQCHH (ERRIND, CHH)

    INTEGER ERRIND   error indicator
    REAL CHH   current character height

1.2.1.32.2. INQUIRE CHARACTER UP VECTOR

SUBROUTINE GQCHUP (ERRIND, CHUX, CHUY)

INTEGER ERRIND	error indicator
REAL CHUX	current character up vector in x
REAL CHUY	current character up vector in y

1.2.1.32.3. INQUIRE TEXT ALIGNMENT

SUBROUTINE GQTXAL (ERRIND, TXALH, TXALV)

INTEGER ERRIND	error indicator
INTEGER TXALH	current text alignment horizontal
INTEGER TXALH	current text alignment vertical

1.2.1.32.4. INQUIRE PICK IDENTIFIER

SUBROUTINE GQPKID (ERRIND, PCID)

INTEGER ERRIND	error indicator
INTEGER PCID	current pick identifier

1.2.1.33. INQUIRE DEFAULT CHOICE DEVICE DATA

SUBROUTINE GQDCH (WTYPE, DEVNO, N, MLDR, ERRIND, MALT,
                  OL, PET, EAREA, LDR, DATREC)

INTEGER WTYPE	workstation type
INTEGER DEVNO	logical input device number
INTEGER N	list element requested
INTEGER MLDR	maximum length of data record
INTEGER ERRIND	error indicator
INTEGER MALT	maximum number of alternatives
INTEGER OL	number of av. prompt/echo types
INTEGER PET	Nth element of list of prompt/echo types
REAL EAREA(4)	default echo area
INTEGER LDR	length of data record
CHARACTER*80 DATREC(MLDR)	data record

1.2.1.34. INQUIRE DEFAULT LOCATOR DEVICE DATA

```
SUBROUTINE GQDLC (WTYPE, DEVNO, N, MLDR, ERRIND, DPX, DPY,
                  OL, PET, EAREA, LDR, DATREC)

    INTEGER WTYPE                   workstation type
    INTEGER DEVNO                   logical input device number
    INTEGER N                       list element requested
    INTEGER MLDR                    maximum length of data record
    INTEGER ERRIND                  error indicator
    REAL DPY, DPY                   default init. locator position
    INTEGER OL                      number of av. prompt/echo types
    INTEGER PET                     Nth element of list of prompt/echo types
    REAL EAREA(4)                   default echo area
    INTEGER LDR                     length of data record
    CHARACTER*80 DATREC(MLDR)       data record
```

1.2.1.35. INQUIRE DEFAULT PICK DEVICE DATA

```
SUBROUTINE GQDPK (WTYPE, DEVNO, N, MLDR, ERRIND, OL, PET,
                  EAREA, LDR, DATREC)

    INTEGER WTYPE                   workstation type
    INTEGER DEVNO                   logical input device number
    INTEGER N                       list element requested
    INTEGER MLDR                    maximum length of data record
    INTEGER ERRIND                  error indicator
    INTEGER OL                      number of av. prompt/echo types
    INTEGER PET                     Nth element of list of prompt/echo types
    REAL EAREA(4)                   default echo area
    INTEGER LDR                     length of data record
    CHARACTER*80 DATREC(MLDR)       data record
```

1.2.1.36. INQUIRE DEFAULT STRING DEVICE DATA

```
SUBROUTINE GQDST (WTYPE, DEVNO, N, MLDR, ERRIND, MBUFF, OL,
                  PET, EAREA, BUFLEN, INIPOS, LDR, DATREC)

    INTEGER WTYPE                   workstation type
    INTEGER DEVNO                   logical input device number
    INTEGER N                       list element requested
    INTEGER MLDR                    maximum length of data record
    INTEGER ERRIND                  error indicator
    INTEGER MBUFF                   maximum string buffer size
    INTEGER OL                      number of av. prompt/echo types
    INTEGER PET                     Nth element of list of prompt/echo types
    REAL EAREA(4)                   default echo area
    INTEGER BUFLEN                  buffer length of string
    INTEGER INIPOS                  initial cursor position
    INTEGER LDR                     length of data record
    CHARACTER*80 DATREC(MLDR)       data record
```

1.2.1.37. INQUIRE DEFAULT STROKE DEVICE DATA

      SUBROUTINE GQDSK (WTYPE, DEVNO, N, MLDR, ERRIND, DBUFSK,
               OL, PET, EAREA, BUFLEN, LDR, DATREC)

INTEGER WTYPE	workstation type
INTEGER DEVNO	logical input device number
INTEGER N	list element requested
INTEGER MLDR	maximum length of data record
INTEGER ERRIND	error indicator
INTEGER DBUFSK	max. input buffer size
INTEGER OL	number of av. prompt/echo types
INTEGER PET	Nth element of list of prompt/echo types
REAL EAREA(4)	default echo area
INTEGER BUFLEN	buffer lenght for stroke
INTEGER LDR	length of data record
CHARACTER*80 DATREC(MLDR)	data record

1.2.1.38. INQUIRE DEFAULT VALUATOR DEVICE DATA

      SUBROUTINE GQDVL (WTYPE, DEVNO, N, MLDR, ERRIND, DVAL, OL,
               PET, EAREA, LOVAL, HIVAL, LDR, DATREC)

INTEGER WTYPE	workstation type
INTEGER DEVNO	logical input device number
INTEGER N	list element requested
INTEGER MLDR	maximum length of data record
INTEGER ERRIND	error indicator
REAL DVAL	default initial value
INTEGER OL	number of av. prompt/echo types
INTEGER PET	Nth element of list of prompt/echo types
REAL EAREA(4)	default echo area
REAL LOVAL, HIVAL	minimal and maximal value
INTEGER LDR	length of data record
CHARACTER*80 DATREC(MLDR)	data record

1.2.1.39. INQUIRE DYNAMIC MODIFICATION OF SEGMENT ATTRIBUTES

      SUBROUTINE GQDSGA (WTYPE, ERRIND, SGTR, VONOFF, VOFFON, HIGH,
                SGPR, ADD, SGDEL)

INTEGER WTYPE	workstation type
INTEGER ERRIND	error indicator
INTEGER SGTA	segment transf. changeable (IRG, IMM)
INTEGER VONOFF	visibility changeable from ON to OFF (IRG, IMM)
INTEGER VOFFON	visibility changeable from OFF to ON (IRG, IMM)
INTEGER HIGH	highlighting changeable (IRG, IMM)
INTEGER SGPR	segment priority changeable (IRG, IMM)
INTEGER ADD	adding primitives to open segment (IRG, IMM)
INTEGER SGDEL	segment deletion immediately visible (IRG, IMM)

1.2.1.40. INQUIRE FILL AREA FACILITIES

SUBROUTINE GQFAF (WTYPE, NI, NH, ERRIND, NIS, IS, NHS, HS, NPFAI)

INTEGER WTYPE	workstation type
INTEGER NI	list element of IS requested
INTEGER NH	list element of HS requested
INTEGER ERRIND	error indicator
INTEGER NIS	number fill interior styles
INTEGER IS	Nth element fill interiors
INTEGER NHS	number fill hatch styles
INTEGER HS	Nth element fill hatch styles
INTEGER NPFAI	number predefined fill indices

1.2.1.41. INQUIRE LEVEL OF GKS

SUBROUTINE GQLVKS (ERRIND, LEVEL)

INTEGER ERRIND	error indicator
INTEGER LEVEL	level of GKS (LMA,LMB,LMC,etc)

1.2.1.42. INQUIRE LIST element OF AVAILABLE GENERALIZED DRAWING PRIMITIVES

SUBROUTINE GQEGDP (WTYPE, N, ERRIND, NGDP, GDPL)

INTEGER WTYPE	workstation type
INTEGER N	list element requested
INTEGER ERRIND	error indicator
INTEGER NDGP	number of av. gen. drawing primitives
INTEGER GDPL	Nth element of list of GDP identifiers

1.2.1.43. INQUIRE LIST element OF COLOR INDICES

SUBROUTINE GQCI (WKID, N, ERRIND, OL, COLIND)

INTEGER WKID	workstation identifier
INTEGER N	list element requested
INTEGER ERRIND	error indicator
INTEGER OL	number of color table entries
INTEGER COLIND	Nth element of color indices

1.2.1.44. INQUIRE LOCATOR DEVICE STATE

```
            SUBROUTINE GQLCS (WKID, LCDNR, TYPE, MLDR, ERRIND, MODE, ESW,
                             ITNR, ILPX, ILPY, PET, EAREA, LDR, DATREC)

            INTEGER WKID                   workstation identifier
            INTEGER LCNDR                  locator device number
            INTEGER TYPE                   type of returned values
            INTEGER MLDR                   maximum length of data record
            INTEGER ERRIND                 error indicator
            INTEGER MODE                   operating mode
            INTEGER ESW                    echo switch (no echo, echo)
            INTEGER ITNR                   initial transformation number
            REAL ILPX, ILPY                initial locator position
            INTEGER PET                    prompt/echo type
            REAL EAREA (4)                 echo area
            INTEGER LDR                    length of data record
            CHARACTER*80 DATREC(MLDR)      data record
```

1.2.1.45. INQUIRE MAXIMUM DISPLAY SURFACE SIZE

```
            SUBROUTINE GQMDS (WTYPE, ERRIND, DCUNIT, RX, RY, LX, LY)

            INTEGER WTYPE                  workstation type
            INTEGER ERRIND                 error indicator
            INTEGER DCUNIT                 device coordinates flag
            REAL RX, RY                    maximum display surface size
            INTEGER LX, LY                 maximum display surface size
```

1.2.1.46. INQUIRE NAME OF OPEN SEGMENT

```
            SUBROUTINE GQOPSG (ERRIND, SEGNAM)

            INTEGER ERRIND                 error indicator
            INTEGER SEGNAM                 name of open segment
```

1.2.1.47. INQUIRE NORMALIZATION TRANSFORMATION

```
            SUBROUTINE GQNT (NTNR, ERRIND, WINDOW, VIEWPT)

            INTEGER NTNR                   norm. transformation number
            INTEGER ERRIND                 error indicator
            REAL WINDOW (4)                window limits in WC
            REAL VIEWPT (4)                viewport limits in NDC
```

1.2.1.48. INQUIRE NUMBER OF AVAILABLE LOGICAL INPUT DEVICES

        SUBROUTINE GQALI (WTYPE, ERRIND, NLCD, NSKD, NVLD, NCHD, NPCD, NSTD)

        INTEGER WTYPE   workstation type
        INTEGER ERRIND   error indicator
        INTEGER NLCD   number of locator devices
        INTEGER NSKD   number of stroke devices
        INTEGER NVLD   number of valuator devices
        INTEGER NCHD   number of choice devices
        INTEGER NPCD   number of pick devices
        INTEGER NSTD   number of string devices

1.2.1.49. INQUIRE NUMBER OF SEGMENT PRIORITES SUPPORTED

        SUBROUTINE GQSGP (WTYPE, ERRIND, NSG)

        INTEGER WTYPE   workstation type
        INTEGER ERRIND   error indicator
        INTEGER NSG   number of priorities supported

1.2.1.50. INQUIRE PICK DEVICE STATE

        SUBROUTINE GQPKS (WKID, PCDNR, TYPE, MLDR, ERRIND, MODE, ESW, ISTAT,
                   ISGNA, IPCID, PET, EAREA, LDR, DATREC)

        INTEGER WKID   workstation identifier
        INTEGER PCDNR   pick device number
        INTEGER TYPE   type of returned values
        INTEGER MLDR   maximum length of data record
        INTEGER ERRIND   error indicator
        INTEGER MODE   operating mode
        INTEGER ESW   echo switch
        INTEGER ISTAT   initial status
        INTEGER ISGNA   initial segment
        INTEGER IPCID   initial pick identifier
        INTEGER PET   prompt/echo type
        REAL EAREA (4)   echo area
        INTEGER LDR   length of data record
        CHARACTER*80 DATREC(MLDR)   data record

1.2.1.51. INQUIRE POLYLINE FACILITIES

        SUBROUTINE GQPLF (WTYPE, N, ERRIND, NLT, LT, NLW, NOMLW, RLWMIN,
                   RLWMAX, NPPLI)

        INTEGER WTYPE   workstation type
        INTEGER N   list element requested
        INTEGER ERRIND   error indicator
        INTEGER NLT   number of linetypes
        INTEGER LT   Nth element of linetypes
        INTEGER NLW   number of linewidths

```
REAL NOMLW                      nominal linewidth
REAL RLWMIN, RLWMAX             range of linewidths
INTEGER NPPLI                   number predefined polyline indices
```

1.2.1.52. INQUIRE POLYMARKER FACILITIES

```
SUBROUTINE GQPMF (WTYPE, N, ERRIND, NMT, MT, NMS, NOMMS, RMSMIN,
                  RMSMAX, NPPMI)

INTEGER WTYPE                   workstation type
INTEGER N                       list element requested
INTEGER ERRIND                  error indicator
INTEGER NMT                     number of marker types
INTEGER MT                      Nth element of marker types
INTEGER NMS                     number of marker sizes
REAL NOMMS                      nominal marker size
REAL RMSMIN, RMSMAX             range of marker sizes
INTEGER NPPMI                   number predefined polymarker indices
```

1.2.1.53. INQUIRE SEGMENT ATTRIBUTES

```
SUBROUTINE GQSGA (SGNA, ERRIND, SEGTM, VIS, HIGH, SGPR, DET)

INTEGER SGNA                    segment name
INTEGER ERRIND                  error indicator
REAL SEGTM(6)                   segment transformation matix
INTEGER VIS                     visibility
INTEGER HIGH                    highlighting
REAL SGPR                       segment priority
INTEGER DET                     detectability
```

1.2.1.54. INQUIRE SET member of SEGMENT NAMES ON WORKSTATION

```
SUBROUTINE GQSGWK (WKID, N, ERRIND, OL, SEGNAM)

INTEGER WKID                    workstation identifier
INTEGER N                       set member requested
INTEGER ERRIND                  error indicator
INTEGER OL                      number of segment names
INTEGER SEGNAM                  Nth member of segment names
```

1.2.1.55. INQUIRE SET member OF ASSOCIATED WORKSTATIONS

```
SUBROUTINE GQASWK (SGNA, N, ERRIND, OL, WKID)

INTEGER SGNA                    segment name
INTEGER N                       set member requested
INTEGER ERRIND                  error indicator
INTEGER OL                      number of associated workstations
INTEGER WKID                    Nth member of associated workstations
```

1.2.1.56. INQUIRE SET member OF SEGMENT NAMES IN USE

SUBROUTINE GQSGUS (N, ERRIND, OL, SEGNAM)

INTEGER N	set member requested
INTEGER ERRIND	error indicator
INTEGER OL	number of segment names in use
INTEGER SEGNAM	nth member of names in use

1.2.1.57. INQUIRE STRING DEVICE STATE

SUBROUTINE GQSTS (WKID, STDNR, MLDR, ERRIND, MODE, ESW, LOSTR,
                 ISTR, PET, EAREA, BUFLEN, INIPOS, LDR, DATREC)

INTEGER WKID	workstation identifier
INTEGER STDNR	string device number
INTEGER MLDR	maximum length of data record
INTEGER ERRIND	error indicator
INTEGER MODE	operating mode
INTEGER ESW	echo switch
INTEGER LOSTR	number of characters returned
CHARACTER *(*) ISTR	initial string
INTEGER PET	prompt/echo type
REAL EAREA (4)	echo area
INTEGER BUFLEN	buffer length of string
INTEGER INIPOS	initial cursor position
INTEGER LDR	length of data record
CHARACTER*80 DATREC(MLDR)	data record

1.2.1.58. INQUIRE STRING DEVICE STATE (FORTRAN 77 subset version)

SUBROUTINE GQSTSS (WKID, STDNR, MSTR, MLDR, ERRIND, MODE, ESW, LOSTR,
                  ISTR, PET, EAREA, BUFLEN, INIPOS, LDR, DATREC)

INTEGER WKID	workstation identifier
INTEGER STDNR	string device number
INTEGER MSTR	maximum number of characters in ISTR
INTEGER MLDR	maximum length of data record
INTEGER ERRIND	error indicator
INTEGER MODE	operating mode
INTEGER ESW	echo switch
INTEGER LOSTR	number of characters returned
CHARACTER *(*) ISTR	initial string
INTEGER PET	prompt/echo type
REAL EAREA (4)	echo area
INTEGER BUFLEN	buffer length of string
INTEGER INIPOS	initial cursor position
INTEGER LDR	length of data record
CHARACTER*80 DATREC(MLDR)	data record

1.2.1.59. INQUIRE STROKE DEVICE STATE

SUBROUTINE GQSKS (WKID, SKDNR, TYPE, N, MLDR, ERRIND, MODE, ESW, ITNR,
                  NP, PX, PY, PET, EAREA, BUFLEN, INIPOS, LDR, DATREC)

```
INTEGER WKID                    workstation identifier
INTEGER SKDNR                   stroke device number
INTEGER TYPE                    type of returned values (SET, REALIZED)
INTEGER N                       maximum number of points
INTEGER MLDR                    maximum length of data record
INTEGER ERRIND                  error indicator
INTEGER MODE                    operating mode
INTEGER ESW                     echo switch
INTEGER ITNR                    init. norm. transformatin number
INTEGER NP                      number of points
REAL PX(N), PY(N)               initial points in stroke (WC)
INTEGER PET                     prompt/echo type
REAL EAREA (4)                  echo area
INTEGER BUFLEN                  buffer length for stroke
INTEGER INIPOS                  editing position
INTEGER LDR                     length of data record
CHARACTER*80 DATREC(MLDR)       data record
```

1.2.1.60. INQUIRE TEXT EXTENT

SUBROUTINE GQTXX (WKID, PX, PY, STR, ERRIND, CPX, CPY, TXEXPX,
                  TXEXPY)

```
INTEGER WKID                    workstation identifier
REAL PX, PY                     text position in WC
CHARACTER *(*) STR              character string
INTEGER ERRIND                  error indicator
REAL CPX, CPY                   concatenation point in WC
REAL TXEXPX (4), TXEXPY (4)     text extent rectangle
```

1.2.1.61. INQUIRE TEXT EXTENT (FORTRAN 77 subset version)

SUBROUTINE GQTXXS (WKID, PX, PY, LSTR, STR, ERRIND, CPX, CPY,
                   TXEXPX, TXEXPY)

```
INTEGER WKID                    workstation identifier
REAL PX, PY                     text position in WC
INTGER LSTR                     length of string (in characters)
CHARACTER *(*) STR              character string
INTEGER ERRIND                  error indicator
REAL CPX, CPY                   concatenation point in WC
REAL TXEXPX (4), TXEXPY (4)     text extent rectangle
```

1.2.1.62. INQUIRE TEXT FACILITIES

SUBROUTINE GQTXF (WTYPE, N, ERRIND, NFPP, FONT, PREC, NCHH, MINCHH,
                  MAXCHH, NCHX, MINCHX, MAXCHX, NPTXI)

INTEGER WTYPE	workstation type
INTEGER N	list element requested
INTEGER ERRIND	error indicator
INTEGER NFPP	number of text font and precision pairs
INTEGER FONT	Nth element of fonts
INTEGER PREC	Nth element of text precisions
INTEGER NCHH	number of available character heights
REAL MINCHH	minimum character height (DC)
REAL MAXCHH	maximum character height (DC)
INTEGER NCHX	number of character expansion factors
REAL MINCHX	minimum character expansion factor
REAL MAXCHX	maximum character expansion factor
INTEGER NPTXI	number of predefined text indices

1.2.1.63. INQUIRE VALUATOR DEVICE STATE

SUBROUTINE GQVLS (WKID, VLDNR, MLDR, ERRIND, MODE, ESW, IVAL, PET,
                  EAREA, LOVAL, HIVAL, LDR, DATREC)

INTEGER WKID	workstation identifier
INTEGER VLDNR	valuator device number
INTEGER MLDR	maximum length of data record
INTEGER ERRIND	error indicator
INTEGER MODE	operating mode
INTEGER ESW	echo switch
REAL IVAL	initial value
INTEGER PET	prompt/echo type
REAL EAREA (4)	echo area
REAL LOVAL, HIVAL	minimum and maximum value
INTEGER LDR	length of data record
CHARACTER*80 DATREC(MLDR)	data record

1.2.1.64. INQUIRE WORKSTATION CONNECTION AND TYPE

SUBROUTINE GQWKC (WKID, ERRIND, CONID, WTYPE)

INTEGER WKID	workstation identifier
INTEGER ERRIND	error indicator
INTEGER CONID	connection identifier
INTEGER WTYPE	workstation type

1.2.1.65. INQUIRE WORKSTATION TRANSFORMATION

```
SUBROUTINE GQWKT (WKID, ERRIND, TUS, RWINDO, CWINDO, RVIEWP, CVIEWP)

INTEGER WKID                    workstation identifier
INTEGER ERRIND                  error indicator
INTEGER TUS                     workstation update state
REAL RWINDO (4)                 requested workstation window
REAL CWINDO (4)                 current workstation window
REAL RVIEWP (4)                 requested workstation viewport
REAL CVIEWP (4)                 current workstation viewport
```

1.2.1.66. INSERT SEGMENT

```
SUBROUTINE GINSG (SGNA, M)

INTEGER WKID                    workstation identifier
REAL M (6)                      transformation matrix
```

1.2.1.67. OPEN GSS

```
SUBROUTINE GSOPN (NTYPES, WNAMES, WTYPES, VERNUM)

INTEGER NTYPES                  number of workstation types
CHARACTER *(*) WNAMES           workstation logical device names to use
             (single array of semicolon terminated devices names,
              binding interface will have to covert semicolons to
              nulls for the C function interface)
INTEGER WTYPES(NTYPES)          workstation types mapped to logical
                                device name
REAL VERNUM                     version number
```

1.2.1.68. OPEN GSS (FORTRAN 77 subset version)

```
SUBROUTINE GSOPNS (NTYPES, LNAMES, WNAMES, WTYPES, VERNUM)

INTEGER NTYPES                  number of workstation types
INTEGER LNAMES                  length of WNAMES array (in characters)
CHARACTER*(*) WNAMES            workstation logical device names to use
INTEGER WTYPES(NTYPES)          workstation types mapped to logical
                                device name
REAL VERNUM                     version number
```

1.2.1.69. OPEN GKS

```
SUBROUTINE GOPKS (ERRFIL, SIZE)

INTEGER ERRRIL                  error message file (a logical unit number
                                from a standard FORTRAN OPEN statement. It
                                is assumed that the application has opened
                                an error file for use by Kernel System).
INTEGER SIZE                    size of buffer area
```

1.2.1.70. OPEN WORKSTATION

SUBROUTINE GOPWK (WKID, CONID, WTYPE)

INTEGER WKID	workstation identifier
INTEGER CONID	connection identifier
INTEGER WTYPE	workstation type

1.2.1.71. PACK DATA RECORD

SUBROUTINE GPREC (IL, IA, RL, RA, SL, LSTR, STR, MLDR, DATREC)

INTEGER IL	number of integer entries >= 0
INTEGER IA (*)	array containing integer entries
REAL RL	number of real entries >= 0
REAL RA (*)	array containing real entries
INTEGER SL	number of character entries >=0
INTEGER LSTR (*)	size of each individual entry, in characters
CHARACTER *(*) STR(*)	character entries
INTEGER MLDR	maximum length of data record
CHARACTER*80 DATREC(MLDR)	resulting data record

1.2.1.72. POLYLINE

SUBROUTINE GPL (N, PX, PY)

INTEGER N	number of points
REAL PX (N), PY (N)	coordinates of points in WC

1.2.1.73. POLYMARKER

SUBROUTINE GPM (N, PX, PY)

INTEGER N	number of points
REAL PX (N), PY (N)	coordinates of points in WC

1.2.1.74. REDRAW ALL SEGMENTS ON WORKSTATION

SUBROUTINE GRSGWK (WKID)

INTEGER WKID	workstation identifier

1.2.1.75. RENAME SEGMENT

SUBROUTINE GRENSG (OLD, NEW)

INTEGER OLD	old segment name
INTEGER NEW	new segment name

1.2.1.76. REQUEST CHOICE

SUBROUTINE GRQCH (WKID, CHDNR, STAT, CHNR)

INTEGER WKID	workstation identifier
INTEGER CHDNR	choice device number
INTEGER STAT	status (none, ok)
INTEGER CHNR	choice number

1.2.1.77. REQUEST LOCATOR

SUBROUTINE GRQLC (WKID, LCDNR, STAT, TNR, PX, PY)

INTEGER WKID	workstation identifier
INTEGER LCDNR	locator device number
INTEGER STAT	status (none, ok)
INTEGER TNR	normalization transformation number
REAL PX, PY	locator position

1.2.1.78. REQUEST PICK

SUBROUTINE GRQPK (WKID, PKDNR, STAT, SGNA, PKID)

INTEGER WKID	workstation identifier
INTEGER PKDNR	pick device number
INTEGER STAT	status (none, ok)
INTEGER SGNA	segment name
INTEGER PKID	pick identifier

1.2.1.79. REQUEST STRING

SUBROUTINE GRQST (WKID, STDNR, STAT, LOSTR, STR)

INTEGER WKID	workstation identifier
INTEGER STDNR	string device number
INTEGER STAT	status (none, ok)
INTEGER LOSTR	length of string
CHARACTER*(*) STR	character string

1.2.1.80. REQUEST STRING (FORTRAN 77 subset version)

SUBROUTINE GRQSTS (WKID, STDNR, MSTR, STAT, LOSTR, STR)

INTEGER WKID	workstation identifier
INTEGER STDNR	string device number
INTEGER MSTR	maximum number of characters in STR
INTEGER STAT	status (none, ok)
INTEGER LOSTR	length of string
CHARACTER*(*) STR	character string

1.2.1.81. REQUEST STROKE

SUBROUTINE GRQSK (WKID, SKDNR, N, STAT, TNR, NP, PX, PY)

INTEGER WKID	workstation identifier
INTEGER SKDNR	stroke device number
INTEGER N	maximum number of points
INTEGER STAT	status (none, ok)
INTEGER TNR	normalization transformation number
INTEGER NP	number of points
REAL PX(N), PY(N)	points in stroke

1.2.1.82. REQUEST VALUATOR

SUBROUTINE GRQVL (WKID, VLDNR, STAT, VAL)

INTEGER WKID	workstation identifier
INTEGER VLDNR	valuator device number
INTEGER STAT	status (none, ok)
REAL VAL	value

1.2.1.83. SAMPLE CHOICE

SUBROUTINE GSMCH (WKID, CHDNR, CHNR)

INTEGER WKID	workstation identifier
INTEGER CHDNR	choice device number
INTEGER CHNR	choice number

1.2.1.84. SAMPLE LOCATOR

SUBROUTINE GSMLC (WKID, LCDNR, TNR, PX, PY)

INTEGER WKID	workstation identifier
INTEGER LCDNR	locator device number
INTEGER TNR	normalization transformation number
REAL PX, PY	locator position

1.2.1.85. SAMPLE PICK

SUBROUTINE GSMPK (WKID, PKDNR, SGNA, PKID)

INTEGER WKID	workstation identifier
INTEGER PKDNR	pick device number
INTEGER SGNA	segment name
INTEGER PKID	pick identifier

1.2.1.86. SAMPLE STRING

    SUBROUTINE GSMST (WKID, STDNR, LOSTR, STR)

        INTEGER WKID   workstation identifier
        INTEGER STDNR   string device number
        INTEGER LOSTR   length of string
        CHARACTER*(*) STR   character string

1.2.1.87. SAMPLE STRING (FORTRAN 77 subset version)

    SUBROUTINE GSMSTS (WKID, STDNR, MSTR, LOSTR, STR)

        INTEGER WKID   workstation identifier
        INTEGER STDNR   string device number
        INTEGER MSTR   maximum number of characters in STR
        INTEGER LOSTR   length of string
        CHARACTER*(*) STR   character string

1.2.1.88. SAMPLE STROKE SAMPLE STROKE

    SUBROUTINE GSQSK (WKID, SKDNR, N, TNR, NP, PX, PY)

        INTEGER WKID   workstation identifier
        INTEGER SKDNR   stroke device number
        INTEGER N   maximum number of points
        INTEGER TNR   normalization transformation number
        INTEGER NP   number of points
        REAL PX(N), PY(N)   points in stroke

1.2.1.89. SAMPLE VALUATOR

    SUBROUTINE GSMVL (WKID, VLDNR, VAL)

        INTEGER WKID   workstation identifier
        INTEGER VLDNR   valuator device number
        REAL VAL   value

1.2.1.90. SELECT NORMALIZATION TRANSFORMATION

    SUBROUTINE GSELNT (TNR)

        INTEGER TNR   normalization transformation number

1.2.1.91. SET CHARACTER HEIGHT

    SUBROUTINE GSCHH (CHH)

        REAL CHH   character height

1.2.1.92. SET CHARACTER UP VECTOR

    SUBROUTINE GSCHUP (CHUX, CHUY)

    REAL CHUX, CHUY   character up vector

1.2.1.93. SET CHOICE MODE

    SUBROUTINE GSCHM (WKID, IDNR, MODE, ESW)

    INTEGER WKID   workstation identifier
    INTEGER IDNR   choice device number
    INTEGER MODE   operating mode (request, sample, event)
    INTEGER ESW   echo switch (noecho, echo)

1.2.1.94. SET CLIPPING INDICATOR

    SUBROUTINE GSCLIP (CLSW)

    INTEGER CLSW   clipping indicator (noclip, clip)

1.2.1.95. SET COLOR REPRESENTATION

    SUBROUTINE GSCR (WKID, CI, CR, CG, CB)

    INTEGER WKID   workstation identifier
    INTEGER CI   color index
    REAL CR, CG, CB   red/green/blue intensities

1.2.1.96. SET DETECTABILITY

    SUBROUTINE GSDTEC (SGNA, DET)

    INTEGER SGNA   segment name
    INTEGER DET   detectability (undetect, detect)

1.2.1.97. SET FILL AREA COLOR INDEX

    SUBROUTINE GSFACI (COLI)

    INTEGER COLI   color index

1.2.1.98. SET FILL AREA INTERIOR STYLE

    SUBROUTINE GSFAIS (INTS)

    INTEGER INTS   fill area interior style

1.2.1.99. SET FILL AREA STYLE INDEX

    SUBROUTINE GSFASI (STYLI)

    INTEGER STYLI   fill area style index

1.2.1.100. SET HIGHLIGHTING

    SUBROUTINE GSHLIT (SGNA, HIL)

    INTEGER SGNA   segment name
    INTEGER HIL   highlighting (norm, highlight)

1.2.1.101. SET LOCATOR MODE

    SUBROUTINE GSLCM (WKID, IDNR, MODE, ESW)

    INTEGER WKID   workstation identifier
    INTEGER IDNR   locator device number
    INTEGER MODE   operating mode (request, sample, event)
    INTEGER ESW   echo switch (noecho, echo)

1.2.1.102. SET PICK IDENTIFIER

    SUBROUTINE GSPKID (PCID)

    INTEGER PCID   pick identifier

1.2.1.103. SET PICK MODE

    SUBROUTINE GSPKM (WKID, IDNR, MODE, ESW)

    INTEGER WKID   workstation identifier
    INTEGER IDNR   pick device number
    INTEGER MODE   operating mode (request, sample, event)
    INTEGER ESW   echo switch (noecho, echo)

1.2.1.104. SET POLYLINE COLOR INDEX

    SUBROUTINE GSPLCI (COLI)

    INTEGER COLI   color index

1.2.1.105. SET POLYLINE TYPE

    SUBROUTINE GSLN (LTYPE)

    INTEGER LTYPE   linetype

1.2.1.106. SET POLYLINE WIDTH SCALE FACTOR

    SUBROUTINE GSLWSC (LWIDTH)

    REAL LWIDTH   linewidth scale factor

1.2.1.107. SET POLYMARKER COLOR INDEX

    SUBROUTINE GSPMCI (COLI)

    INTEGER COLI   color index

1.2.1.108. SET POLYMARKER HEIGHT SCALE FACTOR

    SUBROUTINE GSMKSC (MSZSF)

    REAL MSZSF   polymarker height scale factor

1.2.1.109. SET POLYMARKER TYPE

    SUBROUTINE GSMK (MTYPE)

    INTEGER MTYPE   marker type

1.2.1.110. SET SEGMENT PRIORITY

    SUBROUTINE GSSGP (SGNA, PRIOR)

    INTEGER SGNA   segment name
    REAL PRIOR   priority

1.2.1.111. SET SEGMENT TRANSFORMATION

    SUBROUTINE GSSGT (SGNA, M)

    INTEGER SGNA   segment name
    REAL M (6)   segment image transformation matrix

1.2.1.112. SET STRING MODE

    SUBROUTINE GSSTM (WKID, IDNR, MODE, ESW)

    INTEGER WKID   workstation identifier
    INTEGER IDNR   string device number
    INTEGER MODE   operating mode (request, sample, event)
    INTEGER ESW   echo switch (noecho, echo)

1.2.1.113. SET STROKE MODE

    SUBROUTINE GSSKM (WKID, IDNR, MODE, ESW)

    INTEGER WKID   workstation identifier
    INTEGER IDNR   stroke device number
    INTEGER MODE   operating mode (request, sample, event)
    INTEGER ESW   echo switch (noecho, echo)

1.2.1.114. SET TEXT ALIGNMENT

    SUBROUTINE GSTXAL (TXALH, TXALV)

    INTEGER TXALH   text alignment horizontal
    INTEGER TXALV   text alignment vertical

1.2.1.115. SET TEXT COLOR INDEX

    SUBROUTINE GSTXCI (COLI)

    INTEGER COLI   color index

1.2.1.116. SET TEXT FONT AND PRECISION

    SUBROUTINE GSTXFP (FONT,PREC)

    INTEGER FONT   text font
    INTEGER PREC   text precision

1.2.1.117. SET VALUATOR MODE

    SUBROUTINE GSVLM (WKID, IDNR, MODE, ESW)

    INTEGER WKID   workstation identifier
    INTEGER IDNR   valuator device number
    INTEGER MODE   operating mode (request, sample, event)
    INTEGER ESW   echo switch (noecho, echo)

1.2.1.118. SET VIEWPORT

    SUBROUTINE GSVP (TNR, XMIN, XMAX, YMIN, YMAX)

    INTEGER TNR   transformation number
    REAL XMIN, XMAX, YMIN, YMAX   viewport limits in NDC

1.2.1.119. SET VIEWPORT INPUT PRIORITY

   SUBROUTINE GSVPIP (TNR, RTNR, RELPRI)

   INTEGER TNR   transformation number
   INTEGER RTNR   reference transformation number
   INTEGER RELPRI   relative priority

1.2.1.120. SET VISIBILITY

   SUBROUTINE GSVIS (SGNA, VIS)

   INTEGER SGNA   segment name
   INTEGER VIS   visibility (no, yes)

1.2.1.121. SET WINDOW

   SUBROUTINE GSWN (TNR, XMIN, XMAX, YMIN, YMAX)

   INTEGER TNR   transformation number
   REAL XMIN, XMAX, YMIN, YMAX   window limits in WC

1.2.1.122. SET WORKSTATION VIEWPORT

   SUBROUTINE GSWKVP (WKID, XMIN, XMAX, YMIN, YMAX)

   INTEGER WKID   workstation identifier
   REAL XMIN, XMAX, YMIN, YMAX   workstation viewport limits in DC

1.2.1.123. SET WORKSTATION WINDOW

   SUBROUTINE GSWKWN (WKID, XMIN, XMAX, YMIN, YMAX)

   INTEGER WKID   workstation identifier
   REAL XMIN, XMAX, YMIN, YMAX   workstation window limits in NDC

1.2.1.124. TEXT

   SUBROUTINE GTX (PX, PY, CHARS)

   REAL PX, PY   text position of string in WC
   CHARACTER*(*) CHARS   character string

1.2.1.125. TEXT (FORTRAN 77 subset version)

```
SUBROUTINE GTXS (PX, PY, LSTR, CHARS)

REAL PX, PY                       text position of string in WC
INTEGER LSTR                      length of string (in characters)
CHARACTER*(*) CHARS               character string
```

1.2.1.126. UNPACK DATA RECORD

```
SUBROUTINE GUREC (LDR, DATREC, IIL, IRL, ISTR, MSTR,
                  IL, IA, RL, RA, SL, LSTR, STR)

INTEGER LDR                       length of data record
CHARACTER*80 DATREC(LDR)          data record
INTEGER IIL                       maximum length of integer array
INTEGER IRL                       maximum length of real array
INTEGER ISTR                      maximum length of character string
INTEGER MSTR                      maximum size of individual
                                  character strings
INTEGER IL                        number of integer entries >= 0
INTEGER IA (IL)                   array containing integer entries
REAL RL                           number of real entries >= 0
REAL RA (RL)                      array containing real entries
INTEGER SL                        number of character entries >= 0
INTEGER LSTR (*)                  size of each individual entry,
                                  in characters
CHARACTER *(*) STR(*)             character entries
```

1.2.1.127. UPDATE WORKSTATION

```
SUBROUTINE GUWK (WKID, REGFL)

INTEGER WKID                      workstation identifier
INTEGER REGFL                     regeneration flag
```

Standardization of Animation Commands for Computer Animation System

Hidemaru Sato
Nippon Univac Information Systems Kaisha, Ltd.
17-22, Akasaka 2-chome, Minato-ku
Tokyo 107, Japan

ABSTRACT

The ideal computer animation system should be designed for artists. Designing the system, it is very important for system designer to understand requirements or needs from artists, and to make the system more suitable for them. This paper defines three necessary effects for computer assisted animation, and proposes to standardize the recommended animation commands and parameters. Also, command levels separated by functional features are presented, in order to clarify the functional ability of the system. This standardization trial of animation commands will surely be one guide or step for future system design.

1. BACKGROUNDS

Computer animation forms one field of computer graphics just as same as CAD/CAM and Business graphics. In the latest few years, computer animation techniques on both two dimensional (2D) and three dimensional (3D) have made a remarkable progress. Not to speak of in Europe and United States, in Japan some computer animation systems have already been introduced for commercial use. But people still can not avoid thinking that computer animation is extremely expensive. It maybe comes from two problems as follows:

    1) Problems from introducers

        *Powerful processor is essential in order to deal with a lot of picture data
        *Intelligent graphic display terminal which has high resolution and can show many colors at the same time is necessary
        *Usually needs expensive recording device like high resolution film recorder or professional video tape recorder

    2) Problems from users

        *In the latest few years, some computer generated pictures by using sofisticated algorithms like

ray-tracing and fractal, are remarkably attracted by people. It makes an impression on artists that computer animation needs not only a lot of time and money, but also high-technique.
*It is very difficult for artists to find suitable knowledge or information, if they want to try to use computer animation system.

Characteristics of computer animation is very different from that of CAD/CAM and Business graphics. The most notable difference is that people who operate system should be artists, not computer engineers.

So the ideal computer animation system should be designed for artists. For them, the system is nothing but their tool. They are not interested in how or what computer works. They are interested in how easy they can use it, also how effectively they can exhibit their artistic ability. Moreover, they usually want to try to use different systems, after they finish their work by using one system.

Since different systems have their own different hardwares, it is natural that each system has each operation method. But, if it is possible for every system to be designed by almost the same way for animation commands at least, which is the most creative part for artists, computer animation will be accepted more smoothly by artists.

This paper defines three necessary effects for computer assisted animation, and proposes to standardize recommended animation commands and their parameters. Also, three functional levels of animation commands are prepared in order to clarify guides for system design.

2. RECOMMENDED ANIMATION COMMANDS

2.1 Classification of Animation Effects

Before choosing necessary animation commands for computer animation system, we should consider about usual effects which are often used by artists. It is not easy to define completely essential animation effects, but conventional effects which are usually used by camera artists and graphic designers, are discussed in references (1),(4) and (7). Conventional camera effects(HOLD,PAN,TILT,ZOOM,SPIN,etc) and conventional graphic effects(distortions like twisting and stretching a picture, making it wave, etc) should be at least included in recommended animation commands, and these command names should be the same as far as possible, because artists are very accustomed to use conventional command names.

From this point of view, animation effects by computer can be devided into three classes according to its function.

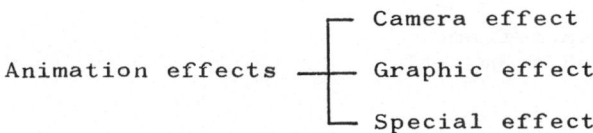

Camera effect means the effect which can only change a position or viewing direction of an original drawing without changing its shape. Graphic effect means the effect which alters only its shape by adding some physical force. And, special effect includes any effects except camera and graphic effects, for example, inbetweening effect between two different drawings and film processing effect such as fade in/out, are categorized in this area.

It is not necessary that computer animation system should have all three effects. Only camera effects can sufficiently produce a kind of graphic animation, but more complicated or high level animation will be possible by adding graphic and special effects. From functional point of view, animation commands are separated by three levels shown in Table 1.

Table 1. Levels of Animation Commands

	Camera effect	Graphic effect	Special effect
LEVEL 1	○	X	X
LEVEL 2	○	○	X
LEVEL 3	○	○	○

2.2 Command <u>LEVEL 1</u>

Animation commands in LEVEL 1 produce camera effect. Several commands are recommended.

1) **HOLD**

    Effect: holds a drawing with no action between start and end frame

    Parameters: start frame
                   end frame

2) **PAN**

    Effect: moves a drawing horizontally between start and end frame

    Parameters: start frame
                   end frame
                   distance D (right+, left-)

3) **TILT**

    Effect: moves a drawing vertically between start and end frame

    Parameters: start frame
                   end frame
                   distance D (up+, down-)

4) **ZOOM**

    Effect: zooms a drawing big or small between start and ebd frame

    Parameters: start frame
                   end frame
                   zooming size at start frame (%)
                   zooming size at end frame (%)
                   coordinates of vanishing point (VX,VY)

5) **SPIN**

    Effect: spins a drawing around between start and end frame

    Parameters: start frame
                   end frame
                   spin angle θ (clockwise+)
                   coordinates of spin center (CX,CY)

6) **PATH**

    Effect: makes a drawing move along path-line between start frame and end frame

        Parameters: start frame
                     end frame
                     path-line information
                     bounds for moving D
                     coordinates of reference position (X,Y)

7) <u>TRACK</u>

   Effect: moves a drawing towards perspective direction
            between start and end frame

   Parameters: start frame
                end frame
                distance D (near+, far-)
                coordinates of camera(eye) position (VX,VY)
                camera(eye) angle θ (deg)

8) <u>FLIP</u>

   Effect: spins a drawing towards perspective direction
            between start and end frame

   Parameters: start frame
                end frame
                direction of spin-axis (H/V)
                position of spin-axis (Y/X)
                spin angle θ1 (deg)
                coordinates of camera(eye) position (VX,VY)
                camera(eye) angle θ2 (deg)

2.3 Command <u>LEVEL 2</u>

Animation commands in LEVEL 2 produce both camera effect
and graphic effect. Several graphic effects are added to
LEVEL 1. These are as follows:

9) <u>PINCH</u>

   Effect: pinches and stretches a drawing like a piece
            of rubber between start and end frame

   Parameters: start frame
                end frame
                direction of pinch-axis (H/V)
                position of pinch-axis (X1/Y1)
                position of no-pinch-axis (X2/Y2)
                pinch amount (%)

10) <u>WAVE</u>

    Effect: makes a wave travel through a drawing between

           start and end frame

Parameters: start frame
              end frame
              direction of wave-axis (H/V)
              wavelength L
              wavesize H
              wave-cycle θ (deg)
              reference position (X,Y)

11) <u>WOBBLE</u>

   Effect: makes a drawing wobble like a bag of jelly
              between start and end frame

   Parameters: start frame
                 end frame
                 coordinates of wobble center (CX,CY)
                 wobble-size (%)
                 wobble-cycle θ (deg)

12) <u>TUMBLE</u>

   Effect: takes a flat drawing and wrap it around a
              cylinder between start and end frame

   Parameters: start frame
                 end frame
                 direction of wrapping (H/V)
                 position of first handle (X1/Y1)
                 position of second handle (X2/Y2)
                 tipping distance D
                 spin angle θ (deg) (clockwise+)

13) <u>SPHERE</u>

   Effect: takes a flat drawing and wraps it around a
              sphere between start and end frame

   Parameters: start frame
                 end frame
                 position of left edge (X1)
                 position of right edge (X2)
                 position of bottom edge (Y1)
                 position of top edge (Y2)
                 spin angle θ (deg) (clockwise+)

14) <u>TWIST</u>

   Effect: twists a drawing into a spiral between start
              and end frame

Parameters: start frame
             end frame
             direction of twist-axis (H/V)
             position of twist-axis (Y/X)
             position of first handle (X1/Y1)
             position of second handle (X2/Y2)
             angle of first handle θ1 (deg)
             angle of second handle θ2 (deg)

15) **SQUASH**

　　Effect: makes a drawing squash-in and stretch-out between start and end frame

　　Parameters: start frame
                end frame
                direction of squash-axis (H/V)
                position of first handle (X1/Y1)
                position of second handle (X2/Y2)
                animation position of 1st handle (AX1/AY1)
                animation position of 2nd handle (AX2/AY2)

16) **FREAK**

　　Effect: makes the line of a drawing go wobbly and spiky between start and end frame

　　Parameters: start frame
                end frame
                maximum freak distance D
                frames between key positions
                points per freak

2.4 Command **LEVEL 3**

Animation commands in LEVEL 3 produce camera effect, graphic effect, and also special effect. A few recommended special effects are as follows: Examples are not everything, this effect depends on computer system.

17) **FADE**

　　Effect: makes a drawing fade in or fade out like an optical fade between start and end frame

　　Parameters: start frame
                end frame
                types of fade (in/out)

18) **INBETWEEN**

Effect: takes a drawing and changes it into another drawing between start and end frame

Parameters: start frame
end frame
a drawing to be changed
change amount (%)

19) **SKELETON**

Effect: changes a drawing with a basic skeleton by various key-skeletons between start and end frame

Parameters: start frame
end frame
key-skeletons at key-frames

3. SUMMARY

In chapter 2, three levels of animation commands are presented, and recommended commands and their parameters of each level are briefly explained. Command name is decided by the way which is easy to understand from artist's point of view. Also, distance(screen measure), degree and percent, are only used for the setting units of parameters except confusing.

Command levels separated by functional feature are very useful and helpful to design the animation software. All recommended commands and parameters described in chapter 2, are based on two dimensional processing. Basic idea of these can be applied to three dimensional extension.

Table 2 shows each functional feature of three levels. The relation between commands and their levels is summarized in Table 3.

With the recently rapid progress of IC technology, a cheap and efficient processor will be realized in the near future. If hardware prices are going down, the computer animation system is increasingly popularizeing among many artists.

We are still developing to make computer animation system better, with an important policy. It is that requirements and needs from artists should be accepted as many as possible in the system. The recommended animation commands described in this paper are decided and modeled by many pieces of advice from artists. In other words, it is no exaggeration to say that these commands are suggested and proposed by artists

We firmly believe that the standardization trial of animation commands will be one guide or step for future system design.

Table 2. Functional Features of Levels

Command Levels	Functional Features
LEVEL 1	*It includes camera effect which can only change a position or viewing direction from eye towards an original drawing, without changing its shape. *It is enough to create art and graphic animation. *Even personal computer will be possible to use, because there is no heavy mathematical calculation.
LEVEL 2	*It includes camera effect(LEVEL 1), and graphic effect which alters the shape of an original drawing by adding some physical force. *Artists can easily exhibit their artistic character, because the original drawing can have a movement on itself. *Application field reaches to educational animation, handmadelike animation, etc.
LEVEL 3	*It includes camera and graphic effects(LEVEL 2), and special effect. *It is possible to make high level art and graphic animation and character animation.

Table 3. Commands in each Levels

Command Level			Animation Commands
LEVEL3	LEVEL2	LEVEL1	HOLD PAN TILT ZOOM SPIN PATH TRACK FLIP
			PINCH WAVE WOBBLE TUMBLE SPHERE TWIST SQUASH FREAK
			FADE INBETWEEN SKELETON

4. ACKNOWLEDGEMENT

The author greatfully acknowledges the suggestions and advice of all members of Antics project at Nippon Univac Information Systems Kaisha, Ltd.

Thanks also go to Shigekazu Sakai for helpful suggestions.

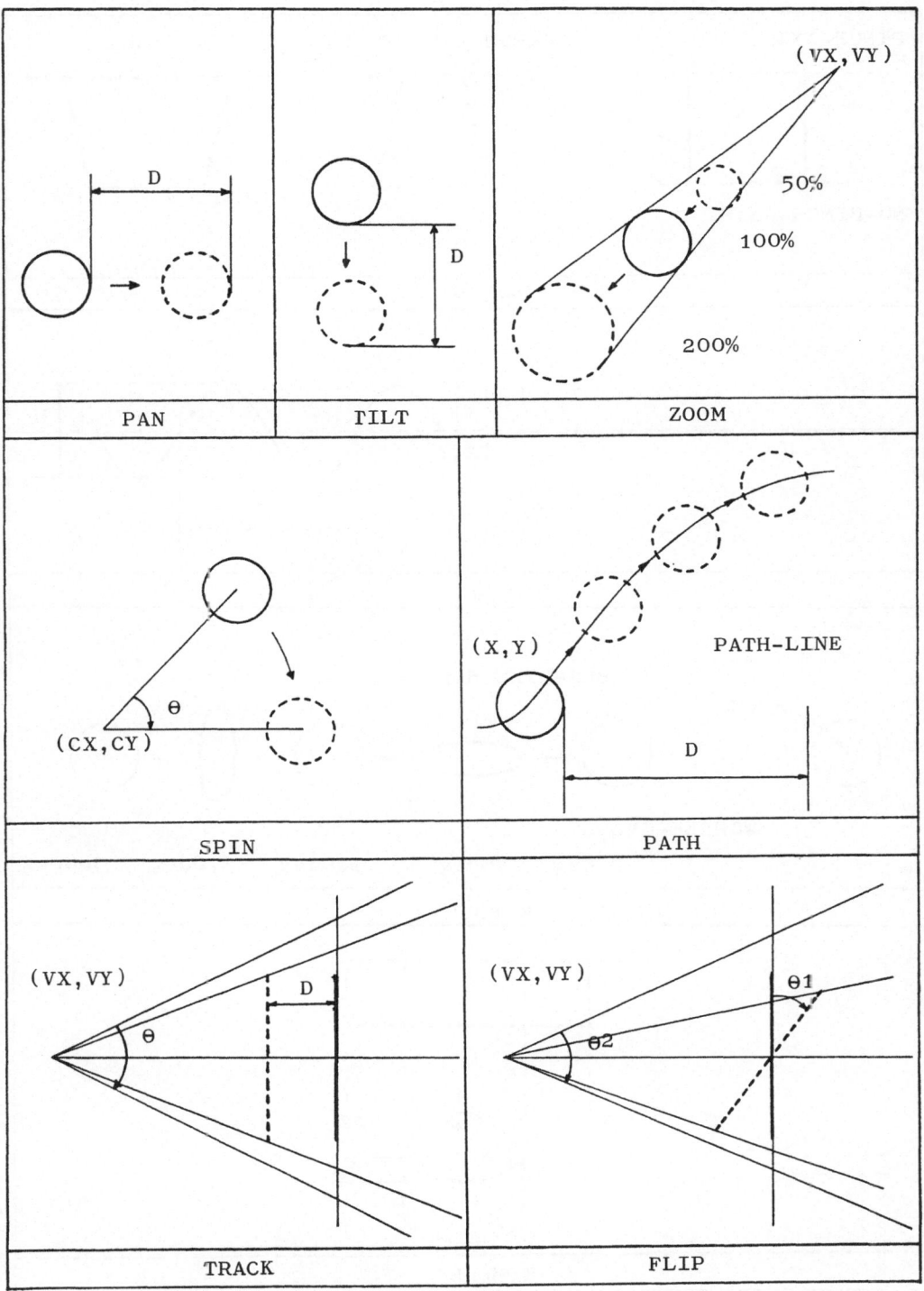

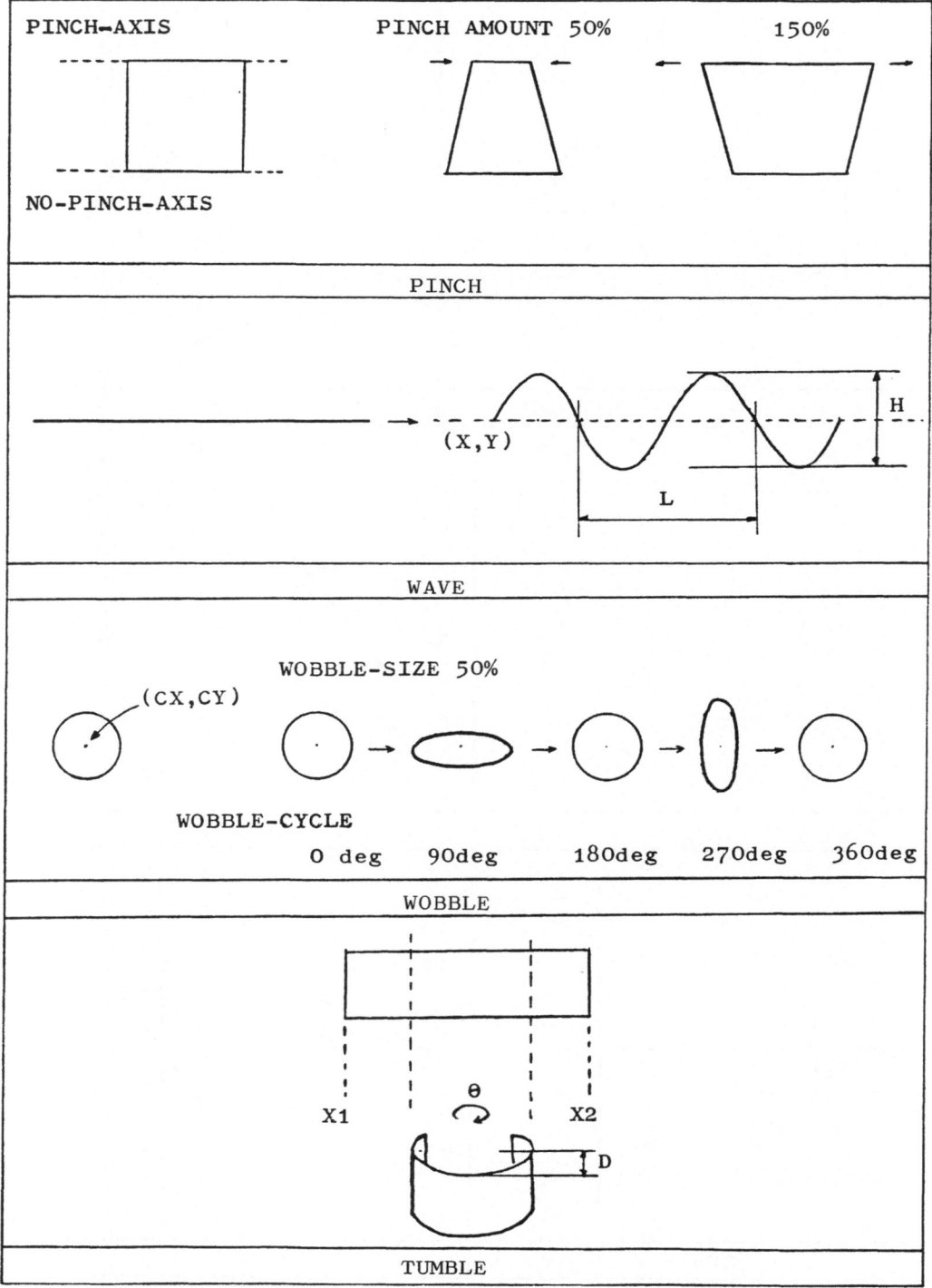

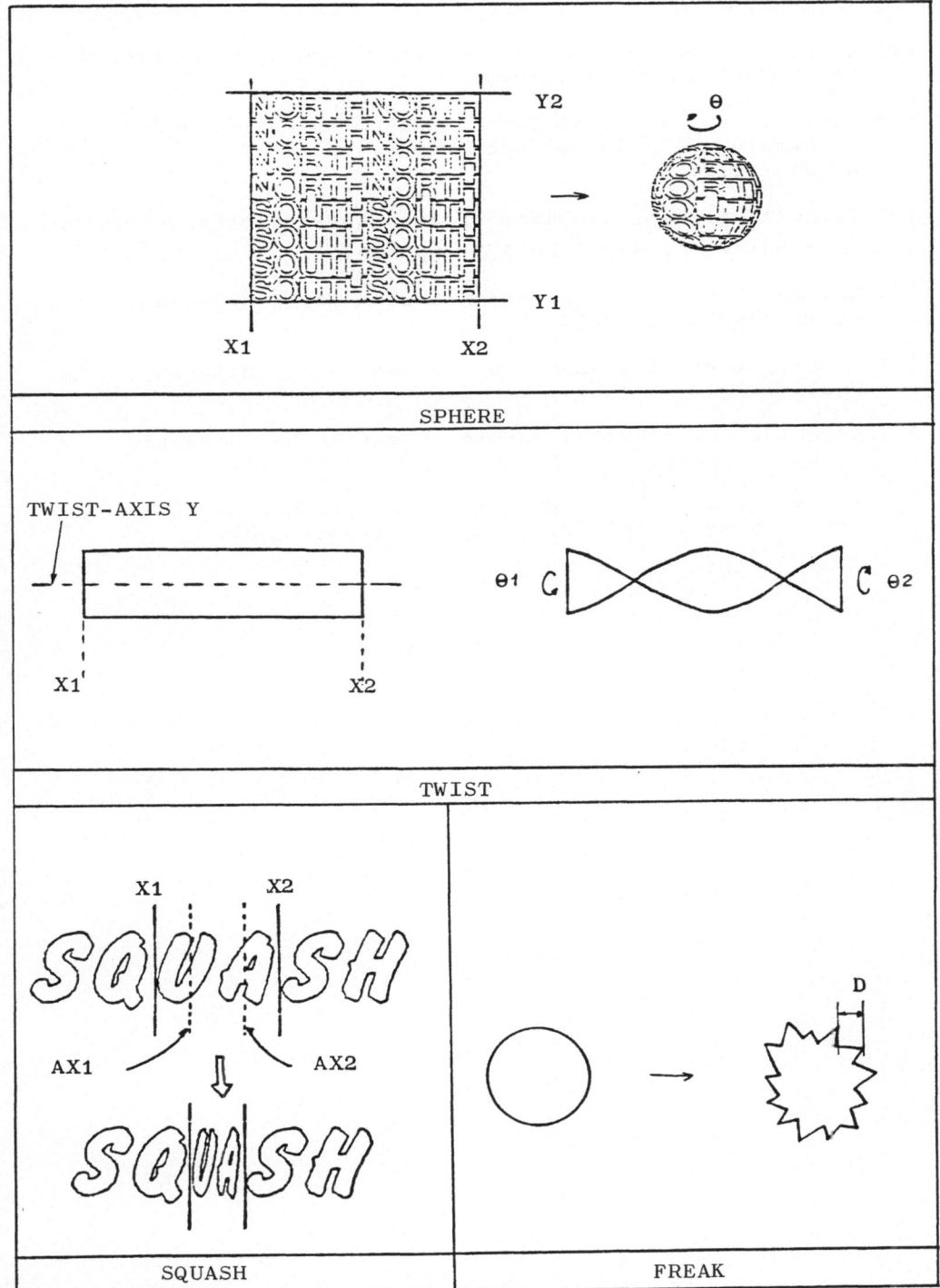

5. REFERENCES

(1) Agui, T., Nakajima, M. and Ohe, S., Computer Animation, Sanpo Publishing Co., 1983.

(2) Catmull, E., A system for computer generated movies, Proceedings ACM Annual Conference, pp422-431., August 1972.

(3) Catmull, E., The problems of computer-assisted animation, Proceedings of SIGGRAPH '79, pp348-353.

(4) Hayama, K. et al., Animation Lesson No.6, Bijutsu Publishing Co., 1983.

(5) Ikeda, H. et al., Animation Lesson No.4, Bijutsu Publishing Co., 1983.

(6) Kitching, A., ANTICS-graphic animation by computer, Comput Graphics, Vol.2, No.4, pp219-223, 1977.

(7) Kitching, A., ANTICS-from stone-age to steam-age, BKSTS Journal, Vol.62, No.8, pp394-404, 1980.

Author Index

The page numbers refer to the list of references provided by each contributor.

Abramatic, J.F.,
   Faugeras, O.D.
   343
Ackerman, W.B. 95
Adachi, T.,
   Kitazawa, H.,
   Nagatani, M.,
   Sudo, T. 285
Adams, J.A., see
   Rogers, D.F.
   73, 265
Agui, T.,
   Nakajima, M.,
   Ohe, S. 430
Akeo, M. 272
Aldefeld, B. 306
Anderson, D.M.
   236
Angell, I.O. 145
Arcelli, C.,
   Sanniti Di
   Baja, G. 342
Arnold, D.B. 306
Aucella, A.F., see
   Smith, S.L.
   183
Auger, B. 306
Auger, B.,
   Butlin, G.,
   Hubbold, R.J.
   306

Badler, N.I., see
   Platt, S.M.
   164
Baer, A.,
   Eastman, C.,
   Henrion, M. 20
Barney, H., see
   Gruber, L.S.
   353
Baumgart, B.G.
   35, 58
Bazjanac, V. 306

Belliston, L., see
   Hanks, K. 237
Bernard, A.
   153, 236
Bergeron, R.D.,
   Bono, P.R.,
   Foley, J.D. 416
BIJI, A., see
   Swinson, P.S.G.
   307
Blinn, J.F.
   164, 265
Blinn, J.F.,
   Newell, M.E.
   113, 265
Boehm, W. 164
Bono, P.R.,
   Encarnacao, J.L.,
   Hopgood, F.R.A.,
   ten Hagen P.J.W.
   374, 416
Bono, P.R., see
   Bergeron, R.F.
   416
Bone, R.O., see
   Ocvirk, O.G.
   236, 237
Braid, I.C.,
   Hillyard, R.C.,
   Stroud, I.A.
   35, 58
Bui-Tuong, P.
   113, 265
Butlin, G., see
   Auger, B. 306

Candlish, J.B., see
   Svetkoff, D.J.
   343
Card, S.K.,
   Moran, T.P.,
   Newell, A. 183
Carlson, W., see
   Marshall, R. 164

Carpenter, L., see
   Fournier, A.
   113
Catmull, E. 430
Chiyokura, H.,
   Kimura, F. 35
Clark, J.H.
   12, 210
Cohen, E.,
   Lyche, T.,
   Riesenfeld, R.
   164
Cook, R.L.,
   Torrance, K.
   113, 164
Cook, R.L., see
   Feibush, E.A.
   265
Cooper, T.J.,
   Pratt, W.K.
   343
Crow 209
Crow, F. 113

Dahl, O.-J., see
   Dijkstra, E.M.
   306
Daly, F.J., see
   Welch, J.E.
   145
Davis, E.G., see
   Wezey, W.R.
   197
Davis, J.C.,
   McCullagh, M.J.
   153
de Bone, E. 306
De Boor, C. 164
Dennis, J.B.,
   Fossen, J.B.,
   Linderman, J.P.
   95
Dijkstra, E.M.
   306

Doctor, L.J.,
   Torborg, J.G.
   12
Duce, D.A., see
   Hopgood, F.R.A.
   416

Earl, D.J. 306
Eastman, C., see
   Baer, A. 20
Edwards, D., see
   Hanks, K. 237
Ellingson, D.G.
   236, 237
Encarnacao, J.L.,
   see Bono, P.R.
   374, 416
Engel, S.E.,
   Granda, R.E.
   183

Faugeras, O.D.,
   see Abramatic,
   J.F. 343
Feibush, E.A.,
   Levoy, M.,
   Cook, R.L. 265
Foley, J.D.,
   Van Dam, A.
   153
Foley, J.D.,
   Wallace, V.L.
   416
Foley, J.D., see
   Bergeron, R.D.
   416
Fossen J.B., see
   DEnnis, J.B. 95
Fournier, A.,
   Fussel, D.,
   Carpenter, C.
   113

Freedman, D.P., see
   Weinberg, G.M.
   183
Frye, N. 237
Fujimoto, A.,
   Perrott, C.G.,
   Iwata, K. 316
Fujimura, K.,
   Kunii, T.L. 12
Fujimura, K., see
   Yamaguchi, K.
   20
Fussel, D., see
   Fournier, A.
   113

Gajski,
   Kuhn 210
Gallop, J.R., see
   Hopgood, F.R.A.
   416
Gates, D. 236

George, F.H. 306

Gero, see
   Sambura 210
Goldberg,
   Robson 209
Goto, S., see
   Sudo, T. 285
Gostelow, K.P.,
   Thomas, R.E. 95
Gouraud, H.
   113, 164, 265
Granda, R.E., see
   Engel, S.E. 183
Greenberg, see
   Hall 209
Gruber, L.S.,
   Barney, H. 353
Guedji,
   Tucker. 209
Guedj, et al. 209

Hall,
   Greenberg 209
Hanks, K.,
   Belliston, L.,
   Edwards, D.
   237
Harlow, F.H., see
   Welch, J.E.
   145
Hatakenaka, K., see
   Hirasawa, I.
   253
Hayama, K., et al.
   430
Heap, B.R. 73
Heller, W.R.,
   Sorkin, G.,
   Maling, K. 285
Heller, W.R., see
   Maling, K. 285
Henrion, M., see
   Baer, A. 20
Hillyard, R.C., see
   Braid, I.C.
   35, 58
Hirasawa, I.,
   Hatakenaka, K.
   253
Hoare, C.A., see
   Dijkstra, E.M.
   306
Hodgman, G.W., see
   Sutherland, I.E.
   12
Hopgood, F.R.A.,
   Duce, D.A.,
   Gallop, J.R.,
   Sutcliffe, D.C.
   416
Hopgood, F.R.A.,
   see Bono, P.R.
   374, 416
Horng, C.S.,
   Lie, M. 285
Hosaka, M., et al.
   80

Hubbold, R.J., see
  Auger, B. 306
Huelskoetter, W.R.
  237
Huitric, H.,
  Nahas, M. 164
Hunter, G.M. 12

Ikeda, H., et al.
  430
Ikedo, T. 316
Inamoto, N., see
  Yamaguchi, K.
  20
Iwata, K., see
  Fujimoto, A.
  316

Jern, M. 353
Johnson, S.C. 95
Jones, K.M., see
  Kobori, K.
  253

Kanakubo, T.,
  Nonomura, K.
  153
Kernighan, B.W.,
  Ritchie, D.M.
  95
Kessener, L.R.A.,
  see Rosenthal,
  D.S.H. 416
Kimura, F., see
  Chiyokura, H.
  35
King, R.G. 223
Kitazawa, H.,
  Ueda, K. 285

Kitazawa, H., see
  Adachi, T. 285
Kitazawa, H., see
  Ueda, K. 285
Kitching, A. 430
Kobayashi, M.,
  et al. 353
Kobori, K.,
  Sato, Y.,
  Nagato, Y.,
  Jones, K.M.,
  Nishioka, I.
  253
Krause, F.-C.,
  Vassilakopoulos,
  V. 306
Kubo, S. 353
Kuhn, see
  Gajski 210
Kunii, H., see
  Yamaguchi, K.
  20
Kunii, T.L., see
  Fujimura, K. 12
Kunii, T.L., see
  Yamaguchi, K.
  20

Langdon, G.G. Jr.,
  Reisner, P.,
  Silberberg, D.
  183
Latombe, J.C. 306
Leblond, A. 285
Lesk, M.E. 95
Levoy, M., see
  Feibush, E.A.
  265
Lie, M., see
  Horng, C.S. 285
Linderman, J.P.,
  see Dennis, J.B.
  95

Lougheed, R.M.,
  see Mudge, T.N.
  342
Lyche, T., see
  Cohen, E. 164

Magnenat-Thalmann,
  N., Thalmann, D.
  113
Mahieu, A.P., see
  Ooms, G. 128
Maling, K.,
  Mueller, S.H.,
  Heller, W.R.
  285
Maling, K., see
  Heller, W.R.
  285
Mantyla,
  Takala 210
Mantyla, M.,
  Sulonen, R.
  35, 210
March, L. 306
Marcus, A. 223
Marshall, R.,
  Wilson, R.,
  Carlson, W.
  164
Matherton, G. 342
Matt-Smith, J.C.
  343
McCubbrey, D.L.
  343
McCullagh, M.J.,
  see Davis, J.C.
  153
McGraw, J.R. 95
Meagher, D. 12
Michener, J.C.,
  see Rosenthal,
  D.S.H. 416
Mitchell, W.J.
  306

Moog, R.A.   360
Moran, T.P.   183
Moran, T.P., see
   Card, S.K.   183
Mudge, T.N.,
   Teel W.B.,
   Lougheed, R.M.
   342
Mueller, S.H., see
   Maling, K.   285
Munari, B.   197

Nagata, Y., see
   Kobori, K.   253
Nagatani, M., see
   Adachi, T.   285
Nagy, G.,
   Wagle, S.   153
Nahas, M., see
   Huitric, H.
   164
Najima, M., see
   Aui, T.   430
Newell, S., see
   Card, S.K.   183
Newell, M.E., see
   Blinn, J.F.
   113, 265
Newman,
   van Dam   209
Newman, W.M.,
   Sproull, R.F.
   164
Nishimura, T.,
   et al.   353
Nishioka, I., see
   Kobori, K.   253
Nonomura, K., see
   Kanakubo, T.
   153
Norman, D.A.   183

Ocvirk, O.G.,
   Bone, R.O.,
   Stinson, R.E.,
   Wigg, P.R.
   236, 237
Ohe, S., see
   Agui, T.   430
Ohtsuki, T., see
   Sudo, T.   285
Okino, N., et al.
   80
Ooms, G.,
   Mahieu, A.P.,
   Zelis, F.   128
Orr, J.N.   353
Otten, R.H.J.M.
   285

Parke, F.E.   164
Pavlidis, T.   342
Pereira, F.C.N.,
   see Swinson,
   P.S.G.   307
Perrott, C.G., see
   Fujimoto, A.
   316
Pfaff, G., see
   Rosenthal, D.S.H.
   416
Pile, J.F.
   236, 237
Platt, S.M.,
   Badler, N.I.   164
   164
Pope, A.   353
Pratt, W.K.   343
Pratt, W.K., see
   Cooper, T.J.   343

Reisner, P.   183
Requicha, A.A.G.
   12, 35, 209

Riesenfeld, R.,
   see Cohen, E.
   164
Ritchie, D.M.,
   Thompson, K.
   95
Ritchie, D.M.,
   see Kernighan,
   B.W.   95
Reisner, P., see
   Langdon, G.G. Jr.
   183
Robson, see
   Goldberg   209
Rodriguez, F., see
   Rogers, D.F.   73
Rogers, D.F.,
   Adams, J.A.
   73, 265
Rogers, D.F.,
   Rodriguez, F.,
   Satterfield, S.G.
   73
Rogers, D.F.,
   Satterfield, S.G.
   73
Rosenfeld, A.   342
Rosenthal   209
Rosenthal, D.S.H.,
   Michener, J.C.,
   Pfaff, G.,
   Kessener, L.R.A.,
   Sabin, M.A.   416
Roth, S.D.   12
Rubin, S.M.,
   Whitted, T.   12

Sabella,
   Wozny   209
Sabin, M.A., see
   Rosenthal, D.S.H.
   416
Salvemini, M.   197

Sambura, Gero 210
Sanniti Di Baja, G., see Arcelli, C. 342
Sargent, W. 236
Sato, Y., Yamaguchi, Y. 272
Sato Y., see Kobori, K. 253
Satterfield, S.G., see Rogers, D.F. 73
Sawada, Y. 128
Schmandt, C. 197
Sequin, Strauss 209
Serra, J. 342
Shannon, J.P., see Welch, J.E. 145
Shigley, J.E. 265
Shneiderman, B. 183, 360
Silberberg, D., see Langdon G.G. Jr. 183
Simon, H.A. 307
Smith, A.R. 164
Smith, S.L., Aucella, A.F. 183
Sorkin, G., see Heller, W.R. 285
Sproull, P.F., see Newman, W.M. 164
Srihari, S.N. 12
Srihari, S.N., see Yau, M.M. 20
Stankowski, A. 237
Stern, G. 360

Sternberg, S.R. 342, 343
Stinson, R.E., see Ocvirk, O.G. 236, 237
Straayer, D. 374
Strauss, see Sequin 209
Stroud, I.A., see Braid, I.C. 35, 58
Sudo, T., Ohtsuki, T., Goto, S. 285
Sudo, T., see Adachi, T. 285
Sulonen, R., see Mantyla, M. 35, 210
Sutcliffe, D.C., see Hopgood, F.R.A. 416
Sutherland 12
Sutherland, I.E., Hodgman, G.W. 12
Svetkoff, D.J., Candlish, J.B., Van Atta, P.W. 343
Swezey, W.R., Davis, E.G. 197
Swinson, P.S.G., Pereira, F.C.N., Biji, A. 307

Takala 209
Takala, see Mantyla 210
Teel, W.B., see Mudge, T.N. 342
ten Hagen, P.J.W. 416

ten Hagen, P.J.W., see Bono, P.R. 374, 416
Thalmann, D., see Magnenat-Thalmann, N. 113
Thomas, R.E., see Gostelow, K.P. 95
Thompson, K., see Ritchie, D.M. 95
Tokieda, T., see Yamaguchi, F. 58
Tokumasu, S., et al. 80
Toller, D.R., Willey, D.S. 307
Torborg, J.G., see Doctor, L.J. 12
Toriya, H., see Yamaguchi, K. 20
Torrance, K., see Cook, R.L. 113, 164
Tucker, see Guedj 209

Ueda, K. 285
Ueda, K., Kitazawa, H. 285
Ueda, K., see Kitazawa, H. 285

Van Atta, P.W., see Suetkoff, D.J. 343

Van Dam, see
    Newman 209
Van Dam, A., see
    Foley, J.D.
    153
Vanderschel, D.J.
    12
Van Uchelen, R.
    236, 237
Vassilakopoulos, V.,
    see Krause, F.-C.
    306
Voss, R.F. 163

Wagle, S., see
    Nagy, G. 153
Wallace, V.L., see
    Foley, J.D. 416
Weimer, see
    Whitted 209
Weinberg, G.M.,
    Freedman, D.P.
    183

Weinzapfel, G. 197
Welch, J.E.,
    Harlow, F.H.,
    Shannon, J.P.,
    Daly, B.J. 145
Whitted, T. 113
Whitted,
    Weimer 209
Whitted, T., see
    Rubin, S.M. 12
Whitton, M.C. 316
Wigg, P.R., see
    Ocvirk, O.G.
    236, 237
Willey, D.S. 307
Willey, D.S., see
    Toller, D.R.
    307
Williams, L. 164
Wilson, R., see
    Marshall, R. 164
Wozny, see
    Sabella 209

Yamaguchi, F. 272
Yamaguchi, F.,
    Tokieda, T. 58
Yamaguchi, K.,
    Inamoto, N.,
    Kunii, H.,
    Kunii, T.L. 20
Yamaguchi, K.,
    Kunii, T.L.,
    Fujimura, K.,
    Toriya, H. 20
Yamaguchi, Y., see
    Sato, Y. 272
Yau, M.M.,
    Srihari, S.N.
    20
Yessios, C.I. 307
Yoshikawa 210

Zelis, F., see
    Ooms, G. 128

Subject Index

The page numbers refer to the page on which term is defined.

actor 101
animated object 111
animation 220
artwork data 250
atmospheric pollution 116
attribute 202, 367

Bezier curve 76
BDAS system 266
bi-cubic Bezier surface 76
bi-cubic B-Spline 159
block packing 283
body 14, 46
Boolean shape operations 48
bottom-up 199
boundary representation 5, 13, 26, 74
bridge edge 44
brightness 163
B-Spline 159, 161
B-Spline surface 66, 69

CAD/CAM 66, 74, 240, 310, 355
CAE 310
camera effect 419
CAP graph system 240
center of gravity 78
CHIP floor plan 282
clipping 3
color 106

color ink jet printer 344
color printer 345
computer aided design (CAD) 27, 32, 74, 130, 198, 266, 294, 311
computer animation 101, 417
computer simulation 116
concavity 53
constant shading 105
constructure solid geometry (CSG) 5, 27, 75, 119
contour 148
contour line 66
contour plane 69
control point 161
convexity 53
coons patch 268
creative process 228
cross reference
cursor 191
curricula 216
cutter path 265

data base 242
data flow language 91
data flow program 90
design guideline 230
design process 228
design rule 297
design work station 245
device dependency 199

DFIG 91
diffusion calculation 118
digital terrain model(DTM) 148
digitizer 191
directed graph 90
display data structure 93
display list 313
display list processor 312
dot pattern 347
drowing 267, 297

E&S PS300 graphic 90
edge 3, 14, 28, 46, 75, 101
ergonomy 194, 198
erosion 331
Euler operation 29, 32
Euler-Poincare characteristic 46

face 28, 46, 49, 75, 102
facet 150
fifth generation system 294
figure 101
flow velocity vector 131
fourth generation graphic 310
fractal 126, 418
FREEDOM-II 44
free-form shape 33

function network 91

geometric editor 247
geometric (meta)model 207
geometric model 32, 74, 198
geometric modeller 74
geometry co-processor 311
geometry processor 313
Gourand intensity interpolation method 262
Gourand's shading 105
GRADAS 77
graphical kernel system (GKS) 376
GKS work station 367
graphic design 233
graphics software 371
graphic symbol 246

hardcopy 344
Heap algorithm 68, 71
HICAD/3D 74
hierarchical display list 312

hierarchical operator 337
hierarchical representation 2
hidden face elimination 149
hidden line 58
history model 207
hemogeneous coordinate 52
Hue 163
human factor 170

image analysis 321
image enhancement 321
image processing 322
intelligent graphic display 92
intelligent knowledge based system(IKBS) 294, 302
input device 355
input system 215
interface 214
interference 58
intersection 55
interprocessor communication 314

joystick 190

keyboard 190
kinematic simulation 264

LAMBERT's law 163
light pen 192
light source 262
linear convolution 323
local display data structure 93
local neighborhood 322
local operation 28
loop 28, 29, 45

macro function 93
man-machine interface 170, 300, 354
mass property 58, 74, 78
mechanically feedbacked touch sensor 354
menu 151
metafile 204
metamodel 201
MIRA-shading 101
model 201
modeller 74
MODIF 26
morphological image processing 321

Navier Stokes Equation 133
N/C 265
node 28
North American Presentation Level Protocol Syntax(NAPLPS) 378
numerical model 129

octree   2, 4, 13
office automation   224
OSLO algorithm   162

parallel execution   93
part library   257
peripheral device   189
Phong's shading   105
pipeline   315, 322
pixel   323, 353
plane   14
polyhedral object   7
polyhedron   48
polygon   3, 7, 74, 77, 161, 204, 365
polygon division   74
polytree   2, 5
portability   199
primitive shape   172
PROLOG   304

quadtree   4

random dot pattern   350
ray-tracing   418
ray-tracing techniques   3
relief map   146
rendering   10, 202
resolution   10
ring   29
ROBART   171
robot arm   94
RODIN   159

saturation   163
segment   367
segment storage   198
set operations   34
shaded computer animation   111
shading   77, 105, 148
shadow   163
Sheridan Computer Graphics Laboratory   218
Simplified Marker-and-Cell (SMAC)   129
skeletonization   337
solid generation   31
solid model   26, 27, 44, 116
spatial processor   323
standardize   418
standards   230
steam plume   116
structured graphic language   101
subdivision   7, 162
sufficiently simple   5
surface   3

task dispatching generator   151
task-scheduler generator   152
terrain   146
text   106
texture   161, 255, 262
texture mapping   255

three-dimensional flow   129
three-dimensional modeling   311
3D CAD/CAM system   242, 254
3-view drawings   267
top-down design   200
topographic data base   146
topology   29, 75, 201, 321
touch sensitive panel   192
trackball   190
transformation   106
triangular element   69
triangular surface   68
triangulation   44
typefaces   243

user defined macro   93
user interface manager (UIMS)   198

vector   101
vertex   14, 28, 46, 75, 101
videotex   219
virtual camera   111
Virtual Device Interface (VDI)   378
visible-surface calculation   3

visual
    communication
    231, 233
visual language
    225
VLSI   310
VLSI design   281

winged-edge data
    structure
    14, 32, 45
wire frame
    77, 101
wire-frame model
    27, 116
working station
    190, 254, 367
world coodinates
    369

Computer Graphics

Theory and Applications

Editor: **T. L. Kunii**

Proceedings of InterGraphics '83

1983. 292 figures, some in color.
X, 530 pages
ISBN 3-540-70001-3

Contents: Graphics Techniques. – Graphics Standards and 3D Models. – CAD/CAM. – Office Automation. – Computer Animation. – Graphic Applications. – Image Processing. – Author Index.

This book is an extensive treatise on the most up-to-date advances in computer graphics technology and its applications. Intended both for business and industry as well as for research and development, this book reflects the incredible development of new methods and tools for enhancing the productivity and quality of human work through computer graphics and applications. The book contains the proceedings of Inter-Graphics '83, a truly international computer graphics conference and exhibit held in Tokyo. InterGraphics was sponsored by the World Computer Graphics Association (WCGA) and organized by the Japan Management Association (JMA) in cooperation with ACM-SIGGRAPH, and attracted over 15,000 participants.

Springer-Verlag
Tokyo
Berlin
Heidelberg
New York

J. Encarnação, E. G. Schlechtendahl

Computer Aided Design

Fundamentals and System Architectures

1983. 176 figures (12 of them in color). IX, 346 pages
(Symbolic Computation, Computer Graphics)
ISBN 3-540-11526-9

The book is a thorough introduction to the fundamentals of Computer Aided Design (CAD). Both Computer Science and Engineering Sciences contribute to the particular flavor of CAD. Design is interpreted as an iterative process involving specification, synthesis, analysis, and evaluation, with CAD as a tool to provide computer assistance in all these phases.
The major issues treated in the book are: System architecture; components and interfaces; data base aspects in CAD; man-machine communication; computer graphics for geometrical design; drafting and data representation; the interrelationship between CAD and numerical methods; and simulation, and optimization. Economic, ergonomic, and social aspects are considered as well.

G. Enderle, K. Kansy, G. Pfaff

Computer Graphics Programming

GKS – The Graphics Standard

1984. 93 figures, some in color. XVI, 542 pages
(Symbolic Computation, Computer Graphics)
ISBN 3-540-11525-0

The book covers computer graphics programming on the base of the Graphical Kernel System, GKS. GKS is the first international standard for the functions of a computer graphics system. It offers capabilities for creation and representation of two-dimensional pictures, handling input from graphical workstations, structuring and manipulating pictures, and for storing and retrieving them. It represents a methodological framework for the concepts of computer graphics and establishes a common understanding for computer graphics systems, methods and applications. This book gives an overview over the GKS concepts, the history of the GKS design and the various system interfaces. A significant part of the book is devoted to a detailed description of the application of GKS functions both in a Pascal and a FORTRAN-language environment.

Springer-Verlag
Berlin
Heidelberg
New York
Tokyo